Engineering Problem Solving with ANSI C:
Fundamental Concepts

Delores M. Etter

Department of Electrical and Computer Engineering
University of Colorado, Boulder

An Alan R. Apt Book

Prentice Hall, Englewood Cliffs, New Jersey 07632

Library of Congress Cataloging–in–Publication Data

Etter, Delores M.

Engineering problem solving with ANSI C: fundamental concepts /
Delores M. Etter.

p. cm.

"An Alan R. Apt book."

Includes bibliographical references and index.

ISBN 0-13-061607-9

1. Engineering--Data processing. 2. C (Computer program language)
I. Title.

TA345.E87 1995

620'.0028553--dc20

94-17480
CIP

Publisher: Alan Apt
Editor-in-Chief: Marcia Horton
Project Manager: Mona Pompili
Developmental Editor: Sondra Chavez
Copy Editor: Peter Zurita
Marketing Manager: Tom McElwee
Design Director: Anne T. Neiglos
Designers: Meryl Poweski , Mona Pompili, Delores M. Etter
Cover Designer: Anthony Gemmelaro
Production Coordinator: Linda Behrens
Editorial Assistant: Shirley McGuire
Cover Photo: Satellite image of Earth's biosphere showing the distribution of vegetation
and phytoplankton (the microscopic plants that drift with the ocean currents and that
are the basis of the ocean's complex food chain).

© 1995 by Prentice-Hall, Inc.
A Simon & Schuster Company
Englewood Cliffs, New Jersey 07632

The author and publisher of this book have used their best efforts in preparing this book. These efforts include the development, research, and testing of the theories and programs to determine their effectiveness. The author and publisher shall not be liable in any event for incidental or consequential damages in connection with, or arising out of, the furnishing, performance, or use of these programs.

Printed in the United States of America

10 9 8 7 6 5 4 3 2

ISBN   0-13-061607-9

PRENTICE-HALL INTERNATIONAL (UK) LIMITED, *London*
PRENTICE-HALL OF AUSTRALIA PTY. LIMITED, *Sydney*
PRENTICE-HALL CANADA, INC., *Toronto*
PRENTICE-HALL HISPANOAMERICANA, S.A., *Mexico*
PRENTICE-HALL OF INDIA PRIVATE LIMITED, *New Delhi*
PRENTICE-HALL OF JAPAN, INC., *Tokyo*
SIMON & SCHUSTER ASIA PTE. LTD., *Singapore*
EDITORA PRENTICE-HALL DO BRASIL, LTDA., *Rio de Janeiro*

TRADEMARK INFORMATION

MATLAB is a registered
trademark of
The MathWorks, Inc.

In memory of my dearest Mother,
Muerladene Janice Van Camp

Preface

Engineers use computers to solve a variety of problems ranging from the evaluation of a simple function to solving a system of nonlinear equations. C has become the language of choice of many engineers and scientists not only because it has powerful commands and data structures, but also because it can easily be used for system-level operations. Since C is the language that a new engineer is most likely to encounter in a job, it is a good choice for an introduction to computing for engineers. Therefore, this text was written to introduce engineering problem solving with the following objectives:

- to develop a consistent **methodology for solving engineering problems,**
- to present the **fundamental capabilities of C,** the language of choice of many practicing engineers and scientists, and
- to illustrate the problem solving process with C through a variety of **engineering examples and applications.**

To accomplish these objectives, Chapter 1 presents a five-step process that is used consistently in the rest of the text for solving engineering problems. Chapters 2–7 present the fundamental capabilities of C for solving engineering problems. Throughout all these chapters, we present a large number of examples from many different engineering and science disciplines. The solutions to these examples are developed using the five-step process and ANSI C, the standard developed by the American National Standards Institute.

PREREQUISITES

No prior experience with the computer is assumed. The mathematical prerequisites are **college algebra and trigonometry.** Of course, the initial material can be covered much faster if the student has used other computer languages or software tools.

COURSE STRUCTURE

The material in these chapters was selected to provide the basis for a **one-term course** in engineering computing. These chapters contain the essential topics of mathematical computations, control structures, functions, arrays, pointers, and character handling. Students with background in another computer language should be able to complete this material in less than a semester. A minimal course that provides only an introduction to C can be designed using the nonoptional sections of the text. (Optional sections are indicated in the Contents.) Three ways to use the text, along with the recommended chapter sections, are

- **Introduction to C**   Many freshman introductory courses introduce the student to several computer tools in addition to an introduction to a language. For these courses, we recommend covering the nonoptional sections of Chapters 1–5. This material introduces students to the fundamental capabilities of C, and they will be able to write substantial programs using mathematical computations, control structures, functions, and arrays.
- **Problem Solving with C**   In a semester course devoted specifically to teaching students to master the C language, we recommend covering all nonoptional sections of Chapters 1–7. This material covers all the fundamental concepts of the C language, including mathematical computations, control structures, functions, arrays, pointers, and character handling.
- **Problem Solving with C and Numerical Techniques**   Upper-level students or students who are already familiar with other high-level languages will be able to cover the material in this text very quickly. In addition, they will be able to apply the numerical technique material to their other courses. Therefore, we recommend that these students cover all sections of Chapters 1–7, including the optional material.

PROBLEM-SOLVING METHODOLOGY

The **emphasis on engineering and scientific problem solving** is an integral part of the text. Chapter 1 introduces a **five-step process for solving engineering problems** using the computer:

1. State the problem clearly.
2. Describe the input and output information.
3. Work a simple example by hand.
4. Develop an algorithm and convert it to a computer program.
5. Test the solution with a variety of data.

To reinforce the development of problem solving skills, each of these five steps is clearly identified each time that a complete engineering problem is solved. In addition, **top-down design** and **stepwise refinement** are presented with the use of **decomposition outlines, pseudocode,** and **flowcharts.**

ENGINEERING AND SCIENTIFIC APPLICATIONS

Throughout the text, emphasis is placed on incorporating real-world engineering and scientific examples and problems. This emphasis is centered around a theme of **grand challenges,** which include:

- prediction of weather, climate, and global change
- computerized speech understanding
- mapping of the human genome
- improvements in vehicle performance
- enhanced oil and gas recovery

Each chapter begins with a photograph and a discussion of some aspect of one of these grand challenges that provides a glimpse of some of the exciting and interesting areas in which engineers might work. Later in the chapter, we solve a problem that not only relates to the introductory problem, but also has applications in other problem solutions. The grand challenges are also referenced in many of the other examples and problems.

ANSI C

The statements presented and all programs developed use the C standards developed by the **American National Standards Institute.** By using ANSI C, students learn to write **portable** code that can be transferred from one computer platform to another. Many of the capabilities of ANSI C are contained in the Standard C Library; some of these capabilities are discussed in the text and additional ones are discussed in Appendix A.

SOFTWARE ENGINEERING CONCEPTS

Engineers and scientists are expected to develop and implement **user-friendly** and **reusable** computer solutions. Learning software engineering techniques is therefore crucial to successfully developing these computer solutions. **Readability** and **documentation** are stressed in the development of programs. Additional topics that relate to software engineering issues are discussed throughout the text and include issues such as **software life cycle, portability, maintenance, modularity, recursion, abstraction, reusability, structured programming, validation, and verification.**

THREE TYPES OF PROBLEMS

Learning any new skill requires practice at a number of different levels of difficulty. We have developed three types of exercises that are used throughout the text to develop problem solving skills. The first set of exercises are **Practice!** problems. These are short-answer questions that relate to the section of material just presented. Most sections are immediately followed by a set of Practice! problems so that students can determine if they are ready to continue to the next section. Complete solutions to all the Practice! problems are included at the end of the text.

The **Modify!** problems are designed to provide hands-on experiences with the programs developed in the Problem Solving Applied sections. In these sections, we develop a complete C program using the five-step process. The Modify! problems ask students to run the program (which is stored on the text diskette) with different sets of data to test their understanding of how the program works and of the relationships among the engineering variables. These exercises also ask the students to make simple modifications to the program and then run the program to test their changes. Selected solutions to some of the Modify! problems are included at the end of the text.

Finally, each chapter ends with a set of **end-of-chapter** problems. These are new problems that relate to a variety of engineering applications, and the level of difficulty ranges from very straightforward to longer project assignments. Each problem requires that the student develop a complete C program or function. Engineering data sets are included for many of the problems to use in testing. Selected solutions to some of the end-of-chapter problems are included at the end of the text.

STUDY AND PROGRAMMING AIDS

Margin notes are used to help the reader not only identify the important concepts, but also to easily locate specific topics. In addition, margin notes are used to identify programming style guidelines and debugging information. Style guidelines show students how to write C programs that incorporate good software discipline; debugging sections help students recognize common errors so that they can avoid them. The programming style notes are indicated with the margin note *Style,* and the debugging notes are indicated with a **bug icon.** Each Chapter Summary contains a summary of the style notes and debugging notes, plus a list of the **Key Terms** from the chapter and a **C Statement Summary** of the new statements to make the book easier to use as a reference. The combined list of these key terms, along with their definitions, is included in a **Glossary** at the end of the text.

OPTIONAL NUMERICAL TECHNIQUES

Numerical techniques that are commonly used in solving engineering problems are also discussed in optional sections in the chapters, and include **interpolation, linear modeling (regression), root finding,** and the **solution to simultaneous equations.** The concept of a **matrix** is also introduced and then illustrated using a number of examples. All of these topics are presented assuming only a trigonometry and college algebra background.

Matlab AND VISUALIZATION

The visualization of the information related to a problem and its solution is a critical component in understanding and developing the intuition necessary to be a creative engineer. Therefore, we have included a number of plots of data throughout the text to illustrate the relationships of the information needed to solve specific problems. All the plots were generated using Matlab, a powerful environment for numerical computations, data analysis, and visualization. We have also included an appendix that shows how to generate a simple plot from data that have been stored in an ASCII data file; this ASCII file could be generated with a word processor or it could be generated by a C program. If a course is planned that will include material on both C and MATLAB, a special package that includes this text and *Engineering Problem Solving with MATLAB®* is available from Prentice Hall.

APPENDICES

To further enhance reference use, the appendices include a number of important topics. Appendix A contains a discussion of the components in the **ANSI C Standard Library.** Appendix B presents the **ASCII character codes.** Appendix C shows how to use MATLAB **to plot data from ASCII files;** this allows students to generate ASCII files with their C programs and to then plot the values using MATLAB. Finally, Appendix D contains a list of **references** used throughout the text.

SOFTWARE DISKETTE

Since the text includes a large number of examples that illustrate the various engineering applications, a **program** and **data file diskette** is included, which contains all the example programs and data files so that students can have immediate access to them. Also, additional data files that are referenced in the end-of-chapter problems are included on the diskette, including climatology data and speech signals. A **diskette icon** is included in the margin next to items that are contained on the diskette. The files on the diskette are ASCII files in a DOS format; they are ready to upload to other computer systems or to be converted to a Macintosh format.

STUDENT WORKBOOK

An **optional student workbook** has been developed to provide additional exercises for mastering the material in the textbook. This workbook contains **fill-in-the-blank problems, true-or-false problems,** and **multiple-choice problems** to test the student's understanding of the material. In addition, a number of programming problems are presented with **short but instructive computer solutions.** Students are then asked to provide memory snapshots at different points in the solutions or to show the output generated by the program. Multiple solutions are given for many of the problems to illustrate the different ways in which problems can be solved. The material in this workbook has been organized to follow the outline of the text, and thus assignments can be made in the workbook to follow the progression through the text.

INSTRUCTOR'S MANUAL

An **Instructor's Manual** is available, which contains complete solutions to all the Modify! problems and end-of-chapter problems. Also, transparency masters and a disk are included to assist in preparing lecture material.

NONTECHNICAL SKILLS

The engineer of the 21st century needs many skills and capabilities in addition to the technical ones learned in an engineering program. In Chapter 1 we present a brief discussion on some of these nontechnical skills that are so important to engineers. Specifically, we discuss developing both oral and written **communications skills,** understanding the **design/process/manufacture path** that takes an idea and leads to a product, working in interdisciplinary teams, understanding the **world and its marketplace,** the importance of **synthesis as well as analysis,** and the importance of **ethics** and other **societal concerns** in engineering solutions. While this text is devoted primarily to teaching problem solving skills and the C language, we have attempted to tie these other nontechnical topics into many of the problems and discussions in the text.

ACKNOWLEDGMENTS

I appreciate the encouragement of a number of people relative to the development of this text, and would like to especially recognize Bernard Goodwin (who was the first person to begin telling me that I should write a C text) and Alan Apt (who convinced me that the time was right). I also want to acknowledge the outstanding work of the publishing team at Prentice Hall, including Tom McElwee, Marcia Horton, Gary June, Kathleen Schiaparelli, Mona Pompili, Sondra Chavez, Alice Dworkin, and Mike Sutton. This text has been significantly improved by the suggestions and comments of the reviewers, who included Arnold Robbins (Georgia Tech College of Computing), Avelino Gonzalez (University of Central Florida), Thomas Cargill (Private Consultant), Jonathan Haines (Software/Hardware/Systems Consultant), Thomas Walker (Virginia Polytechnic Institute and State University), Christopher Skelly (Insight Resource Inc.), Betty Barr (The University of Houston), John Cordero (University of Southern California), A. R. Marundarajan (Cal Poly, Pomona), Lawrence Genalo (Iowa State University), Karen Davis (University of Cincinnati), Petros Gheresus (General Motors Institute), Leon Levine (UCLA), Harry Tyrer (University of Missouri—Columbia), Caleb Drake (University of Illinois at Chicago), John Miller (University of Michigan—Dearborn), Elden Heiden (New Mexico State University), Joe Hootman (University of North Dakota), and Nazeih Botros (Southern Illinois University).

I also want to recognize the important contributions of three groups of students (ranging from freshmen who had never used the computer, to undergraduates who had done a little computing with other languages, to graduate students who wanted to use C to do their research) who class-tested and carefully reviewed the various drafts of the manuscript and gave their feedback on the explanations, the examples, and the problems. A final note of gratitude goes to my husband, a mechanical engineer, for his help in developing some of the engineering application problems, and to my daughter, a veterinarian student, for her help in developing some of the genetic engineering problems.

Delores M. Etter
Department of Electrical/Computer Engineering
University of Colorado, Boulder

Contents

*Optional Section

[*]Optional Section

[*]Optional Section

*Optional Section

Engineering Applications

Aerospace Engineering

Biomedical Engineering

Chemical Engineering

Electrical Engineering

Environmental Engineering

Genetic Engineering

Manufacturing Engineering

Mechanical Engineering

Petroleum Engineering

Power Engineering

Engineering Problem Solving with ANSI C

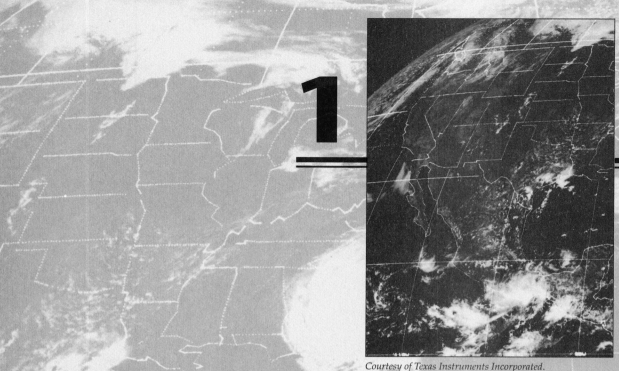

1

Courtesy of Texas Instruments Incorporated.

GRAND CHALLENGE:
Weather Prediction

Weather satellites provide a great deal of information to meteorologists who attempt to predict the weather. Large volumes of historical weather data can also be analyzed and used to test models for predicting weather. In general, we can do a reasonably good job of predicting the overall weather patterns; however, local weather phenomena such as tornadoes, water spouts, and microbursts are still very difficult to predict. Even predicting heavy rainfall or large hail from thunderstorms is often difficult. Although Doppler radar is useful in locating regions within storms that could contain tornadoes or microbursts, the radar detects the events as they occur and thus gives little time for issuing appropriate warnings to populated areas or aircraft. Accurate and timely prediction of weather and associated weather phenomena is still an elusive goal.

Engineering Problem Solving

Objectives

OBJECTIVES

Although most of this text is focused on teaching you to use the C language, we begin by describing some of the recent outstanding engineering achievements, and then we introduce a group of grand challenges—problems yet to be solved that will require technological breakthroughs in both engineering and science. One of the grand challenges includes the prediction of weather, which we used in the chapter-opening discussion. We also discuss some of the specific skills and nontechnical capabilities that are needed by engineers, such as communication

3

skills, the ability to work in interdisciplinary teams, and the need for a societal responsibility in the development of problem solutions. Because most solutions to engineering problems use computers, we next describe computer systems with a discussion of both computer hardware and computer software. Solving engineering problems effectively with the computer also requires a design plan or procedure, and in this chapter we define a problem-solving methodology with five steps for describing a problem and then developing a solution. Finally, after discussing computing and the problem-solving methodology, we return to the problem of weather prediction and discuss some of the different types of weather data that are currently being collected. These data are critical for developing the understanding and intuition needed to create a mathematical model to predict weather. The data are also important because they can be used to test hypothetical models as they are developed. Data analysis helps engineers and scientists better understand complex physical phenomena so that they can then apply that knowledge to developing solutions to new problems.

1.1   Engineering in the Twenty-First Century

Engineers solve real-world problems using scientific principles from disciplines that include computer science, mathematics, physics, and chemistry. It is this variety of subjects, and the challenge of real problems, that makes engineering so interesting and so rewarding. In this section, we present some of the outstanding engineering achievements of recent years, followed by a discussion of some of the important engineering challenges we face as we go into the next century. Finally, we consider some of the nontechnical skills and capabilities needed by the engineers of the twenty-first century.

RECENT ENGINEERING ACHIEVEMENTS

Since the development of the computer in the late 1950s, a number of very significant engineering achievements [1, 2]* have occurred. In 1989, the National Academy of Engineering selected the **10 engineering achievements** that it considered to be the most important accomplishments during the previous 25 years. These achievements illustrate the multidisciplinary nature of engineering, and demonstrate how engineering has improved our lives and expanded the possibilities for the future while providing a wide variety of interesting and challenging careers. We now briefly discuss these 10 achievements; a set of suggested readings at the end of the chapter includes more detailed information on these topics.

The development of the **microprocessor**, a tiny computer smaller than a postage stamp, is one of the top engineering achievements of the last 25 years. Microprocessors are used in electronic equipment, household appliances, toys, and games, as well as in automobiles, aircraft, and space shuttles, because they

---

*The references in the text material are summarized in Appendix D.

provide powerful yet inexpensive computing capabilities. Microprocessors also provide the computing power inside calculators and personal computers.

Several of the top 10 achievements relate to the exploration of space. The **moon landing** was probably the most complex and ambitious engineering project ever attempted. Major breakthroughs were required in the design of the Apollo spacecraft, the lunar lander, and the three-stage Saturn V rocket. Even the design of the spacesuit was a major engineering project that resulted in a system that included a three-piece suit and backpack, which together weighed 190 pounds. The computer played a key role not only in the designs of the various systems, but it also played a critical role in the communications required during a individual moon flight; a single flight required the coordination of over 450 people in the launch control center and over 7000 others on nine ships, in 54 aircraft, and at stations located around the earth.

MICROPROCESSOR
Courtesy of Texas Instruments Incorporated.

MOON LANDING
Courtesy of National Aeronautics and Space Administration.

The space program also provided much of the impetus for the development of **application satellites** that are used to provide weather information, relay communication signals, map uncharted terrain, and provide environmental updates on the composition of the atmosphere. The Global Positioning System (GPS) is a constellation of 24 satellites that broadcasts position, velocity, and time information worldwide. GPS receivers measure the time it takes for signals to travel from the GPS satellite to the receiver. Using information received from four satellites, a microprocessor in the receiver can then determine very precise measurements of the receiver's location; the accuracy varies from a few meters to centimeters, depending on the computation techniques used.

Another of the top engineering achievements recognizes the contributions of **computer-aided design and manufacturing** (CAD/CAM). CAD/CAM has generated a new industrial revolution by increasing the speed and efficiency of many types of manufacturing processes. CAD allows the design to be done using the computer, which then produces the final schematics, parts lists, and computer simulation results. CAM uses design results to control machinery or industrial robots to manufacture, assemble, and move components.

SATELLITE
Courtesy of National Aeronautics and Space Administration.

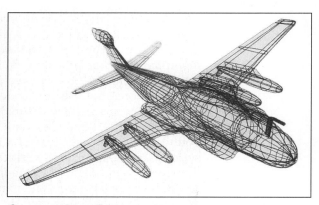

COMPUTER-AIDED DESIGN
Courtesy of Computervision Corporation.

The origins of the **jumbo jet** came from the U.S. Air Force C-5A cargo plane that began operational flights in 1969. Much of the success of the jumbo jets can be attributed to the high-bypass fanjet that allows them to fly farther with less fuel and with less noise than previous jet engines. The core of the engine operates like a pure turbojet, in which compressor blades pull air into the engine's combustion chamber. The hot expanding gas thrusts the engine forward, and at the same time spins a turbine that in turn drives the compressor and the large fan on the front of the engine. The spinning fan provides the bulk of the engine's thrust.

The aircraft industry was also the first industry to develop and use **advanced composite materials** that consist of materials that can be bonded together in such a way that one material reinforces the fibers of the other material. Advanced composite materials were developed to provide lighter, stronger, and more temperature-resistant materials for aircraft and spacecraft. New markets for composites now exist in sporting goods. For example, downhill snow skis use layers of woven Kevlar fibers to increase their strength and reduce weight, and golf club shafts of graphite/epoxy are stronger and lighter than the steel in conventional shafts. Composite materials are also used in the design of prosthetics for artificial limbs.

JUMBO JET   *Courtesy of United Parcel Service.*

ADVANCED COMPOSITE MATERIALS *Courtesy of Mike Valeri.*

The areas of medicine, bioengineering, and computer science were teamed for the development of the CAT (**computerized axial tomography**) scanner machine. This instrument can generate three-dimensional images or two-dimensional slices of an object using X-rays that are generated from different angles around the object. Each X-ray measures a density from its angle, and very complicated computer algorithms combine the information from all the X-rays to reconstruct a clear image of the inside of the object. CAT scans are routinely used to identify tumors, blood clots, and brain abnormalities. The U.S. Army is developing a rugged, lightweight CAT scanner that can be transported to medical stations in combat zones.

The work of geneticists and engineers have resulted in many new products as a result of **genetic engineering**. These products range from insulin, to growth hormones, to infection-resistant vegetables. A genetically engineered product is produced by splicing a gene that produces a valuable substance from one organism into another organism that will multiply itself and the foreign gene along with it. The first commercial genetically engineered product was human insulin, which appeared under the trade name Humulin. Current work is investigating the use of genetically altered microbes to clean up toxic waste and to degrade pesticides.

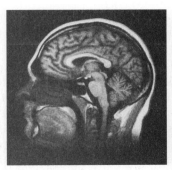

CAT SCAN
Courtesy of General Electric.

GENETIC ENGINEERING
Courtesy of Matt Meadows.

Lasers are light waves that have the same frequency and travel in a narrow beam that can be directed and focused. CO_2 lasers are used to drill holes in materials that range from ceramics to composite materials. Lasers are also used in medical procedures to weld detached retinas, seal leaky blood vessels, vaporize brain tumors, and perform delicate inner-ear surgery. Three-dimensional pictures called holograms are also generated with lasers.

Fiber-optic communications use **optical fiber**, a transparent glass thread that is thinner than a human hair. This optical fiber can carry more information than either radio waves or electric waves in copper telephone wires, and it does not produce electromagnetic waves that can cause interference on communication lines. Transoceanic fiber-optic cables provide communication channels between continents. Fiber optics is also used in medical instrumentation to allow surgeons to thread light into the human body for examination and laser surgery.

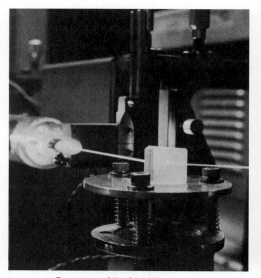
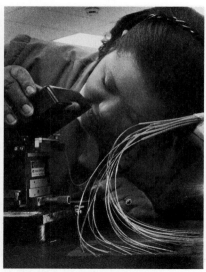

LASERS   *Courtesy of Perkin-Elmer.*

FIBER OPTICS
Courtesy of Photo Researchers, Inc.

GRAND CHALLENGES FOR THE FUTURE

Grand challenges

Although the recent achievements of engineers have produced dramatic results, there are still many important problems to be solved. In this section we present a group of **grand challenges**—fundamental problems in science and engineering with broad potential impact. The grand challenges were identified by the Office of Science and Technology Policy in Washington, D.C., as part of a research and development strategy [3] for high-performance computing. We have selected five of these grand challenges to use as a general theme for this text; these challenges are discussed in the chapter-opening applications, and problems related to these challenges are solved in examples. The following paragraphs briefly present these grand challenges and outline the types of benefits that will come with their solutions. Just as the computer played an important part in the top 10 engineering achievements of the last 25 years, the computer will play an even greater role in solving problems related to these grand challenges.

The **prediction of weather, climate, and global change** requires that we understand the coupled atmosphere and ocean biosphere system. This includes understanding CO_2 dynamics in the atmosphere and ocean, ozone depletion, and climatological changes due to the releases of chemicals or energy. This complex interaction also includes solar interactions. A major eruption from a solar storm near a "coronal hole" (a venting point for the solar wind) can eject vast amounts of hot gases from the sun's surface toward the earth's surface at speeds over a million miles per hour. This ejection of hot gases bombards the earth with X-rays, and can interfere with communication and cause power fluctuations in power lines. Learning to predict changes in weather, climate, and global change involves collecting large amounts of data for study and developing new mathematical models that can represent the interdependency of many variables. We will analyze the weather patterns at Denver International Airport over a 1-year period in later chapters. We will also develop a model for predicting ozone mixing ratios in the middle atmosphere using satellite data, and we analyze the altitude and velocity information for a helium-filled weather balloon.

Computerized speech understanding could revolutionize our communication systems, but many problems are involved. Teaching a computer to understand words from a small vocabulary spoken by the same person is currently possible. However, to develop systems that are speaker-independent and that understand words from large vocabularies and from different languages is very difficult. Subtle changes in one's voice, such as those caused by a cold or stress, can affect the performance of speech-recognition systems. Even assuming that the computer can recognize the words, it is not simple to determine their meaning. Many words are context-dependent, and thus cannot be analyzed separately. Intonation such as raising one's voice can change a statement into a question. Although there are still many difficult problems left to address in automatic speech recognition and understanding, exciting applications are everywhere. Imagine a telephone system that determines the languages being spoken and translates the speech signals so that each person hears the conversation in his or her native language. We will analyze actual speech data stored on the diskette in the back of this book to demonstrate some of the techniques used in word recognition.

The goal of the **Human Genome Project** is to locate, identify, and determine the function of each of the 50,000 to 100,000 genes that are contained in human DNA (deoxyribonucleic acid), which is the genetic material found in cells. The deciphering of the human genetic code will lead to many technical advances, including the ability to detect most, if not all, of the over 4000 known human genetic diseases such as sickle-cell anemia and cystic fibrosis. However, deciphering the code is complicated by the nature of genetic information. Each gene is a double-helix strand composed of base pairs (adenine bonded with thymine or cytosine bonded with guanine) arranged in a steplike manner with phosphate groups along the side. These base pairs can occur in any sequential order, and represent the hereditary information in the gene. The number of base pairs in human DNA has been estimated to be around 3 billion. DNA directs the production of proteins for all metabolic needs, so the proteins produced by a cell may provide a key to the sequence of base pairs in the DNA. We will write programs to compute the molecular weights of amino acids, the building blocks of proteins, and to compute the molecular weights of general molecular formulas.

Substantial **improvements in vehicle performance** requires more complex physical modeling in the areas of fluid dynamic behavior for three-dimensional flow fields and flow inside engine turbomachinery and ducts. Turbulence in fluid flows impacts the stability and control, thermal characteristics, and fuel performance of aerospace vehicles, and modeling this flow is necessary for the analysis of new configurations. The analysis of the aeroelastic behavior of vehicles also affects new designs. The efficiency of combustion systems is also related because attaining significant improvements in combustion efficiency requires understanding the relationships between the flows of the various substances and the chemistry that causes the substances to react. Vehicle performance is also being addressed through the use of onboard computers and microprocessors. Transportation systems are currently being studied in which cars have computers with small video screens mounted on the dash. The driver enters the destination location, and the video screen shows the street names and path to go from the current location to the desired location. A communication network keeps the car's computer aware of any traffic jams so that it can automatically reroute the car if necessary. Other transportation research addresses totally automated driving, with computers and networks handling all the control and information interchange. Using data collected from a wind tunnel, we will use linear interpolation to compute information for flight-path angles not in the original data set collected during wind-tunnel experiments. We also analyze the velocity and acceleration data for an advanced turboprop engine.

Enhanced oil and gas recovery will allow us to locate the estimated 300 billion barrels of oil reserves in the United States. Current techniques for identifying structures likely to contain oil and gas use seismic techniques that can evaluate structures 20,000 feet below the surface. These techniques use a group of sensors (called a sensor array) that is located near the area to be tested. A ground-shock signal is sent into the earth, reflected by the different geological layer boundaries, and received by the sensors. By using sophisticated signal processing, the boundary layers can be mapped and some estimate can be made as to the materials in the various layers, such as sandstone, shale, and water. The ground-shock signals can be generated in several ways—a hole can be drilled and an explosive charge can be exploded in the hole; a ground shock can be generated by an explosive charge on the surface; or a special truck that uses a hydraulic hammer can be used to pound the earth several times per second. Continued research is needed to improve the resolution of the information and to find methods of production and recovery that are economical and ecologically sound. We will write programs that analyze seismometer data to determine the locations of reflections in the data.

These grand challenges are only a few of the many interesting problems waiting to be solved by engineers and scientists. The solutions to problems of this magnitude will be the result of organized approaches that combine ideas and technologies. The use of computers and engineering problem-solving techniques will be a key element in the solution process.

CHANGING ENGINEERING ENVIRONMENT

The engineer of the twenty-first century will work in an environment that requires many nontechnical skills and capabilities [4]. Although the computer will be the primary computational tool of most engineers, the computer will also be useful in developing additional nontechnical abilities.

Engineers need strong **communication skills** for both oral presentations and for preparing written materials. Computers provide the software to assist in writing outlines and developing materials and graphs for presentations and technical reports. The problems at the end of this chapter include written and oral presentations to provide practice of these important skills.

The **design/process/manufacture path**, which consists of taking an idea from a concept to a product, is one that engineers must understand first-hand. Every step of this process uses computers in areas from design analysis, machine control, robotic assembly, quality assurance, and market analysis. Several problems in the text relate to these topics. For example, in Chapter 4, programs are developed to simulate the reliability of systems that use multiple components.

Engineering teams of the future will be **interdisciplinary teams**, just as the engineering teams of today are interdisciplinary teams. The discussions of the top 10 engineering achievements of the last 25 years clearly show the interdisciplinary nature of those achievements. The teams that address, and will eventually solve, the grand challenges will also be interdisciplinary teams. Learning to interact in teams and to develop organizational structures for effective team communication is an important skill for engineers. A good way to begin developing engineering team skills is to organize teams to study for exams. Assign specific topics to members of the team with the assignment that they then review these topics for the team, with examples and potential test questions.

The engineers of the twenty-first century need to understand the **world marketplace**. This involves understanding different cultures, political systems, and business environments. Courses in these topics and in foreign languages help provide some understanding, but exchange programs with international experiences provide invaluable knowledge in developing a broader world understanding.

Engineers are problem solvers, but problems are not always formulated carefully. An engineer must be able to extract a problem statement from a problem discussion, and then determine the important issues related to the problem. This involves not only developing order, but also learning to correlate chaos. It means not only **analyzing** the data, but **synthesizing** a solution using many pieces of information. The integration of ideas can be as important as the decomposition of the problem into manageable pieces. A problem solution may involve not only abstract thinking about the problem, but also experimental learning from the problem environment.

Problem solutions must also be considered in their **societal context**. Environmental concerns should be addressed as alternative solutions to problems are being considered. Engineers must also be conscious of ethical issues in providing test results, quality verifications, and design limitations. It is unfortunate that tragedies like the Challenger explosion are sometimes the impetus for bringing issues of responsibility and accountability into the forefront. Ethical issues are never easy to resolve, and some of the exciting new technological achievements will bring more ethical issues with them. For example, the mapping of the genome will potentially provide ethical, legal, and social implications. Should the gene therapy that allows doctors to combat diabetes also be used to enhance athletic ability? Should prospective parents be given detailed information related to the physical and mental characteristics of an unborn child? What kind of privacy should an individual have over his or her genetic code? Very complicated issues arise with any technological advancement because the same capabilities that can do a great deal of good can often be applied in ways that are harmful.

The material presented in this text is only one step in building the knowledge, confidence, and understanding needed by engineers of the twenty-first century. However, we enthusiastically begin the process with an introduction to the range of computing systems available to engineers and an introduction to a problem-solving methodology that will be used throughout this text as we use C to solve engineering problems.

1.2   Computing Systems: Hardware and Software

Before we begin discussing the C language, a brief discussion on computing is useful, especially for those who have not had prior experience with computers. A **computer** is a machine that is designed to perform operations that are specified with a set of instructions called a **program**. Computer **hardware** refers to the computer equipment, such as the keyboard, the mouse, the terminal, the hard disk, and the printer. Computer **software** refers to the programs that describe the steps that we want the computer to perform.

Computer
Program
Hardware

Software

COMPUTER HARDWARE

All computers have a common internal organization, as shown in Figure 1.1. The **processor** is the part of the computer that controls all the other parts. It accepts input values (from a device such as a keyboard) and stores them in the **memory**. It also interprets the instructions in a computer program. If we want to add two values, the processor will retrieve the values from memory, and send them to the **arithmetic logic unit**, or ALU. The ALU performs the addition and the processor then stores the result in memory. The processing unit and the ALU use internal memory composed of read-only memory (ROM) and random-access memory (RAM) in their processing; most data are stored in external memory or secondary memory using hard-disk drives or floppy-disk drives that are attached to the processor. The processor and ALU together are called the **central processing**

Processor
Memory

Arithmetic
logic unit

Central
processing unit

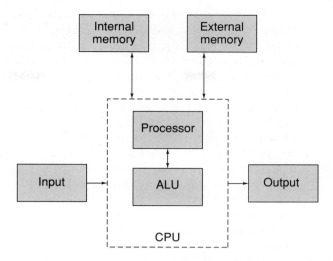

Figure 1.1 *Internal organization of a computer.*

Microprocessor

unit, or CPU. A **microprocessor** is a CPU that is contained in a single integrated-circuit chip, which contains millions of components in an area smaller than a postage stamp.

We usually instruct the computer to print the values that it has computed on the terminal screen or on paper using a printer. Dot-matrix printers use a matrix (or grid) of pins to produce the shape of a character on paper, whereas a laser printer uses a light beam to transfer images to paper. The computer can also write information to diskettes, which store the information magnetically. A printed copy of information is called hard copy, and a magnetic copy of informa-

Electronic copy

tion is called an **electronic copy** or a soft copy.

Personal computers (PCs)

Computers come in all sizes, shapes, and forms (see photos next page). **Personal computers (PCs)** are small inexpensive computers that are commonly used in offices, homes, and laboratories. PCs are also referred to as microcomputers, and their design is built around a microprocessor, such as the Intel 486 microprocessor, that can process millions of instructions per second (mips). Minicomputers are more powerful than microcomputers; mainframes are even more powerful computers that are often used in businesses and research laboratories. A

Workstation
Supercomputers

workstation is a minicomputer or mainframe computer that is small enough to fit on a desktop. **Supercomputers** are the fastest of all computers, and can process billions of instructions per second. As a result of their speed, supercomputers are capable of solving very complex problems that cannot be feasibly solved on other computers. Mainframes and supercomputers require special facilities and a specialized staff to run and maintain the computer systems.

The type of computer needed to solve a particular problem depends on the problem requirements. If the computer is part of a home security system, a microprocessor is sufficient; if the computer is running a flight simulator, a main-

Networks

frame is probably needed. Computer **networks** allow computers to communicate with each other so that they can share resources and information. For example, ethernet is a commonly-used local area network (LAN).

Courtesy of Johnson Space Center.

Courtesy of The Image Works.

Courtesy of Apple Computer Inc.

Courtesy of The Image Works.

Courtesy of CRAY Research.

Courtesy of IBM.

PREDICTION OF WEATHER, CLIMATE, AND GLOBAL CHANGE

To predict weather, climate, and global change, we must understand the complex interactions of the atmosphere and the oceans. These interactions are influenced by many things, including temperature, winds, ocean currents, precipitation, soil moisture, snow cover, glaciers, polar sea ice, and the absorption of ultraviolet radiation by ozone in the earth's atmosphere. As a result of concern over the ozone depletion in the atmosphere, weather balloons (**Photo 1**) were launched in Sweden in 1990 as part of an experiment conducted by engineers and scientists from France, Germany, and the United States to measure the atmospheric ozone and various pollutants near the Arctic pole.

Photo 1   *Weather Balloon*

Photo 2 illustrates the total atmospheric ozone concentration in the southern hemisphere in October 1993. These data come from the Total Ozone Mapping Spectrometer instrument on the Russian Meteor-3 satellite; the white region shows a 60% decrease in the ozone levels from 1975.

To be able to predict weather phenomena such as tornadoes, we must understand the combination of events required for them to develop. **Photo 3** shows equipment designed to generate miniature tornadoes; results from experiments such as this one provide new insights to the field of meteorology. ∎

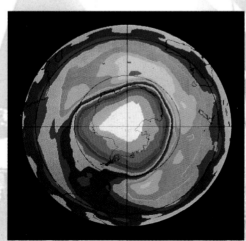

Photo 2   *Ozone Model*

Photo 3   *Tornado Machine*

IMPROVEMENTS IN VEHICLE PERFORMANCE

Significant improvements in vehicle performance will not only affect the modes of transportation available to us, but can also improve the environment by reducing

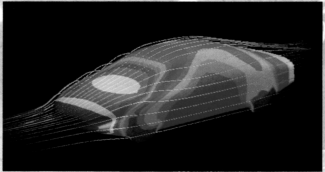

Photo 4   *Car Aerodynamics*

pollution and by providing more efficient energy consumption. Computer-aided design techniques allow us to analyze the three-dimensional fluid flow around a vehicle (**Photo 4**). We can also analyze new designs using wind tunnels, which can generate various wind speeds to test the performance of new structures (**Photo 5**). Improvements in transportation will take advantage of engineering breakthroughs in other areas, such as satellite navigation. The Global Positioning System (GPS) satellites can be used to determine the exact position of a GPS receiver, and that information could be used in an onboard computer to direct a driver to a desired location, as shown in **Photo 6**. ■

Photo 5   *Wind Tunnel*

Photo 6   *Computer-navigated Car*

COMPUTERIZED SPEECH UNDERSTANDING

Computerized speech understanding could revolutionize our communication systems. We still cannot converse normally with computers, but there are applications that use some forms of speech understanding. Educational games such as the one illustrated in **Photo 7** use speech input to teach skills such as language and mathematics; these programs understand words from limited vocabularies. Other computer programs are designed to understand and respond to words from a specific person. For example, motorized wheelchairs can be designed to respond to verbal commands, or computers can take their input from verbal instructions instead of through a keyboard (**Photo 8**).

Photo 7   *Educational Game*

Photo 8   *Speech Input to Computer*

ENHANCED OIL AND GAS RECOVERY

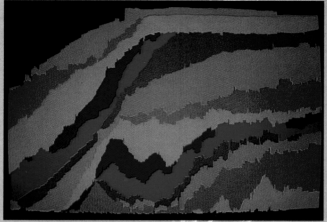

Photo 10   *Oil Platform*

Photo 11   *Computer Model of Earth Layers*

Photo 12   *Geological Experiments in a Volcano*

Economical and ecologically sound techniques are needed for the identification and recovery of oil and gas reserves. Sonar signal processing techniques are being developed to identify potential reserves under the ocean, which are then recovered by oil platforms (**Photo 10**). Underground reserves can be located by techniques that map the geological structure, as shown in the computer model in **Photo 11** that was developed using seismic signal processing. This information can be used to determine the materials in the various layers, and thus to indicate areas that are likely to contain oil or gas. Understanding the geological structure and relationships of different regions, such as the Mauna Loa volcano rift shown in **Photo 12**, gives engineers and scientists new information in understanding the earth's structure and the materials of which it is composed. ■

Photo 9   *Airline Cockpit*

Researchers are currently exploring the use of speech to simplify access to the information contained in the hundreds of gauges and instruments in an airline cockpit (**Photo 9**). For instance, in a future airliner, the pilot may be able to verbally ask for information, such as fuel status, and a computer will respond in synthesized speech with the amount of fuel remaining. ■

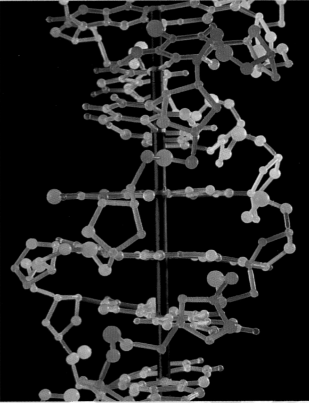

Photo 13　*DNA molecule model*

Photo 14　*Equipment for DNA Sequencing*

HUMAN GENOME PROJECT

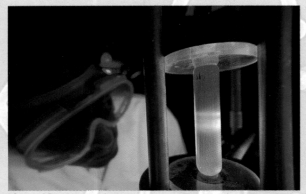

Photo 15　*Bands of DNA*

The goal of the Human Genome Project is to locate, identify, and determine the function of each of the 50,000 to 100,000 genes contained in human DNA (deoxyribonucleic acid). A model of the double-helix DNA molecule is shown in **Photo 13**. Each gene is composed of base pairs arranged in a step-like manner, and it is the identification of the order of these base pairs that provides the key to the human genome. The structure of genes can be studied using equipment such as the electrophoresis machine in **Photo 14**. This machine contains a gel that can separate radioactively tagged DNA fragments using an electric field. **Photo 15** shows an engineer separating bands of DNA for a gene-splicing experiment. ■

COMPUTER SOFTWARE

Computer software contains the instructions or commands that we want the computer to perform. There are several important categories of software, which include operating systems, software tools, and language compilers. Figure 1.2 illustrates the interaction between these categories of software and the computer hardware. We now discuss each of these software categories in more detail.

Operating systems

Operating Systems. Some software, such as the operating system, typically comes with the computer hardware when it is purchased. The operating system provides an interface between you (the user) and the hardware by providing a convenient and efficient environment in which you can select and execute the software on your system.

Utilities

Operating systems also contain a group of programs called utilities that allow you to perform functions such as printing files, copying files from one diskette to another, and listing the files that you have saved on a diskette. Whereas these utilities are common to most operating systems, the commands themselves vary from operating system to operating system. For example, to list your files using DOS (a disk operating system used mainly with PCs), the command is `dir`; to list your files with UNIX (a powerful operating system frequently used with workstations), the command is `ls`. Some operating systems simplify the interface with the operating system by using icons and menus; examples

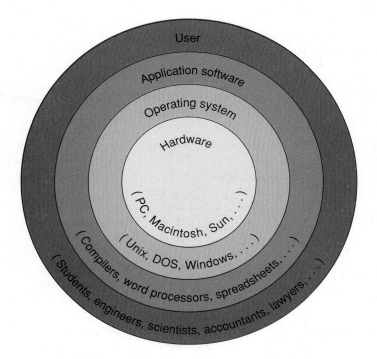

Figure 1.2 *Software interface to the computer.*

of user-friendly systems are the Macintosh environment and the Windows environment.

Because C programs can be run on many different platforms or hardware systems and because a specific computer can use different operating systems, it is not feasible to discuss the wide variety of operating systems that you might use while taking this course. We assume that your professor will provide the specific operating system information that you need to know to use the computers available at your university; this information is also contained in the operating system manuals.

Software tools
Word processors

Software Tools. Software tools are programs that have been written to perform common operations. For example, **word processors** such as Microsoft Word and WordPerfect are programs that have been written to help you enter and format text. Word processors allow you to move sentences and paragraphs, and often have capabilities that allow you to enter mathematical equations and to check your spelling and grammar. Word processors are also used to enter computer programs and store them in files. Very sophisticated word processors allow you to produce well-designed pages that combine elaborate charts and graphics with text and headlines; these word processors use a technology called **desktop**

Desktop publishing

publishing which combines a very powerful word processor with a high-quality printer to produce professional-looking documents.

Spreadsheet

Spreadsheet programs are software tools that allow you to easily work with data that can be displayed in a grid of rows and columns. Spreadsheets were initially used for financial and accounting applications, but many science and engineering problems can be easily solved using spreadsheets. Most spreadsheet packages include plotting capabilities, so they can be especially useful in analyzing and displaying information. Lotus 1–2–3, Quattro, and Excel are popular spreadsheet packages.

Database management

Another popular group of software tools are **database management** programs, such as dBASE IV and Paradox. These programs allow you to store a large amount of data, and then easily retrieve pieces of the data, and format them into reports. Databases are used by large organizations such as banks, hospitals, hotels, and airlines. Scientific databases are also used to analyze large amounts of data. Meteorology data is an example of scientific data that require large databases for storage and analysis.

Computer-aided design packages, such as AutoCAD, AutoSketch, and CADKEY, allow you to define objects and then manipulate them graphically. For example, you can define an object and then view it from different angles or observe a rotation of the object from one position to another.

Mathematical computation tools
Graphics tools

There are also some very powerful **mathematical computation tools**, such as MATLAB, Mathematica, MATHCAD, and Maple. Not only do these tools have very powerful mathematical commands, but they are also **graphics tools** that provide extensive capabilities for generating graphs. This combination of computational power and visualization power make them particularly useful tools for engineers. Appendix C contains a discussion on using MATLAB to plot data from a data file generated by a C program.

If an engineering problem can be solved using a software tool, it is usually more efficient to use the software tool than to write a program in a computer language to solve the problem. However, many problems cannot be solved using software tools, or a software tool may not be available on the computer system that must be used for solving the problem; thus, we also need to know how to write programs using computer languages. The distinction between a software tool and a computer language is becoming less clear as some of the more powerful tools such as MATLAB and Mathematica include their own language in additional to specialized operations.

Computer Languages. Computer languages can be described in terms of levels. Low-level languages or **machine languages** are the most primitive languages. Machine language is tied closely to the design of the computer hardware. Because computer designs are based on two-state technology (devices with two states such as open or closed circuits, on or off switches, positive or negative charges), machine language is written using two symbols, which are usually represented using the digits 0 and 1. Therefore, machine language is also a **binary** language, and the instructions are written as sequences of 0's and 1's called binary strings. Since machine language is closely tied to the design of the computer hardware, the machine language for a Sun computer is different from the machine language for a VAX computer.

An **assembly language** is also unique to a specific computer design, but its instructions are written in Englishlike statements instead of binary. Assembly languages usually do not have very many statements, and thus writing programs in assembly language can be tedious. In addition, to use an assembly language you must also know information that relates to the specific computer hardware. Instrumentation that contains microprocessors often requires that the programs operate very fast, and thus the programs are called **real-time programs**. These real-time programs are usually written in assembly language to take advantage of the specific computer hardware in order to perform the steps faster.

High-level languages are computer languages that have Englishlike commands and instructions, and include languages such as C, Fortran, Ada, Pascal, COBOL, and Basic. Writing programs in high-level languages is certainly easier than writing programs in machine language or in assembly language. However, a high-level language contains a large number of commands and an extensive set of **syntax** (or grammar) rules for using the commands. To illustrate the syntax

Margin notes:
MATLAB
Machine languages
Binary
Assembly language
Real-time programs
High-level languages
Syntax
MATLAB

TABLE 1.1 Comparison of Software Statements

Software	Example Statement
C	`area = 3.141593*(diameter/2)*(diameter/2);`
MATLAB	`area = pi*((diameter/2)^2);`
Fortran	`area = 3.141593*(diameter/2.0)**2`
Ada	`area := 3.141593*(diameter/2)**2;`
Pascal	`area := 3.141593*(diameter/2)*(diameter/2)`
Basic	`let a = 3.141593*(d/2)*(d/2)`
COBOL	`compute area = 3.141593*(diameter/2)*(diameter/2).`

and punctuation required by both software tools and high-level languages, we compute the area of a circle with a specified diameter in Table 1.1 using several different languages and tools. Notice both the similarities and the differences in this simple computation. Although we included C as a high-level language, many people like to describe C as a midlevel language because it allows access to low-level routines and is often used to define programs that are converted to assembly language.

Languages are also defined in terms of **generations**. The first generation of computer languages is machine language, the second generation is assembly language, and the third generation is high-level language. Fourth-generation languages, also referred to as **4GLs,** have not been developed yet, and are described only in terms of characteristics and programmer productivity. The fifth generation of languages is called **natural language**. To program in a fifth-generation language, one would use the syntax of natural speech. Clearly, the implementation of a natural language would require the achievement of one of the grand challenges—computerized speech understanding.

Fortran (FORmula TRANslation) was developed in the mid 1950s for solving engineering and scientific problems. New standards updated the language over the years, and the current standard, Fortran 90, contains strong numerical computation capabilities, along with many of the new features and structures in languages such as C. **COBOL** (COmmon Business-Oriented Language) was developed in the late 1950s to solve business problems. **Basic** (Beginner's All-purpose Symbolic Instruction Code) was developed in the mid-1960s and was used as an educational tool, and is often included with the system software for a PC. **Pascal** was developed in the early 1970s and is widely used in computer science programs to introduce students to computing. **Ada** was developed at the initiative of the U.S. Department of Defense with the purpose of developing a high-level language appropriate to embedded computer systems, which are typically implemented using microprocessors. The final design of the language was accepted in 1979, and the language was named in honor of Ada Lovelace, who developed instructions for doing computations on an analytical machine in the early 1800s. **C** is a general-purpose language that evolved from two languages, BCPL and B, which were developed at Bell Laboratories in the late 1960s. In 1972, Dennis Ritchie developed and implemented the first C compiler on a DEC PDP-11 computer at Bell Laboratories. The language became very popular for system development because it was hardware-independent. Because of its popularity in both industry and in academia, it became clear that a standard definition was needed. A committee of the American National Standards Institute (ANSI) was created in 1983 to provide a machine-independent and unambiguous definition of C. In 1989, the **ANSI C** standard was approved; that language is described in this text.

ANSI C

C has become the language of choice of many engineers and scientists because it has not only powerful commands and data structures, but also because it can easily be used for operating system operations. Because C is the language that a new engineer is most likely to encounter in a job, it is a good choice for an introduction to computing for engineers. However, it is more important to establish a good foundation in an introductory course in computing than it is to cover all the features of the language. Therefore, we have selected the most important features of C for solving engineering problems, and we have incorporated them in this text. Thus, we cover the fundamental concepts of C, but we do not attempt to cover all elements of the language.

Executing a Computer Program. A program written in a high-level language such as C must be translated into machine language before the instructions can be executed by the computer. A special program called a **compiler** is used to perform this translation. Thus, in order to be able to write and execute C programs on a computer, the computer's software must include a C compiler. C compilers are available for the entire range of computer hardware, from supercomputers to personal computers. Most C compilers are based on the ANSI standards, but you should check the documentation of your compiler to see if it is an ANSI C compiler. If it is not an ANSI C compiler, there will be some differences between the C language that we discuss in this text and the C language accepted by the compiler.

Compiler

Bugs

Compiler errors

Debugging

Source program
Object program

If any errors (often called **bugs**) are detected by the compiler during compilation, corresponding error messages are printed. We must correct our program statements and then perform the compilation step again. The errors identified during this stage are called **compiler errors**, or compile-time errors. For example, if we want to divide the value stored in a variable called `sum` by 3, the correct expression in C is `sum/3`; if we incorrectly write the expression using the backslash, as in `sum\3`, we will have a compiler error. The process of compiling, correcting statements (or **debugging**), and recompiling must often be repeated several times before the program compiles without compiler errors. When there are no compiler errors, the compiler generates a program in machine language that performs the steps specified by the original C program. The original C program is referred to as the **source program**, and the machine language version is called an **object program**. Thus, the source program and the object program specify the same steps, but the source program is specified in a high-level language and the object program is specified in machine language.

Execution
Linking
Loading

Logic errors

Once the program has compiled correctly, additional steps are necessary to prepare the object program for **execution**. This preparation involves **linking** other machine language statements to the object program and then **loading** the program into memory. After this linking/loading, the program steps are then executed by the computer. New errors called execution errors, run-time errors, or **logic errors** may be identified in this stage; they are also called program bugs. Execution errors often cause termination of a program. For example, the program statements may attempt to perform a division by zero, which generates an execution error. Some execution errors do not stop the program from executing, but they cause incorrect results to be computed. These types of errors can be caused by programmer errors in determining the correct steps in the solutions and by errors in the data processed by the program. When execution errors occur due to errors in the program statements, we must correct the errors in the source program and then begin again with the compilation step. Even when a program appears to execute properly, we must check the answers carefully to be sure that they are correct. The computer will perform the steps precisely as we specify, and

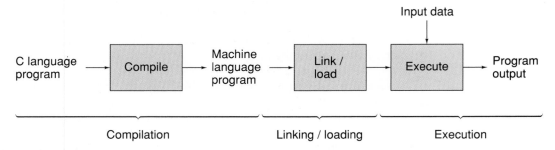

Figure 1.3 *Program compilation/linking/execution.*

if we specify the wrong steps, the computer will execute these wrong (but syntactically legal) steps and thus present us with an answer that is incorrect.

The processes of compilation, linking/loading, and execution are outlined in Figure 1.3. The process of converting an assembly language program to binary **Assembler** is performed by an **assembler** program, and the corresponding processes are called assembly, linking/loading, and execution.

A C compiler often has additional capabilities that provide a user-friendly environment for implementing and testing C programs. For example, some C environments contain text processors so that program files can be generated, compiled, and executed in the same software package, as opposed to using a separate word processor that requires the use of operating system commands to transfer back and forth between the word processor and the compiler. Many C program**Debugger** ming environments include **debugger** programs, which are useful in identifying errors in a program. Debugger programs allow us to see values stored in variables at different points in a program and to step through the program line by line.

As we present new statements in C, we will also point out common errors associated with the statements or useful techniques for locating errors associated with the statements. The **debugging aids** will be identified with a bug icon in the margin, and they will also be summarized at the end of each chapter.

Software life cycle   **Software Life Cycle.** In 1955, the cost of a typical computer solution was estimated to be 15% for software development and 85% for associated computer hardware [5]. Over the years, the cost of the hardware has dramatically dropped, whereas the cost of the software has increased, and in 1985, it was estimated that these numbers had essentially switched, with 85% of the cost for the software and 15% for the hardware. With the majority of the cost of a computer solution residing in software development, a great deal of attention has been given to understanding the development of a software solution.

The development of a software project generally follows definite steps or cycles, which are collectively called the **software life cycle.** These steps typically include project definition, detailed specification, coding and modular testing, integrated testing, and maintenance [5]. (These steps will be explained in more detail in later chapters.) Data indicate that the corresponding percentages of effort involved can be estimated as shown in Table 1.2. From these estimates, it is clear

TABLE 1.2 Software Life-Cycle Phases

Life Cycle	Percent of Effort
Definition	3
Specification	15
Coding and modular testing	14
Integrated testing	8
Maintenance	60

Software
maintenance

that **software maintenance** is a significant part of the cost of a software system. This **maintenance** includes adding enhancements to the software, fixing errors identified as the software is used, and adapting the software to work with new hardware and software. The ease of providing maintenance is directly related to the original definition and specification of the solution because these steps lay the foundation for the rest of the project. The problem-solving process that we present in the next section emphasizes the need to define and specify the solution carefully before beginning to code or test it.

Software
prototypes

One of the techniques that has been successful in reducing the cost of software development both in time and in cost is the development of **software prototypes**. Instead of waiting until the software system is developed and then letting the users work with it, a prototype of the system is developed early in the life cycle. This prototype does not have all the functions required of the final software, but it allows the user to use it early in the life cycle, and to make desired modifications to the specifications. Making changes earlier in the life cycle is both cost- and time-effective.

As an engineer, it is very likely that you will need to modify or add additional capabilities to existing software. These modifications will be much simpler if the existing software is well-structured and readable, and if the documentation that accompanies the software is up-to-date and clearly written. For these reasons, we stress developing good habits that make programs more readable and self-documenting. As new C statements are presented and new techniques are demonstrated, we include guidelines for writing well-structured and readable code. These **style guidelines** are indicated with margin notes and are also summarized at the end of the chapter.

1.3   An Engineering Problem-Solving Methodology

Problem solving is a key part of not only engineering courses, but also of courses in computer science, mathematics, physics, and chemistry. Therefore, it is important to have a consistent approach to solving problems. It is also helpful if the approach is general enough to work for all these different areas, so that we do not have to learn one technique for mathematics problems, a different technique for physics problems, and so on. The problem-solving process

Problem-
solving process

that we present works for engineering problems and can be tailored to solve problems in other areas as well; however, it does assume that we are using the computer to help solve the problem.

The process or methodology for problem solving that we will use throughout this text has five steps:

1.   State the problem clearly.
2.   Describe the input and output information.
3.   Work the problem by hand (or with a calculator) for a simple set of data.
4.   Develop a solution and convert it to a computer program.
5.   Test the solution with a variety of data.

We now discuss each of these steps using an example of computing the distance between two points in a plane.

1.   PROBLEM STATEMENT

The first step is to state the problem clearly. It is extremely important to give a clear, concise problem statement to avoid any misunderstandings. For this example, the problem statement is the following:

Compute the straight-line distance between two points in a plane.

2.   INPUT/OUTPUT DESCRIPTION

The second step is to describe carefully the information that is given to solve the problem and then identify the values to be computed. These items represent the input and the output for the problem, and collectively can be called input/output, or I/O. For many problems, a diagram that shows the input and output is useful. At this point, the program is an "abstraction" because we are not defining the steps to determine the output; instead, we are only showing **I/O diagram** the information that is used to compute the output. The **I/O diagram** for this example follows.

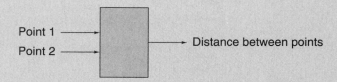

3.   HAND EXAMPLE

The third step is to work the problem by hand or with a calculator, using a simple set of data. This is a very important step, and should not be skipped even for simple problems. This is the step in which you work out the details of the problem solution. If you cannot take a simple set of numbers and compute the output (either by hand or with a calculator), then you are not ready to move on to the next step; you should reread the problem, and perhaps consult reference material. The solution by hand for this specific example follows:

Let the points p_1 and p_2 have the following coordinates:

$$p_1 = (1,5); \qquad p_2 = (4,7)$$

We want to compute the distance between the two points, which is the hypotenuse of a right triangle, as shown in Figure 1.4. Using the Pythagorean theorem, we can compute the distance with the following equation:

$$
\begin{aligned}
\text{distance} &= \sqrt{(\text{side}_1)^2 + (\text{side}_2)^2} \\
&= \sqrt{(4-1)^2 + (7-5)^2} \\
&= \sqrt{13} \\
&= 3.61
\end{aligned}
$$

4.   ALGORITHM DEVELOPMENT

Algorithm

Once you can work the problem for a simple set of data, you are then ready to develop an **algorithm**, or a step-by-step outline, of the problem solution. For

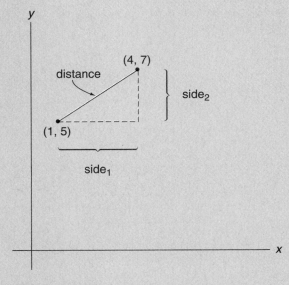

Figure 1.4 *Straight-line distance between two points.*

simple problems such as this one, the algorithm can be listed as operations that are performed one after another. This outline of steps decomposes the problem into simpler steps, as shown by the following outline of the steps required to compute and print the distance between two points.

Decomposition Outline
1. *Give values to the two points.*
2. *Compute the lengths of the two sides of the right triangle generated by the two points.*
3. *Compute the distance between the two points, which is equal to the length of the hypotenuse of the triangle.*
4. *Print the distance between the two points.*

Decomposition outline

This **decomposition outline** is then converted to C commands so that we can use the computer to perform the computations. From the following solution, you can see that the commands are very similar to the steps used in the hand example. The details of these commands are explained in Chapter 2. The diskette icon in the margin indicates that this program is included on the diskette at the end of the text.

ch1_1.c

```c
/*------------------------------------------------------------*/
/*   Program chapter1_1                                       */
/*                                                            */
/*   This program computes the                                */
/*   distance between two points.                             */

#include <stdio.h>
#include <stdlib.h>
#include <math.h>

main()
{
   /*   Declare and initialize variables.   */
   double x1=1, y1=5, x2=4, y2=7,
          side_1, side_2, distance;

   /*   Compute sides of a right triangle.   */
   side_1 = x2 - x1;
   side_2 = y2 - y1;
   distance = sqrt(side_1*side_1 + side_2*side_2);

   /*   Print distance.   */
   printf("The distance between the two points is "
          "%5.2f \n",distance);

   /*   Exit program.   */
   return EXIT_SUCCESS;
}
/*------------------------------------------------------------*/
```

5.   **TESTING**

The final step in our problem-solving process is testing the solution. We should first test the solution with the data from the hand example because we have already computed the solution. When the C statements in this solution are executed, the computer displays the following output:

```
The distance between the points is  3.61
```

This output matches the value that we calculated by hand. If the C solution did not match the hand solution, then we should review both solutions to find the error. Once the solution works for the hand example, we should also test it with additional sets of data to be sure that the solution works for other valid sets of data.

The set of steps demonstrated in this example are used in developing the programs in the Problem Solving Applied sections in the chapters that follow.

1.4   Data Collection for Weather Prediction

In each of the following chapters, we include Problem Solving Applied sections that use the new C statements presented in the chapter to solve a problem related to the grand challenge discussed in the chapter introduction. Although we have shown you a C program, we do not have the background yet to develop a new program related to weather prediction (the grand challenge discussed in this chapter introduction), but we can discuss the types of weather data that are collected, and we can discuss the preliminary analyses that accompany the search for a solution that predicts the weather.

The first step in attempting to develop an equation or a model to predict the weather is to study the past history of the weather. Fortunately, a number of national agencies are interested in collecting and storing weather information [2, 6]. NOAA (National Oceanic and Atmospheric Administration) is a research-oriented organization that studies the oceans and the atmosphere. It also funds environmental research in data analysis, modeling, and experimental work relative to global changes. The National Environmental Satellite, Data, and Information Service collects and distributes information relative to the weather. The National Climatic Data Center collects and compiles climatology information from National Weather Service offices across the country. It is also the National Weather Service offices that interact with state and local weather forecasters to keep the general public aware of current weather information.

The National Climatic Data Center in North Carolina is responsible for maintaining climatological data from National Weather Service offices. These data are available in many forms, including local climatology data by month,

Figure 1.5 *Local climatological data.*

data by state, and data for the world. The center also maintains historical climatology data beginning with 1931. Figure 1.5 contains a month summary of local climatology data that was collected by the National Weather Service office at Stapleton International Airport in Denver, Colorado, for the month of January 1991. The summary contains 23 different pieces of weather information collected for each day, including maximum and minimum temperatures, amount of precipitation, peak wind gust, and minutes of sunshine. These data are then analyzed to generate the monthly summary information at the bottom of the form, which includes average temperature, total rainfall, total snowfall, and the number of days that were partly cloudy.

To analyze these weather data for one month, one of the first things that we might do is plot some of the different pieces of data in order to see if we could observe any visible trends in the data. For example, we should be able to observe if the maximum temperature seems to stay the same, or increases, or decreases, or fluctuates around a common point. Figure 1.6 contains a graph of the maximum temperatures for January 1991. We can see that the temperature has some wide fluctuations or variations, but there is not a steady increase or decrease. We could also analyze temperature data for a year in the same way; Figure 1.7 con-

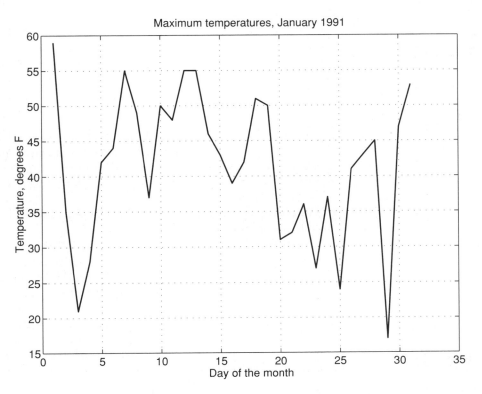

Figure 1.6 *Maximum temperatures for January 1991.*

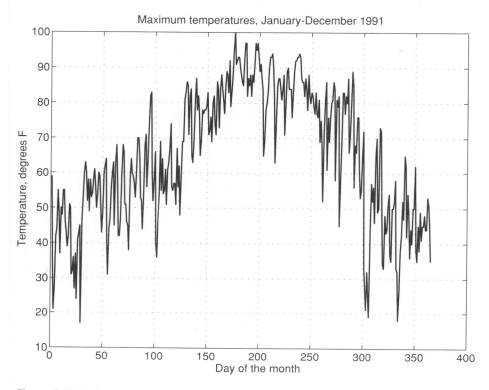

Figure 1.7 *Maximum temperatures for 1991.*

tains the maximum daily temperatures from January through December 1991. To observe gradual warming trends, it would be important to look at the temperatures over many years. From observing Figures 1.6 and 1.7, it is clear that a straight line (linear model) is not a good model for either set of data; the models for these sets of data are more complicated.

We often are interested in analyzing several different sets of data at the same time to see if there are relationships. For example, we would expect that the maximum temperatures and the average temperatures over a period of time would be related. That is, we expect that days with higher maximum temperatures will also have higher average temperatures. However, we also expect that on some days, the maximum temperature and the average temperature are close together, and on other days, the maximum temperature and the average temperature are not close together. Figure 1.8 contains plots of the maximum temperatures and the average temperatures for the month of January 1991 at Stapleton International Airport, and illustrates the relationship between the maximum temperatures and average temperatures. There are mathematical computations that we can perform to measure the relationship, or correlation, between variables. Several of the problems in the text will compute and analyze these correlation coefficients.

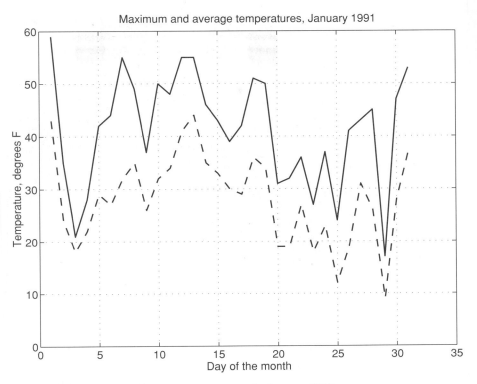

Figure 1.8 *Maximum and average temperatures for January 1991.*

Graphs give us a quick intuitive feel for data trends, but we need more analytical methods for using past history to predict the future. Analytical methods commonly used to model data include developing linear or polynomial models to represent the data. We discuss these types of computations later in the text. Also, predictions of weather at a specific location cannot be made entirely on the past information. A good prediction model will need to take into account other factors such as the weather in surrounding areas and worldwide weather patterns.

SUMMARY

A group of outstanding recent engineering achievements was presented to demonstrate the diversity of engineering applications. A set of grand challenges was then presented to illustrate some of the exciting and difficult problems that currently face engineers and scientists. We also discussed some of the nontechnical skills required to be a successful engineer. Because the solutions to most engineering problems, including the grand challenges, will be by computer, we also presented a summary of the components of a computer system, from computer hardware to computer software. We also introduced a five-step problem-solving methodology that we will use to develop a computer solution to a problem. These five steps are as follows:

1.   State the problem clearly.
2.   Describe the input and output information.
3.   Work the problem by hand (or with a calculator) for a simple set of data.
4.   Develop an algorithm and convert it to a computer program.
5.   Test the solution with a variety of data.

This process will be used throughout the text as we develop solutions to problems.

KEY TERMS

algorithm	machine language
ANSI C	mathematical computation tool
arithmetic logic unit (ALU)	memory
assembler	microprocessor
assembly language	network
binary	object program
bug	operating system
central processing unit (CPU)	personal computer (PC)
compiler	problem-solving process
compiler error	processor
computer	program
database management	real-time program
debug	software
debugger	software life cycle
decomposition outline	software maintenance
desktop publishing	software prototype
electronic copy	software tool
execution	source program
grand challenges	spreadsheet
graphics tool	supercomputer
hardware	syntax
high-level language	utility
I/O diagram	word processor
linking/loading	workstation
logic error	

PROBLEMS

The following problems combine an assignment in which you will learn more about one of the topics in this chapter with an opportunity to improve your written communication skills. (Perhaps your professor will even select some of the written reports for oral presentation in class.) Each report should include at least two references, so you will want to learn how to use library computers to locate reference information. Prepare your report using word processor software. If you do not already know how to use a word processor, ask your professor for guidance on locating manuals or seminars to help you learn to use one of the word processors available on your university's computer systems.

1. Write a short report on one of these outstanding engineering achievements:

Moon landing	Composite materials
Application satellites	Jumbo jets
Microprocessors	Lasers
CAD/CAM	Fiber optics
CAT scans	Genetically engineered products

   A good starting point for finding references is the set of suggested readings at the end of this chapter.

2. Write a short report on one of these grand challenges:

   Predication of weather, climate, and global change

   Computerized speech understanding

   Mapping of the human genome

   Improved vehicle performance

   Enhanced oil and gas recovery

   A good starting point for finding references is the set of suggested readings at the end of this chapter.

3. Write a short report on an outstanding engineering achievement that is not included in the list given in this chapter. Past issues of *Scientific American* would provide some good ideas of recent achievements.

4. Write a short report on a topic that you think is a grand engineering challenge that was not included in the list given in this chapter. Recent issues of *Scientific American* would provide some results in topics of current research that could be a potential grand challenge.

5. Write a short report discussing an ethical issue that you think relates to one of the top 10 achievements. Present several potential ways in which one might view the issue.

6. Write a short report discussing an ethical issue that you think relates to one of the grand challenges. Present several potential ways in which one might view the issue.

7. Write a short report on the history of computing. You can choose to focus on either computer hardware or computer software.

8. Write a short report discussing the equipment used in the collection of climatological data. A good source of information would be a National Weather Service Office or a local television station.

9. Write a short report discussing the types of climatology data that have been collected over the years. Your university library may contain climatological data in its government records section. Climatological information can also be ordered from the National Climatic Data Center, Federal Building, Asheville, North Carolina 28801-2696. Also, use a software tool to prepare at least one graph for your report.

SUGGESTED READINGS

For further reading on the top 10 achievements or on the grand challenges, we recommend the following articles from Scientific American.

Barton, John H. "Patenting Life." *Scientific American*, March 1991, pp. 40–46.

Berns, Michael W. "Laser Surgery." *Scientific American*, June 1991, pp. 84–90.

Biship, David J., Peter L. Gammel, and David A. Huse. "Resistance in High-Temperature Superconductors." *Scientific American*, Feb. 1993, pp. 48–55.

Brown, Barbara E. and John C. Ogden. "Coral Bleaching." *Scientific American*, Jan. 1993, pp. 64–71.

Bugg, Charles E., William M. Carson, and John A. Montgomery. "Drugs by Design." *Scientific American*, December 1993, pp. 92–101.

Capecchi, Mario R. "Targeted Gene Replacement." *Scientific American*, Mar. 1994, pp. 52–61.

Cava, Robert J. "Superconductors beyond 1–2–3." *Scientific American*, August 1990, pp. 42–49.

Charlson, Robert J. and Tom M. L. Wigley. "Sulfate Aerosol and Climatic Change." *Scientific American*, Feb. 1994, pp. 48–57.

Chou, Tsu-Wei, Roy L. McCullough, and R. Byron Pipes. "Composites." *Scientific American*, October 1986, pp. 192–203.

Coffin, Millard F., and Olav Eldholm. "Large Igneous Provinces." *Scientific American*, October 1993, pp. 42–49.

Conn, Robert W., et al. "The International Thermonuclear Experimental Reactor." *Scientific American*, April 1992, pp. 103–110.

Corcoran, Elizabeth. "Calculating Reality." *Scientific American*, January 1991, pp. 100–109.

Curl, Robert F., and Richard E. Smalley. "Fullerenes." *Scientific American*, October 1991, pp. 54–63.

Depp, Steven W. and Webster E. Howard. "Flat-Panel Displays." *Scientific American*, Mar. 1993, pp. 90–99.

Desurvire, Emmanuelf. "Lightwave Communications: The Fifth Generation." *Scientific American*, January 1992, pp. 114–121.

Ditto, William L., and Louis M. Pecora. "Mastering Chaos." *Scientific American*, August 1993, pp. 78–85.

Doolittle, Russell F., and Peer Bork. "Evolutionarily Mobile Modules in Proteins." *Scientific American*, October 1993, pp. 50–57.

Drexhage, Martin G., and Cornelius T. Moynihan. "Infrared Optical Fibers." *Scientific American*, November 1988, pp. 110–116.

Dunker, Kenneth F. and Basile G. Rabbat. "Why America's Bridges are Crumbling." *Scientific American*, Mar. 1993, pp. 66–73.

Gasser, Charles S., and Robert T. Fraley. "Transgenic Crops." *Scientific American*, June 1992, pp. 62–69.

Goulding, Michael. "Flooded Forests of the Amazon." *Scientific American*, April 1993, pp. 114–121.

Greenberg, Donald P. "Computers and Architecture." *Scientific American*, February 1991, pp. 104–109.

Halsey, Thomas C., and James E. Martin. "Electrorheological Fluids." *Scientific American*, October 1993, pp. 58–67.

Hess, Wilmot, et al. "The Exploration of the Moon." *Scientific American*, October 1969, pp. 55–72.

Holloway, Marguerite. "Sustaining the Amazon." *Scientific American*, June 1992, pp. 90–100.

Holloway, Marguerite. "Nurturing Nature." *Scientific American*, Apr. 1994, pp. 98–109.

Homer-Dixon, Thomas F., Jeffrey H. Boutwell, and George W. Rathjens. "Environmental Change and Violent Conflict." *Scientific American*, Feb 1993, pp. 38–47.

Jewell, Jack L., James P. Harbison, and Axel Scherer. "Microlasers." *Scientific American*, November 1991, pp. 86–94.

Johnston, Arch C., and Lisa R. Kanter. "Earthquakes in Stable Continental Crust." *Scientific American*, March 1990, pp. 68–75.

Keyes, Robert W. "The Future of the Transistor." *Scientific American*, June 1993, pp. 70–99.

Kusler, Jon A., William J. Mitsch, and Joseph S. Larson. "Wetlands." *Scientific American*, January 1994, pp. 16–72.

Lents, James M., and William J. Kelly. "Clearing the Air in Los Angeles." *Scientific American*, October 1993, pp. 32–41.

Likharev, Konstantin K. and Tord Claeson. "Single Electronics." *Scientific American*, June 1992, pp. 80–86.

Luhmann, Janet G., James B. Pollack and Lawrence Colin. "The Pioneer Mission to Venus." *Scientific American*, Apr 1994, pp. 90–97.

Mahowald, Misha A., and Carver Mead. "The Silicon Retina." *Scientific American*, May 1991, pp. 76–82.

Matthews, Dennis L., and Mordecai D. Rosen. "Soft-X-Ray Lasers." *Scientific American*, December 1988, pp. 86–91.

Osada, Yoshihito and Simon B. Ross-Murphy. "Intelligent Gels." *Scientific American*, May 1993, pp. 82–87.

Paabo, Svante. "Ancient DNA." *Scientific American*, November 1993, pp. 86–93.

Pollack, Henry N. and David S. Chapman. "Underground Records of Changing Climate." *Scientific American*, June 1993, pp. 44–53.

Rennie, John. "DNA's New Twists." *Scientific American*, April 1993, pp. 122–133.

Repetto, Robert. "Accounting for Environmental Assets." *Scientific American*, June 1992, pp. 94–101.

Rhodes, Daniela and Aaron Klug, "Zinc Fingers." *Scientific American*, Feb. 1993, pp. 56–65.

Richelson, Jeffrey T. "The Future of Space Reconnaissance." *Scientific American*, January 1991, pp. 38–44.

Ross, Philip E. "Eloquent Remains." *Scientific American*, May 1992, pp. 114–125.

Steinberg, Morris A. "Materials for Aerospace." *Scientific American*, October 1986, pp. 67–72.

Swade, Doron D. "Redeeming Charles Babbage's Mechanical Computer." *Scientific American*, Mar 1993, pp. 86–91.

Veldkamp, Wilfrid B., and Thomas J. McHugh. "Binary Optics." *Scientific American*, May 1992, pp. 92–97.

Wallich, Paul. "Silicon Babies." *Scientific American*, December 1991, pp. 124–134.

Courtesy of National Aeronautics and Space Administration.

GRAND CHALLENGE:
Vehicle Performance

Wind tunnels are test chambers built to generate precise wind speeds. Accurate scale models of new aircraft can be mounted on force-measuring supports in the test chamber, and measurements of the forces on the model then can be made at many different wind speeds and angles. Some wind tunnels can operate at hypersonic velocities, generating wind speeds of thousands of miles per hour. The size of wind-tunnel test sections vary from a few inches across to sizes large enough to accommodate a jet fighter. At the completion of a wind-tunnel test series, many sets of data have been collected that can be used to determine lift, drag, and other aerodynamic performance characteristics of a new aircraft at its various operating speeds and positions.

Simple C Programs

Objectives

OBJECTIVES

In this chapter, we outline the structure of a simple C program that defines variables, performs computations, and then prints the results. We then present the syntax and the semantics for the C statements that define and initialize constants and variables, that compute new values using simple arithmetic operations, that read user-supplied information from the keyboard during the execution of a program, and that print information on the screen. Additional functions are presented for most of the numerical computations commonly used to solve engineering problems. With these C statements and functions, we then have the capability to write complete programs. We also graphically explain linear interpolation, which is then used to solve a problem that analyzes wind-tunnel data. An additional problem is solved that analyzes the velocity and acceleration values of an advanced turboprop engine. Finally, a C program is presented that allows you to check the specific limitations of values for constants and variables for your system.

2.1   Program Structure

In this section, we analyze the structure of a specific C program, and then we present the **general structure** of a C program. The program that follows was first introduced in Chapter 1; it computes and prints the distance between two points.

ch1_1.c

```
/*------------------------------------------------------*/
/*   Program chapter1_1                                 */
/*                                                      */
/*   This program computes the                          */
/*   distance between two points.                       */

#include <stdio.h>
#include <stdlib.h>
#include <math.h>

main()
{
  /*  Declare and initialize variables.  */
  double x1=1, y1=5, x2=4, y2=7,
         side_1, side_2, distance;

  /*  Compute sides of a right triangle.  */
  side_1 = x2 - x1;
  side_2 = y2 - y1;
  distance = sqrt(side_1*side_1 + side_2*side_2);

  /*  Print distance.  */
  printf("The distance between the two points is "
         "%5.2f \n",distance);

  /*  Exit program.  */
  return EXIT_SUCCESS;
}
/*------------------------------------------------------*/
```

We now briefly discuss the statements in this specific example; each of the statements is discussed in detail in later sections of this chapter.

Comments   The first five lines of this program contain **comments** that give the program a name (**chapter1_1**) and that define its purpose:

```
/*-------------------------------------------------------*/
/*  Program chapter1_1                                   */
/*                                                       */
/*  This program computes the                            */
/*  distance between two points.                         */
```

Comments begin with the characters /* and end with the characters */. A comment can be on a line by itself, or it can be on the same line as a command; a comment can also extend over several lines. Each of the comment lines here is a separate comment because each line begins with /* and ends with */. *Although comments are optional, good style requires that comments be used throughout a program to improve its readability and to document the computations.* In the text programs, we always use initial comments to give a name to the program and to describe the general purpose of the program; additional explanation comments are also included throughout the program. ANSI C allows comments and statements to begin anywhere on a line; we begin the initial comments of a program in the first column.

Preprocessor directives give instructions to the compiler that are performed before the program is compiled. The most common directive inserts additional statements in the program; it contains the characters **#include** followed by the name of the file containing the additional statements. This program contains the following three preprocessor directives:

```
#include <stdio.h>
#include <stdlib.h>
#include <math.h>
```

These directives specify that statements in the files **stdio.h**, **stdlib.h**, and **math.h** should be included in place of these three statements before the program is executed. The < and > characters around the file names indicate that the files are included with the **Standard C library** [7]; this library is contained in the files that accompany an ANSI C compiler. The **stdio.h** file contains information related to the output statement used in this program, the **stdlib.h** file contains a constant we will use in exiting the program, and the **math.h** file contains information related to the function used in this program to compute the square root of a value. The **h** extension on these file names specifies that they are header files; more information on header files is included later in this chapter and in Chapter 4. Preprocessor directives are generally included after the initial comments describing the program's purpose.

Every C program contains a set of statements called a **main** function. The body of the function is enclosed by braces, { }. In order to easily identify the body of the function, we place these braces on lines by themselves. Thus, the two lines following the preprocessor directives specify the beginning of the main function:

```
main()
{
```

Style

Preprocessor directives

Standard C library

Declarations

Initial values

The **main** function contains two types of commands: declarations and state-ments. The **declarations** define the memory locations that will be used by the statements, and therefore the declarations must precede the statements. The dec-larations may or may not give **initial values** to be stored in the memory loca-tions. A comment precedes the declaration statement in this program:

```
/* Declare and initialize variables. */
double x1=1, y1=5, x2=4, y2=7,
       side_1, side_2, distance;
```

These declarations specify that the program will use seven variables named **x1**, **y1**, **x2**, **y2**, **side_1**, **side_2**, and **distance**. The term **double** indicates that the vari-ables will store **double-precision floating-point** values; these variables can store noninteger values such as 12.5 and -0.0005 with many digits of precision. In ad-dition, this statement specifies that **x1** should be initialized (given an initial value) to the value 1, **y1** should be initialized to the value 5, **x2** should be initial-ized to the value 4, and **y2** should be initialized to the value 7. The initial values of **side_1**, **side_2**, and **distance** are not specified, and should not be assumed to be initialized to zero. *Because the declaration was too long for one line, we split it over two lines; the indenting of the second line indicates that it is a continuation of the previous line.*

Style

Statements

The statements that specify the operations to be performed in the example program are the following:

```
/* Compute sides of a right triangle.  */
side_1 = x2 - x1;
side_2 = y2 - y1;
distance = sqrt(side_1*side_1 + side_2*side_2);

/* Print distance.  */
printf("The distance between the two points is "
       "%5.2f \n",distance);
```

These statements compute the lengths of the two sides of the right triangle formed by two points (see Figure 1.5, page 21) and then compute the length of the hypotenuse of the right triangle. The details of the syntax of these statements are discussed later in the chapter. After the distance is computed, it is printed with the **printf** statement. This output statement is too long for a single line, so we separate the statement into two lines; the indenting of the second line again indicates that it is a continuation of the previous line. Additional comments were used to explain the computations and the output statement. **Also, note that the declarations and statements are all required to end with a semicolon.**

To exit the program, we use a **return** statement. The constant **EXIT_SUCCESS** is defined in the **stdlib.h** file, and indicates a successful exit from the program.

```
/* Exit program.  */
return EXIT_SUCCESS;
```

The use of a `return` statement at the end of the `main` function is optional in ANSI C; we use it for documentation purposes.

The body of the `main` function then ends with the right brace on a line by itself, and another comment line to delineate the end of the `main function`.

```
}
/*--------------------------------------------------------*/
```

Style

Note that we have also included blank lines (also called white space) in the program to separate different components. *These blank lines make a program more readable and easier to modify.* The declarations and statements within the main function were indented three columns in order to show the structure of the program. This spacing provides a consistent style, and makes our programs easier to read.

Now that we have closely examined the C program from Chapter 1, we can compare its structure to the **general form** of a C program:

```
preprocessing directives
main()
{
      declarations;
      statements;
}
```

This structure is evident in the programs developed in this chapter and in the chapters that follow.

Modify!

`ch1_1.c`

1. Create a file containing the sample program discussed in this section using either an editor that is part of your C compiler or using a word processor.* Or, you can copy the file `ch1_1.c` from the diskette at the end of this text to your computer work area. Then compile and execute the program. You should get this output:

    `The distance between the two points is   3.61`

2. Change the values given to the two points to the coordinates $(-1, 6)$ and $(2, 4)$. Run the program with these new values. Did the distance change? Explain.

3. Change the values given to the two points so that they represent the coordinates $(1,0)$ and $(5,7)$. Check the program's answer with your calculator.

4. Change the values given to the two points so that they represent the same coordinates $(2, 4)$ and $(2, 4)$. Does the program give the correct answer?

---

* If you use a word processor to generate the file, be sure to save it as a text file.

2.2   Constants and Variables

Constants

Variables
Identifier

Constants and variables represent values that we use in our programs. **Constants** are specific values such as 2, 3.1416, or −1.5 that we include in the C statements, and **variables** are memory locations that are assigned a name or **identifier**. The identifier is used to reference the value stored in the memory location. A useful analogy for a memory location and its corresponding identifier is a mailbox that is associated with the name of an individual; the memory location (or mailbox) then contains a value. The following shows the variables, their identifiers, and their initial values after the following declaration statement from program **Chapter1_1**:

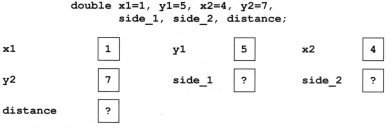

```
double x1=1, y1=5, x2=4, y2=7,
       side_1, side_2, distance;
```

Garbage values

Memory
snapshot

The values of variables that were not given initial values are unspecified, and thus indicated with a question mark; sometimes these values are called **garbage values** because they are values from the previous program. A diagram such as this that shows a variable along with its identifier and its value is called a **memory snapshot** because it shows the contents of a memory location at a specified point in the execution of a program; the preceding memory snapshot shows the variables and their contents as specified by the declaration statement. We frequently use memory snapshots to show the contents of variables both before and after a statement is executed in order to show its effect.

The rules for selecting a valid identifier are as follows:

- an identifier must begin with an alphabetic character or the underscore character _
- alphabetic characters in an identifier can be lowercase or uppercase letters
- an identifier can contain digits, but not as the first character
- an identifier can be of any length, but the first 31 characters of the identifier must be unique

Case-sensitive

Keywords

C is **case-sensitive**, and thus uppercase letters are different from lowercase letters; thus **Total**, **TOTAL**, and **total** represent three different variables. Also the variable **distance_in_miles_from_earth_to_mars** would not be distinguished from **distance_in_miles_from_earth_to_venus** because the first 31 characters are the same. C also includes **keywords** with special meaning to the C compiler that cannot be used for identifiers; a complete list is given in Table 2.1.

Examples of valid identifiers are **distance, x_1, X_Sum, average_measurement**, and **initial_time**. Examples of invalid identifiers are **1x** (begins with a digit), **minimum-x** (contains an invalid character −), **I/O** (contains an invalid character /), **switch** (a keyword), **$sum** (contains an invalid character $), and **rate%** (contains an invalid character %).

TABLE 2.1 Keywords			
auto	double	ints	truct
break	else	long	switch
case	enum	register	typedef
char	extern	return	union
const	float	short	unsigned
continue	for	signed	void
default	goto	sizeof	volatile
do	if	static	while

Style

An identifier name should be carefully selected so that it reflects the contents of the variable. *If possible, the name should also indicate the units of measurement.* For example, if a variable represents a temperature measurement in degrees Fahrenheit, use an identifier such as **temp_F** or **degrees_F**, or if a variable represents an angle, name it **theta_rad** to indicate that the angle is measured in radians or **theta_deg** to indicate that the angle is measured in degrees.

The declarations at the beginning of the **main** function (and also at the beginning of other C functions that we write) must include not only all identifiers of the variables that we plan to use in our program, but they must also specify the types of values that will be stored in the variables. These data types are presented after a discussion on scientific notation.

Practice!

Determine which of the following names are valid identifiers. If a name is not a valid identifier, give the reason that it is not acceptable, and suggest a valid replacement.

1.	**density**	2.	**area**	3.	**Time**
4.	**xsum**	5.	**x_sum**	6.	**tax-rate**
7.	**perimeter**	8.	**sec^2**	9.	**degrees_C**
10.	**break**	11.	**#123**	12.	**x&y**
13.	**count**	14.	**void**	15.	**f(x)**
16.	**f2**	17.	**Final_Value**	18.	**w1.1**
19.	**reference1**	20.	**reference_1**	21.	**m/s**

SCIENTIFIC NOTATION

Floating-point value
Scientific notation
Mantissa

A **floating-point value** is one that can represent both integer and noninteger values, such as 2.5, −0.004, and 15.0. A floating-point value expressed in **scientific notation** is rewritten as a mantissa times a power of 10, where the **mantissa** has

Exponential notation

an absolute value greater than or equal to 1.0 and less than 10.0. For example, in scientific notation, 25.6 is written as 2.56×10^1, -0.004 is written as -4.0×10^{-3}, and 1.5 is written as 1.5×10^0. In **exponential notation**, the letter e is used to separate the mantissa from the exponent of the power of 10. Thus, in exponential notation, 25.6 is written as 2.56e1, -0.004 is written as $-4.0e-3$, and 1.5 is written as 1.5e0.

Precision

Range

The number of digits allowed by the computer for the decimal portion of the mantissa determines the **precision** or accuracy, and the number of digits allowed for the exponent determines the **range**. Thus, values with one digit of accuracy and an exponent range of -8 to 7 could include values such as 2.3×10^5 (230,000) and 5.9×10^{-8} (0.000000059). This precision and exponent range would not be sufficient for many of the types of values that we use in engineering problem solutions. For example, the distance in miles from Mars to the Sun, with seven digits of precision, is 141,517,510 or 1.4151751×10^8; to represent this value, we would need at least seven digits of accuracy and an exponent range that included the integer 8.

Practice!

In problems 1 to 6, express the value in scientific notation. Specify the number of digits of precision needed to represent each value.

1.	35.004	2.	0.00042
3.	$-50,000$	4.	3.15723
5.	-0.0999	6.	10,000,002.8

In problems 7 to 12, express the value in floating-point notation.

7.	03e-5	8.	$-1.05e5$
9.	$-3.552e6$	10.	6.67e-4
11.	9.0e-2	12.	$-2.2e-2$

NUMERIC DATA TYPES

Numeric data types are used to specify the types of numbers that will be contained in variables. In C, numeric values are either integers or floating-point values. Nonnumeric data types (such as characters) are discussed in later chapters. The diagram on the next page shows the numeric data types that are discussed in the following paragraphs:

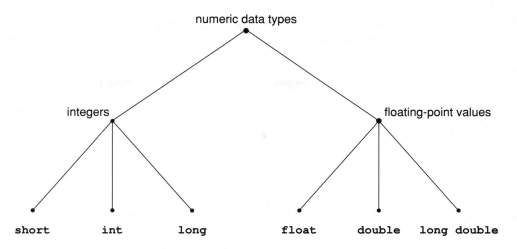

The **type specifiers** for signed integers are **short, int** and **long**, for short integer, integer, and long integer, respectively. The specific ranges of values are **system-dependent**, which means that the ranges can vary from one system to another. In the last section of this chapter, we present a program that you can use to determine the ranges of the numeric data types on your system. On many systems, the short integer and the integer data types range from −32,768 to 32,767, and the long integer type often represents values from −2,147,483,648 to 2,147,483,647. (The unusual limits such as 32,767 and 2,147,483,647 relate to conversions of binary values to decimal values.) C also allows an **unsigned** qualifier to be added to integer specifiers, where an unsigned integer represents only positive values. Signed and unsigned integers can represent the same number of values, but the ranges are different. For example, if an **unsigned short** has the range of values from 0 to 65,535, then a **short** integer has the range of values from −32,768 to 32,767; both variables can represent a total of 65,536 values.

The type specifiers for floating-point values are **float** (single-precision), **double** (double-precision), and **long double** (extended precision). The following statement from program **chapter1_1** thus defines seven variables that all contain double-precision floating-point values:

```
double x1=1, y1=5, x2=4, y2=7,
       side_1, side_2, distance;
```

The difference between the **float, double**, and **long double** types relates to the precision (or accuracy) and the range of the values represented. The precision and range are system-dependent. Table 2.2 contains precision and range information for integers and floating-point values used by the Borland C++ compiler that can be used to run C programs as well as C++ programs. (C++ is an extension of C.) A program given in Section 2.9 allows you to obtain this information for your computer system. On most systems, a **double** data type stores about twice as many decimal digits of precision as are stored with a **float** data type. In addition,

TABLE 2.2 Example Data-Type Limits*	
Integers	
short	Maximum = 32,767
int	Maximum = 32,767
long	Maximum = 2,147,483,647
Floating Point	
float	6 digits of precision Maximum exponent = 38 Maximum value = 3.402823e + 38
double	15 digits of precision Maximum exponent = 308 Maximum value = 1.797693e + 308
long double	19 digits of precision Maximum exponent = 4932 Maximum value = 1.189731e + 4932

*Borland Turbo C++ 3.0 compiler.

a **double** value will have a wider range of exponent values than a **float** value. The **long double** value may have more precision and a still wider exponent range, but this is again system-dependent. A floating-point constant such as 2.3 is assumed to be a **double** constant. To specify a **float** constant or a **long double** constant, the letter (or suffix) **F** or **L** must be appended to the constant. Thus, **2.3F** and **2.3L** represent a **float** constant and a **long double** constant, respectively.

SYMBOLIC CONSTANTS

Symbolic
constant

Style

A **symbolic constant** is defined with a preprocessor directive that assigns an identifier to the constant. The directive can appear anywhere in a C program; the compiler will replace each occurrence of the directive identifier with the constant value in all statements that follow the directive. *Engineering constants such as π or the acceleration of gravity are good candidates for symbolic constants.* For example, consider the following preprocessing directive to assign the value 3.141593 to the variable PI with the following statement:

```
#define PI 3.141593
```

Statements that need to use the value of π would then use the symbolic constant identifier instead of 3.141593, as illustrated in this statement:

```
area = PI*radius*radius;
```

which computes the area of a circle.

Style

Symbolic constants are usually defined with uppercase identifiers (as in PI *instead of* pi*) to indicate that they are symbolic constants, and, of course, the* *identifiers should be selected so that they are easy to remember.* Finally, only one symbolic constant can be defined in a directive; if several symbolic constants are desired, several separate directives are required. Note that preprocessor directives, which include the `#define` statement, do not end with a semicolon.

In the next section we discuss C statements that allow us to assign values to variables. These assignment statements could be used to assign constant values to variables, but we will see later that there are some special advantages to using symbolic constants in many cases.

Practice!

Give preprocessor directives to assign symbolic constants for these constants [8]:

1. Speed of light, $c = 2.99792 \times 10^8$ m/s
2. Charge of an electron, $e = 1.602177 \times 10^{-19}$ C
3. Avogadro's number, $N_A = 6.022 \times 10^{23}$ mol^{-1}
4. Acceleration of gravity, $g = 9.8$ m/s^2
5. Acceleration of gravity, $g = 32$ ft/s^2
6. Mass of the Earth, $M_E = 5.98 \times 10^{24}$ kg
7. Radius of the Moon, $r = 1.74 \times 10^6$ m

2.3   Assignment Statements

Assignment statement

An **assignment statement** is used to assign a value to an identifier. The general form of the assignment statement is

        identifier = expression;

Expression

where an **expression** can be a constant, another variable, or the result of an operation. Consider the following two sets of statements that declare and give values to the variables **sum** and **x1**:

```
double sum=10.5;        double sum;
int x1=3;               int x1;
                        ...
                        sum = 10.5;
                        x1 = 3;
```

After either set of statements is executed, the value of **sum** is 10.5 and the value of **x1** is 3, as shown in the following memory snapshot.

        sum | 10.5 | x1 | 3 |

The statements on the left define and initialize the variables at the same time; the assignment statements on the right could be used at any point in the program, and thus may be used to change (as opposed to initialize) the values in variables.

Multiple assignments are also allowed in C, as in the following statement, which assigns a value of zero to each of the variables **x**, **y**, and **z**:

```
x = y = z = 0;
```

Multiple assignments are discussed further at the end of this section.

We can also assign a value from one variable to another with an assignment statement:

```
rate = state_tax;
```

The equal sign should be read as "is assigned the value of"; thus, this statement is "**rate** is assigned the value of **state_tax**." If **state_tax** contains the value 0.06, then **rate** also contains the value 0.06 after the statement is executed; the value in **state_tax** is not changed. Thus, the memory snapshots before and after this statement is executed are the following:

Before: rate [?   ]   state_tax [0.06]

After: rate [0.06]   state_tax [0.06]

If we assign a value to a variable that has a different data type, then a conversion must occur during the execution of the statement. Sometimes the conversion can result in information being lost. For example, consider the following declaration and assignment statement:

```
int a;
...
a = 12.8;
```

Because **a** is defined to be an integer, it cannot store a value with a nonzero decimal portion. Therefore, in this case, the memory snapshot after executing the assignment statement is the following:

a   [12]

To determine if a numeric conversion will work properly or not, we use the following order, which is from high to low:

high: long double
          double
          float
          long integer
          integer
low: short integer

If a value is moved to a data type that is higher in order, no information will be lost; if a value is moved to a data type that is lower in order, information may be lost. Thus, moving an integer to a double will work properly, but moving a float to an integer may result in the loss of some information or in an incorrect result. In general, use only assignments that do not cause potential conversion problems. (Unsigned integers were not included in the list because errors can occur in both directions.)

ARITHMETIC OPERATORS

An assignment statement can be used to assign the result of an arithmetic operation to a variable, as shown in this statement that computes the area of a square:

```
area_square = side*side;
```

where * is used to indicate multiplication. The symbols + and – are used to indicate addition and subtraction, and the symbol / is used for division. Thus, each of the following statements is a valid computation for the area of a triangle:

```
area_triangle = 0.5*base*height;

area_triangle = (base*height)/2;
```

The use of parentheses in the second statement is not required but is used for readability.

Consider this assignment statement:

```
x = x + 1;
```

In algebra, this statement is invalid because a value cannot be equal to itself plus 1. However, this assignment statement should not be read as an equality; instead, it should be read as "x is assigned the value of x plus 1." With this interpretation, the statement indicates that the value stored in the variable x is incremented by 1. Thus, if the value of x is 5 before this statement is executed, then the value of x will be 6 after the statement is executed.

Modulus   C also includes a **modulus** operator % that is used to compute the remainder in a division between two integers. For example, 5%2 is equal to 1, 6%3 is equal to 0, and 2%7 is equal to 2. (The quotient of 2/7 is zero with a remainder of 2.) If a and b are integers, then the expression a/b computes the integer quotient, whereas the expression a%b computes the integer remainder. Thus, if a is equal to 9 and b is equal to 4, the value of a/b is 2 and the value of a%b is 1. An execution error occurs if the value of b is equal to zero in either a/b or a%b because the computer cannot perform **division by zero**. If either of the integer values in a and b is negative, the result of a%b is system-dependent.

The modulus operator is useful in determining if an integer is a multiple of another number. For example, if a%2 is equal to zero, then a is even; otherwise, a is odd. If a%5 is equal to zero, then a is a multiple of 5. We will use the modulus operator frequently in the development of engineering solutions.

Binary operators
Unary operators

The five operators (+, -, *, /, %) discussed in the previous paragraphs are **binary operators**—operators that operate on two values. C also includes **unary operators**—operators that operate on a single value. For example, plus and minus signs can be unary operators when they are used in an expression such -*x*.

The result of a binary operation with values of the same type is another value of the same type. For example, if a and b are double values, then the result of a/b is also a double value. Similarly, if a and b are integers, then the result of a/b is also an integer; however, an integer division can sometimes produce unexpected results because any decimal portion of the integer division is dropped; the

Truncated result

result is a **truncated result**, not a rounded result. Thus, 5/3 is equal to 1, and 3/6 is equal to 0.

An operation between values with different types is a **mixed operation**. Before the operation is performed, the value with the lower type is converted or promoted to the higher type (as discussed in conversions within assignment statements), and thus the operation is performed with values of the same type. For example, if an operation is specified between an integer and a float, the integer will be converted to a float before the operation is performed; the result will be a float.

Suppose that we want to compute the average of a set of integers. If the sum and the count of the integers have been stored in the integer variables sum and count, it would seem that the following statements should correctly compute the average:

```
int sum, count;
float average;
. . .
average = sum/count;
```

However, the division between two integers gives an integer result that is then converted to a float value. Thus, if sum is 18, and count is 5, then the value of av-

Cast operator

erage is 3.0, not 3.6. To compute this sum correctly, we use a **cast operator**—a unary operator that allows us to specify a type change in the value before the next computation. In this example, the cast (float) is applied to sum:

```
average = (float)sum/count;
```

The value of sum is converted to a float value before the division is performed. The division is then a mixed operation between a float value and an integer, so the value of count is converted to a float value; the result of the division is then a float value that is stored in average. If the value of sum is 18, and the value of count is 5, the value of average is now correctly computed to be 3.6. Note that the cast operator affects only the value used in the computation; it does not change the value stored in the variable sum.

Practice!

Give the value computed by each of the following sets of statements.

1.  ```
    int a=27, b=6; c;
    ...
    c = b%a;
    ```

2.  ```
    int a=27, b=6;
    float c;
    ...
    c = a/(float)b;
    ```

3.  ```
    int a;
    float b=6, c = 18.6;
    ...
    a = c/b;
    ```

4.  ```
    int b=6;
    float a, c=18.6;
    ...
    a = (int)c/b;
    ```

PRIORITY OF OPERATORS

Precedence

In an expression that contains more than one arithmetic operator, we need to be concerned about the order in which the operations are performed. Table 2.3 contains the **precedence** of the arithmetic operators, which matches the standard algebraic precedence. Operations within parentheses are always evaluated first; if the parentheses are nested, the operations within the innermost parentheses are evaluated first. Unary operators are evaluated before the binary operations *, /, and %; binary addition and subtraction are evaluated last. If there are several operators of the same precedence level in an expression, the variables or constants are grouped (or associated) with the operators in a specific order, as specified in Table 2.3. For example, consider the following expression:

```
a*b + b/c*d
```

Associativity

Because multiplication and division have the same precedence level, and because the **associativity** (the order for grouping the operations) is from left to right, this expression will be evaluated as if it contained the following:

```
(a*b) + ((b/c)*d)
```

The precedence order does not specify whether `a*b` is evaluated before `(b/c)*d`; the order of evaluation of these terms is system-dependent.

Style

The spacing within an arithmetic expression is a style issue. Some people prefer to put spaces around each operator. We prefer to put spaces only around binary addition and subtraction because they are evaluated last. *Choose the spacing style that you prefer, but then use it consistently.*

Assume that we want to compute the area of a trapezoid, and that we have declared four **double** variables: **base**, **height_1**, **height_2**, and **area**. Assume further that the variables **base**, **height_1**, and **height_2** already have values. A statement to correctly compute the area of the trapezoid is:

```
area = 0.5*base*(height_1 + height_2);
```

TABLE 2.3 Precedence of Arithmetic Operators		
Precedence	**Operator**	**Associativity**
1	Parentheses: ( )	Innermost first
2	Unary operators: + - (type)	Right to left
3	Binary operators: * / %	Left to right
4	Binary operators: + -	Left to right

Suppose that we omitted the parentheses in the expression:

```
area = 0.5*base*height_1 + height_2;
```

The statement would be executed as if it were this statement:

```
area = ((0.5*base)*height_1) + height_2;
```

Note that although an incorrect answer has been computed, there is no error message to alert us to the error. Therefore, it is important to be very careful when converting expressions into C. In general, use parentheses to indicate the order of operations in a complicated expression to avoid confusion and to be sure that the expression is evaluated in the manner desired.

You may have noticed that there is no operator for exponentiation to compute values such as x^4. A special mathematical function will be discussed later in this chapter to perform exponentiations. Of course, exponentiations with integer exponents such as a^2 can be computed with repeated multiplications, as in **a*a**.

Style   *The evaluation of long expressions should be broken into several statements.*
For example, consider the following equation:

$$f = \frac{x^3 - 2x^2 + x - 6.3}{x^2 + 0.05005x - 3.14}$$

If we try to evaluate the expression in one statement, it becomes too long to be easily read:

```
f = (x*x*x - 2*x*x + x - 6.3)/(x*x + 0.05005*x - 3.14);
```

We could break the statement into two lines:

```
f = (x*x*x - 2*x*x + x - 6.3)/
    (x*x + 0.05005*x - 3.14);
```

Another solution is to compute the numerator and denominator separately:

```
numerator = x*x*x - 2*x*x + x - 6.3;
denominator = x*x + 0.05005*x - 3.14;
f = numerator/denominator;
```

The variables x, numerator, denominator, and f must be floating-point variables in order to compute the correct value of f.

Practice!

In problems 1 to 3, give C statements to compute the indicated values [8]. Assume that the identifiers in the expressions have been defined as double variables, and have also been assigned appropriate values. Use the following constant:

Acceleration of gravity: $g = 9.80665$ m/s^2

1. Distance traveled:

   Distance $= x_0 + v_0 t + \frac{1}{2} a t^2$

2. Tension in a cord:

   Tension $= \dfrac{2m_1 m_2}{m_1 + m_2} \cdot g$

3. Fluid pressure at the end of a pipe:

   $$P_2 = P_1 + \frac{\rho v_2^2 (A_2^2 - A_1^2)}{2A_1^2}$$

In problems 4 to 6, give the mathematical equations computed by the C statements. Assume that the following symbolic constants have been defined, where the units of G are m^3/(kg $\cdot$ s^2):

```
#define PI 3.141593
#define G 6.67259e-11
```

4. Centripetal acceleration:

   ```
   centripetal = 4*PI*PI*r/(T*T);
   ```

5. Potential energy:

   ```
   potential_energy = -G*M_E*m/r;
   ```

6. Change in potential energy:

   ```
   change = G*M_E*m(1/R_E - 1/(R_E + h));
   ```

OVERFLOW AND UNDERFLOW

The values stored in a computer have a wide range of allowed values. However, if the result of a computation exceeds the range of allowed values, an error occurs. For example, assume that the exponent range of a floating point value is from -38 to 38. This range should accommodate most computations, but it is possible for the results of an expression to be outside of this range. For example, suppose that we execute the following commands:

```
x = 2.5e30;
y = 1.0e30;
z = x*y;
```

Overflow

Underflow

The values of **x** and **y** are within the allowable range. However, the value of **z** should be 2.5e60, but this value exceeds the range. This error is called exponent **overflow** because the exponent of the result of an arithmetic operation is too large to store in the memory assigned to the variable. The action generated by an exponent overflow is system-dependent.

Exponent **underflow** is a similar error caused by the exponent of the result of an arithmetic operation being too small to store in the memory assigned to the variable. Using the same allowable range as in the previous example, we obtain an exponent underflow with the following commands:

```
x = 2.5e-30;
y = 1.0e30;
z = x/y;
```

Again, the values of **x** and **y** are within the allowable range, but the value of **z** should be 2.5e$-$60. Because the exponent is less than the minimum value allowed, we have caused an exponent underflow. Again the action generated by an exponent underflow is system-dependent; on some systems, the result of an operation with exponent underflow is set to zero.

INCREMENT AND DECREMENT OPERATORS

The C language contains unary operators for incrementing and decrementing variables; these operators cannot be used with constants or expressions. The increment operator ++ and the decrement operator -- can be applied either in a **prefix** position (before the identifier) as in ++count or in a **postfix** position (after the identifier) as in count++. If an increment or decrement operator is used by itself, it is equivalent to an assignment statement that increments or decrements the variable. Thus, the statement

Prefix
Postfix

```
y--;
```

is equal to this statement:

```
y = y - 1;
```

If the increment or decrement operator is used in an expression, then the expression must be evaluated carefully. If the increment or decrement operator is in a prefix position, the identifier is modified, and then the new value is used in evaluating the rest of the expression. If the increment or decrement operator is in a postfix position, the old value of the identifier is used to evaluate the rest of the expression, and then the identifier is modified. Thus, the execution of this statement:

```
w = ++x - y;
```
(2.1)

is equivalent to the execution of this pair of statements:

```
x = x + 1;
w = x - y;
```

Similarly, this statement:

```
w = x++ - y;
```
(2.2)

is equivalent to this pair of statements:

```
w = x - y;
x = x + 1;
```

When executing either (2.1) or (2.2), if we assume that the value of **x** is equal to 5 and the value of **y** is equal to 3, then the value of **x** increases to 6. However, after executing (2.1), the value of **w** is 3, but after executing (2.2), the value of **w** is 2.

The increment and decrement operators have the same precedence as the other unary operators. If several unary operators are in an expression, they are associated from right to left.

ABBREVIATED ASSIGNMENT OPERATORS

C allows simple assignment statements to be abbreviated. For example, each pair of statements contains equivalent statements:

```
x = x + 3;
x += 3;

sum = sum + x;
sum += x;
```

```
d = d/4.5;
d /= 4.5;

r = r%2;
r %= 2;
```

In fact, any statement of this form:

identifier = identifier operator expression;

can be written in this form:

identifier operator = expression;

Abbreviated assignment statements are usually used because they are shorter.

Earlier in this section, we used the following **multiple-assignment** statement:

```
x = y = z = 0;
```

The interpretation of this statement is clear, but the interpretation of the following statement is not as evident:

```
a = b += c + d;
```

To evaluate this properly, we use Table 2.4, which indicates that the assignment operators are evaluated last, and their associativity is right to left. Thus, the statement is equivalent to the following:

```
a = (b += (c + d));
```

If we replace the abbreviated forms with the longer forms of the operations, we have

```
a = (b = b + (c + d));
```

or

```
b = b + (c + d);
a = b;
```

Evaluating this statement was good practice with the precedence/associativity table, but in general, statements used in a program should be more readable. Therefore, using abbreviated assignment statements in a multiple-assignment statement is not recommended. *Also, note that the spacing convention that we use inserts spaces around abbreviated operators and multiple-assignment operators because these operators are evaluated after the arithmetic operators.*

Abbreviated
assignment
Multiple-
assignment

Style

TABLE 2.4 Precedence of Arithmetic and Assignment Operators		
Precedence	Operator	Associativity
1	Parentheses: ( )	Innermost first
2	Unary operators: + - ++ -- (type)	Right to left
3	Binary operators: * / %	Left to right
4	Binary operators: + -	Left to right
5	Assignment operators: = += -= *= /= %=	Right to left

Practice!

Give a memory snapshot after each statement is executed, assuming that **x** is equal to 2 and that **y** is equal to 4 before the statement is executed. Also, assume that all the variables are integers.

1. `z = x++ * y;`   2. `z = ++x * y;`
3. `x += y;`   4. `y %= x;`

2.4   Standard Input and Output

We have discussed statements for declaring variables and then using the variables to compute new values. We now present a statement that allows us to print the new values computed. In addition, we also discuss a statement that allows us to enter values from the keyboard when the program is executed. To use either of these statements in a program, we must include the following preprocessor directive:

```
#include <stdio.h>
```

This directive gives the compiler the information that it needs to check references to the input/output functions in the Standard C library.

printf FUNCTION

The **printf** function allows us to print values and explanatory text to the screen. For example, consider the following statement that prints the value of a **double** variable named **angle** along with the corresponding units:

```
printf("Angle = %f radians \n",angle);
```

This `printf` statement contains two arguments: a control string and an identifier to specify the value to be printed. A **control string** is enclosed in double quotation marks, and can contain text, or conversion specifiers, or both. A **conversion specifier** describes the format to use in printing the value of a variable. In the previous example, the control string specifies that the characters `Angle =` are to be printed. The next group of characters (`%f`) represents a conversion specifier that indicates that a value is to be printed next, which will then be followed by the characters `radians`. The next combination of characters (`\n`) represents a **new line** indicator; it causes a skip to a new line on the screen after the information has been printed. The second argument in the `printf` statement is a variable `angle`; it is matched to the conversion specifier in the control string. Thus, the value in `angle` is printed according to the specification `%f`, which will be explained later. If the value of `angle` is 2.84, then the output generated by the previous statement is

```
Angle = 2.840000 radians
```

Now that we have analyzed a simple statement and its corresponding output, we are ready to look closer at the conversion specifiers.

To select a conversion specifier for a value to be printed, first select the correct type of specifier as indicated in Table 2.5. For example, to print a `short` or an `int`, use an `%i` (integer) or `%d` (decimal) specifier (either specifier gives the same results), and to print a `long`, use an `%li` or `%ld` specifier. To print a `float` or a `double`, use an `%f` (floating-point form), `%e` (exponential form, as in `2.3e+02`), or `%E` (exponential form, as in `2.3E+02`). The `%g` (general) specifier prints the value using an `%f` or `%e` specifier, depending on the size of the value; the `%G` specifier is the same as the `%g`, except that it prints the value using an `%f` or `%E` specifier.

After selecting the correct specifier, additional information can be added. A minimum **field width** can be specified, along with an optional precision that controls the number of characters printed. The field width and the **precision** can be

**TABLE 2.5 Numeric Conversion Specifiers
for Output Statements**

Variable Type	Output Type	Specifier
Integer Values		
short, int	int	%i, %d
int	short	%hi, %hd
long	long	%li, %ld
int	unsigned int	%u
int	unsigned short	%hu
long	unsigned long	%lu
Floating-Point Values		
float, double	double	%f, %e, %E, %g, %G
long double	long double	%Lf, %Le, %LE, %Lg, %LG

used together or separately. If the precision is omitted, a default of 6 is used for the %f specifier. The decimal portion of a value is rounded to the specified precision; thus, the value 14.51678 will be printed as **14.52** if a **%.2f** specification is used. The specification **%5i** indicates that a **short** or an **int** is to be printed with a minimum field width of 5. The field width will be increased if necessary to print the corresponding value. If the field width specifies more positions than are needed for the value, the value is **right-justified**, which means that the extra positions are filled with blanks on the left of the value. To **left-justify** a value, a minus sign is inserted before the field width, as in **% -8i**. If a plus sign is inserted before the field width, as in **%+6f**, a sign will always be printed with the value.

Right-justfied
Left-justified

The following list shows several conversion specifiers and the resulting output fields for a given value; the character $_b$ is used to indicate the location of blanks within the field. In these examples, assume that the corresponding integer value is −145:

Specifier	Value Printed
%i	−145
%4d	−145
%3i	−145
%6i	$_{bb}$−145
%-6i	−145$_{bb}$

The next list shows several conversion specifiers and the resulting output fields for the **double** value 157.8926:

Specifier	Value Printed
%f	157.892600
%6.2f	157.89
%+8.2f	b+157.89
%7.5f	157.89260
%e	1.578926e+02
%.3E	1.579E+02
%g	157.893

Note the rounding that occurred with the last two specifiers.

If a control argument contains three conversion specifiers, then three corresponding identifiers or expressions would need to follow the control string, as in this statement:

```
printf("Results: x = %5.2f, y = %5.2f, z = %5.2f \n",
       x, y, z+3);
```

An example output from this statement is

```
Results: x =   4.52, y =   0.15, z = -1.34
```

Note that the last conversion specifier matches to an arithmetic expression instead of a simple variable.

The backslash (\) is called an **escape character** when it is used in a control string. The compiler combines it with the character that follows it and then attaches a special meaning to the combination of characters. For example, we have already seen that \n represents a skip to a new line. In addition, the sequence \\ is used to insert a single backslash in a control string, and the sequence \" will insert a double quote in a control string. Thus, the output of this statement

```
printf("\"The End.\"\n");
```

is a line containing:

```
"The End."
```

The other escape sequences recognized by C are listed below:

sequence	character represented
\a	alert(bell) character
\b	backspace
\f	formfeed
\n	newline
\r	carriage return
\t	horizontal tab
\v	vertical tab
\\	backslash
\?	question mark
\'	single quote
\"	double quote

If a `printf` statement is long, you should split it into two lines. In general, long lines should be split at a point that preserves readability. However, to split text that is contained in quotation marks, you should split the text into two separate pieces of text, each in its own set of quotation marks. The following statements show several different ways to correctly separate a statement:

```
printf("The distance between the points is %5.2f \n",
       distance);

printf("The distance between the points is"
       " %5.2f \n",distance);

printf("The distance between the "
       "points is %5.2f \n",distance);
```

Style

Conversion specifiers can be used to make the output of your program readable and usable. *For engineering values, it is also very important to include the corresponding units in the output along with the numerical values.*

Although the purpose of the `printf` function is to print information, it also returns a value that represents the number of characters printed.

Practice!

Assume that the integer variable **sum** contains the value 150, and that the **double** variable **average** contains the value 12.368. Show the output line (or lines) generated by the following statements.

1.   `printf("Sum = %5i; Average = %7.1f \n",sum,average);`

2.   `printf("Sum = %4i \n Average = %8.4f \n",sum,average);`

3.   `printf("Sum and Average \n\n %d %.1f \n",sum,average);`

4.   `printf("%7.2f is the average; \n",average);`
     `printf("%8d is the sum \n",sum);`

5.   `printf("%7.2f is the average;",average);`
     `printf("%8d is the sum \n",sum);`

scanf FUNCTION

The **scanf** function allows you to enter values from the keyboard when the program is executed. For example, suppose that a program computes the number of acres of new forest growth after a specified period of time elapses. If the time elapsed is a constant in the program, we would have to change the value of the constant, and then recompile and reexecute the program to obtain the output for a different time period. Alternatively, if we use the **scanf** function to read the time period, we do not need to recompile the program; we only need to reexecute it and enter the desired time period from the keyboard.

The first argument of the **scanf** function is a control string that specifies the types of the variables whose values are to be entered from the keyboard. The type specifiers are shown in Table 2.6; thus, for example, the specifiers for an integer variable are **%i** or **%d**; the specifiers for a **float** variable are **%f**, **%e**, and **%g**; and the specifiers for a **double** variable are **%lf**, **%le**, and **%lg**. It is very important to use a correct specifier. For example, errors will occur if you use an **%f** specifier to read the value for a **double** variable. The remaining arguments in the **scanf** function are memory locations that correspond to the specifiers in the control string. **Address operator** These memory locations are indicated with the **address operator &**. This operator is a unary operator that determines the memory address of the identifier with which it is associated. Thus, if the value to be entered through the keyboard is an integer that is to be stored in the variable **year**, we could use this statement to read the value

`scanf("%i",&year);`

TABLE 2.6 Numeric Conversion Specifiers for Input Statements

Variable Type	Specifier
Integer Values	
int	%i, %d
short	%hi, %hd
long int	%li, %ld
unsigned int	%u
unsigned short	%hu
unsigned long	%lu
Floating-Point Values	
float	%f, %e, %E, %g, %G
double	%lf, %le, %lE, %lg, %lG
long double	%Lf, %Le, %LE, %Lg, %LG

The precedence level of the address operator is the same as the other unary operators; if there are several unary operators in the same statement, they are associated from right to left. A common error in the `scanf` statement is to omit the address operator for the identifiers.

If we wish to read more than one value from the keyboard, we can use statements such as the following:

```
scanf("%lf %lf",&distance,&velocity);
```

When this statement is executed, the program will read two values from the keyboard and convert them into two **double** values. The values must be separated by at least one blank; they can be on the same line or on different lines. In order to

Prompt

prompt the program user to enter the values, a `scanf` statement is usually preceded by a `printf` statement that describes the information that the user should enter from the keyboard:

```
printf("Enter the distance(ft) and velocity(ft/s): \n");
scanf("%lf %lf",&distance,&velocity);
```

The control string of the `printf` statement ended with a new line specifier, so the values entered by the user will be on the line (or lines) following the prompt text. Thus, after the previous statements are executed and the user has responded to the prompt, an example of the information on the screen is

```
Enter the distance(ft) and velocity(ft/s):
10 15.5
```

If the characters entered by the user cannot be successfully converted to the types of values indicated by conversion specifiers in the `scanf` statement, the result is system-dependent. These conversion errors include entering values such as 14.2 for integer values, including commas in large values, and forgetting to separate values with blanks.

Although the main purpose of the **scanf** function is to read input from the keyboard, it also returns a value that is equal to the number of successful conversions. This value is used in programs in later chapters.

Modify!

Write a short program that can be modified to include the following errors. How does your system respond to each of these errors?

1.   Division by zero
2.   Input conversion error:
        enter 1,245 instead of 1245 for an **%i** specifier
3.   Input conversion error:
        use **%f** for the input of an integer variable
4.   Input conversion error:
        use **%f** for the input of a **double** variable
5.   Exponent overflow error:
        use the example statements in the related discussion in this section
6.   Exponent underflow error
        use the example statements in the related discussion in this section

2.5   Numerical Technique—Linear Interpolation

The collection of data from an experiment or from observing a physical phenomenon is an important step in developing a problem solution. These data points can generally be considered to be coordinates of points of a function $f(x)$. We would often like to use these data points to determine estimates of the function $f(x)$ for values of x that were not part of the original set of data. For example, suppose that we have data points $(a,f(a))$ and $(c,f(c))$. If we want to estimate the value of $f(b)$, where $a < b < c$, we could assume that a straight line joined $f(a)$ and $f(c)$, and then use **linear interpolation** to obtain the value of $f(b)$. If we assume that the points $f(a)$ and $f(c)$ are joined by a cubic (third-degree) polynomial, we could use a cubic spline interpolation method to obtain the value of $f(b)$. Most interpolation problems can be solved using one of these two methods [6,9]. Figure 2.1 contains a set of six data points that have been connected with straight-line segments and that have been connected with cubic degree polynomial segments. It should be clear that the values determined for the function between sample points depend on the type of interpolation that we select. In this section, we discuss linear interpolation.

Linear
interpolation

A graph with two arbitrary data points $f(a)$ and $f(c)$ is shown in Figure 2.2. If we assume that the function between the two points can be estimated by a straight line, we can then compute the function value at any point $f(b)$ using an

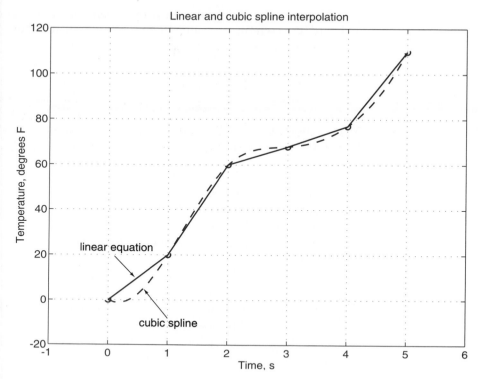

Figure 2.1 *Linear and cubic spline interpolation.*

$$\frac{f(a) - f(b)}{b - a} = \frac{f(a) - f(c)}{c - a}$$

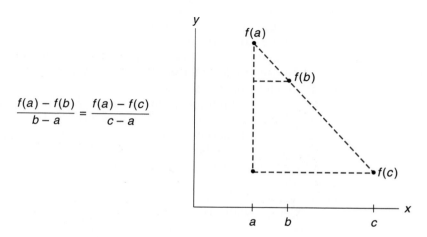

Figure 2.2 *Similar triangles.*

equation derived from similar triangles:

$$f(b) = f(a) + \frac{b - a}{c - a} [f(c) - f(a)]$$

Recall that we are also assuming that $a < b < c$.

To illustrate using this interpolation equation, assume that we have a set of temperature measurements taken from the cylinder head in a new engine that is being tested for possible use in a race car. These data are plotted with straight lines connecting the points in Figure 2.3, and they are also listed here:

Time, s	Temperature, °F
0.0	0.0
1.0	20.0
2.0	60.0
3.0	68.0
4.0	77.0
5.0	110.0

Assume that we want to interpolate a temperature to correspond to the value 2.6 seconds. We then have the following situation:

a	2.0	60.0	$f(a)$
b	2.6	?	$f(b)$
c	3.0	68.0	$f(c)$

Using the interpolation formula, we have

$$f(b) = f(a) + \frac{b - a}{c - a}[f(c) - f(a)]$$

$$= 60.0 + \frac{0.6}{1.0}(8.0)$$

$$= 64.8$$

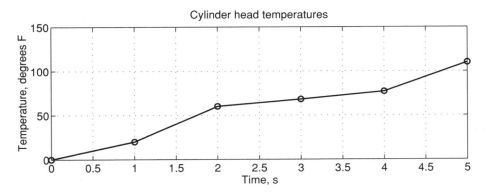

Figure 2.3 *Cylinder head temperatures.*

In this example, we used linear interpolation to find the temperature that corresponds to a specified time. We could also interchange the roles of temperature and time, so that we plot temperature on the x axis and time on the y axis. In this case, we can use the same process to compute the time that a specified temperature occurred, assuming that we have a pair of data points with temperatures below and above the specified temperature.

Practice!

Assume that we have the following set of data points, which is also plotted in Figure 2.4:

Time, s	Temperature, °F
0.0	72.5
0.5	78.1
1.0	86.4
1.5	92.3
2.0	110.6
2.5	111.5
3.0	109.3
3.5	110.2
4.0	110.5
4.5	109.9
5.0	110.2

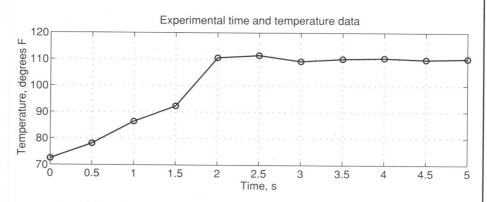

Figure 2.4 *Temperature values.*

1. Use your calculator to compute temperatures at the following times using linear interpolation:

   0.3,   1.25,   2.36,   4.48

2. Use your calculator to compute time values that correspond to the following temperatures using linear interpolation:

   81,   96,   100,   106

3. Suppose problem 2 asked you to compute the time value that corresponds to the temperature 110°F. What complicates this problem? How many time values correspond to the temperature 110°F? Find each of the corresponding time values using linear interpolation. (You may want to refer to Figure 2.5, which contains a plot of these data with the temperature data on the x axis and the time values on the y axis.)

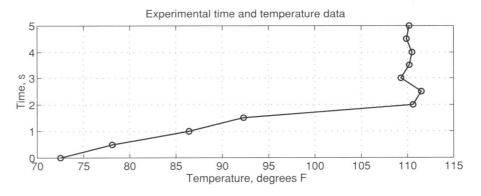

Figure 2.5 *Time values.*

2.6   Problem Solving Applied: Wind-Tunnel Data Analysis

In this section, we use the new statements presented in this chapter along with linear interpolation to solve a problem related to the grand challenge discussed in the chapter-opening section.

A **wind-tunnel** is a test chamber built to generate different wind speeds, or Mach numbers (which is the wind speed divided by the speed of sound). Accurate scale models of aircraft can be mounted on force-measuring supports in the test chamber, and then measurements of the forces on the model can be made at many different wind speeds and angles. At the end of an extended wind-tunnel test, many sets of data have been collected and can be used to determine the coefficient of lift, drag, and other aerodynamic performance characteristics of the new aircraft at its various operating speeds and positions [2,6]. Data collected from a wind-tunnel test are plotted in Figure 2.6, and follow:

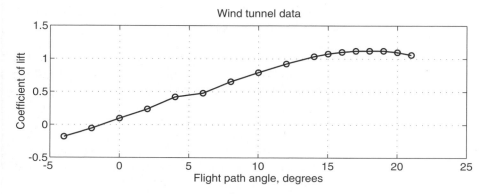

Figure 2.6 *Coefficients of lift.*

Flight-Path Angle (degrees)	Coefficient of Lift
−4	−0.182
−2	−0.056
0	0.097
2	0.238
4	0.421
6	0.479
8	0.654
10	0.792
12	0.924
14	1.035
15	1.076
16	1.103
17	1.120
18	1.121
19	1.121
20	1.099
21	1.059

Assume that we would like to use linear interpolation to determine the coefficient of lift for additional flight-path angles that are between −4 degrees and 21 degrees. Write a program that allows the user to enter the data for two points and a flight-path angle between those points. The program should then compute the corresponding coefficient of lift.

1.   PROBLEM STATEMENT

Use linear interpolation to compute a new coefficient of lift for a specified flight-path angle.

2.   INPUT/OUTPUT DESCRIPTION

The following diagram shows that the input to the program includes two consecutive points $(a, f(a))$ and $(c, f(c))$ and new flight-path angle b. The output is the new coefficient of lift, $f(b)$.

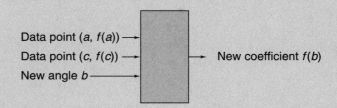

3.   HAND EXAMPLE

Suppose that we want to determine the coefficient of lift for a flight-path angle of 8.7 degrees. From the data, we see that this point falls between 8 and 10 degrees:

a	8.0	0.654	$f(a)$
b	8.7	?	$f(b)$
c	10.0	0.792	$f(c)$

Using the linear equation formula, we can compute f(b):

$$f(b) = f(a) + \frac{b - a}{c - a}[f(c) - f(a)]$$

$$= 0.654 + \frac{0.7}{2.0}\,(0.792 - 0.654)$$

$$= 0.702$$

As expected, this value of f(b) falls between f(a) and f(c).

4.   ALGORITHM DEVELOPMENT

The first step in the development of an algorithm is the decomposition of the problem solution into a set of sequentially executed steps:

Decomposition Outline
1. *Read the coordinates of the adjacent points and the new flight-path angle.*
2. *Compute the new coefficient of lift.*
3. *Print the new coefficient of lift.*

This program has a simple structure, so we can convert the decomposition directly into C.

ch2_1.c

```
/*----------------------------------------------------------*/
/*  Program chapter2_1                                      */
/*                                                          */
/*  This program uses linear interpolation to              */
/*  compute the coefficient of lift for an angle.          */

#include <stdio.h>
#include <stdlib.h>
#include <math.h>

main()
{
   /*  Declare variables.  */
   double a, f_a, b, f_b, c, f_c;

   /*  Get user input from the keyboard.  */
   printf("Use degrees for all angle measurements. \n");
   printf("Enter first angle and lift coefficient: \n");
   scanf("%lf %lf",&a,&f_a);
   printf("Enter second angle and lift coefficient: \n");
   scanf("%lf %lf",&c,&f_c);
   printf("Enter new angle: \n");
   scanf("%lf",&b);

   /*  Use linear interpolation to compute new lift.  */
   f_b = f_a + (b-a)/(c-a)*(f_c - f_a);

   /*  Print new lift value.  */
   printf("New lift coefficient: %6.3f \n",f_b);

   /*  Exit program.  */
   return EXIT_SUCCESS;
}
/*----------------------------------------------------------*/
```

5.   TESTING

We first test the program using the data from the hand example. This generates the following interaction:

```
Use degrees for all angle measurements.
Enter first angle and lift coefficient:
8 0.654
Enter second angle and lift coefficient:
10 0.792
Enter new angle
8.7
New lift coefficient: 0.702
```

The value computed matches the hand example, so we can then test the program with other time values. If the new coefficient value had not matched the result from the hand example, we would then need to determine if the error is in the hand example or in the C program.

For the linear interpolation to work properly, the new angle must be between the first and second angle that we entered. For this program, we assume that this relationship is maintained. In the next chapter, we learn how to use new C commands to be sure that the new angle is between the first and second angles.

Modify!

These problems relate to the program developed in this section for computing new data values with linear interpolation.

ch2_1.c

1. Use the program to determine the coefficients of lift to go with the following flight-path angles:

   −3.2,   −0.1,   5,   16.5,   19.5

2. Modify the program so that it prints the new angle in radians. (Recall that $180° = \pi$ radians.)

3. Suppose that the data used with the program contained values with the angles in radians instead of degrees. Would the program need to be changed? Explain.

4. Modify the program so that it interpolates for a new angle, instead of a new coefficient. (You may want to refer to Figure 2.7, which contains a plot of this data with the coefficients of lift on the x axis and the flight path angle on the y axis.)

2.7   Mathematical Functions

Arithmetic expressions that solve engineering problems often require computations other than addition, subtraction, multiplication, and division. For example, many expressions require the use of exponentiation, logarithms, exponentials, and trigonometric functions. In this section, we discuss the mathematical functions that are available in the Standard C library. The following preprocessor directive should be used in programs referencing the mathematical functions:

```
#include <math.h>
```

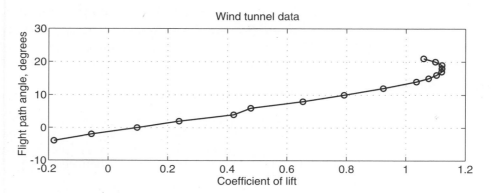

Figure 2.7 *Flight path angles.*

This directive specifies that information be added to the program to aid the compiler when it converts references to the mathematical functions in the Standard C library.

Before we discuss the rules relating to functions, we present a specific example. The following statement computes the sine of an angle **theta** and stores the result in the variable **b**:

```
b = sin(theta);
```

The **sin** function assumes that the argument is in radians. If the variable **theta** contains a value in degrees, we can convert the degrees to radians with a separate statement. (Recall that $180° = \pi$ radians.)

```
#define PI 3.141593
...
theta_rad = theta*PI/180;
b = sin(theta_rad);
```

The conversion can also be specified within the function reference:

```
b = sin(theta*PI/180);
```

Performing the conversion with a separate statement is usually preferable because it is easier to understand.

A function reference, such as **sin(theta)**, represents a single value. The parentheses following the function name contain the inputs to the function, which are called **parameters** or **arguments**. A function may contain no arguments, one argument, or many arguments, depending on its definition. If a function contains more than one argument, it is very important to list the arguments in the correct order. Some functions also require that the arguments be in specific units. For example, the trigonometric functions assume that arguments are in radians. Most of the mathematical functions assume that the arguments are **double** values; if a different type argument is used, it is converted to a **double** before the function is executed.

Parameters
Arguments

A function reference can also be part of the argument of another function reference. For example, the following statement computes the logarithm of the absolute value of **x**:

```
b = log(fabs(x));
```

Composition

When one function is used to compute the argument of another function, be sure to enclose the argument of each function in its own set of parentheses. This nesting of functions is also called **composition** of functions.

We now discuss several categories of functions that are commonly used in engineering computations. Other functions will be presented throughout the remaining chapters as we discuss relevant subjects. Tables of common functions are included on the inside front cover. Appendix A also contains more information on the functions included in the Standard C library.

ELEMENTARY MATH FUNCTIONS

Math functions

The elementary **math functions** include functions to perform a number of common computations such as computing the absolute value of a number and the square root of a number. In addition, they also include a group of functions used to perform rounding. These functions assume that the type of all arguments is **double**, and the functions all return a **double**; if an argument is not a **double**, a conversion will occur using the rules described in Section 2.3. We now list these functions with a brief description:

fabs(x)	This function computes the absolute value of **x**.
sqrt(x)	This function computes the square root of **x**, where $x \geq 0$.
pow(x,y)	This function is used for exponentiation, and computes the value of **x** to the **y** power, or x^y. Errors occur if $x = 0$ and $y \leq 0$, or if $x < 0$ and **y** is not an integer.
ceil(x)	This function rounds **x** to the nearest integer toward ∞ (infinity). For example, **ceil(2.01)** is equal to 3.
floor(x)	This function rounds **x** to the nearest integer toward $-\infty$ (negative infinity). For example, **floor(2.01)** is equal to 2.
exp(x)	This function computes the value of e^x, where e is the base for natural logarithms, or approximately 2.718282.
log(x)	This function returns ln **x**, the natural logarithm of **x** to the base e. Errors occur if $x \leq 0$.
log10(x)	This function returns $\log_{10} x$, the common logarithm of **x** to the base 10. Errors occur if $x \leq 0$.

Remember that the logarithm of a negative value or zero does not exist, and thus an execution error occurs if you use a logarithm function with a negative value for its argument.

An additional mathematical function that you may find useful is the **abs** function. This function computes the absolute value of an integer, and returns an integer value. The header file containing information relative to this function is **stdlib.h**, and it should be included in programs referencing this function.

Practice!

Evaluate the following expressions:

1. `floor(-2.6)`   2. `ceil(-2.6)`
3. `pow(2,-3)`   4. `sqrt(floor(10.7))`
5. `fabs(-10*2.5)`   6. `floor(ceil(10.8))`
7. `log10(100) + log10(0.001)`   8. `fabs(pow(-2,5))`

TRIGONOMETRIC FUNCTIONS

Trigonometric functions

The **trigonometric functions** assume that all arguments are of type **double**, and they return values of type **double**. In addition, as previously stated, the trigonometric functions also assume that angles are represented in radians. To convert radians to degrees, or degrees to radians, use the following conversions:

```
#define PI 3.141593
...
angle_deg = angle_rad*(180/PI);
angle_rad = angle_deg*(PI/180);
```

The trigonometric functions are included in the Standard C library, and a preprocessor directive including the information in **math.h** should be used with these functions. A brief summary of the functions follows:

sin(x)	This function computes the sine of **x**, where **x** is in radians.
cos(x)	This function computes the cosine of **x**, where **x** is in radians.
tan(x)	This function computes the tangent of **x**, where **x** is in radians.
asin(x)	This function computes the arcsine or inverse sine of **x**, where **x** must be in the range $[-1, 1]$. The function returns an angle in radians in the range $[-\pi/2, \pi/2]$.
acos(x)	This function computes the arccosine or inverse cosine of **x**, where **x** must be in the range $[-1, 1]$. The function returns an angle in radians in the range $[0, \pi]$.
atan(x)	This function computes the arctangent or inverse tangent of **x**. The function returns an angle in radians in the range $[-\pi/2, \pi/2]$.
atan2(y,x)	This function computes the arctangent or inverse tangent of the value **y/x**. The function returns an angle in radians in the range $[-\pi, \pi]$.

Note that the **atan** function always returns an angle in Quadrant I or IV, whereas the **atan2** function returns an angle that can be in any quadrant, depending on the signs of **x** and **y**. Thus, in many applications, the **atan2** function is preferred over the **atan** function.

The other trigonometric and inverse trigonometric functions can be computed using the following equations [10]:

$$\sec x = \frac{1}{\cos x} \qquad \operatorname{asec} x = \operatorname{acos}\left(\frac{1}{x}\right)$$

$$\csc x = \frac{1}{\sin x} \qquad \operatorname{acsc} x = \operatorname{asin}\left(\frac{1}{x}\right)$$

$$\cot x = \frac{1}{\tan x} \qquad \operatorname{acot} x = \operatorname{acos}\left(\frac{x}{\sqrt{1 + x^2}}\right)$$

Using degrees instead of radians is a common error in programs with trigonometric functions.

Practice!

In problems 1 to 3, give assignment statements for computing the indicated values [8], assuming that the variables have been declared and given appropriate values. Also assume that the following declarations have been made:

```
#define g 9.8
#define PI 3.141563
```

1. Velocity computation:

    $$\text{Velocity} = \sqrt{v_0^2 + 2 \cdot a \cdot (x - x_0)}$$

2. Length contraction:

    $$\text{Length} = k \sqrt{1 - \left(\frac{v}{c}\right)^2}$$

3. Distance of the center of gravity from a reference plane in a hollow cylinder sector:

    $$\text{Center} = \frac{38.1972 \cdot (r^3 - s^3)\sin a}{(r^2 - s^2) \cdot a}$$

In problems 4 to 6, give the equations that correspond to the assignment statement.

4.   Electrical oscillation frequency:

```
frequency = 1/sqrt(2*pi*c/L);
```

5.   Range for a projectile:

```
range = (v0*v0/g)*sin(2*theta);
```

6.   Speed of a disk at the bottom of an incline:

```
v = sqrt(2*g*h/(1 + I/(m*pow(r,2))));
```

HYPERBOLIC FUNCTIONS*

Hyperbolic
functions

Hyperbolic functions are functions of the natural exponential function e^x; the inverse hyperbolic functions are functions of the natural logarithm function ln x. These functions are useful in specialized applications such as the design of some types of digital filters. C includes several hyperbolic functions, as shown in these descriptions:

sinh(x)   This function computes the hyperbolic sine of **x**, which is equal to

$$\frac{e^x - e^{-x}}{2}$$

cosh(x)   This function computes the hyperbolic cosine of **x**, which is equal to

$$\frac{e^x + e^{-x}}{2}$$

tanh(x)   This function computes the hyperbolic tangent of **x**, which is equal to

$$\frac{\sinh x}{\cosh x}$$

Additional hyperbolic functions and the inverse hyperbolic functions can be computed using these relationships [10]:

$$\coth x = \frac{\cosh x}{\sinh x} \quad (\text{for } x \neq 0)$$

$$\text{sech } x = \frac{1}{\cosh x}$$

$$\text{csch } x = \frac{1}{\sinh x}$$

*Optional section.

$$\text{asinh } x = \ln\left(x + \sqrt{x^2 + 1}\right)$$

$$\text{acosh } x = \ln\left(x + \sqrt{x^2 - 1}\right) \qquad (\text{for } x \geq 1)$$

$$\text{atanh } x = \frac{1}{2} \ln\left(\frac{1 + x}{1 - x}\right) \qquad (\text{for } \mid x \mid < 1)$$

$$\text{acoth } x = \frac{1}{2} \ln\left(\frac{x + 1}{x - 1}\right) \qquad (\text{for } \mid x \mid > 1)$$

$$\text{asech } x = \ln\left(\frac{1 + \sqrt{1 - x^2}}{x}\right) \qquad (\text{for } 0 < x \leq 1)$$

$$\text{acsch } x = \ln\left(\frac{1}{x} + \frac{\sqrt{1 + x^2}}{\mid x \mid}\right) \qquad (\text{for } x \neq 0)$$

Many of the hyperbolic functions and inverse trigonometric functions have restrictions on the range of acceptable values for arguments. If the arguments are entered from the keyboard, remind the user of the range restrictions. In the next chapter, we introduce C statements that allow you to determine if a value is in the proper range within the program.

Practice!

Give assignment statements for calculating the following values, given the value of **x**. (Assume that the value of **x** is in the proper range of values for the calculations.)

1.	coth x	2.	sec x
3.	csc x	4.	acoth x
5.	acosh x	6.	acsc x

2.8   Problem Solving Applied: Velocity Computation

In this section, we perform computations in another application related to the vehicle performance grand challenge. An advanced turboprop engine called the **unducted fan (UDF)** is one of the promising new propulsion technologies being developed for future transport aircraft [6]. Turboprop engines, which have been in use for decades, combine the power and reliability of jet engines with the efficiency of propellers. They are a significant improvement over earlier piston-powered propeller engines. Their application has been limited to smaller commuter-type aircraft, however, because they are not as fast or powerful as the fanjet engines used on larger airliners. The UDF engine employs significant advancements in propeller technology, which narrow the performance gap between turboprops and fanjets. New materials, blade shapes, and higher rotation advancements in propeller technology, which narrow the performance gap between turboprops and fanjets. New materials, blade shapes, and higher rotation speeds enable UDF-powered aircraft to fly almost as fast as fanjets, and with greater fuel efficiency. The UDF is also significantly quieter than the conventional turboprop.

During a test flight of a UDF-powered aircraft, the test pilot has set the engine power level at 40,000 newtons, which causes the 20,000-kg aircraft to attain a cruise speed of 180 m/s (meters/second). The engine throttles are then set to a power level of 60,000 newtons, and the aircraft begins to accelerate. As the speed of the plane increases, the aerodynamic drag increases in proportion to the square of the airspeed. Eventually, the aircraft reaches a new cruise speed where the thrust from the UDF engines is just offset by the drag. The equations used to estimate the velocity and acceleration of the aircraft from the time that the throttle is reset until the plane reaches its new cruise speed (at approximately 120 s) are the following:

$$\text{Velocity} = 0.00001 \, \text{time}^3 - 0.00488 \, \text{time}^2 + 0.75795 \, \text{time} + 181.3566$$
$$\text{Acceleration} = 3 - 0.000062 \, \text{velocity}^2$$

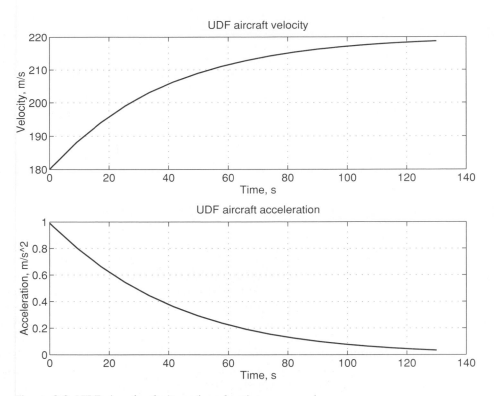

Figure 2.8 *UDF aircraft velocity and acceleration.*

Write a program that asks the user to enter a time value that represents the time elapsed (in seconds) since the power level was increased. Compute and print the corresponding acceleration and velocity of the aircraft at the new time value.

1.   PROBLEM STATEMENT

Compute the new velocity and acceleration of the aircraft after a change in power level.

2.   INPUT/OUTPUT DESCRIPTION

The following diagram shows that the input to the program is a time value, and that the output of the program is the pair of new velocity and acceleration values.

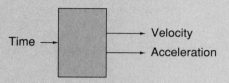

3.   HAND EXAMPLE

Suppose that the new time value is 50 seconds. Using the equations given for the velocity and accelerations, we can compute these values:

Velocity   = 208.3 m/s

Acceleration = 0.31 m/s^2

4.   ALGORITHM DEVELOPMENT

The first step in the development of an algorithm is the decomposition of the problem solution into a set of sequentially executed steps:

Decomposition Outline

1. *Read new time value.*
2. *Compute corresponding velocity and acceleration values.*
3. *Print new velocity and acceleration.*

Because this program is a very simple program, we can convert the decomposition directly to C.

ch2_2.c

```
/*-------------------------------------------------------*/
/*  Program chapter2_2                                   */
/*                                                       */
/*  This program estimates new velocity and             */
/*  acceleration values for a specified time.           */

#include <stdio.h>
#include <stdlib.h>
#include <math.h>

main()
{
   /*  Declare variables.  */
   double time, velocity, acceleration;

   /*  Get time value from the keyboard.  */
   printf("Enter new time value in seconds: \n");
   scanf("%lf",&time);

   /*  Compute velocity and acceleration.  */
   velocity = 0.00001*pow(time,3) - 0.00488*pow(time,2)
              + 0.75795*time + 181.3566;
   acceleration = 3 - 0.000062*velocity*velocity;

   /*  Print velocity and acceleration.  */
   printf("Velocity = %8.3f m/s \n",velocity);
   printf("Acceleration = %8.3f m/s^2 \n",acceleration);

   /*  Exit program.  */
   return EXIT_SUCCESS;
}
/*-------------------------------------------------------*/
```

5.   TESTING

We first test the program using the data from the hand example. This generates the following interaction:

```
Enter new time value in seconds:
50
Velocity = 208.304 m/s
Acceleration =    0.310 m/s^2
```

Because the values computed match the hand example, we can then test the program with other time values. If the values had not matched the hand example, we would need to determine if the error is in the hand example or in the program.

Modify!

These problems relate to the program developed in this section for computing velocity and acceleration values.

ch2_2.c

1. Use this program to find the time at which the velocity is equal to 210 m/s.
2. Use this program to find the time at which the acceleration is equal to 0.5 m/s^2.
3. Modify the program so that the input values are entered in minutes instead of seconds. Remember that the equations will still assume that the time values are in seconds.
4. Modify the program so that the output values are printed in feet per second, and feet per second^2. (Recall that 1 meter = 39.37 inches.)

2.9   System Limitations

In Section 2.2, we presented a table that contained the maximum values for the various types of integers and floating-point values for the Borland Turbo C++ 3.0 compiler. To print a similar table for your system, use the following program. Note that the program includes four header files. The **stdio.h** header file is necessary because the program references output functions; the **stdlib.h** header file is necessary because the **return** function references a constant defined in **stdlib.h**; the **limits.h** header file is necessary because it contains information relative to the ranges of integer types; and the **float.h** header file is necessary because it contains information relative to the ranges of floating-point types [7]. Appendix A contains more information on the constants and limits that are system-dependent.

ch2_3.c

```
/*------------------------------------------------*/
/*  Program chapter2_3                            */
/*                                                */
/*  This program prints the system limitations.   */

#include <stdio.h>
#include <stdlib.h>
#include <limits.h>
#include <float.h>

main()
{
   /*  Print integer type maximums. */
   printf("short maximum: %i \n",SHRT_MAX);
   printf("int maximum: %i \n",INT_MAX);
   printf("long maximum: %li \n\n",LONG_MAX);
```

```
      /*  Print float precision, range, maximum.  */
      printf("float precision digits: %i \n",FLT_DIG);
      printf("float maximum exponent: %i \n",
             FLT_MAX_10_EXP);
      printf("float maximum: %e \n\n",FLT_MAX);

      /*  Print double precision, range, maximum.  */
      printf("double precision digits: %i \n",DBL_DIG);
      printf("double maximum exponent: %i \n",
             DBL_MAX_10_EXP);
      printf("double maximum: %e \n\n",DBL_MAX);

      /*  Print long precision, range, maximum.  */
      printf("long double precision: %i \n",LDBL_DIG);
      printf("long double maximum exponent: %i \n",
             LDBL_MAX_10_EXP);
      printf("long double maximum: %Le \n",LDBL_MAX);

      /*  Exit program.  */
      return EXIT_SUCCESS;
}
/*-------------------------------------------------------*/
```

Modify!

ch2_3.c

Once you have run this program, change the conversion specifiers such that the following values are printed with full precision, instead of the default six digits of precision.

1.   float maximum
2.   double maximum
3.   long double maximum

SUMMARY

In this chapter, we presented the C statements necessary to write simple programs that compute and print new values. We also presented the statement that allows us to enter information through the keyboard when the program is executing. The computations that were presented included the standard arithmetic operations and a large number of functions that can be used to perform the types of computations needed for engineering solutions.

KEY TERMS

abbreviated assignment
address operator
argument
assignment statement
associativity
binary operator
case-sensitive
cast operator
comment
composition
constant
control string
conversion specifier
declaration
exponential notation
expression
field width
floating-point value
garbage value
hyperbolic function
identifier
initial value
keyword
linear interpolation
mantissa

math function
memory snapshot
modulus
multiple assignment
overflow
parameter
postfix
precedence
precision
prefix
preprocessor directive
prompt
range
scientific notation
Standard C library
statement
symbolic constant
system-dependent
trigonometric function
truncate
type specifier
unary operator
underflow
variable

C STATEMENT SUMMARY

Preprocessor directives to include information from the files in the Standard C library:

```
#include <stdio.h>
#include <stdlib.h>
#include <math.h>
```

Preprocessor directive to define a symbolic constant:

```
#define PI 3.141593
```

Declarations for integers:

```
short sum=0;
int year_1, year_2;
long k;
```

Declarations for floating-point values:

```
float height_1, height_2;
double length=10, side1, side2;
long double distance, velocity;
```

Assignment statement:

```
area = 0.5*base*(height_1 + height_2);
```

Keyboard input statement:

```
scanf("%i",&year);
```

Screen output statement:

```
printf("The area is %f square feet. \n",area);
```

Program exit statement:

```
return EXIT_SUCCESS;
```

Style NOTES

1. Use comments throughout a program to improve the readability and to document the steps in it.
2. Use blank lines and indenting to identify the structure of a program.
3. Use the units in a variable name when possible.
4. Symbolic constants should be used for engineering constants such as π, and they should be uppercase so that they are easily identified.
5. Use consistent spacing around arithmetic and assignment operators.
6. Use parentheses in complicated expressions to improve readability.
7. The evaluation of long expressions should be broken into several statements.

8. Be sure to include units along with numerical values in the output of a program.
9. Use a prompt to the user to describe the information and units for values to be entered from the keyboard.

DEBUGGING NOTES

1. Remember that declarations and C statements must end with a semicolon.
2. Preprocessor directives do not end with a semicolon.
3. If possible, avoid assignments that could potentially cause information to be lost.
4. Use parentheses in a long expression to be sure that it is evaluated as desired.
5. Use double precision or extended precision to avoid problems with exponent overflow or underflow.
6. Be sure that the specifier matches the variable type in a `scanf` statement.
7. Errors can occur if user input values cannot be converted correctly to the specifier variable type in a `scanf` statement.
8. Do not forget the address operator with identifiers in the `scanf` statement.
9. Remember that symbolic constant definitions do not end with a semicolon.
10. In nested function references, each set of arguments must be in its own set of parentheses.
11. Remember that the logarithm functions cannot be used with negative values for arguments.
12. Be sure to use angles in radians with the trigonometric functions.
13. Remember that many of the inverse trigonometric functions and hyperbolic functions have restrictions on the ranges of allowable input values.

PROBLEMS

Conversions. This set of problems involves conversions of a value in one unit to another unit. Each program should prompt the user for a value in the specified units, and then print the converted value, along with the new units.

1. Write a program to convert miles to kilometers. (Recall that 1 mi = 1.6093440 km.)
2. Write a program to convert meters to miles. (Recall that 1 mi = 1.6093440 km.)
3. Write a program to convert pounds to kilograms. (Recall that 1 kg = 2.205 lb.)
4. Write a program to convert newtons to pounds. (Recall that 1 lb = 4.448 N.)

5. Write a program that converts degrees Fahrenheit (T_F) to degrees Rankin (T_R). (Recall that $T_F = T_R - 459.67°R$.)

6. Write a program that converts degrees Celsius (T_C) to degrees Rankin (T_R). (Recall that $T_F = T_R - 459.67°R$ and that $T_F = (9/5) T_C + 32°F$.)

7. Write a program that converts degrees Kelvin (T_K) to degrees Fahrenheit (T_F). (Recall that $T_R = (9/5) T_K$ and that $T_F = T_R - 459.67°R$.)

Areas and Volumes. These problems involve computing an area or a volume using input from the user. Each program should include a prompt to the user to enter the variables needed.

8. Write a program to compute the area of a rectangle with sides a and b. (Recall that $A = a \cdot b$.)

9. Write a program to compute the area of a triangle with base b and height h. (Recall that $A = \frac{1}{2} b \cdot h$.)

10. Write a program to compute the area of a circle with radius r. (Recall that $A = \pi r^2$.)

11. Write a program to compute the area of a sector of a circle when θ is the angle in radians between the radii. (Recall that $A = r^2\theta/2$.)

12. Write a program to compute the area of a sector of a circle when d is the angle in degrees between the radii. (Recall that $A = r^2\theta/2$, where θ is in radians.)

13. Write a program to compute the area of an ellipse with semiaxes a and b. (Recall that $A = \pi a \cdot b$.)

14. Write a program to compute the area of the surface of a sphere of radius r. (Recall that $A = 4\pi r^2$.)

15. Write a program to compute the volume of a sphere of radius r. (Recall that $V = (4/3)\pi r^3$.)

16. Write a program to compute the volume of a cylinder of radius r and height h. (Recall that $V = \pi r^2 h$.)

Amino Acid Molecular Weights. The amino acids in proteins are composed of atoms of oxygen, carbon, nitrogen, sulfur, and hydrogen, as shown in Table 2.7. The molecular weights of the individual elements follow:

Element	Atomic Weight
Oxygen	15.9994
Carbon	12.011
Nitrogen	14.00674
Sulfur	32.066
Hydrogen	1.00794

TABLE 2.7 Amino Acid Molecules					
Amino Acid	O	C	N	S	H
Alanine	2	3	1	0	7
Arginine	2	6	4	0	15
Asparagine	3	4	2	0	8
Aspartic	4	4	1	0	6
Cysteine	2	3	1	1	7
Glutamic	4	5	1	0	8
Glutamine	3	5	2	0	10
Glycine	2	2	1	0	5
Histidine	2	6	3	0	10
Isoleucine	2	6	1	0	13
Leucine	2	6	1	0	13
Lysine	2	6	2	0	15
Methionine	2	5	1	1	11
Phenylanlanine	2	9	1	0	11
Proline	2	5	1	0	10
Serine	3	3	1	0	7
Threonine	3	4	1	0	9
Tryptophan	2	11	2	0	11
Tyrosine	3	9	1	0	11
Valine	2	5	1	0	11

19. Write a program that asks the user to enter the number of atoms of each of the five elements for an amino acid. Then compute and print the molecular weight for this amino acid.

20. Write a program that asks the user to enter the number of atoms of each of the five elements for an amino acid. Then compute and print the average weight of the atoms in the amino acid.

Logarithms to the Base b. To compute the logarithm of x to base b, we can use the following relationship [11]:

$$log_b x = \frac{log_e x}{log_e b}$$

21. Write a program that reads a positive number and then computes and prints the logarithm of the value to base 2. For example, the logarithm of 8 to base 2 is 3 because $2^3 = 8$.

22. Write a program that reads a positive number and then computes and prints the logarithm of the value to base 8. For example, the logarithm of 64 to base 8 is 2 because $8^2 = 64$.

3

Courtesy of National Center for Atmospheric Research/
University Corporation for Atmospheric Research/
National Science Foundation.

GRAND CHALLENGE:
Global Change

Weather balloons are used to collect data from the upper atmosphere. The
balloons are filled with helium and rise to an equilibrium point where the
difference between the densities of the helium inside the balloon and the air
outside the balloon is just enough to support the weight of the balloon. During the
day, the sun warms the balloon, causing it to rise to a new equilibrium point; in
the evening, the balloon cools, and it descends to a lower altitude. The balloon
can be used to measure the temperature, pressure, humidity, chemical
concentrations, or other properties of the air around the balloon. A weather
balloon may stay aloft for only a few hours or as long as several years collecting
environmental data. The balloon falls back to earth as the helium leaks out or is
released.

Control Structures and Data Files

OBJECTIVES

In this chapter, we present structured programming in terms of sequence, selection, and repetition structures. After defining these structures using pseudocode and flowcharts, we then discuss the C statements for implementing these structures. Sequence structures do not require new statements. The selection structure requires conditional expressions and `if` statements to provide alternative paths in a program. The repetition structure is implemented with three different loop structures—`while` loops, `do while` loops, and `for` loops. An example that applies to weather balloons is used to illustrate conditional statements and loops. We also

*Optional sections.

introduce simple data files **at this point** because they are commonly used in solving engineering problems. The numerical technique of linear modeling (or linear regression) is described with both equations and graphs, **and a specific example is presented** that uses a linear model for predicting ozone mixing ratios in the middle atmosphere.

3.1   Algorithm Development

In Chapter 2, the C programs that we developed were very simple. The steps were sequential, and typically involved reading information from the keyboard, computing new information, and then printing the new information. In solving engineering problems, most of the solutions require more complicated steps, and thus we need to expand the algorithm development part of our problem-solving process.

TOP–DOWN DESIGN

Top–down design

Top–down design presents a "big picture" description of the problem solution in sequential steps. This overall description of the problem is then refined until the steps are detailed enough to translate to language statements.

Decomposition outlines

Decomposition Outline. We used **decomposition outlines** in Chapters 1 and 2 to provide the first definition of a problem solution. This outline is written in sequential steps, and can be shown in a diagram or a step-by-step outline. For very simple problems, such as the one that follows, which was developed in Chapter 2, we can go from the decomposition outline directly to the C statements:

Decomposition Outline
1. *Read the new time value.*
2. *Compute the corresponding velocity and acceleration values.*
3. *Print the new velocity and acceleration.*

Divide-and-conquer
Stepwise refinement

However, for most problem solutions, we need to refine the decomposition outline into a description with more detail. This process is often referred to as a **divide-and-conquer** strategy, because we keep breaking the problem solution into smaller and smaller portions. To describe this **stepwise refinement**, we use pseudocode or flowcharts.

Pseudocode
Flowchart

Refinement with Pseudocode and Flowcharts. The refinement of an outline into more detailed steps can be done with pseudocode or a flowchart. **Pseudocode** uses Englishlike statements to describe the steps in an algorithm, and a **flowchart** uses a diagram to describe the steps in an algorithm. The fundamental steps in most algorithms are shown in Figure 3.1, along with the corresponding notation in pseudocode and flowcharts.

Pseudocode and flowcharts are tools to help us determine the order of steps to solve a problem. Both tools are commonly used, although they are not gener-

Basic Operation	Pseudocode Notation	Flowchart Symbol

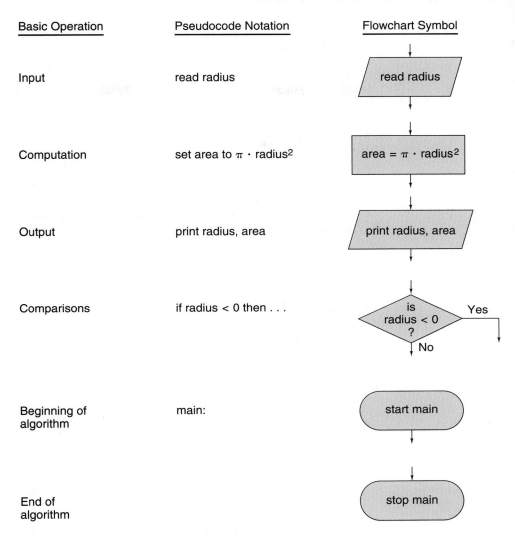

Input — read radius

Computation — set area to $\pi \cdot radius^2$

Output — print radius, area

Comparisons — if radius < 0 then . . .

Beginning of algorithm — main:

End of algorithm

Figure 3.1 *Pseudocode notation and flowchart symbols.*

ally both used with the same problem. In order to give examples of both tools, some problem solutions will use pseudocode and others will use flowcharts; the choice between pseudocode and flowcharts is usually a personal preference. Sometimes we need to go through several levels of pseudocode or flowcharts to develop complex problem solutions; this is the stepwise refinement that we mentioned previously in this section. Decomposition outlines, pseudocode, and flowcharts are working models of the solution, and thus are not unique. Each person working on a solution will have different decomposition outlines and pseudocode or flowchart descriptions, just like the C programs developed by different people will be somewhat different, although they solve the same problem.

STRUCTURED PROGRAMMING

A **structured program** is one written using simple control structures to organize the solution to a problem. A simple structure is usually defined to be a sequence, a selection, or a repetition. A **sequence** structure contains steps that are performed one after another; a **selection** structure contains one set of steps that is performed if a condition is true, and another set of steps that is performed if the condition is false; a **repetition** structure contains a set of steps that is repeated as long as a condition is true. We now discuss each of these simple structures, and use pseudocode and flowcharts to give specific examples.

Sequence. A sequence contains steps that are performed one after another. All the programs developed in Chapter 2 have a sequence structure. For example, the pseudocode for the program that performed the linear interpolation follows, and the flowchart for the program that computed the velocity and acceleration of the aircraft with the unducted engine is shown in Figure 3.2.

Sequence
Selection

Repetition

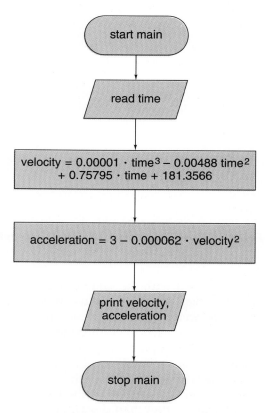

Figure 3.2 *Flowchart for unducted fan problem solution from Section 2.8.*

Refinement in Pseudocode

main: *read a, f_a*
        read c, f_c

$$\text{set } f\_b \text{ to } f\_a + \frac{b-a}{c-a} \cdot (f\_c - f\_a)$$

        print f_b

Condition

Selection. A selection structure contains a **condition** that can be evaluated as either true or false. If the condition is true, then one set of statements is executed; if the condition is false, then another set of statements is executed. For example, suppose that we have computed values for the numerator and denominator of a fraction. Before we compute the division, we want to be sure that the denominator is not close to zero. Therefore, the condition that we want to test is "denominator close to zero." If the condition is true, then we want to print a message indicating that we cannot compute the value. If the condition is false, which means that the denominator is not close to zero, then we compute and print the value of the fraction. In defining this condition, we need to define "close to zero." For this example, we will assume that close to zero means that the absolute value is less than 0.0001. A pseudocode description follows, and a flowchart description of this structure is shown in Figure 3.3.

if $|denominator| < 0.0001$
        print "Denominator close to zero"
else
            set fraction to numerator/denominator
            print fraction

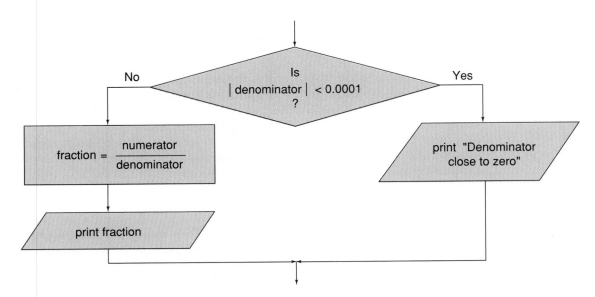

Figure 3.3 *Flowchart for selection structure.*

Note that this structure also contains a sequence structure (compute a fraction and then print the fraction) that is executed when the condition is false. We give more variations of the selection structure later in this chapter.

Loop

Repetition. The repetition structure allows us to repeat (or **loop** through) a set of steps as long as a condition is true. For example, we might want to compute a set of velocity values that correspond to time values of 0, 1, 2, . . . , 10 seconds. We do not want to develop a sequential structure that has a statement to compute the velocity for a time of 0, then another statement to compute the velocity for a time of 1, and then another statement to compute the velocity for a time of 2, and so on. Although this structure would require only 11 statements in this case, it could require hundreds of statements if we wanted to compute the velocity values over a long period of time. If we use the repetition structure, we can develop a solution in which we initialize the time to 0. Then, as long as the time value is less than or equal to 10, we compute and print a velocity value, and increment the time value by 1. When the time value is greater than 10, we exit the structure. Figure 3.4 contains the flowchart for this repetition structure, and the pseudocode follows:

> *set time to 0*
> *while time ≤ 10*
> > *compute velocity*
> > *print velocity*
> > *increment time by 1*

In the remaining sections of this chapter, we present the C statements for performing selections and repetitions, and then develop example programs that use these structures.

EVALUATION OF ALTERNATIVE SOLUTIONS

There are usually many ways to solve the same problem. In most cases, there is not a single best solution, but some solutions are better than others. Selecting a good solution becomes easier with experience, and we will give examples of the elements that contribute to good solutions in this text. For example, a good solution is one that is readable; therefore, a good solution is not necessarily the shortest solution because short solutions are often not very readable. We will strive to avoid subtle or clever steps that shorten a program but are difficult to understand.

As you begin to develop a solution to a problem, it is a good idea to try to think of several ways to solve it. Sketch the decomposition outline and pseudocode or flowchart for several solutions. Then choose the solution that you think will be the easiest to translate into C statements. Some algorithms fit different languages better than others, so you also want to pick a solution that is a good fit to the C language. Occasionally, other aspects of a solution must also be considered, such as execution speed and memory requirements.

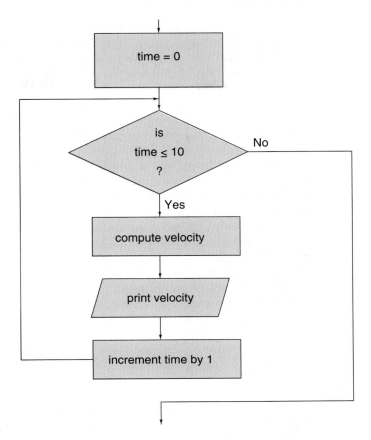

Figure 3.4 *Flowchart for repetition structure.*

ERROR CONDITIONS

As we develop an algorithm, we usually assume that the input data are correct. However, in real applications, there are often errors in the input data. Therefore, it may be important to test for errors in the input data that could occur and would cause the program to work incorrectly. There may also be conditions that could arise as we compute new values that could cause problems. For example, suppose that we are performing a computation in which the denominator value for a division operation turns out to be zero. Or suppose that the result of an altitude computation is negative. These are examples of **error conditions** (which are separate from errors in the algorithm) that could occur when a program is run.

Error conditions

Some error conditions can be checked within the program itself using statements that we present in this chapter, but if we check for every possible error condition, our programs become long, and a large percentage of the statements are checking for error conditions. Therefore, how do we decide which error conditions to check in our programs? Sometimes the problem statement will include information on error conditions that could occur, and the response to take if they are detected. Usually, though, error conditions are not mentioned. In these cases, we suggest that you develop an algorithm based on the problem statement, and then generate a list of potential error conditions that could arise. If possible, discuss these with the person or group that will be using the program. Otherwise, include error checks that seem to catch the most common types of errors, and then include written documentation to go with the program that describes the error conditions that your program will catch and the ones that your program does not catch.

Once you have decided which error conditions you will incorporate in your algorithm, you still need to decide what to do if one of the error conditions occurs. There are usually two possibilities—you can exit the program or you can attempt to correct the error and continue with the program. In either case, you should probably print an error message that describes the error condition that occurred and the action that you are taking. Be sure that the error message gives as much information as possible. Instead of printing "Error occurred in input data," print messages such as "Temperature out of bounds," "Time value is negative," or "Pressure exceeds safety limits."

In this chapter we discuss how to read and write data files, which are files (similar to program files) that contain information used in other programs. Sometimes programs called **data filters** are written that check the information in the data files for error conditions. Then, programs that use the data files do not need to check for the same error conditions.

GENERATION OF TEST DATA

Test data

The generation of **test data** is a very important part of developing problem solutions. Test data should include data to test each of the error conditions that is checked in our programs. Test data should also test each path through our program. As programs become longer, generating test data to completely test the program becomes very difficult. Entire courses and books are based on this **validation and verification** topic.

Validation and verification

We now give some suggestions on generating test data sets. First, use the data from the hand example. If this does not work properly, we are not off to a good start! Once these data work correctly, begin using test data that are correct, but cover different ranges of values. Be sure to use test data that test the boundary conditions, or limits, if the data are supposed to be in certain ranges. Once the program seems to work for valid data, then begin including the error conditions to see if the program handles them properly. In general, use many small sets of data instead of one large set of data to test the program.

If you find an error in testing the program, go back to the algorithm development step. Correct the error in the decomposition outline and the pseudocode or flowchart, and then correct the C program. When you make a major change in the program, you should completely retest the program. Sometimes changes affect parts of the program that we had not anticipated. This retesting is easier if we keep a log of the test sets used so that we can repeat them.

Program
walkthrough

Finally, we want to mention a technique called a **program walkthrough** that is commonly used in industry in the development of large programs. In a program walkthrough, the people who have developed an algorithm for a complicated problem present their solution to a small group of people who are knowledgeable about the problem, but did not take part in the algorithm development. The interaction between the people who developed the algorithm and the people who are analyzing it usually results in identifying potential problems with the algorithm and the generation of potential test data for the software after it is coded. The result is that the final program is completed sooner with more confidence in its accuracy. You might try simple program walkthroughs with other students in your class as you solve more complicated problems.

3.2   Conditional Expressions

Condition

Because both selection and repetition structures use conditions, we must discuss conditions before presenting the statements that implement selection and repetition structures. A **condition** is an expression that can be evaluated to be true or false, and it is composed of expressions combined with relational operators; a condition can also include logical operators. In this section, we present relational operators and logical operators, and discuss the evaluation order when they are combined in a single condition.

RELATIONAL OPERATORS

Relational
operators

The **relational operators** that can be used to compare two expressions in C are shown in the following list:

Relational Operator	Interpretation
<	is less than
<=	is less than or equal to
>	is greater than
>=	is greater than or equal to
==	is equal to
!=	is not equal to

Blanks can be used on either side of a relational operator, but blanks cannot be used to separate a two-character operator such as ==.

Example conditions are the following:

```
a < b
x+y >= 10.5
fabs(denominator) < 0.0001
```

Given the values of the identifiers in these conditions, we can evaluate each one to be true or false. For example, if **a** is equal to 5, and **b** is equal to 8.4, then **a<b** is

a true condition. If **x** is equal to 2.3 and **y** is equal to 4.1, **then x+y >= 10.5** is a false condition. If **denominator** is equal to -0.0025, then **fabs(denominator) < 0.0001** is a false condition. *Note that we use spaces around the relational operator in a logial expression but not around the arithmetic operators in the conditions.*

In C, a true condition is assigned a value of 1 and a false condition is assigned a value of zero. Therefore, the following statement is valid:

```
d = b>c;
```

If **b>c**, then the value of **d** is 1; otherwise, the value of **d** is zero. Because a condition is given a value, it is then valid to use a value in place of a condition. For example, consider the following statement:

```
if (a)
    count++;
```

If the condition value is zero, then the condition is assumed to be false; if the value is nonzero, then the condition is assumed to be true. Therefore, in the previous statement, the value of **count** will be incremented if **a** is nonzero.

LOGICAL OPERATORS

Logical operators can also be used within conditions. However, logical operators compare conditions, not expressions. C supports three **logical operators**: and, or, and not. These logical operators are represented by the following symbols:

Logical Operator	Symbol
and	&&
or	||
not	!

For example, consider the following condition:

```
a<b && b<c
```

The relational operators have higher precedence than the logical operator; therefore, this condition is read "**a** is less than **b**, and **b** is less than **c**." *In order to make a logical statement more readable, we insert spaces around the logical operator, but not around the relational operators.* Given values for **a**, **b**, and **c**, we can evaluate this condition as true or false. For example, if **a** is equal to 1, **b** is equal to 5, and **c** is equal to 8, then the condition is true. If **a** is equal to -2, **b** is equal to 9, and **c** is equal to 2, then the condition is false.

If **A** and **B** are conditions, then the logical operators can be used to generate new conditions **A && B, A || B, !A**, and **!B**. The condition **A && B** is true only if both **A** and **B** are true. The condition **A || B** is true if either or both **A** and **B** are true. The **!** operator changes the value of the condition with which it is used.

TABLE 3.1 Logical Operators					
A	B	A && B	A || B	!A	!B
False	False	False	False	True	True
False	True	False	True	True	False
True	False	False	True	False	True
True	True	True	True	False	False

Thus, the condition !A is true only if A is false, and the condition !B is true only if B is false. These definitions are summarized in Table 3.1.

When expressions with logical operators are executed, C will only evaluate as much of the expression as necessary to evaluate it. For example, if A is false, then the expression A && B is also false, and there is no need to evaluate B. Similarly, if A is true, then the expression A || B is true, and there is no need to evaluate B.

PRECEDENCE AND ASSOCIATIVITY

A condition can contain several logical operators, as in the following:

```
! (b==c || b==5.5)
```

The hierarchy, from highest to lowest, is !, &&, ||, but parentheses can be used to change the hierarchy. In the previous example, the expressions b==c and b==5.5 are evaluated first. Suppose b is equal to 3 and c is equal to 5. Then neither expression is true, so the expression b==c || b==5.5 is false. We then apply the ! operator to the false condition, which gives a true condition. Blanks cannot be used to separate the characters in either the || or &&. A common error is to use = instead of == in a logical expression.

A condition can contain both arithmetic operators and relational operators, as well as logical operators. Table 3.2 contains the precedence and the associativity order for the elements in a condition.

TABLE 3.2 Operator Precedence for Arithmetic, Relational, and Logical Operators		
Precedence	Operation	Associativity
1	( )	innermost first
2	++ -- + - ! (type)	right to left (unary)
3	* / %	left to right
4	+ -	left to right
5	< <= > >=	left to right
6	== !=	left to right
7	&&	left to right
8	||	left to right
9	= += -= *= /= %=	right to left

Practice!

Determine if the following conditions in problems 1 through 8 are true or false. Assume that the following variables have been declared and given these values:

$$a = 5.5 \qquad b = 1.5 \qquad k = -3$$

1. `a < 10.0+k`
2. `a+b >= 6.5`
3. `k != a-b`
4. `b-k > a`

5. `!(a == 3*b)`
6. `-k <= k+6`
7. `a<10 && a>5`
8. `fabs(k)>3 || k<b-a`

3.3   Selection Statements

The `if` statement allows us to test conditions, and then perform statements based on whether the conditions are true or false. C contains two forms of if statements—the simple `if` statement and the `if/else` statement. C also contains a `switch` statement that allows us to test multiple conditions and then execute groups of statements based on whether the conditions are true or false.

SIMPLE `if` STATEMENT

The simplest form of an `if` statement has the following general form:

```
if (condition)
    statement 1;
```

Style

If the condition is true, we execute statement 1; if the condition is false, we skip statement 1. *The statement within the `if` statement is indented so that it is easier to visualize the structure of the program from the statements.*

Compound statement

If we wish to execute several statements (or a sequence structure) when the condition is true, we use a **compound statement**, or **block**, which is composed of a set of statements enclosed in braces. The location of the braces is a matter of style; two common styles are shown:

```
Style 1
if (condition)
{
    statement 1;
    statement 2;
    . . .
    statement n;
}
```

```
Style 2
if (condition) {
    statement 1;
    statement 2;
    . . .
    statement n;
}
```

In the text solutions, we use the first style convention; thus, both braces are on lines by themselves. *Although this makes the program a little longer, it also makes it easier to notice if a brace has been mistakenly omitted.* Figure 3.5 contains flowcharts of the control flow with simple **if** statements containing either one statement to execute, or several statements to execute, if the condition is true.

A specific example of an **if** statement follows:

```
if (a < 50)
{
    ++count;
    sum += a;
}
```

If **a** is less than 50, then **count** is incremented by 1 and **a** is added to **sum**; otherwise, these two statements are skipped.

If statements can also be nested; the following example includes an **if** statement within an **if** statement:

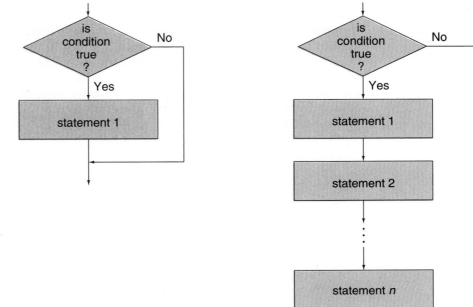

Figure 3.5 *Flowcharts for selection statements.*

```
if (a < 50)
{
    ++count;
    sum += a;
    if (b > a)
        b = 0;
}
```

If **a** is less than 50, we increment **count** by 1 and add **a** to **sum**. In addition, if **b** is greater than **a**, then we also set **b** to zero. If **a** is not less than 50, then we skip all these statements. *Be sure to indent the statements in each* **if** *statement when they are nested.*

Style

if/else STATEMENT

An **if/else** statement allows us to execute one set of statements if a condition is true and a different set if the condition is false. The simplest form of an **if/else** statement is the following:

```
if (condition)
    statement 1;
else
    statement 2;
```

Statements 1 and 2 can also be replaced by compound statements. Statement 1 or statement 2 can also be an **empty statement,** which is just a semicolon. If statement 2 is an empty statement, then the **if/else** statement should probably be posed as a simple **if** statement. There are situations in which it is convenient to use an empty statement for statement 1; however, these statements can also be rewritten as simple **if** statements with the conditions reversed. For example, the following two statements are equivalent:

```
if (a < b)              if (a >= b)
    ;                       count++;
else
    count++;
```

Consider this **if/else** statement:

```
if (d <= 30)
    velocity = 0.425 + 0.00175*d*d;
else
    velocity = 0.625 + 0.12*d - 0.0025*d*d;
```

In this example, **velocity** is computed with the first assignment statement if the distance **d** is less than or equal to 30; otherwise, **velocity** is computed with the second assignment statement. A flowchart for this **if/else** statement is shown in Figure 3.6.

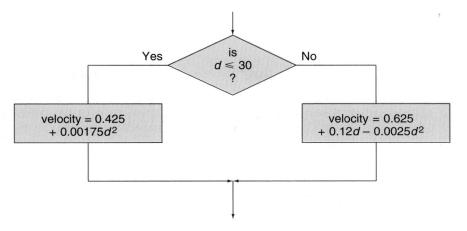

Figure 3.6 *Flowchart for if/else statement.*

Another example of the **if/else** statement is the following:

```
if (fabs(denominator) < 0.0001)
    printf("Denominator close to zero");
else
{
    x = numerator/denominator;
    printf("x = %f \n",x);
}
```

In this example, we examine the absolute value of the variable **denominator**. If this value is close to zero, we print a message indicating that we cannot perform the division. If the value of **denominator** is not close to zero, we compute and print the value of **x**. The flowchart for this statement was shown in Figure 3.3.
Consider the following set of nested **if/else** statements:

```
if (x > y)
    if (y < z)
        k++;
    else
        m++;
else
    j++;
```

The value of **k** is incremented when **x > y** and **y < z**. The value of **m** is incremented when **x > y** and **y >= z**. The value of **j** is incremented when **x <= y**. With careful indenting, this statement is straightforward to follow. Suppose that we now eliminate the **else** portion of the inner **if** statement. If we keep the same indention, the statements become the following:

```
if (x > y)
    if (y < z)
        k++;
else
    j++;
```

It might appear that **j** is incremented when **x <= y**, but that is not correct. The C compiler will associate an **else** statement with the closest **if** statement within a block. Therefore, no matter what indenting is used, the previous statement is executed as if it were the following:

```
if (x > y)
    if (y < z)
        k++;
    else
        j++;
```

Thus, **j** is incremented when **x > y** and **y >= z**. If we intended for **j** to be incremented when **x <= y**, then we would need to use braces to define the inner statement as a block:

```
if (x > y)
{
    if (y < z)
        k++;
}
else
    j++;
```

Style

To avoid confusion and possible errors when using nested if/else statements, you should routinely use braces to clearly define the blocks of statements that go together.

C allows a **conditional operator** to be used in place of a simple **if/else** statement. This conditional operator is a ternary operator because it has three arguments—a condition, a statement to perform if the condition is true, and a statement to perform if the condition is false. The operation is indicated with a question mark following the condition, and with a colon between the two statements. To illustrate, the following two statements are equivalent:

```
if (a<b)                a<b ? count++ : c = a + b;
    count++;
else
    c = a + b;
```

The conditional operator (specified as **?:**) is evaluated before assignment operators, and if there is more than one conditional operator in an expression, they are associated from right to left.

In this section, we have presented a number of ways to compare values in selection statements. A caution is necessary when comparing floating-point values. As we saw in Chapter 2, floating-point values can sometimes be slightly different than we expect them to be because of the conversions between binary and decimal values. For example, earlier in this section, we did not compare **denominator** to zero, but instead used a condition to see if the absolute value of **denominator** was less than a small value. Similarly, if we wanted to know if **y** were close to the value 10.5, we should use a condition such as **fabs(y-10.5) <= 0.0001** instead of **y == 10.5**. In general, do not use the equality operator with floating-point values.

Practice!

In problems 1 through 7, draw a flowchart to perform the steps indicated. Then give the corresponding C statements. Assume that the variables have been declared and have reasonable values.

1. If **time** is greater than 15.0, increment **time** by 1.0.
2. When the square root of **poly** is less than 0.5, print the value of **poly**.
3. If the difference between **volt_1** and **volt_2** is larger than 10.0, print the values of **volt_1** and **volt_2**.
4. If the value of **den** is less than 0.05, set **result** to zero; otherwise, set **result** equal to **num** divided by **den**.
5. If the natural logarithm of **x** is greater than or equal to 3, set **time** equal to zero and decrement **count**.
6. If **dist** is less than 50.0 and **time** is greater than 10.0, increment **time** by 2; otherwise, increment **time** by 2.5.
7. If **dist** is greater than or equal to 100.0, increment **time** by 2.0. If **dist** is between 50 and 100, increment **time** by 1. Otherwise, increment **time** by 0.5.

switch STATEMENT

The **switch** statement is used for multiple-selection decision making. In particular, it is often used to replace nested **if/else** statements. Before giving the general discussion of the **switch** statement, we present a simple example that uses nested **if/else** statements and then an equivalent solution that uses the **switch** statement.

Suppose that we have a temperature reading from a sensor inside a large piece of machinery. We want to print a message on the control screen to inform the operator of the temperature status. If the status code is 10, the temperature is too hot, and the equipment should be turned off; if the status code is 11, the operator should check the temperature every 5 minutes; if the status code is 13, the operator should turn on the circulating fan; for all other status codes, the equipment is operating in a normal mode. The correct message could be printed with the following set of nested **if/else** statements:

```
if (code == 10)
   printf("Too hot - turn equipment off \n");
else
{
   if (code == 11)
      printf("Caution - recheck in 5 minutes \n");
   else
   {
      if (code == 13)
         printf("Turn on circulating fan \n");
      else
         printf("Normal mode of operation \n");
   }
}
```

An equivalent statement is the following **switch** statement:

```
switch (code)
{
   case 10:
      printf("Too hot - turn equipment off \n");
      break;
   case 11:
      printf("Caution - recheck in 5 minutes \n");
      break;
   case 13:
      printf("Turn on circulating fan \n");
      break;
   default:
      printf("Normal temperature range \n");
      break;
}
Statement 1;
```

The **break** statement causes the execution of the program to continue with the statement following the **switch** statement (statement 1), thus skipping the rest of the statements in the braces.

Nested **if/else** statements do not always easily translate to a **switch** statement. However, when the conversion works, the **switch** statement is usually easier to read. It is also easier to determine the punctuation needed for the **switch** statement. In fact, if the punctuation is not correct in the **if/else** statements, the compiler may not execute the statements as expected.

Controlling expression

Case labels

Case structure

The **switch** statement selects the statements to perform based on a **controlling expression**, which must be an integer expression. In the general form that follows, **case labels** (**label_1, label_2,** . . .) determine which statements are executed, and thus in some languages, this structure is called a **case structure**. The statements executed are the ones that correspond to the case for which the label is equal to the controlling expression. The case labels must be unique constants; an error occurs if two or more of the case labels have the same value. The

Default label

default label is used to give a statement to execute if none of the other statements is executed; the default label is optional.

```
switch  (controlling expression)
{
    case label_1:
        statements;
    case label_2:
        statements;
    . . .
    default:
        statements;
}
```

The statements in the **switch** structure usually contain the **break** statement. When the **break** statement is executed, the execution of the program breaks out of the **switch** structure, and continues executing with the statement following the **switch** structure. Without the **break** statement, all statements will be executed that follow the ones selected with the case label.

Although the default *clause in the* switch *statement is optional, we recommend that it be included so that the steps are clearly specified for the situation in which none of the case labels is equal to the controlling expression.* We also use the **break** statement in the default clause to emphasize that the program continues with the statement following the **switch** statement.

It is valid to use several case labels with the same statement, as in

```
switch (status)
{
    case 1: case 2:
        printf("Normal operating range \n");
        break;
    case 3:
        printf("Maintenance needed \n");
        break;
    default:
        printf("Error in code value \n");
        break;
}
```

When more than one case label is used for the same statement, the evaluation is performed as if the logical **or** operator joined the cases. For this example, the first statement is executed if **status** is equal to 1 or if **status** is equal to 2.

Practice!

Convert the following nested **if/else** statements to a **switch** statement:

```
if (rank==1 || rank==2)
   printf("Lower division \n");
else
{
   if (rank==3 || rank==4)
      printf("Upper division \n");
   else
   {
      if (rank==5)
         printf("Graduate student \n");
      else
         printf("Invalid rank \n");
   }
}
```

3.4   Loop Structures

Loops are used to implement repetitive structures. C contains three different loop structures—the **while** loop, the **do/while** loop, and the **for** loop. In addition, C allows us to use two additional statements with loops to modify their performance—the **break** statement (which we used with the **switch** statement) and the **continue** statement.

Before presenting these loop structures, we would like to present two debugging suggestions that are useful when trying to find errors in programs that contain loops. When compiling longer programs, it is not uncommon to have a large number of compiler errors. Rather than trying to find each error separately, we suggest that you recompile your program after correcting several obvious syntax errors. One error will often generate several error messages. Some of these error messages may describe errors that are not in your program, but were printed because the original error confused the compiler.

The second debugging suggestion relates to errors inside a loop. When you want to determine if the steps in a loop are working the way that you want, include **printf** statements in the loop to provide a memory snapshot of key variables each time the loop is executed. Then, if there is an error, you have much of the information that you need to determine what is causing the error.

while LOOP

while loop

The general form of a **while loop** follows:

```
while (condition)
{
   statements;
}
```

The condition is evaluated before the statements within the loop are executed. If the condition is false, the loop statements are skipped, and execution continues with the statement following the **while** loop. If the condition is true, then the loop statements are executed, and the condition is evaluated again. If it is still true, then the statements are executed again, and the condition is evaluated again. This repetition continues until the condition is false. The statements within the loop must modify variables that are used in the condition; otherwise, the value of the condition will never change, and we will either never execute the statements in the loop or we will never be able to exit the loop. An **infinite loop** is generated if the condition in a `while` loop is always true. Most systems have a system-defined limit on the amount of time that can be used by a program, and will generate an execution error when this limit is exceeded. Other systems require that the user enter a special set of characters, such as the control key followed by the character c (abbreviated as ^c) to stop or **abort** the execution of a program. Nearly everyone eventually writes a program that inadvertently contains an infinite loop, so be sure you know the special characters to abort the execution of a program for your system.

The following pseudocode and program use a `while` loop to generate a conversion table for converting degrees to radians. The degree values start at 0°, increment by 10°, and go through 360°.

Refinement in Pseudocode

main: *set degrees to zero*
           while degrees ≤ 360
                 convert degrees to radians
                 print degrees, radians
                 add 10 to degrees

ch3_1.c

```
/*--------------------------------------------------------*/
/*   Program chapter3_1                                   */
/*                                                        */
/*   This program prints a degree-to-radian table         */
/*   using a while loop structure.                        */

#include <stdio.h>
#include <stdlib.h>
#define PI 3.141593

main()
{
   /*  Declare and initialize variables.  */
   int degrees=0;
   double radians;

   /*  Print radians and degrees in a loop.  */
   printf("Degrees to Radians \n");
   while (degrees <= 360)
   {
      radians = degrees*PI/180;
      printf("%6i %9.6f \n",degrees,radians);
      degrees += 10;
   }

   /*  Exit program.  */
   return EXIT_SUCCESS;
}
/*--------------------------------------------------------*/
```

The first few lines of output from the program follow:

```
Degrees to Radians
     0   0.000000
    10   0.174533
    20   0.349066
     .   .   .
```

do/while LOOP

The **do/while** loop is similar to the **while** loop except that the condition is tested at the end of the loop instead of at the beginning of the loop. Testing the condition at the end of the loop ensures that the **do/while** loop is always executed at least once; a **while** loop may not be executed at all if the condition is initially false. The general form of the **do/while** loop is as follows:

```
do
{
    statements;
} while (condition);
```

The following pseudocode and program print the degree-to-radian conversion table using a **do/while** loop instead of a **while** loop:

Refinement in Pseudocode

main: set degrees to zero
           do
                   convert degrees to radians
                   print degrees, radians
                   add 10 to degrees
           while degrees ≤ 360

ch3_2.c

```
/*-----------------------------------------------------*/
/*  Program chapter3_2                                 */
/*                                                     */
/*  This program prints a degree-to-radian table       */
/*  using a do-while loop structure.                   */

#include <stdio.h>
#include <stdlib.h>
#define PI 3.141593

main()
{
    /*  Declare and initialize variables.  */
    int degrees=0;
    double radians;
```

```
    /*  Print degrees and radians in a loop.  */
    printf("Degrees to Radians \n");
    do
    {
       radians = degrees*PI/180;
       printf("%6i %9.6f \n",degrees,radians);
       degrees += 10;
    } while (degrees <= 360);

    /*  Exit program.  */
    return EXIT_SUCCESS;
}
/*------------------------------------------------------*/
```

for LOOP

Many programs require loops that are based on the value of a variable that increments (or decrements) by the same amount each time through the loop. When
the variable reaches a specified value, we then want to exit the loop. This type of
loop can be implemented as a **while** loop, but it can also be easily implemented
with the **for loop**. The general form of the **for** loop is as follows:

for loop

```
for (expression_1; expression_2; expression_3)
{
    statements;
}
```

Loop-control variable

Expression_1 is used to initialize the **loop-control variable**, expression_2 specifies the condition that should be true to continue the loop repetition, and expres-
sion_3 specifies the modification to the loop-control variable.

For example, if we want to execute a loop 10 times, with the value of the
variable **k** going from 1 to 10 in increments of 1, we could use the following **for**
loop structure:

```
for (k=1; k<=10; k++)
{
    statements;
}
```

Style

*Braces should be used to delineate the statements in a loop, even when they are not
necessary.*

If we want to execute a loop with the value of the variable **n** going from 20
to 0 in increments of −2, we could use this loop structure:

```
for (n=20; n>=0; n=n-2)
{
    statements;
}
```

The **for** loop could also have been written in this form:

```
for (n=20; n>=0; n - =2)
{
    statements;
}
```

Both forms are valid, but the abbreviated form is commonly used because it is shorter.

The following expression computes the number of times that a **for** loop will be executed:

$$\text{floor}\left(\frac{\text{final value} - \text{initial value}}{\text{increment}}\right) + 1$$

If this value is negative, the loop is not executed. Thus, if a **for** statement has the following structure:

```
for (k=5; k<=83; k+=4)
{
    statements;
}
```

then it would be executed the following number of times:

$$\text{floor}\left(\frac{83 - 5}{4}\right) + 1 = \text{floor}\left(\frac{78}{4}\right) + 1 = 20$$

The value of **k** would be 5, then 9, then 13, and so on, until the final value of 81. The loop would not be executed with the value of 85 because the loop condition is not true when **k** is equal to 85.

The following pseudocode and program print the degree-to-radian conversion table shown earlier with a **while** loop, now modified to use a **for** loop. Note that the pseudocode for the **while** loop solution to this problem and the pseudocode for the **for** loop solution to this problem are identical.

Refinement in Pseudocode

main: set degrees to zero
         while degrees ≤ 360
             convert degrees to radians
             print degrees, radians
             add 10 to degrees

ch3_3.c

```
/*------------------------------------------------------------*/
/*  Program chapter3_3                                        */
/*                                                            */
/*  This program prints a degree-to-radian table             */
/*  using a for loop structure.                              */
```

```
#include <stdio.h>
#include <stdlib.h>
#define PI 3.141593

main()
{
  /*  Declare the variables.  */
  int degrees;
  double radians;

  /*  Print degrees and radians in a loop.  */
  printf("Degrees to Radians \n");
  for (degrees=0; degrees<=360; degrees+=10)
  {
    radians = degrees*PI/180;
    printf("%6i %9.6f \n",degrees,radians);
  }

  /*  Exit program.  */
  return EXIT_SUCCESS;
}
/*----------------------------------------------------*/
```

Note that the value of **degrees** did not need to be initialized in the declaration because it is initialized in the **for** loop statement.

Practice!

Determine the number of times that the following **for** loops are executed.

1.
```
for (k=3; k<=20; k++)
{
    statements;
}
```

2.
```
for (k=3; k<=20; ++k)
{
    statements;
}
```

3.
```
for (count=-2; count<=14; count++)
{
    statements;
}
```

4.
```
for (k= -2; k>= -10; k--)
{
    statements;
}
```

5.
```
for (time=10; time>=5; time++)
{
    statements;
}
```

The initialization and modification expressions in a `for` loop can contain more than one statement, as shown in this statement that initializes and updates two variables in the loop:

```
for (k=1, j=5; k<=10; k++, j++)
{
    sum_1 += k;
    sum_2 += j;
}
```

When more than one statement is used, they are separated by commas, and are executed from left to right. This comma operator is executed last in operator precedence.

break AND continue STATEMENTS

We used the **break** statement in a previous section with the **switch** statement. The **break** statement can also be used with any of the loop structures presented in this section to immediately exit from the loop in which it is contained. In contrast, the **continue** statement is used to skip the remaining statements in the current pass or **iteration** of the loop, and then continue with the next iteration of the loop. Thus, in a **while** loop or a **do/while** loop, the condition is evaluated after the **continue** statement is executed to determine if the statements in the loop are to be executed again. In a **for** loop, the loop-control variable is modified, and the repetition-continuation condition is evaluated to determine if the statements in the loop are to be executed again. Both the **break** and **continue** statements are useful in exiting either the current iteration or the entire loop when error conditions are encountered.

Iteration

To illustrate the difference between the **break** and the **continue** statements, consider the following loop that reads values from a data file:

```
sum = 0;
for (k=1; k<=20; k++)
{
    scanf("%lf",&x);
    if (x > 10.0)
        break;
    sum += x;
}
printf("Sum = %f \n",sum);
```

This loop reads up to 20 values from the keyboard. If all 20 values are less than or equal to 10.0, then the statements compute the sum of the values and print the sum. But, if a value is read that is greater than 10.0, then the **break** statement causes control to break out of the loop, and execute the **printf** statement. Thus, the sum printed is only the sum of the values up to the value greater than 10.0.

Now, consider this variation of the previous loop:

```
sum = 0;
for (k=1; k<=20; k++)
{
    scanf("%lf",&x);
    if (x > 10.0)
        continue;
    sum += x;
}
printf("Sum = %f \n",sum);
```

In this loop, the sum of all 20 values is printed if all values are less than or equal to 10.0. However, if a value is greater than 10.0, then the **continue** statement causes control to skip the rest of the statements in that iteration of the loop, and to continue with the next iteration of the loop, Hence, the sum printed is the sum of all values in the 20 values that are less than or equal to 10.

3.5   Problem Solving Applied: Weather Balloons

Weather balloons are used to gather temperature and pressure data at various altitudes in the atmosphere. The balloon rises because the density of the helium in the balloon is less than the density of the surrounding air outside the balloon. As the balloon rises, the surrounding air becomes less dense, and thus the balloon's ascent slows until it reaches a point of equilibrium. During the day, sunlight warms the helium trapped inside the balloon, which causes the helium to expand and become less dense and the balloon to rise higher. During the night, however, the helium in the balloon cools and becomes more dense, causing the balloon to descend to a lower altitude. The next day, the sun heats the helium again and the balloon rises. Over time, this process generates a set of altitude measurements that can be approximated with a polynomial equation.

Assume that the following polynomial represents the altitude or height in meters during the first 48 hours following the launch of a weather balloon:

$$alt(t) = -0.12t^4 + 12t^3 - 380t^2 + 4100t + 220$$

where the units of t are hours. The corresponding polynomial model for the velocity in meters per hour of the weather balloon is as follows:

$$v(t) = -0.48t^3 + 36t^2 - 760t + 4100$$

Print a table of the altitude and the velocity for this weather balloon using units of meters and meters/second. Let the user enter the start time, increment in time between lines of the table, and ending time, where all the time values must be less than 48 hours. In addition to printing the table, also print the peak altitude and its corresponding time.

1.   PROBLEM STATEMENT

Using the polynomials that represent the altitude and velocity for a weather balloon, print a table using units of meters and meters/second. Also find the maximum altitude (or height) and its corresponding time.

2.   INPUT/OUTPUT DESCRIPTION

The following I/O diagram shows the user input that represents the starting time, time increment, and ending time for the table. The output is the table of altitude and velocity values and the maximum altitude and its corresponding time.

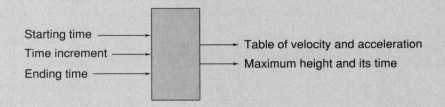

3.   HAND EXAMPLE

Assume that the starting time is 0 hours, the time increment is 1 hour, and the ending time is 5 hours. To obtain the correct units, we need to divide the velocity value in meters/hour by 3600 in order to get meters/second. Using our calculator, we can then compute the following values:

Time	Altitude (m)	Velocity(m/s)
0	220.00	1.14
1	3,951.88	0.94
2	6,994.08	0.76
3	9,414.28	0.59
4	11,277.28	0.45
5	12,645.00	0.32

We can also determine the maximum altitude for this table, which is 12,645.00 meters; it occurred at 5 hours.

4.   ALGORITHM DEVELOPMENT

We first develop the decomposition outline because it breaks the solution into a series of sequential steps.

Decomposition Outline

1. *Get user input to specify times for the table.*
2. *Generate and print conversion table and find maximum height and corresponding time.*
3. *Print maximum height and corresponding time.*

The second step in the decomposition outline represents a loop in which we generate the table and, at the same time, keep track of the maximum height. As we refine this outline, and particularly step 2 into more detail, we need to think carefully about finding the maximum height. Look back at the hand example. Once the table has been printed, it is easy to look at it and select the maximum height. However, when the computer is computing and printing the table, it does not have all the data at one time; it only has the information for the current line in the table. Therefore, to keep track of the maximum, we need to specify a separate variable to store the maximum value. Each time that we compute a new height, we will compare that value to the maximum value. If the new value is larger, we replace the maximum with this new value. We will also need to keep track of the corresponding time. The following refinement in pseudocode outlines these new steps:

Refinement in Pseudocode

```
main:      read initial, increment, final values from keyboard
           set max_height to zero
           set max_time to zero
           print table heading
           set time to initial
           while time<=final
                compute height and velocity
                print height and velocity
                if height>max_height
                     set max_height to height
                     set max_time to time
                add increment to time
           print max_time and max_height
```

The steps in the pseudocode are now detailed enough to convert into C. Note that we convert the velocity from meters/hour to meters/second in the **printf** statement.

ch3_4.c

```
/*-------------------------------------------------------*/
/*  Program chapter3_4                                   */
/*                                                       */
/*  This program prints a table of height and           */
/*  velocity values for a weather balloon.               */

#include <stdio.h>
#include <stdlib.h>
#include <math.h>

main()
{
   /*  Declare and initialize variables.  */
   double initial, increment, final, time, height,
         velocity, max_time=0, max_height=0;

   /*  Get user input.  */
   printf("Enter initial value for table (in hours) \n");
   scanf("%lf",&initial);
   printf("Enter increment between lines (in hours) \n");
   scanf("%lf",&increment);
   printf("Enter final value for table (in hours) \n");
   scanf("%lf",&final);

   /*  Print report heading.  */
   printf("\n\nWeather Balloon Information \n");
   printf("Time     Height    Velocity \n");
   printf("(hrs)    (meters)   (meters/s) \n");

   /*  Compute and print report information.  */
   for (time=initial; time<=final; time+=increment)
   {
      height = -0.12*pow(time,4) + 12*pow(time,3)
              - 380*time*time + 4100*time + 220;
      velocity = -0.48*pow(time,3) + 36*time*time
              - 760*time + 4100;
      printf("%6.2f   %8.2f    %7.2f \n",
             time,height,velocity/3600);
      if (height > max_height)
      {
         max_height = height;
         max_time = time;
      }
   }
```

```
                /*  Print maximum height and corresponding time.  */
                printf("\nMaximum balloon height was %8.2f meters \n",
                       max_height);
                printf("and it occurred at %6.2f hours \n",max_time);

                /*  Exit program.  */
                return EXIT_SUCCESS;
           }
           /*-------------------------------------------------------*/
```

5.   **TESTING**

If we use the data from the hand example, we have the following interaction
with the program:

```
Enter initial value for table (in hours)
0
Enter increment between lines (in hours)
1
Enter final value for table (in hours)
5

Weather Balloon Information
Time     Height     Velocity
(hrs)    (meters)   (meters/s)
 0.00     220.00      1.14
 1.00    3951.88      0.94
 2.00    6994.08      0.76
 3.00    9414.28      0.59
 4.00   11277.28      0.45
 5.00   12645.00      0.32

Maximum balloon height was 12645.00 meters
and it occurred at    5.00 hours
```

Figure 3.7 contains a plot of the altitude and velocity of the balloon for a period of 48 hours. From the plots, we can see the periods during which the balloon rises or falls.

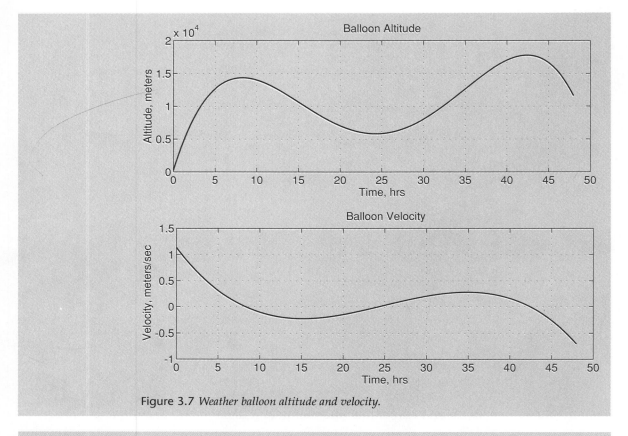

Figure 3.7 *Weather balloon altitude and velocity.*

Modify!

ch3_4.c

These problems relate to the program developed in this section that prints a table of weather balloon information.

1.   Use this program to generate a table showing the weather balloon information for every 10 minutes for 2 hours, starting at 4 hours after the balloon was launched.

2.   Modify the program to include a check to be sure that the final time is greater than the initial. If it is not, ask the user to reenter the complete set of report information.

3.   The equations given in this section were developed to be accurate only for time from 0 to 48 hours, so modify the program to print a message to the user that specifies an upper bound of 48 hours. Also check the user input to be sure that it stays within the proper bounds. If there are any errors, ask the user to reenter the complete set of report information.

4.   If there are two times with the same maximum height, this program will print the first time that the maximum height occurred. Modify the program so that it will print the last time that the maximum height occurred.

3.6   Data Files

Engineering problem solutions often involve large amounts of data. These data can be data generated by the program as output, or they can be input data that are used by the program. It is not generally feasible to either print large amounts of data to the screen or to read large amounts of data from the keyboard. In these

Data files

cases, we usually use **data files** to store the data. These data files are similar to the program files that we create to store our C program. In fact, a C program file is an input data file to the C compiler and the object program is an output file from the C compiler. In this section we discuss the C statements for interacting with data files and give examples that generate and read information from data files.

When debugging programs that read information from data files, echo (or print) the information read from the file to be sure that the data are being read properly. If the data values are all zero, or are unusual numbers, it may be possi-

ble that the program cannot find the file because it is in a directory that the program cannot access. The solution is either to move the file to a directory that the program can access, or to change some of the operating system parameters so that the program can find the file.

In the examples that follow, we use data files containing sensor data. For this discussion we assume that the sensor is a **seismometer**. Seismometers are usually buried near the surface of the earth and record earth motion. These sensors are very sensitive, and can record tidal motion even though they may be located hundreds of miles from the ocean. Seismometer data are collected from sensors all over the earth, and are sent by satellite to central locations for collection and analysis. By studying this motion, scientists and engineers may be able predict earthquakes from seismometer data.

I/O STATEMENTS

File pointer

Each data file used in a program must have a **file pointer** associated with it. If a program uses two files, then each file requires a different file pointer. A file pointer is defined with a **FILE** declaration, as in

```
FILE *sensor1;
```

The **FILE** data type is defined in the header file **stdio.h**, and thus the word **FILE** is capitalized to match the definition in the header file. The asterisk before the identifier specifies that the identifier is a pointer. Later chapters include more information on pointers; in this section we present only the statements needed to work with file pointers.

After a file pointer is defined, it must then be associated with a specific file. The **fopen** function obtains the information needed to assign a file pointer to a specific file. The two arguments for this function are the file name and a character

File open mode

that indicates the file status, which is also called the **file open mode**; both the file name and the character need to be enclosed in double quotes. If we are going to read information from a file with a program, the file open mode is **r** for read. If we are going to write information to a file with a program, the file open mode is **w** for write. Thus, the following statement specifies that the file pointer **sensor1** is going to be used with a file named **sensor1.dat** from which we will read information:

```
sensor1 = fopen("sensor1.dat","r");
```

Once an input file and its pointer have been specified, we can read information from it much as we would read information from the keyboard. However, instead of using the **scanf** function, we use the **fscanf** function. If each line in the **sensor1.dat** file contains a time and sensor reading, we can read one line of this information and store the values in the variables **t** and **motion** with this statement:

```
fscanf(sensor1,"%lf %lf",&t,&motion);
```

Note that the difference between the **scanf** function and the **fscanf** function is that the first argument in the **fscanf** function is the file pointer. Otherwise, both statements are the same. The **scanf** statement converts the characters received from the keyboard to values, and the **fscanf** statement converts the characters from the lines in the data file to values.

If the file is an output file, we can write information to the file with the **fprintf** function. The first argument of the **fprintf** statement is the file pointer, and the rest of the arguments define the variables and the form in which the corresponding values are to be written in the file. For example, consider the program developed earlier in this chapter that computed and printed a table of time, altitude, and velocity data. If we wanted to modify this program so that it generated a data file containing this set of data, we could use a pointer **balloon** that would be associated with an output file named **ballon.dat** using these statements:

```
FILE *balloon;
...
balloon = fopen("balloon.dat","w");
```

Then, as we compute the time, height, and velocity information, we can write it to the file with this statement:

```
fprintf(balloon,"%f %f %f\n",
        time,height,velocity);
```

The newline indicator causes a skip to a new line after each group of three values is written to the file.

The **fclose** function is used to close a file after we are finished with it; the function argument is the file pointer. To close the two files used in these example statements, we use the following statements:

```
fclose(sensor1);
fclose(balloon);
```

There is no distinction between closing an input file and closing an output file. If a file has not been closed when the **return EXIT_SUCCESS** statement is executed, it will automatically be closed.

A preprocessor directive is often used to specify the data file name because we frequently use the same program with different data files. It is easier to modify the preprocessor directive than it is to search through the statements for the **fopen** function. An example of a preprocessor directive and a corresponding **fopen** function are the following:

```
#define FILENAME "sensor1.dat"
...
sensor1 = fopen(FILENAME,"r");
```

This combination of statements is used in all the example programs that use files in this and the following chapters.

READING DATA FILES

In order to read information from a data file, we must first know some details about the file. Obviously we must know the file name so that we can use the **fopen** statement to associate the file with its pointer. We must also know the order and data type of the values stored in the file so that we can declare corresponding identifiers correctly. Finally, we need to know if there is any special information in the file to help us determine how much information is in the file. If we attempt to execute an **fscanf** statement after we have read all the data in the file, an error occurs. In order to avoid this error, we need to know when we have read all the data.

Data files generally have one of three common structures. Some files have been generated such that the first line in the file contains the number of lines (also called records) with information that follow. For example, suppose that a file containing sensor data has 150 sets of time and sensor information. The data file could be constructed such that the first line contains only the value 150, and that line would then be followed by 150 lines containing the sensor data. To read the data from this file, we read the value from the first line in the file, and then use a **for** loop to read the rest of the information. This type of loop is also called a **counter-controlled loop**.

Trailer signal
Sentinel signal

Another form of file structure uses a **trailer signal** or **sentinel signal**. These signals are special data values that are used to indicate or signal the last record of a file. For example, the sensor data file constructed with a sentinel signal would contain the 150 lines of information followed by a line with special values, such as -999.0 for the time and sensor value. These sentinel signals must be values that could not appear as regular data in order to avoid confusion. To read data from this type of file, we use a **while** loop with a condition that is true as long as the data value is not the sentinel signal. This type of loop is also called a **sentinel-controlled loop.**

The third data file structure does not contain an initial line with the number of valid data records that follow, and it does not contain a trailer or sentinel signal. For this type of data file, we use the value returned by the **fscanf** function to help us determine when we have reached the end of the file. To read data from this type of file, we use a **while** loop with a condition that is true as long as we are not at the end of the file.

Style

Since some operating systems are case-sensitive, we will use all lower-case letters in file names to avoid any potential problems. The data file used with a program often changes, so it is helpful if the file name is easy to locate and change. *Therefore, use a preprocessor directive to define the filename; otherwise, the file-name becomes embedded in the program and cannot be as easily changed.*

We now present programs for reading sensor information and printing a summary report that contains the number of sensor readings, the average value, the maximum value, and the minimum value. Each of the three common file formats discussed will be used in the following programs.

Specified Number of Records. Assume that the first record in the sensor data file contains an integer that specifies the number of records of sensor information that follow. Each following line contains a time and sensor reading.

sensor1.dat

```
sensor1.dat
10
0.0   132.5
0.1   147.2
0.2   148.3
0.3   157.3
0.4   163.2
0.5   158.2
0.6   169.3
0.7   148.2
0.8   137.6
0.9   135.9
```

The process of first reading the number of data points and then using that to specify the number of times to read data and accumulate information is easily described using a variable-controlled loop. In the following pseudocode and program, the first actual data value is used to initialize the **max** and **min** values. If we set the **min** value initially to zero and all the sensor values were greater than zero, the program would print the erroneous value of zero for the minimum sensor reading.

The pseudocode and program for this solution are as follows:

Refinement in Pseudocode
main: *set sum to zero*
             read number of data points
             set k to 1
             while k < = number of data points
                 read time, motion
                 if k = 1
                     set max to motion
                     set min to motion
                 add motion to sum
                 if motion > max
                     set max to motion
                 if motion < min
                     set min to motion
                 increment k by 1

set average to sum/number of data points
print average, max, min

ch3_5.c
sensor1.dat

```
/*-------------------------------------------------------*/
/*  Program chapter3_5                                   */
/*                                                       */
/*  This program generates a summary report from         */
/*  a data file that has the number of data points       */
/*  in the first record.                                 */

#include <stdio.h>
#include <stdlib.h>
#define FILENAME "sensor1.dat"

main()
{
   /*  Declare and initialize variables.  */
   int num_data_pts, k;
   double time, motion, sum=0, max, min;
   FILE *sensor1;

   /*  Open file and read the number of data points.  */
   sensor1 = fopen(FILENAME,"r");
   fscanf(sensor1,"%i",&num_data_pts);

   /*  Read data and compute summary information.  */
   for (k=1; k<=num_data_pts; k++)
   {
      fscanf(sensor1,"%lf %lf",&time,&motion);
      if (k == 1)
         max = min = motion;
      sum += motion;
      if (motion > max)
         max = motion;
      if (motion < min)
         min = motion;
   }

   /*  Print summary information.  */
   printf("Number of sensor readings: %i \n",
         num_data_pts);
   printf("Average reading:          %.2f \n",
         sum/num_data_pts);
   printf("Maximum reading:          %.2f \n",max);
   printf("Minimum reading:          %.2f \n",min);

   /*  Close file and exit program.  */
   fclose(sensor1);
   return EXIT_SUCCESS;
}
/*-------------------------------------------------------*/
```

The report printed by this program using the **sensor1.dat** file is the following:

```
Number of sensor readings: 10
Average reading:           149.77
Maximum reading:           169.30
Minimum reading:           132.50
```

Trailer or Sentinel Signals. Assume that the data file **sensor2.dat** contains the same information as the **sensor1.dat** file, but instead of giving the number of valid data records at the beginning of the file, a final record contains a trailer signal. The time value on last line in the file will contain a negative value so that we know that it is not a valid line of information. A second number must be included on the trailer line since the statement that reads each line expects two values; otherwise an error occurs. The contents of the data file are as follows:

sensor2.dat

```
sensor2.dat
0.0    132.5
0.1    147.2
0.2    148.3
0.3    157.3
0.4    163.2
0.5    158.2
0.6    169.3
0.7    148.2
0.8    137.6
0.9    135.9
-99    -99
```

The process of reading and accumulating information until we read the trailer signal is easily described using a **do/while** loop structure as shown in the following pseudocode and program.

Refinement in Pseudocode

main: set sum to zero
          set number of points to 0
          read time, motion
          set max to motion
          set min to motion
          do
                  add motion to sum
                  if motion > max
                          set max to motion
                  if motion < min
                          set min to motion
                  increment number of points by 1
                  read time, motion
          while time ≥ 0
          set average to sum/number of data points
          print average, max, min

ch3_6.c
sensor2.dat

```c
/*--------------------------------------------------*/
/*  Program chapter3_6                              */
/*                                                  */
/*  This program generates a summary report from    */
/*  a data file that has a trailer record with      */
/*  negative values.                                */

#include <stdio.h>
#include <stdlib.h>
#define FILENAME "sensor2.dat"

main()
{
   /*  Declare and initialize variables.  */
   int num_data_pts=0, k;
   double time, motion, sum=0, max, min;
   FILE *sensor2;

   /*  Open file and read the first data point.  */
   sensor2 = fopen(FILENAME,"r");
   fscanf(sensor2,"%lf %lf",&time,&motion);

   /*  Initialize variables using first data point.  */
   max = min = motion;

   /*  Update summary data until trailer record read.  */
   do
   {
      sum += motion;
      if (motion > max)
         max = motion;
      if (motion < min)
         min = motion;
      num_data_pts++;
      fscanf(sensor2,"%lf %lf",&time,&motion);
   } while (time >= 0);

   /*  Print summary information.  */
   printf("Number of sensor readings: %i \n",
          num_data_pts);
   printf("Average reading:           %.2f \n",
          sum/num_data_pts);
   printf("Maximum reading:           %.2f \n",max);
   printf("Minimum reading:           %.2f \n",min);

   /*  Close file and exit program.  */
   fclose(sensor2);
   return EXIT_SUCCESS;
}
/*--------------------------------------------------*/
```

The report printed by this program using the **sensor2.dat** file is exactly the same as the report printed using the **sensor1.dat** file.

End-of-File. A special **end-of-file indicator** is inserted at the end of every data file; the `feof` function in the Standard C library can be used to detect when this indicator has been reached in a data file. The `fscanf` function can also be used to detect when the end of the data has been reached in a file. Recall that the `fscanf` function returns the number of values successfully read each time that it is executed. Thus, if the function returns a value that is different from the number of values that it was supposed to read, then the end of the data file has been reached or there are errors in the information in the data file. If the information in the data file is valid, then the `fscanf` function can be used to determine when the end of the data file is reached. Consider the following statements:

```
while ((fscanf(data1,"%lf",&x)) == 1)
{
   count++;
   sum += x;
}
ave = sum/count;
```

The `fscanf` function attempts to read a value for `x` from a data file. If a value is read, the function returns a value of 1, and the statements within the loop are executed. If the end of the data file is reached, there is no more data; thus the function does not return a value of 1, and control passes to the statement following the `while` loop.

We now assume that the data file `sensor3.dat` contains the same information as the `sensor2.dat` file except that it does not include the trailer signal. In the following pseudocode and program we read and accumulate information until we reach the end of the data file.

Refinement in Pseudocode

main: set sum to zero
         set number of points to 0
         while not at the end of the file
              read time, motion
              add 1 to the number of points
              if number of points is 1
                   set max to motion
                   set min to motion
              add motion to sum
              if motion > max
                   set max to motion
              if motion < min
                   set min to motion
         set average to sum/number of data points
         print average, max, min

ch3_7.c
sensor3.dat

```
/*------------------------------------------------------*/
/*  Program chapter3_7                                  */
/*                                                      */
/*  This program generates a summary report from        */
/*  a data file that does not have a header record      */
/*  or a trailer record.                                 */

#include <stdio.h>
#include <stdlib.h>
#define FILENAME "sensor3.dat"

main()
{
   /*  Declare and initialize variables.  */
   int num_data_pts=0, k;
   double time, motion, sum=0, max, min;
   FILE *sensor3;

   /*  Open file.  */
   sensor3 = fopen(FILENAME,"r");

   /*  While not at the end of the file, */
   /*  read and accumulate information    */
   while ((fscanf(sensor3,"%lf %lf",&time,&motion)) == 2)
   {
      num_data_pts++;
      if (num_data_pts == 1)
         max = min = motion;
      sum += motion;
      if (motion > max)
         max = motion;
      if (motion << min)
         min = motion;
    }

   /*  Print summary information.  */
   printf("Number of sensor readings: %i \n",
          num_data_pts);
   printf("Average reading:           %.2f \n",
          sum/num_data_pts);
   printf("Maximum reading:           %.2f \n",max);
   printf("Minimum reading:           %.2f \n",min);

   /*  Close file and exit program.  */
   fclose(sensor3);
   return EXIT_SUCCESS;
}
/*------------------------------------------------------*/
```

The report printed using the sensor3.dat file is exactly the same as the report printed using sensor1.dat or sensor2.dat.

The programs in this section work properly if the data files exist and contain the information expected. If this program is going to be used routinely with sensor data, statements should be included to be sure that the file structure is the one expected. Also, an error would occur if the program attempted to open a file that did not exist, and a division by zero error would occur if the number of points were zero. Chapter 6 contains a discussion on statements to check to see if a file exists, and the division by zero error could be avoided by comparing the number of points to zero before printing the report.

All three file structures are commonly used in engineering and scientific applications. Therefore, it is important to know which type of structure is used when you work with a data file. If you make the wrong assumption, you may get incorrect answers instead of an error message. Sometimes the only way to be sure of the file structure is to print the first few lines and the last few lines of the file.

Modify!

ch3_5.c
sensor1.dat

ch3_7.c
sensor3.dat

In two of the programs developed in this chapter, the loop contained a condition that tested for the first time that the loop was executed. When the condition was true, the **max** and **min** values were initialized to the first **motion** value. If the data files used with these programs were very long, the time required to execute this selection statement could begin to be substantial. One way to avoid this test is to read the first set of data and initialize the variables before entering the loop. This change may also require other changes in the program.

1.   Modify program **chapter3_5** so that the condition is removed that tests for the first time that the loop is executed.

2.   Modify program **chapter3_7** so that the condition is removed that tests for the first time that the loop is executed.

GENERATING A DATA FILE

Generating a data file is very similar to printing a report; instead of writing the line to the terminal screen, we write it to a data file. Before we generate the data file, though, we must decide what file structure we want to use. In the previous discussion, we presented the three most common file structures—files with an initial record giving the number of valid records that follow, files with a trailer or sentinel record to indicate the end of the valid data, and files with only valid data records and no special beginning or ending records.

There are advantages and disadvantages to each of the three file structures discussed. A file with a trailer signal is simple to use, but choosing a value for the trailer signal must be done carefully so that it does not contain values that could occur in the valid data. If the first record in the data file will contain the number of lines of actual data, we must know how many lines of data will be in the file before we begin to generate the file. It may not always be easy to determine the number of lines before executing the program that generates the file. The simplest file to generate is the one that contains only the valid information, with no special information at the beginning or end of the file. If the information in the file is going to used with a plotting package, it is usually best to use this third file structure which includes only valid information.

We now present a program that is a modification of the program presented earlier in the chapter that printed a table of time, height, and velocity values for a weather balloon. In addition to generating a table of information that is displayed on the screen, we also write the time, height, and velocity information to a data file. Compare this program to the one in section 3.5 on page 116.

ch3_8.c

```c
/*--------------------------------------------------------*/
/*  Program chapter3_8                                    */
/*                                                        */
/*  This program generates a file of height and          */
/*  velocity values for a weather balloon. The           */
/*  information is also printed in a report.             */

#include <stdio.h>
#include <stdlib.h>
#include <math.h>
#define FILENAME "balloon.dat"

main()
{
    /*  Declare and initialize variables.  */
    double initial, increment, final, time, height,
           velocity, max_time=0, max_height=0;
    FILE *balloon;

    /*  Open output file.  */
    balloon = fopen(FILENAME,"w");

    /*  Get user input.  */
    printf("Enter initial value for table (in hours) \n");
    scanf("%lf",&initial);
    printf("Enter increment between lines (in hours) \n");
    scanf("%lf",&increment);
    printf("Enter final value for table (in hours) \n");
    scanf("%lf",&final);

    /*  Print report heading.  */
    printf("\n\nWeather Balloon Information \n");
    printf("Time     Height     Velocity \n");
    printf("(hrs)    (meters)   (meters/s) \n");
```

```
/*   Compute and print report information    */
/*   and write data to a file.               */
for (time=initial; time<=final; time+=increment)
{

    height = -0.12*pow(time,4) + 12*pow(time,3)
             - 380*time*time + 4100*time + 220;
    velocity = -0.48*pow(time,3) + 36*time*time
               - 760*time + 4100;
    printf("%6.2f  %8.2f    %7.2f \n",
            time,height,velocity/3600);
    fprintf(balloon,"%.2f %.2f %.2f \n",
             time,height,velocity/3600);
    if (height > max_height)
    {
        max_height = height;
        max_time = time;
    }
}

/*  Print maximum height and corresponding time.   */
printf("\nMaximum balloon height was %8.2f meters \n",
        max_height);
printf("and it occurred at %6.2f hours \n",max_time);

/*  Close file and exit program.   */
fclose(balloon);
return EXIT_SUCCESS;
}
/*-----------------------------------------------------*/
```

The first few lines of a data file generated by this program using an initial time of 0 hours, an increment of 0.5 hours, and a final time of 48 hours are as follows:

```
0.00 220.00 1.14
0.50 2176.49 1.04
1.00 3951.88 0.94
. . .
```

This file is in a form to be easily plotted using a package such as MATLAB, as discussed in Appendix C; a plot of this specific file was shown in Figure 3.7.

Modify!

ch3_8.c

1. Modify program **chapter3_8** such that it generates a file in which the last line of the data file contains negative values for the time, height and velocity.

2. Modify program **chapter3_8** such that it generates a file in which the first line contains a number that specifies the number of valid lines of data that follow in the data file.

3.7   Numerical Technique: Linear Modeling*

Linear modeling

Linear regression

Linear modeling is the name given to the process that determines the linear equation that is the **best fit** to a set of data points in terms of minimizing the sum of the squared distances between the line and the data points. (This process is also called **linear regression**.) To understand this process, we first consider the set of temperature values presented in Section 2.5, Chapter 2, that were collected from the cylinder head of a new engine [6]:

Time, s	Temperature, °F
0	0
1	20
2	60
3	68
4	77
5	110

If we plot these data points, we find that they appear to be close to a straight line. In fact, we could determine a good estimate of a straight line through these points by drawing it on a graph, and then computing the slope and y intercept. Figure 3.8 contains a plot of the points (with time on the x axis and temperature on the y axis) along with the straight line with the equation

$$y = 20x$$

To measure the quality of the fit of this linear estimate to the data, we first determine the vertical distance from each point to the linear estimate; these distances are shown in Figure 3.9. The first two points fall exactly on the line, so d_1 and d_2 are zero. The value of d_3 is equal to $60 - 40$, or 20; the rest of the distances can be computed in a similar way. If we compute the sum of the distances, some of the positive and negative values would cancel each other and give a sum that is smaller than it should be. To avoid this problem, we could add absolute values

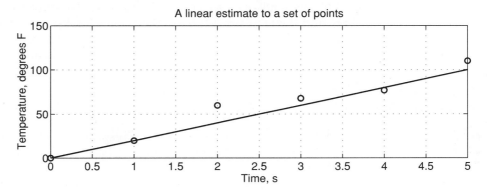

Figure 3.8 *A linear estimate to model a set of points.*

*Optional section.

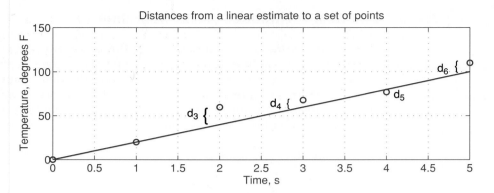

Figure 3.9 *Distances between points and linear estimate.*

or squared values; linear regression uses squared values. Therefore, the measure of the quality of the fit of this linear estimate is the sum of the squared distances between the points and the linear estimates. This sum can be easily computed, and is 573.

If we drew another line through the points, we could compute the sum of squares that corresponds to this new line. Of the two lines, the best fit is provided by the line with the smaller sum of squared distances, or the **least-squares** distance. To find the line with the smallest sum of squared distances, we begin with a general linear equation:

Least-squares

$$y = mx + b$$

We then write an equation that computes the sum of the squared distances between the given data points and this general equation. Using techniques from calculus, we can then compute the derivatives of the equation with respect to m and b, and set the derivatives equal to zero. The values of m and b that are determined in this way represent the straight line with the minimum sum of squared distances. Before giving these equations for m and b, we define **summation notation**.

Summation notation

The set of data points given at the beginning of this section can be represented by the points $(x_1, y_1), (x_2, y_2), \ldots, (x_6, y_6)$. The symbol Σ represents a summation, and thus the sum of the x coordinates can be expressed in the following notation: $\Sigma_{k=1}^{6} x_k$; this summation is read as *the sum of x_k as k goes from 1 to 6*. The value of this summation for the example data points is $(0 + 1 + 2 + 3 + 4 + 5)$, or 15. Other sums that could be computed using the example data points are as follows:

$$\sum_{k=1}^{6} y_k = 0 + 20 + 60 + 68 + 77 + 110 = 335$$

$$\sum_{k=1}^{6} y_k^2 = (0)^2 + (20)^2 + (60)^2 + (68)^2 + (77)^2 + (110)^2 = 26{,}653$$

$$\sum_{k=1}^{6} x_k y_k = 0 \cdot 0 + 1 \cdot 20 + 2 \cdot 60 + 3 \cdot 68 + 4 \cdot 77 + 5 \cdot 110 = 1{,}202$$

We now return to the problem of finding the best linear fit to a set of points. Using the procedure described before that is based on results from calculus, the slope and y intercept for the best linear fit to a set of n data points, in a least-squares sense, are the following [9]:

$$m = \frac{\sum\limits_{k=1}^{n} x_k \cdot \sum\limits_{k=1}^{n} y_k - n \cdot \sum\limits_{k=1}^{n} x_k y_k}{\left(\sum\limits_{k=1}^{n} x_k\right)^2 - n \cdot \sum\limits_{k=1}^{n} x_k^2} \tag{3.1}$$

$$b = \frac{\sum\limits_{k=1}^{n} x_k \cdot \sum\limits_{k=1}^{n} x_k y_k - \sum\limits_{k=1}^{n} x_k^2 \cdot \sum\limits_{k=1}^{n} y_k}{\left(\sum\limits_{k=1}^{n} x_k\right)^2 - n \cdot \sum\limits_{k=1}^{n} x_k^2} \tag{3.2}$$

For the sample set of data, the optimum value for m is 20.83 and the optimum value for b is 3.76. The set of data points and this best fit linear equation are shown in Figure 3.10. The sum of squares for this best fit is 356.82, as compared to 573 for the straight line in Figure 3.8.

One of the advantages of performing a linear regression for a set of data points that is nearly linear in nature is that we can then estimate or predict points for which we had no data. For example, in the cylinder-head temperature example, suppose that we want to estimate the temperature for the cylinder head at 3.3 seconds. By using the equation computed with linear regression, the estimated temperature is

$$y = mx + b$$

$$= (20.83)(3.3) + 3.76$$

$$= 72.5$$

With an equation model, we can compute estimates that we could not compute with linear interpolation. For example, using the linear model, we can compute an estimate of the temperature for 8 seconds, but we could not compute an

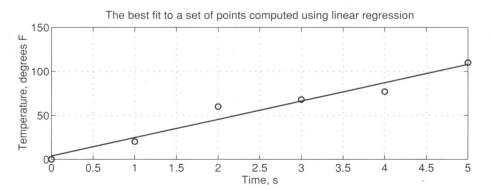

Figure 3.10 *Least squares linear regression model.*

estimate at 8 seconds using linear interpolation because we do not have a point with a time greater than 8 seconds. (This would be extrapolation, not interpolation.)

It is also important to remember that linear models do not provide a good fit to all sets of data. Therefore, it is important to first determine if a linear model is a good model for the data before using it to predict new data points. A technique for measuring the quality of a linear model for a set of data is presented in the problem set at the end of Chapter 5.

In the next section, we develop a problem solution that determines the best fit for a set of sensor data collected from a satellite, and then use that model to estimate or predict other sensor values.

3.8   Problem Solving Applied: Ozone Measurements*

Satellite sensors can be used to measure many different pieces of information that help us understand more about the atmosphere, which is composed of a number of layers around the earth [12]. Starting at the earth's surface, the layers are the troposphere, stratosphere, mesosphere, thermosphere, and exosphere, as shown in Figure 3.11. Each layer of the atmosphere can be characterized by its temperature profile. The **troposphere** is the inner layer of the atmosphere, varying in height from around 5 km at the poles to 18 km at the equator. Most cloud formations occur in the troposphere, and there is a steady fall of temperature with increasing altitude. The **stratosphere** is characterized by relatively uniform temperatures over considerable differences in altitude. It extends from the troposphere to about 50 km (about 31 miles) above the earth. Pollutants that drift into the stratosphere may remain there for many years before they drift back to the troposphere, where they can be diluted and removed by the weather. The **mesosphere** extends from 50 to approximately 85 km (about 53 miles) above the earth's surface. In this layer, the air mixes fairly readily. Above the mesosphere is the **thermosphere**, which extends from 85 to about 140 km (about 87 miles) above the earth. In this region, the heating is due to the absorption of solar energy by atomic oxygen. The **ionosphere** is a relatively dense band of charged particles within the thermosphere. Some types of communications use the reflection of radio waves off the ionosphere. Finally, the **exosphere** is the highest region of the atmosphere. In the exosphere, the air density is so low that an air molecule moving upward is more likely to escape the atmosphere than it is to hit another molecule.

A satellite experiment was launched on the NIMBUS 7 spacecraft in 1978 to collect data on the composition and structure of the middle atmosphere [13]. The instrumentation and sensors collected data from October 25, 1978, to May 28, 1979, returning more than 7000 sets of data to the earth each day. These data were used to determine temperature, ozone, water vapor, nitric acid, and nitrogen dioxide distributions in the stratosphere and mesosphere.

Consider a problem in which we have collected a set of data measuring the ozone mixing ratio in parts per million volume (ppmv). Over small regions, these data are nearly linear, and thus we can use a linear model to estimate the ozone

*Optional section.

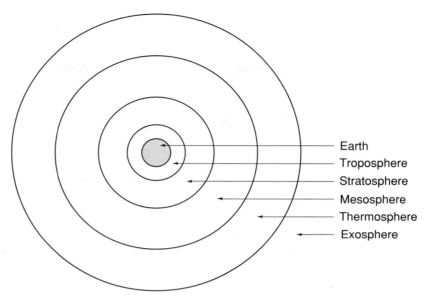

Figure 3.11 *Atmospheric layers around the earth.*

at altitudes other than ones for which we have specific data. Write a program that reads a data file named **zone1.dat** containing the altitude in km and the corresponding ozone mixing ratios in ppmv for a region over which we want to determine a linear model. The data file contains only valid data, and thus does not have a special header line or trailer line. Use the least-squares technique presented in the previous section to determine and print the model. Also print the beginning and ending altitudes to indicate the region over which the model is accurate.

1.   **PROBLEM STATEMENT**

Use the least-squares technique to determine a linear model for estimating the ozone mixing ratio at a specified altitude.

2.   **INPUT/OUTPUT DESCRIPTION**

The following I/O diagram shows that the data file **zone1.dat** is the input, and that the output is the range of altitudes and the linear model.

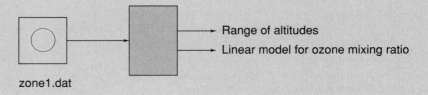

3.   **HAND EXAMPLE**

Assume that the data consist of the following four data points:

zone1.dat

Altitude (km)	Ozone Mixing Ratio (ppmv)
20	3
24	4
26	5
28	6

We now need to evaluate Equations (3.1) and (3.2), which are repeated here for convenience:

$$m = \frac{\sum_{k=1}^{n} x_k \cdot \sum_{k=1}^{n} y_k - n \cdot \sum_{k=1}^{n} x_k y_k}{\left(\sum_{k=1}^{n} x_k\right)^2 - n \cdot \sum_{k=1}^{n} x_k^2}$$

$$b = \frac{\sum_{k=1}^{n} x_k \cdot \sum_{k=1}^{n} x_k y_k - \sum_{k=1}^{n} x_k^2 \cdot \sum_{k=1}^{n} y_k}{\left(\sum_{k=1}^{n} x_k\right)^2 - n \cdot \sum_{k=1}^{n} x_k^2}$$

To evaluate these equations using the hand example data, we need to compute the following group of sums:

$$\sum_{k=1}^{4} x_k = 20 + 24 + 26 + 28 = 98$$

$$\sum_{k=1}^{4} y_k = 3 + 4 + 5 + 6 = 18$$

$$\sum_{k=1}^{4} x_k^2 = (20)^2 + (24)^2 + (26)^2 + (28)^2 = 2436$$

$$\sum_{k=1}^{4} x_k y_k = 20 \cdot 3 + 24 \cdot 4 + 26 \cdot 5 + 28 \cdot 6 = 454$$

Using these sums, we can now compute the values of m and b:

$$m = 0.37$$

$$b = -4.6$$

4.   **ALGORITHM DEVELOPMENT**

We first develop the decomposition outline because it divides the solution into a series of sequential steps.

Decomposition Outline
1. *Read data file values and compute corresponding sums and ranges.*
2. *Compute slope and y intercept.*
3. *Print range of altitudes and linear model.*

The first step in the decomposition outline involves a loop in which we read the data from the file and at the same time add the corresponding values to the sums needed for computing the linear model. We will also need to determine the number of data points as we read the file. The condition to exit the loop will be a test for the end of the file because there is no header or trailer information. Because we want to keep track of the altitude ranges, we also need to save the first altitude value and the last altitude value. Steps 2 and 3 of the decomposition outline are sequential steps involving computations and printing. Therefore, the refinement in pseudocode is as follows:

Refinement in Pseudocode

main: *set count to zero*
        set sumx, sumy, sumxy, sumx2 to zero
        while not at end-of-file
            read x, y
            increment count by 1
            if count = 1
                set first to x
            add x to sumx
            add y to sumy
            add x^2 to sumx2
            add xy to sumxy
        set last to x
        compute slope and y intercept
        print first, last, slope, y intercept

The steps in the pseudocode are now detailed enough to convert into C.

ch3_9.c
zone1.dat

```
/*------------------------------------------------------------*/
/*  Program chapter3_9                                        */
/*                                                            */
/*  This program computes a linear model for a set            */
/*  of altitude and ozone mixing ratio values.                */

#include <stdio.h>
#include <stdlib.h>
#define FILENAME "zone1.dat"
```

```
main()
{
    /*  Declare and initialize variables.  */
    int count=0;
    double x, y, first, last, sumx=0, sumy=0, sumx2=0,
           sumxy=0, denominator, m, b;
    FILE *zone1;

    /*  Open input file.  */
    zone1 = fopen(FILENAME,"r");

    /*  While not at the end of the file,  */
    /*  read and accumulate information.   */
    while ((fscanf(zone1,"%lf %lf",&x,&y)) == 2)
    {
        ++count;
        if (count == 1)
            first = x;
        sumx  += x;
        sumy  += y;
        sumx2 += x*x;
        sumxy += x*y;
    }
    last = x;

    /*  Compute slope and y-intercept.  */
    denominator = sumx*sumx - count*sumx2;
    m = (sumx*sumy - count*sumxy)/denominator;
    b = (sumx*sumxy - sumx2*sumy)/denominator;

    /*  Print summary information.  */
    printf("Range of altitudes in km: \n");
    printf("%.2f to %.2f \n\n",first,last);
    printf("Linear model: \n");
    printf("ozone-mix-ratio = %.2f altitude + %.2f \n",
           m,b);

    /*  Close file and exit program.  */
    fclose(zone1);
    return EXIT_SUCCESS;
}
/*------------------------------------------------------------*/
```

5.   TESTING

Using the data from the hand example as the contents of the data file **zone1.dat**, we get the following program output:

```
Range of altitudes in km:
20.00 to 28.00
```

```
Linear model:
ozone-mix-ratio = 0.37 altitude + -4.60
```

This matches the values computed from the hand example.

Modify!

ch3_9.c
zone1.dat

These problems relate to the program developed in this section. You may need to use the following relationship in some of the problems:

1 km = 0.621 mi

1. Add statements to the program so that it allows you to enter an altitude in km, and then uses the model to estimate a corresponding ozone mix ratio.
2. Modify your program in problem 1 so that it checks that the altitude that you enter is within the range that is appropriate for this model.
3. Modify the program in problem 2 so that it allows you to enter the altitude in miles. (The program should convert miles to kilometers.)
4. Modify the original program so that it also prints a linear model so that it can be used with altitudes that are in miles instead of kilometers. Assume that the data file still contains altitudes in kilometers.

SUMMARY

In this chapter, we covered the use of conditions and **if** statements to select the proper statements to be executed. We also presented techniques for repeating sets of statements that used loops. These loops can be implemented as **while** loops or **for** loops. These selection and repetition structures are used in most programs. In addition, we included the statements necessary to read information from a data file so that we could use the information in the program. We also presented the statements to generate a data file from a program. Data files are commonly used in solving engineering problems; therefore, this concept was presented early in the text so that we could use it in many of the later problem solutions. Finally, we covered the concept of generating a linear model for a set of data points, and included the equations for determining the best fit in terms of least squares.

KEY TERMS

case label	linear regression
case structure	logical operator
compound statement	loop
condition	loop-control variable
controlling expression	program walkthrough
data file	pseudocode
decomposition outline	relational operator
default label	repetition
divide and conquer	selection
end-of-file indicator	sequence
error condition	sentinel signal
file open mode	stepwise refinement
file pointer	summation notation
flowchart	test data
for loop	top–down design
iteration	trailer signal
least squares	validation and verification
linear modeling	while loop

C STATEMENT SUMMARY

Declaration for file pointer:

```
FILE *sensor1;
```

If statement:

```
if (temp > 100)
    printf("Temperature exceeds limit \n");

temp>100 ? printf("Caution \n") : printf("Normal \n");
```

If/else statement:

```
if (d <= 30)
    velocity = 4.25 + 0.00175*d*d;
else
    velocity = 0.65 + 0.12*d - 0.0025*d*d;
```

Switch statement:

```
switch (code)
{
    case 1: case 2:
        printf("Normal Operating range \n");
        break;
    case 3:
        printf("Maintenance needed \n");
        break;
    default:
        printf("Error in code value \n");
        break;
}
```

While loop:

```
while (degrees <= 360)
{
    radians = degrees*PI/180;
    printf("%6.0f %9.0f \n",degrees,radians);
    degrees += 10;
}
```

Do/while loop:

```
do
{
    radians = degrees*PI/180;
    printf("%6.0f %9.6f \n",degrees,radians);
    degrees += 10;
} while (degrees <= 360);
```

For loop:

```
for (degrees=0; degrees<=360; degrees+=10)
{
    radians = degrees*PI/180;
    printf("%6.0f %9.6f \n",degrees,radians);
}
```

Break statement:

```
break;
```

Continue statement;

```
continue;
```

File open function:

```
sensor1 = fopen("sensor1","r");
balloon = fopen(FILENAME,"w");
```

File input function:

```
fscanf(sensor1,"%lf %lf",&t,&motion);
```

File output function:

```
fprintf(balloon,"%f %f %f\n",
        time,height,velocity);
```

File close function:

```
fclose(sensor1);
```

Style NOTES

1. Use spaces around the relational operator in a logical expression in a simple condition; use spaces around the logical operator and not around the relational operators in a complicated condition.
2. Indent the statements within a compound statement or inside a loop. If loops or compound statements are nested, indent each nested set of statements from the previous statement.
3. Use braces even when they are not required to clearly identify the structure of a complicated statement.
4. Use the default case within the **switch** statement to emphasize the action to take when none of the case labels matches the controlling expression.
5. Use braces to identify the body of every loop; put each brace on a line by itself so that the body of the loop is easily identified.
6. Define filenames with preprocessor directives so that they can easily be changed.

DEBUGGING NOTES

1. When you discover and correct an error in a program, start the testing step over again. In particular, rerun the program with all the test data sets again.
2. Be sure to use the relational operator == instead of = in a condition for equality.
3. Put the braces surrounding a block of statements on lines by themselves; this will help you avoid omitting them.
4. Do not use the equality operator with floating-point values; instead, test for values "close to" a desired value.
5. Recompile your program frequently when correcting syntax errors; correcting one error may remove many error messages.
6. Use the **printf** statement to give memory snapshots of the values of key variables when debugging loops.
7. It is easier than you think to generate an infinite loop; be sure you know the

special characters needed to abort the execution of a program on your system if it goes into an infinite loop.

8. When debugging a program that reads data from a data file, print the values as soon as they are read to check for errors in reading the information.

9. When debugging a program that reads a data file, be sure that your program can access the directory that contains the data file.

10. To avoid problems with operating systems that are not case-sensitive, use filenames with lowercase letters.

PROBLEMS

Unit Conversions. The following problems generate tables of unit conversions. Include a table heading and column headings for the tables. Choose the number of decimal places based on the values to be printed.

1. Generate a table of conversions from radians to degrees. Start the radian column at 0.0, and increment by $\pi/10$, until the radian amount is 2π.

2. Generate a table of conversions from degrees to radians. The first line should contain the value for $0°$ and the last line should contain the value for $360°$. Allow the user to enter the increment to use between lines in the table.

3. Generate a table of conversions from inches to centimeters. Start the inches column at 0.0 and increment by 0.5 in. The last line should contain the value 20.0 in. (Recall that 1 in. = 2.54 cm.)

4. Generate a table of conversions from mph to ft/s. Start the mph column at 0, and increment by 5 mph. The last line should contain the value 65 mph. (Recall that 1 mi = 5280 ft.)

5. Generate a table of conversions from ft/s to mph. Start the ft/s column at 0 and increment by 5 ft/s. The last line should contain the value 100 ft/s. (Recall that 1 mi = 5280 ft.)

Currency Conversions. The following problems generate tables of currency conversions. Use title and column headings. Assume the following conversion rates:

1 dollar ($) = 5.3 francs (Fr)

1 yen (Y)   = $ 0.0079

1 dollar ($) = 1.57 deutsche marks (DM)

6. Generate a table of conversions from francs to dollars. Start the francs column at 5 Fr and increment by 5 Fr. Print 25 lines in the table.

7. Generate a table of conversions from deutsche marks to francs. Start the deutsche marks column at 1 DM and increment by 2 DM. Print 30 lines in the table.

8. Generate a table of conversions from yen to deutsche marks. Start the yen column at 100 Y and print 25 lines, with the final line containing the value 10,000 Y.

9. Generate a table of conversions from dollars to francs, deutsche marks, and yen. Start the column with $1 and increment by $1. Print 50 lines in the table.

Temperature Conversions. The following problems generate temperature-conversion tables. Use the following equations that give relationships between temperatures in degrees Fahrenheit (T_F), degrees Celsius (T_C), degrees Kelvin (T_K), and degrees Rankin (T_R):

$$T_F = T_R - 459.67° \text{ R}$$

$$T_F = (9/5)T_C + 32° \text{ F}$$

$$T_R = (9/5)T_K$$

10. Write a program to generate a table of conversions from Fahrenheit to Celsius for values from 0°F to 100°F. Print a line in the table for each 5-degree change. Use a **while** loop in your solution.

11. Write a program to generate a table of conversions from Fahrenheit to Kelvin for values from 0°F to 200°F. Allow the user to enter the increment in degrees Fahrenheit between lines. Use a **do while** loop in your solution.

12. Write a program to generate a table of conversions from Celcius to Rankin. Allow the user to enter the starting temperature and increment between lines. Print 25 lines in the table. Use a **for** loop in your solution.

rocket1.dat
rocket2.dat
rocket3.dat

Sounding Rocket Trajectory. Sounding rockets are used to probe different levels of the atmosphere to collect information such as that used to monitor the levels of ozone in the atmosphere. In addition to carrying the scientific package for collecting data in the upper atmosphere, the rocket also carries a telemetry system in its nose to transmit data to a receiver at the launch site. In addition to the scientific data, performance measurements on the rocket itself are also transmitted to be monitored by range safety personnel and to be later analyzed by engineers. These performance data include altitude, velocity, and acceleration data. Assume that this information is stored in a file, and each line contains contains four values—time, altitude, velocity, and acceleration. Assume that the units are s, m, m/s, and m/s², respectively.

13. Assume that the file **rocket1.dat** contains an initial line that contains the number of actual data lines that follows. Write a program that reads these data and determines the time at which the rocket begins falling back to earth. (*Hint*: Determine the time at which the altitude begins to decrease.)

14. The number of stages in the rocket can be determined by the number of times that the velocity increases to some peak and then begins decreasing. Write a program that reads these data and determines the number of stages on the rocket. Use the data file **rocket2.dat**. It contains a trailer line with the value −99 for all four values.

15. Modify the program in problem 14 such that it prints the times that correspond to the firing of each stage. Assume that the firing corresponds to the point at which the velocity begins to increase.

16. After each stage of the rocket is fired, the acceleration will initially increase and then decrease to -9.8 m/s^2, which is the downward acceleration due to gravity. Find the time periods of the rocket flight during which the acceleration is due only to gravity. Allow the acceleration to range within $\pm 5\%$ of theoretical value for these time periods. Use the data file **rocket3.dat**, which does not contain a header line or a trailer line.

suture.dat

Suture Packaging. Sutures are strands or fibers used to sew living tissue together after an injury or an operation. Packages of sutures must be sealed carefully before they are shipped to hospitals so that contaminants cannot enter the packages. The object that seals the package is referred to as a sealing die. Generally, sealing dies are heated with an electric heater. For the sealing process to be a success, the sealing die is maintained at an established temperature and must contact the package with a predetermined pressure for an established time period. The time period in which the sealing die contacts the package is called the dwell time. Assume that the acceptable range of parameters for an acceptable seal are the following:

Temperature:	150–170° C
Pressure:	60–70 psi
Dwell time:	2–2.5 s

17. A data file named **suture.dat** contains information on batches of sutures that have been rejected during a 1-week period. Each line in the data file contains the batch number, temperature, pressure, and dwell time for a rejected batch. The quality control engineer would like to analyze this information, and needs a report that computes the percent of the batches rejected due to temperature, the percent rejected due to pressure, and the percent rejected due to dwell time. It is possible that a specific batch may have been rejected for more than one reason, and it should be counted in all applicable totals. Write a program to compute and print these three percentages.

18. Modify the program developed in problem 17 such that it also prints the number of batches in each rejection category and the total number of batches rejected. (Remember that a rejected batch should appear only once in the total, but could appear in more that one rejection category.)

19. Write a program to read the data file **suture.dat** and make sure that the information relates only to batches that should have been rejected. If any batch should not be in the data file, print an appropriate message with the batch information.

Timber Regrowth. A problem in timber management is to determine how much of an area to leave uncut so that the harvested area is reforested in a certain period of time. It is assumed that reforestation takes place at a known rate per year, depending on climate and soil conditions. A reforestation equation expresses this growth as a function of the amount of timber standing and the reforestation rate. For example, if 100 acres are left standing after harvesting and the reforestation rate is 0.05, then $100 + 0.05 \times 100$, or 105 acres, are forested at the end of the first year. At the end of the second year, the number of acres forested is $105 + 0.05 \times 105$, or 110.25 acres.

20. Assume that there are 14,000 acres total with 2500 acres uncut, and that the reforestation rate is 0.02. Print a table showing the number of acres forested at the end of each year, for a total of 20 years.

21. Modify the program developed in problem 20 so that the user can enter the number of years to be used for the table.

22. Modify the program developed in problem 20 so that the user can enter a number of acres and the program will determine how many years are required for the number of acres to be completely reforested.

jan91.dat
feb91.dat
mar91.dat
apr91.dat
may91.dat
jun91.dat
jul91.dat
aug91.dat
sep91.dat
oct91.dat
nov91.dat
dec91.dat

Weather Patterns. In Chapter 1, we discussed the types of information that are collected by the National Weather Bureau. Figure 1.5, page 24, contained a sample of the reports that are available with weather information. A group of data files included in the diskette that accompanies this text contains weather information for Stapleton International Airport for the period January–December 1991. Each file contains data from 1 month; each line in the file contains 32 pieces of information, in the order shown in Figure 1.5. The data have been edited so that they are totally numeric. If a field of information contained T, for a trace amount, the corresponding value in the data file contains 0.001. There are nine possible weather types, and because several weather types can occur during a single day, nine fields are used to store this information. For example, if weather type 1 occurred, the first of the nine fields will contain a 1; otherwise, it will contain a 0. If weather type 2 occurred, the second of the nine fields will contain a 1; otherwise, it will contain a 0. The peak wind-gust direction has been converted to an integer using the following:

N	1
NE	2
E	3
SE	4
S	5
SW	6
W	7
NW	8

The values on each line in the data file are separated by blanks, and the data files are named **jan91.dat**, **feb91.dat**, and so on.

23. Write a program to determine the number of days that had temperatures in the following categories for January 1991.

Below 0
0–32
33–50
51–60
61–70
Over 70

Note that the range of temperatures in one day may fall in several of the categories.

24. Modify the program developed in problem 23 so that it prints percentages instead of the number of days.

25. Modify the program developed in problem 23 so that it uses the time period May–August 1991.

26. Write a program that computes the average temperature for days with fog in November 1991.

27. Write a program that determines the date in December 1991 with the largest difference between the maximum temperature and the minimum temperature. Print the date, both temperatures, and the difference.

path.dat

Critical Path Analysis. A critical path analysis is a technique used to determine the time schedule for a project. This information is important in the planning stages before a project is begun, and it is also useful to evaluate the progress of a project that is partially completed. One method for this analysis starts by dividing a project into sequential events and then dividing each event into various tasks. Although one event must be completed before the next one is started, various tasks within an event can occur simultaneously. The time it takes to complete an event, therefore, depends on the number of days required to finish its longest task. Similarly, the total time it takes to finish a project is the sum of time it takes to finish each event.

Assume that the critical path information for a major construction project has been stored in a data file. Each line of the data file contains an event number, a task number, and the number of days required to complete the task. The data have been stored such that all the task data for event 1 are followed by all the task data for event 2, and so on. Thus, a typical set of data might be as follows:

Event	Task	Number of Days
1	15	3
1	27	6
1	36	4
2	15	5
3	18	4
3	26	1
4	15	2
4	26	7
4	27	7
5	16	4

28. Write a program to read the critical path information and print a project completion timetable that lists each event number, the maximum number of days for a task within the event, and the total number of days for the project completion.

29. Write a program to read the critical path information and print a report that lists the event number and task number for all tasks requiring more than 5 days.

30. Write a program to read the critical path information and print a report that lists the number of each event and a count of the number of tasks within the event.

4

Courtesy of Chevron Corporation.

GRAND CHALLENGE:
Enhanced Oil and Gas Recovery

The design and construction of the Alaskan pipeline presented numerous engineering challenges. One of the important problems that had to be addressed was protecting the permafrost (the permanently frozen subsoil in arctic or subarctic regions) from the heat of the pipeline itself. The oil flowing in the pipeline is warmed by pumping stations and by friction from the walls of the pipe, so the supports holding the pipeline must be insulated or even cooled to keep them from melting the permafrost at their bases. In addition, the components of the pipeline had to be very reliable because of the inaccessibility of some locations. More importantly, component failure could cause damage to human life, animal life, and the environment around the pipeline. Therefore, the analysis of the reliability of equipment in applications such as this one is an important topic in engineering.

Modular Programming with Functions

OBJECTIVES

In this chapter, we discuss the importance of dividing programs into functions (or modules) that perform specific operations. In C, modules are available from libraries such as the Standard C library; modules also can be written specifically to accompany a **main** function. This chapter presents several examples of additional library functions from the Standard C library and of programmer-defined functions. The library function for generating a random number is used in an application that discusses instrumentation reliability and presents a computer simulation

*Optional section.

149

to estimate reliability. Numerical techniques for finding real roots to polynomials are discussed, and the incremental search technique is implemented in C using two programmer-defined modules. Optional sections discuss macros that can be used to implement single-line functions and recursive functions that can reference themselves.

4.1   Modularity

Functions
Modules

The execution of a C program begins with the statements in the **main** function. A program may also contain other functions, and it may refer to functions in another file or in a library. These **functions**, or **modules**, are sets of statements that typically perform an operation or that compute a value. For example, the **printf** function prints a line of information on the terminal screen, and the **sqrt** function computes the square root of a value.

Style

To maintain simplicity and readability in longer and more complex problem solutions, we develop programs that use a **main** function and additional functions, instead of using one long **main** function. *By separating a solution into a group of modules, each module is simpler and easier to understand, thus adhering to the basic guidelines of structured programming presented in Chapter 3.*

The process of developing a problem solution is often one of "divide and conquer," as was discussed in Chapter 2 when we first discussed the decomposition outline. The decomposition outline is a set of sequentially executed steps that solves the problem, so it provides a good starting point for selecting potential functions. In fact, it is not uncommon for each step in the decomposition outline to correspond to one or more function references in the **main** function.

Breaking a problem solution into a set of modules has many advantages. Because a module has a specific purpose, it can be written and tested separately from the rest of the problem solution. An individual module is smaller than the complete solution, so testing it is easier. And, once a module has been carefully tested, it can be used in new problem solutions without being retested. For example, suppose that a module is developed to find the average of a group of values. Once this module is written and tested, it can be used in other programs that need to compute an average. This **reusability** is a very important issue in the development of large software systems because it can save development time. In fact, libraries of commonly used modules (such as the Standard C library) are often available on computer systems.

Reusability

Modularity

The use of modules (called **modularity**) often reduces the overall length of a program because many problem solutions include steps that are repeated several places in the program. By incorporating these steps that are repeated in a function, the steps can be referenced with a single statement each time that they are needed.

Several programmers can work on the same project if it is separated into modules because the individual modules can be developed and tested independently of each other. This allows the development schedule to be accelerated because some of the work can be done in parallel.

Abstraction

The use of modules that have been written to accomplish specific tasks supports the concept of **abstraction**. The modules contain the details of the tasks, and the programmer can reference the modules without worrying about these details. The I/O diagrams that we use in developing a problem solution are an example of abstraction—we specify the input information and the output information without giving the details of how the output information is determined. In a similar way, we can think of modules as "black boxes" that have a specified input and that compute specified information; we can use these modules to help develop a solution. Thus, we are able to operate at a higher level of abstraction to solve problems. For example, the Standard C library contains functions that compute the logarithms of values. We can reference these functions without being concerned about the specific details, such as whether the functions are using infinite series approximations or lookup tables to compute the specified logarithms. By using abstraction, we can reduce the development time of software at the same time that we increase its quality.

To summarize, some of the advantages of using modules in a problem solution are the following:

- A module can be written and tested separately from other parts of the solution, and thus module development can be done in parallel for large projects.
- A module is a small part of the solution, and thus testing it separately is easier.
- Once a module is tested carefully, it does not need to be retested before it can be used in new problem solutions.
- The use of modules usually reduces the length of a program, making it more readable.
- The use of modules promotes the concept of abstraction that allows the programmer to "hide" the details in modules; this allows us to use modules in a functional sense without being concerned about the specific details.

Additional benefits of modules will be pointed out as we progress through this chapter.

Structure charts
Module charts

Structure charts or **module charts** show the module structure of a program. The `main` function references additional functions, which may also reference other functions themselves. Figure 4.1 contains structure charts for the programs developed in the Problem Solving Applied sections in this chapter and in the next chapter. Note that a structure chart does not indicate the sequence of steps that are contained in the decomposition outline. The structure chart shows the separation of the program tasks into modules and indicates which modules reference other modules. Therefore, both the decomposition outline and the structure chart provide different but useful views of a problem solution. Also, note that the structure chart does not contain the modules referenced from the Standard C library because they are used so frequently and because they are an integral part of the C environment.

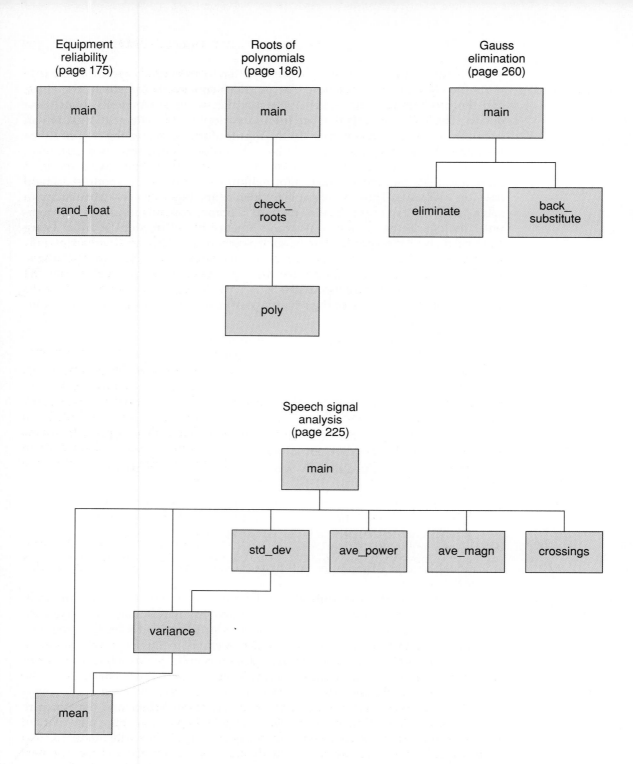

Figure 4.1 *Example structure charts.*

As we begin to develop solutions to more complicated problems, the programs become longer. Therefore, we include here three suggestions for debugging longer programs. First, it is sometimes helpful to run a program using a different compiler because different compilers have different error messages; in fact, some compilers have extensive error messages, whereas others give very little information about some errors. Another useful step in debugging a long program is to add comment indicators (/* and */) around some sections of the code so that you can focus on other parts of the program. Of course, you must be careful that you do not comment out statements that affect variables needed for the parts of the program that you want to test. Finally, test complicated functions by themselves. This is usually done with a special program called a **driver**, whose purpose is to provide a simple interface between you and the function that you are testing. Typically, this program asks you to enter the parameters that you want passed to the function, and it then prints the value returned by the function. The usefulness of a driver program will become more apparent as we cover the next few sections.

4.2 Programmer-Defined Functions

Invoked

Library function
Programmer-
defined
functions

The execution of a program always begins with the **main** function. Additional functions are called, or **invoked**, when the program encounters function names. These additional functions must be defined in the file containing the **main** function or in another available file or library of files. (If the function is included in a system library file, such as the **sqrt** function, it is often called a **library function**; other functions are usually called **programmer-written** or **programmer-defined functions**.) After executing the statements in a function, the program execution continues with the statement that called the function.

FUNCTION DEFINITION

The sinc(x) function, plotted in Figure 4.2, is commonly used in many engineering applications. The most common definition for sinc(x) is the following:

$$f(x) = \text{sinc}(x)$$
$$= \frac{\sin(x)}{x}$$

(The sinc(x) function is also occasionally defined to be $\sin(\pi x)/\pi x$.) The values of this function can be easily computed except for sinc(0), which gives an indeterminant form of $0/0$. In this case, l'Hôpital's theorem [11] from calculus can be used to prove that sinc(0) = 1.

Assume that we want to develop a program that allows the user to enter interval limits, a and b. The program should then compute and print 21 values of sinc(x) for values of x evenly spaced between a and b, inclusively. Thus, the first value of x should be a. An increment should then be added to obtain the next value of x, and so on, until the twenty-first value, which should be b. Therefore, the increment in x is

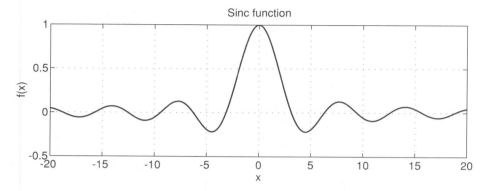

Figure 4.2 *Sinc function in [−20,20].*

$$x\_\text{increment} = \frac{\text{interval width}}{20} = \frac{b - a}{20}$$

Select values for *a* and *b*, and convince yourself that, with this increment, and with *a* as the first value, the twenty-first value will be *b*.

Because sinc(*x*) is not part of the mathematical functions provided by the Standard C library, we implement this problem solution two ways. In one solution, we include the statements to perform the computations of sinc(*x*) in the **main** function; in the other solution, we write a programmer-defined function to compute sinc(*x*), and then reference the programmer-defined function each time that the computations are needed. Both solutions are now presented so that you can compare them.

SOLUTION 1

ch4_1.c

```
/*------------------------------------------------------------*/
/*   Program chapter4_1                                       */
/*                                                            */
/*   This program prints 21 values of the sinc               */
/*   function in the interval [a,b] using                    */
/*   computations within the main function.                  */

#include <stdio.h>
#include <stdlib.h>
#include <math.h>

main()
{
   /* Declare variables.  */
   int k;
   double a, b, x_incr, new_x, sinc_x;

   /* Get interval endpoints from the user.  */
   printf("Enter end points a and b (a<b): \n");
   scanf("%lf %lf",&a,&b);
   x_incr = (b - a)/20;
```

```
   /*  Compute and print table of sinc(x) values.  */
   printf("x and sinc(x) \n");
   for (k=0; k<=20; k++)
   {
      new_x = a + k*x_incr;
      if (fabs(new_x) < 0.0001)
         sinc_x = 1.0;
      else
         sinc_x = sin(new_x)/new_x;
      printf("%f %f \n",new_x,sinc_x);
   }

   /*  Exit program.  */
   return EXIT_SUCCESS;
}
/*-------------------------------------------------------*/
```

SOLUTION 2

ch4_2.c

```
/*-------------------------------------------------------*/
/*  Program chapter4_2                                   */
/*                                                       */
/*  This program prints 21 values of the sinc            */
/*  function in the interval [a,b] using a               */
/*  programmer-defined function.                         */
/*                                                       */

#include <stdio.h>
#include <stdlib.h>
#include <math.h>

main()
{
   /*  Declare variables and function prototypes.  */
   int k;
   double a, b, x_incr, new_x;
   double sinc(double x);

   /*  Get interval endpoints from the user.  */
   printf("Enter endpoints a and b (a<b): \n");
   scanf("%lf %lf",&a,&b);
   x_incr = (b - a)/20;

   /*  Compute and print table of sinc(x) values.  */
   printf("x and sinc(x) \n");
   for (k=0; k<=20; k++)
   {
      new_x = a + k*x_incr;
      printf("%f %f \n",new_x,sinc(new_x));
   }

   /*  Exit program.  */
   return EXIT_SUCCESS;
}
```

```
/*------------------------------------------------------------*/
/*   This function evaluates the sinc function.          */

double sinc(double x)
{
   if (fabs(x) < 0.0001)
      return 1.0;
   else
      return sin(x)/x;
}
/*------------------------------------------------------------*/
```

The following output represents an example interaction that could occur with either program:

```
Enter endpoints a and b (a<b):
-5 5
x and sinc(x)
-5.000000 -0.191785
-4.500000 -0.217229
-4.000000 -0.189201
-3.500000 -0.100224
-3.000000 0.047040
-2.500000 0.239389
-2.000000 0.454649
-1.500000 0.664997
-1.000000 0.841471
-0.500000 0.958851
0.000000 1.000000
0.500000 0.958851
1.000000 0.841471
1.500000 0.664997
2.000000 0.454649
2.500000 0.239389
3.000000 0.047040
3.500000 -0.100224
4.000000 -0.189201
4.500000 -0.217229
5.000000 -0.191785
```

Figure 4.3 contains plots of the 21 values computed for four different intervals [a, b]. The program computes only 21 values, so the resolution in the plots is affected by the size of the interval—a smaller interval has better resolution than a larger interval. Now that you have an example of a program with a programmer-defined function, we present a more general discussion of the statements in a function.

A function consists of a definition statement followed by declarations and statements. The first part of the definition statement defines the type of value that is computed by the function; if the function does not compute a value, the type is void. The function name and parameter list follow the return_type. Thus, the general form of a function is

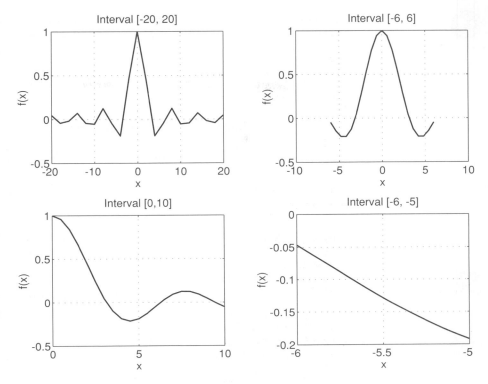

Figure 4.3 *Program output for four intervals.*

```
return_type function_name (parameter declarations)
{
    declarations;
    statements;
}
```

The parameter declarations represent the information passed to the function; if there are no input parameters (also called arguments), then the parameter declarations should be **void**. Additional variables used by a function are defined in the declarations. The declarations and the statements within a function are enclosed in braces. The function name should be selected to help document the purpose of the function. Comments should also be included within the function to further describe the purpose of the function and to document the steps. *We also use a comment line with dashes to separate a programmer-defined function from the* main *function and from other programmer-defined functions.*

Style

All functions should include a **return** statement, which has the following general form:

```
return expression;
```

The expression specifies the value to be returned to the statement that referenced the function. The expression type should match the return_type indicated in the function definition to avoid potential errors. The cast operator (discussed in Chapter 2) can be used to explicitly specify the type of the expression if necessary. A **void** function does not return a value, and thus has this general definition statement:

> **void** function_name (parameter declarations)

The **return** statement in a **void** function does not contain an expresession and has this form:

> **return;**

Compare the general form of a function that has just been described with the **sinc** function defined in program **chapter 4_2**. Also, note that the **main** function of this solution is easier to read because it is shorter than the **main** function in the first solution.

Functions can be defined before or after the **main** function. (Remember that a right brace specifies the end of the **main** function.) However, one function must be completely defined before another function begins; function definitions cannot

Style

be nested within each other. *In our programs, we include the* main *function first, and then additional functions are included in the order in which they are referenced in the program.*

We now look closer at the interaction between a statement that references a function, and the function itself.

FUNCTION PROTOTYPE

The **main** function presented in program **chapter4_2** contained the following statement in its declarations:

> **double sinc(double x);**

Function prototype

This statement is a **function prototype** statement. It informs the compiler that the **main** function will reference a function named **sinc**, that the **sinc** function expects a **double** parameter, and that the **sinc** function returns a **double** value. The identifier **x** is not being defined as a variable; it is just used to indicate that a value is expected as an argument by the **sinc** function. In fact, it is valid to include only the argument types in the function prototype statement:

> **double sinc(double);**

Style

Both of these prototype statements give the same information to the compiler. *We recommend using parameter identifiers in prototype statements because the identifiers help document the order and definition of the parameters.*

A function prototype can be included with preprocessor directives, or, because a function prototype is defining the type of value being returned by the function, it can also be included with other variable declarations. For example, the declarations of program **chapter4_2** are

```
/*  Declare variables and function prototypes.  */
int k;
double a, b, x_incr, new_x;
double sinc(double x);
```

These statements could also have been written in the following form:

```
/*  Declare variables and function prototypes.  */
int k;
double a, b, x_incr, new_x, sinc(double x);
```

In our programs, we list function prototypes on separate declaration statements to make it easier to identify them.

Function prototype statements should be included for all functions referenced in a program. Header files, such as **stdio.h** and **math.h**, contain the prototype statements for many of the functions in the Standard C library; otherwise, we would need to include individual prototype statements for functions such as **printf** and **sqrt** in our programs. If a programmer-defined function references other programmer-defined functions, then it will also need additional prototype statements.

If a program references a large number of programmer-defined functions, it becomes cumbersome to include all the function prototype statements. In these cases, a custom header file can be defined that contains the function prototypes and any related symbolic constants. A header file should have a file name that ends with a suffix of **.h**. The file is then referenced with an **include** statement, using double quotes around the file name. In Chapter 5, we develop a set of functions for computing common statistics from a set of values. If a header file containing the corresponding function prototypes is named **stat_lib.h**, then the prototypes are all included in a program with this statement:

```
#include "stat_lib.h"
```

Custom header files are often used to accompany routines that are shared by programmers.

PARAMETER LIST

The definition statement of a function defines the parameters that are required by the function; these are called **formal parameters**. Any statement that references the function must include values that correspond to the parameters; these are called **actual parameters.** For example, consider the **sinc** function developed earlier in this section. The definition statement of this function is

Style

Formal
parameters

Actual
parameters

```
double sinc(double x)
```

and the statement from the **main** program that references the function is

```
printf("%f %f \n",new_x,sinc(new_x));
```

Thus, the variable **x** is the formal parameter and the variable **new_x** is the actual parameter. When the reference to the **sinc** function in the **printf** statement is executed, the value in the actual parameter is copied to the formal parameter and the steps in the **sinc** function are executed using the new value in **x**. The value returned by the **sinc** function is then printed. It is important to note that the value in the formal parameter is not moved back to the actual parameter when the function is completed. We illustrate these steps with a memory snapshot that shows the transfer of the value from the actual parameter to the formal parameter, assuming that the value of **new_x** is 5.0:

actual parameter   formal parameter

new_x | 5.0 | ⟶   x | 5.0 |

After the value in the actual parameter is copied to the formal parameter, then the steps in the **sinc** function are executed. When debugging a function, it is a good idea to use **printf** statements to provide a memory snapshot of the actual parameters before the function is referenced, and of the formal parameters at the beginning of the function.

Valid references to the **sinc** function can also include expressions, and can include other function references, as shown in these example references to the **sinc** function:

```
printf("%f \n",sinc(x+2.5));

scanf("%lf",&y);
printf("%f \n",sinc(y));

z = x*x + sinc(2*x);

w = sinc(fabs(y));
```

In all these example references, the formal parameter is still **x**, but the actual parameter is **x+2.5**, or **y**, or **2*x**, or **fabs(y)**, depending on the reference selected.

If a function has more than one parameter, the formal parameters and the actual parameters must match in number, type, and order. A mismatch between the number of formal parameters and actual parameters can be detected by the compiler using the function prototype statement. If the type of an actual parameter is not the same as the corresponding formal parameter, then the value of the actual parameter will be converted to the appropriate type; this conversion is also called **coercion of arguments**, and may or may not cause errors. The coercion occurs according to the discussion given in Chapter 2, which discussed moving values stored as one type to a variable with a different type. Converting

Coercion of
arguments

values to a higher type (such as from **float** to **double**) generally works correctly; converting values to a lower type (such as from **float** to **int**) often introduces errors.

To illustrate the coercion of arguments, consider the following function that returns the maximum of two values:

```
/*-----------------------------------------------------------*/
/*   This function returns the maximum of two                */
/*   integer values.                                         */

int max(int a, int b)
{
   if (a > b)
      return a;
   else
      return b;
}
/*-----------------------------------------------------------*/
```

Assume that a reference to this function is **max(x_sum, y_sum)**, and that **x_sum and y_sum** are integers containing the values 3 and 8, respectively. Then, the following memory snapshot shows the transfer of values from the actual parameters to the formal parameters when the reference **max(x_sum, y_sum)** is made:

actual parameters   formal parameters

x_sum   3   ⟶   a   3

y_sum   8   ⟶   b   8

The statements in the function will then return the value 8 as the value of the reference **max(x_sum, y_sum)**.

Now suppose that a reference to the function **max** is made using **float** variables **t_1** and **t_2**. If **t_1** and **t_2** contain the values 2.8 and 4.6, then the following transfer of parameters occurs when the reference **max(t_1, t_2)** is executed:

actual parameters   formal parameters

t_1   2.8   ⟶   a   2

t_2   4.6   ⟶   b   4

The statements in the function will then return the value 4 to the statement containing the reference **max(t_1, t_2)**. Obviously, the wrong value has been returned by the function. However, the problem is not in the function; the problem is that the function was referenced with the wrong types of actual parameters.

Addition errors can be introduced if the actual parameters are out of order. These errors may not be detected by the compiler, and can be difficult to detect; therefore, be especially careful that the order of the formal parameters and the actual parameters match.

Call by value   The function reference in the `sinc` example is a **call by value** reference, or a **reference by value**. When a function reference is made, the value of the actual parameter is passed to the function and is used as the value of the corresponding formal parameter. In general, a C function cannot change the value of an actual parameter. Exceptions occur when the actual parameters are arrays (discussed in Chapter 5) or are pointers (discussed in Chapter 6); these exceptions generate a **Call by reference**   **call by reference** or a reference by address, which will be discussed in these later chapters.

Practice!

Consider the following function:

```
/*-------------------------------------------------*/
/*  This function counts positive parameters.    */

int positive(double a, double b, double c)
{
.   int count;

    count = 0;
    if (a >= 0)
       count++;
    if (b >= 0)
       count++;
    if (c >= 0)
       count++;
    return count;
}
/*-------------------------------------------------*/
```

Assume that the function is referenced with the following statements:

```
x = 25;
total = positive(x, sqrt(x), x-30);
```

1.   Show the memory snapshot of the actual parameters and the formal parameters.
2.   What is the new value of `total`?

STORAGE CLASS AND SCOPE

In the example programs presented thus far, we have declared variables within a **main** function and within programmer-defined functions. It is also valid to define a variable before the **main** function. Therefore, it is important to be able to deter-
Scope   mine the **scope** of a function or a variable, where scope refers to the portion of

the program in which it is valid to reference the function or variable; scope is also sometimes defined in terms of the portion of the program in which the function or variable is visible or accessible. Because the scope of a variable is directly related to its **storage class**, we also discuss the four storage classes—automatic, external, static, and register.

First, we define the difference between local variables and global variables. **Local variables** are defined within a function, and thus include the formal parameters and any other variables declared in the function. A local variable can be accessed only in the function that defines it. A local variable has a value when its function is being executed, but its value is not retained when the function is completed. **Global variables** are defined outside the `main` function or other programmer-defined functions. The definition of a global variable is outside of all functions, so it can be accessed by any function within the program; however, to reference an external variable, a declaration within the function must include the keyword `extern` before the type designation to tell the computer to look outside the function for the variable. The **automatic storage class** is used to represent local variables; this is the default storage class, but it can also be specified with the keyword `auto` before the type designation. The **external storage class** is used to represent global variables; the `extern` designation must be used within functions, and it is optional in the original definition of a global variable.

Consider a program that contains the following statements:

```
#include <stdio.h>
#include <stdlib.h>
int count=0;
...
main()
{
   int x, y, z;
   ...
}
int function calc(int a, int b);
{
   int x;
   extern int count;
   ...
}
void function check(int sum);
{
   extern int count;
   ...
}
```

The variable `count` is a global variable that can be referenced by the functions `calc` and `check`. The variables `x`, `y`, and `z` are local variables that can be referenced only in the `main` program; similarly, the variables `a`, `b`, and `x` are local variables that can be referenced only in the function `calc`, and `sum` is a local variable that can be referenced only in the function `check`. Note that there are two local variables `x`—these are two different variables with different scopes.

Storage class

Local variables

Global variables

Automatic storage class

External storage class

Style

The memory assigned to an external variable is retained for the duration of the program. Although an external variable can be referenced from a function using the proper declaration, using global variables is generally discouraged. *In general, parameters are preferred for transferring information to a function because the parameter is evident in the function prototype, whereas the external variable is not visible in the function prototype.*

Function names also have external storage class, and thus can be referenced from other functions. Function prototypes included outside of any function are also external references, and thus are available to all other functions in the program; this explains why we do not need to include `math.h` in every function that references a mathematical function. However, the parameter variables in the function prototype are known only in the function prototype statement.

Static

The **static** storage class is used to specify that the memory for a local variable should be retained during the entire program execution. Therefore, if a local variable in a function is given a static storage class assignment by using the keyword **static** before its type specification, the variable will not lose its value when the program exits the function in which it is defined. A **static** variable could be used to count the number of times that a function was invoked because the value of the count would be preserved from one function call to another.

Register

The keyword **register** is used before the type designation of a variable to specify that it should be placed in a **register** as opposed to a memory location. Accessing registers is faster than accessing memory, so this class of storage is used for frequently accessed values. Because the number of registers available is system-dependent, and because the time required for a memory access is steadily being reduced, this type of storage class is seldom used.

Practice!

Using the program on page 175 in Section 4.4, give the following information. (You do not need to understand the program to determine the requested information.)

1. List the external identifiers.
2. List the local variables, and identify their scope.

Using the program on page 186 in Section 4.6, give the following information. (You do not need to understand the program to determine the requested information.)

3. List the external identifiers.
4. List the local variables, and identify their scope.

4.3   Random Numbers

Random
numbers

A sequence of **random numbers** is not defined by an equation; instead, it has certain characteristics that define it. These characteristics include the minimum and maximum values, the average, and whether the possible values are equally likely to occur or whether some values are more likely to occur than others. Sequences of random numbers can be generated from experiments, such as tossing a coin, rolling a die, or selecting numbered balls. Sequences of random numbers can also be generated using the computer.

Many engineering problems require the use of random numbers in the development of a solution. In some cases, the numbers are used to develop a simulation of a complicated problem. The simulation can be run over and over to analyze the results, and each computer run represents a repetition of the experiment. We also use random numbers to approximate noise sequences. For example, the static that we hear on a radio is a noise sequence. If we are testing a program that uses an input data file that represents a radio signal, we may want to generate noise and add it to a speech signal or a music signal in order to provide a more realistic signal.

Engineering applications often require random numbers distributed between specified values. For example, we may want to generate random integers between 1 and 500, or we may want to generate random floating-point values between −5 and 5. We now present discussions on generating random numbers between two specified values. The random numbers generated are equally likely to occur; that is, if the random number is supposed to be an integer between 1 and 5, each of the integers in the set {1, 2, 3, 4, 5} is equally likely to occur. Another way of saying this is that each integer should occur approximately 20% of the time. Random numbers that are equally likely to be any value in a specified set are also called **uniform random numbers** or uniformly distributed random numbers.

INTEGER SEQUENCES

The Standard C library contains a function **rand** that generates a **random** integer between 0 and **RAND_MAX**, where **RAND_MAX** is a system-dependent integer defined in **stdlib.h**. (A common value for **RAND_MAX** is 32,767.) The **rand** function has no input arguments, and is referenced by the expression **rand()**. Thus, to generate and print a sequence of two random numbers, we could use this statement:

```
printf("random numbers: %i %i \n",rand(),rand());
```

The same two values are printed each time that a program containing this statement is executed because the **rand** function generates integers in a specified sequence. (Because this sequence eventually begins to repeat, it is sometimes called a **pseudorandom** sequence instead of a random sequence.) However, if we generate additional random numbers in the same program, they will be different. Thus, this pair of statements generates four random numbers:

```
printf("random numbers: %i %i \n",rand(),rand());
printf("random numbers: %i %i \n",rand(),rand());
```

Each time that the **rand** function is referenced in a program, it generates a new value; however, each time that the program is run, it generates the same sequence of values.

In order to cause a program to generate a new sequence of random values each time that it is executed, we need to give a new **random number seed** to the random-number generator. The function **srand** (from **stdlib.h**) specifies the seed for the random-number generator; for each seed value, a new sequence of random numbers is generated by **rand**. The argument of the **srand** function is an unsigned integer that is used in computations that initialize the sequence; the seed value is not the first value in the sequence. If an **srand** function is not used before the **rand** function is referenced, the computer assumes that the seed value is 1. Therefore, if you specify a seed value of 1, you will get the same sequence of values from the **rand** function that you will get without specifying a seed value.

In the following program, the user is asked to enter a seed value, and then the program generates 10 random numbers. Each time that the user executes the program and enters the same seed, the same set of 10 random integers is generated; each time that a different seed is entered, a different set of 10 random integers is generated. The function prototype statements for **rand** and **srand** are included in **stdlib.h**.

Random number seed

ch4_3.c

```
/*-------------------------------------------------------*/
/*   Program chapter4_3                                  */
/*                                                       */
/*   This program generates and prints ten              */
/*   random integers between 1 and RAND_MAX.            */

#include <stdio.h>
#include <stdlib.h>

main()
{
   /*   Declare variables.   */
   unsigned int seed;
   int k;

   /*   Get seed value from the user.   */
   printf("Enter a positive integer seed value: \n");
   scanf("%u",&seed);
   srand(seed);

   /*   Generate and print ten random numbers.   */
   printf("Random Numbers: \n");
   for (k=1; k <= 10; k++)
   {
      printf("%i ",rand());
   }
   printf("\n");
```

```
    /*  Exit program.  */
    return EXIT_SUCCESS;
}
/*---------------------------------------------------------*/
```

A sample output follows, using the Borland Turbo C++ 3.0 compiler:

```
Enter a positive integer seed value:
123
Random Numbers:
9827 6588 24191 6712 22732 10409 17951 18683 8409 12981
```

Experiment with the program on your computer system; use the same seed to generate the same numbers, and use different seeds to generate different numbers.

Because the prototype statements for **rand** and **srand** are included in **stdlib.h**, we do not need to include them separately in a program. However, it is instructive to analyze these prototype statements. Because the **rand** function returns an integer and has no input, its prototype statement is

```
int rand(void);
```

Because the **srand** function returns no value and has an unsigned integer as an argument, its prototype statement is

```
void srand(unsigned int);
```

Generating random integers over a specified range is simple to do with the **rand** function. For example, suppose that we want to generate random integers between 0 and 7. The following statement first generates a random number that will be between 0 and **RAND_MAX**, and then uses the modulus operator to compute the modulus of the random number and the integer 8:

```
x = rand()%8;
```

The result of the modulus operation is the remainder after **rand()** is divided by 8, so the value of **x** can assume integer values between 0 and 7.

Suppose that we want to generate a random integer between -25 and 25. The total number of possible integers is 51, and a single random number in this range can be computed with this statement:

```
y = rand()%51 - 25;
```

This statement first generates a value between 0 and 50, and then subtracts 25 from the value, yielding a new value between -25 and 25.

We can now write a function that generates an integer between two specified integers, a and b. The function first computes n, which is the number of all integers between a and b, inclusive; this value is equal to $b - a + 1$. The function then uses the modulus operation with the **rand()** function to generate a new integer between 0 and $n - 1$. Finally, the lower limit, a, is added to the new integer to give a value between a and b. All three steps can be combined in one expression on the **return** statement in the function:

```
/*--------------------------------------------------------*/
/*   This function generates a random integer             */
/*   between specified limits a and b (a<b).              */

int rand_int(int a, int b)
{
    return rand()%(b-a+1) + a;
}
/*--------------------------------------------------------*/
```

To illustrate the use of this function, the following program generates and prints 10 random integers between user-specified limits. The user also enters the seed to initiate the sequence.

ch4_4.c

```
/*--------------------------------------------------------*/
/*   Program chapter4_4                                   */
/*                                                        */
/*   This program generates and prints ten random        */
/*   integers between user-specified limits.             */

#include <stdio.h>
#include <stdlib.h>

main()
{
    /*   Declare variables and function prototypes.   */
    unsigned int seed;
    int a, b, k;
    int rand_int(int a, int b);

    /*   Get seed value and interval limits.   */
    printf("Enter a positive integer seed value: \n");
    scanf("%u",&seed);
    srand(seed);
    printf("Enter integer limits a and b (a<b): \n");
    scanf("%i %i",&a,&b);

    /*   Generate and print ten random numbers.   */
    printf("Random Numbers: \n");
    for (k=1; k<=10; k++)
    {
        printf("%i ",rand_int(a,b));
    }
    printf("\n");

    /*   Exit program.   */
    return EXIT_SUCCESS;
}
/*--------------------------------------------------------*/
```

```
/*   This function generates a random integer     */
/*   between specified limits a and b (a<b).       */

int rand_int(int a, int b)
{
    return rand()%(b-a+1) + a;
}
/*----------------------------------------------------*/
```

A sample set of values generated from this program follows:

```
Enter a positive integer seed value:
13
Enter integer limits a and b (a<b):
-5 5
Random Numbers:
-3  0 -4  3 -1 -4 -1 -3 -3  5
```

Remember that the values generated are system-dependent; you should not expect to get this same set of random numbers from a different compiler.

Modify!

ch4_4.c

Use the program developed in this section to generate several sets of random integers in each of the following ranges using different seed values.

1. 0 through 500
2. −10 through 200
3. −50 through −10
4. 5 through 5

FLOATING-POINT SEQUENCES

In many engineering problems, we need to generate random floating-point values in a specified interval $[a, b]$. The computation to convert an integer between 0 and RAND_MAX to a floating-point value between a and b has three steps. The value from the rand function is first divided by RAND_MAX to generate a floating-point value between 0 and 1. The value between 0 and 1 is then multiplied by $(b - a)$ (the width of the interval $[a, b]$) to give a value between 0 and $(b - a)$. The value between 0 and $b - a$ is then added to a to adjust it so that it will be between a and b. These three steps are combined in the expression on the return statement in the following function.

rand_rtn.c

```
/*----------------------------------------------------*/
/*   This function generates a random                 */
/*   double value between a and b.                    */

double rand_float(double a, double b)
{
  return ((double)rand()/RAND_MAX)*(b-a) + a;
}
/*----------------------------------------------------*/
```

Note that a cast operator was needed to convert the integer **rand()** to a **double** value so that the result of the division would be a **double** value.

The program presented earlier in this section can easily be modified to generate and print floating-point values. A sample set of values from such a modification follows:

```
Enter a positive integer seed value:
82
Enter limits a and b (a<b):
-5 5
Random Numbers:
3.666341 -0.290994 -3.398389 0.816218 -0.264138 4.970397
-0.623646 0.590991 0.696890 -3.357799
```

Modify!

Modify the program for generating integers to one that generates 10 random floating-point values within a user-specified range. Then, generate several sets of numbers from each of the following ranges using different seed values.

1.   0.0 through 1.0   2.   −0.1 through 1.0
3.   −5.0 through −4.5   4.   5.1 through 5.1

4.4   Problem Solving Applied: Instrumentation Reliability

An analysis of the reliability of a piece of equipment is especially important if it is going to be used in situations that would be dangerous if it should fail, or in environments that are not easily accessible. For example, in the application in the chapter-opening discussion that related to the Alaskan pipeline, failures in instrumentation related to the transport of oil in the pipeline could cause serious problems due to the difficulty of getting replacement equipment to the location of the failure. Also, failure of the instrumentation could cause damage to human life, animal life, and the environment around the pipeline. Therefore, the analysis of the reliability of equipment in applications such as this one is an important topic in engineering.

Reliability

Equations for analyzing the reliability of instrumentation can be developed from the study of statistics and probability, where the **reliability** is the proportion of the time that the component works properly. Thus, if a component has a reliability of 0.8, then it should work properly 80% of the time. The reliability of combinations of components can also be determined if the individual component reliabilities are known. Consider the diagrams in Figure 4.4. In order for information to flow from point a to point b in the series design, all three components must work properly. In the parallel design, only one of the three components must work properly for information to flow from point a to point b. If we know the reliability of an individual component, then the reliability of a specific combination of components can be determined in two ways; an analytical reliability can be computed using theorems and results from probability and statistics, and a computer simulation can be developed to give an estimate of the reliability.

Consider the series configuration of Figure 4.4(a). If r is the reliability of a component, and if all three components have the same reliability, then it can be shown [14] that the reliability of the series configuration is r^3. Thus, if the reliability of each component is 0.8 (which means that a component works properly 80% of the time), then the analytical reliability of the series configuration is $(0.8)^3$, or 0.512. Thus, this series configuration should work properly 51.2% of the time.

Consider the parallel configuration of Figure 4.4(b). If r is the reliability of a component, and if all three components have the same reliability, then it can be

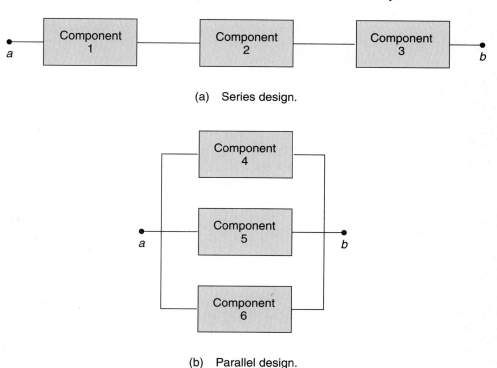

(a)   Series design.

(b)   Parallel design.

Figure 4.4 *Series and parallel configurations.*

shown [14] that the reliability of the parallel configuration is $3r - 3r^2 + r^3$. Thus, if the reliability of each component is 0.8, then the analytical reliability of the parallel configuration is $3(0.8) - 3(0.8)^2 + (0.8)^3$, or 0.992. The parallel configuration should work properly 99.2% of the time. Your intuition probably also tells you that the parallel configuration is more reliable because only one of the components must be working for the overall configuration to perform properly, whereas all three components must work properly in order for the series configuration to perform properly.

Computer
simulation

We can also estimate the reliability of these two designs using random numbers from a **computer simulation**. First, we need to simulate the performance of a single component. If the reliability of a component is 0.8, then it works properly 80% of the time. To simulate this performance, we could generate a random value between 0 and 1. If the value is between 0 and 0.8, we can assume that the component worked properly; otherwise it failed. (We could also have used the values 0 to 0.2 for a failure, and 0.2 to 1.0 for a component that worked properly.) To simulate the series design with three components, we would generate three floating-point random numbers between 0 and 1. If all three numbers are less than or equal to 0.8, then the design works for this one trial; if any one of the numbers is greater than 0.8, then the design does not work for this one trial. If we run hundreds or thousands of trials, we can compute the proportion of the time that the overall design works. This simulation estimate is an approximation to the analytically computed reliability.

To estimate the reliability of the parallel design with a component reliability of 0.8, we again generate three random floating-point numbers between 0 and 1. If any one of the three numbers is less than or equal to 0.8, then the design works for this one trial; if all of the numbers are greater than 0.8, then the design does not work for one trial. To estimate the reliability determined by the simulation, we divide the number of trials for which the design works by the total number of trials performed.

As indicated by the previous discussion, we can use computer simulations to provide a validation for the analytical results because the simulated reliability should approach the analytically computed reliability as the number of trials increases. There are also cases in which it is very difficult to analytically compute the reliability of a piece of instrumentation. In these cases, a computer simulation can be used to provide a good estimate of the reliability.

Develop a program to compare the analytical reliabilities of the series and parallel configurations in Figure 4.4 with simulation results. Allow the user to enter the individual component reliability and the number of trials to use in the simulation.

1.   PROBLEM STATEMENT

Compare the analytical and simulation reliabilities for a series configuration with three components and for a parallel configuration with three components. Assume all components have the same reliability.

2.   INPUT/OUTPUT DESCRIPTION

The I/O diagram shows that the input values are the component reliability, the number of trials, and a random number seed for initiating the sequence. The output consists of the analytical reliability and the simulation reliability for the series and the parallel configurations.

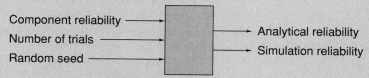

3.   HAND EXAMPLE

For the hand example, we use a component reliability of 0.8 and 3 trials. Since each trial requires three random numbers, assume that the first nine random numbers generated are the following. (These were generated from the **rand_float** function using a seed of 6666 for values between 0 and 1.)

First set of three random values:

    0.448988   0.138737   0.602466

Second set of three random values:

    0.053255   0.436903   0.976379

Third set of three random values:

    0.745872   0.141026   0.591968

From each group of three random numbers, we can determine whether a series configuration would work properly and whether a parallel configuration would work properly. For the first group of three random numbers, all the values are less than 0.8, and so both the series and parallel configurations would work properly. One of the values in the second set of numbers is greater than 0.8, so only the parallel configuration would work properly. Both configurations work properly with the third set of random numbers. Thus, the analytical results (computed earlier in this section)* and the simulation results for three trials are the following:

    Analytical Reliability:
    Series: 0.512 Parallel: 0.992
    Simulation for 3 Trials
    Series: 0.667 Parallel: 1.000

As we increase the number of trials, the simulation results should approach the analytical results. If we change the random number seed, the simulation results may also change even with only three trials.

4.   ALGORITHM DEVELOPMENT

We first develop the decomposition outline because it divides the solution into a series of sequential steps.

Decomposition Outline
1. *Read component reliability, number of trials, and random number seed.*
2. *Compute analytical reliabilities.*
3. *Compute simulation reliabilities.*
4. *Print comparison of reliabilities.*

Step 1 involves prompting the user to enter the necessary information and then reading it. Step 2 uses the equations given earlier to compute the analytical reliabilities. Because the computations are straightforward, we compute them in the **main** function. Step 3 involves a loop to generate the random numbers and to determine whether the configurations would perform properly for each trial. The **rand_float** function is used to compute the random numbers in the loop. In step 4, we print the results of the computations. The structure chart for this solution was shown in Figure 4.1 on page 152. The refinement in pseudocode is the following:

Refinement in Pseudocode

main: read component reliability, number of trials,
              and random number seed
          compute analytical reliabilities
          set series_success to zero
          set parallel_success to zero
          set k to 1
          while k ≤ number of trials
              generate three random numbers between 0 and 1
              if each number < component reliability,
                  increment series_success by 1
              If any number < component reliability,
                  increment parallel_success by 1
              increment k by 1
          print analytical reliabilities
          print $\dfrac{series\_success}{number\ of\ trials}$, $\dfrac{parallel\_success}{number\ of\ trials}$

The steps in the pseudocode are now detailed enough to convert to C. We also include the `rand_float` function in the program.

ch4_5.c

```c
/*----------------------------------------------------------*/
/*  Program chapter4_5                                      */
/*                                                          */
/*  This program estimates the reliability                  */
/*  of a series and a parallel configuration                */
/*  using a computer simulation.                            */

#include <stdio.h>
#include <stdlib.h>
#include <math.h>

main()
{
   /*  Declare variables and function prototypes.  */
   unsigned int seed;
   int n, k;
   double component_reliability, a_series, a_parallel,
          series_success=0, parallel_success=0,
          num1, num2, num3;
   double rand_float(double a, double b);

   /*  Get information for the simulation.  */
   printf("Enter individual component reliability: \n");
   scanf("%lf",&component_reliability);
   printf("Enter number of trials: \n");
   scanf("%i",&n);
   printf("Enter unsigned integer seed: \n");
   scanf("%u",&seed);
   srand(seed);
   printf("\n");

   /*  Compute analytical reliabilities.  */
   a_series = pow(component_reliability,3);
   a_parallel = 3*component_reliability
                - 3*pow(component_reliability,2)
                + pow(component_reliability,3);

   /*  Determine simulation reliability estimates.  */
   for (k=1; k<=n; k++)
   {
     num1 = rand_float(0,1);
     num2 = rand_float(0,1);
     num3 = rand_float(0,1);
     if (((num1<=component_reliability) &&
          (num2<=component_reliability)) &&
          (num3<=component_reliability))
             series_success++;
     if (((num1<=component_reliability) ||
          (num2<=component_reliability)) ||
          (num3<=component_reliability))
             parallel_success++;
   }
```

```
                /*  Print results.  */
                printf("Analytical Reliability \n");
                printf("Series: %.3f  Parallel: %.3f \n",
                        a_series,a_parallel);
                printf("Simulation Reliability, %i trials \n",n);
                printf("Series: %.3f  Parallel: %.3f \n",
                        (double)series_success/n,
                        (double)parallel_success/n);

                /*  Exit program.  */
                return EXIT_SUCCESS;
        }
        /*-------------------------------------------------------*/
        /*  This function generates a random                    */
        /*  double value between a and b.                       */

        double rand_float(double a, double b)
        {
           return ((double)rand()/RAND_MAX)*(b-a) + a;
        }
        /*-------------------------------------------------------*/
```

5.   TESTING

If we use the data from the hand example, we have the following interaction;
this output matches the data that we computed by hand:

```
Enter individual component reliability:
0.8
Enter number of trials:
3
Enter unsigned integer seed:
6666

Analytical Reliability
Series: 0.512  Parallel: 0.992
Simulation Reliability, 3 trials
Series: 0.667  Parallel: 1.000
```

Here are results from two more simulations that demonstrate that the
simulation results approach the analytical results as the number of trials increases.

```
Enter individual component reliability:
0.8
Enter number of trials:
100
Enter unsigned integer seed:
123
```

```
Analytical Reliability
Series: 0.512  Parallel: 0.992
Simulation Reliability, 100 trials
Series: 0.520  Parallel: 0.990

Enter individual component reliability:
0.8
Enter number of trials:
1000
Enter unsigned integer seed:
3535

Analytical Reliability
Series: 0.512  Parallel: 0.992
Simulation Reliability, 1000 trials
Series: 0.513  Parallel: 0.996
```

Modify!

ch4_5.c

These problems relate to the program developed in this section, which compares the analytical and simulated reliabilities.

1. Use this program to compute information comparing the simulation results for 10, 100, 1000, and 10000 trials, assuming that the component reliability is 0.85.

2. Use this program to compute information comparing the simulation results for 1000 trials, using five different random-number seeds. Assume that the component reliability is 0.75.

3. What component reliability is necessary to give a series reliability of 0.7? (*Hint*: Use the analytical reliability equation.) Validate your answer using this program.

4. What component reliability is necessary to give a parallel reliability of 0.9? Using the analytical reliability equation is not as easy in this case. If your calculator does not find roots of polynomial equations, just experiment with the program until you are close to the desired reliability.

4.5   Numerical Technique: Roots of Polynomials*

A polynomial is a function of a single variable that can be expressed in the following general form:

$$f(x) = a_0 x^N + a_1 x^{N-1} + a_2 x^{N-2} + \cdots + a_{N-2} x^2 + a_{N-1} x + a_N \tag{4.1}$$

*Optional section.

where the variable is x and the coefficients are represented by $a_0, a_1, \ldots a_N$. The degree of a polynomial is equal to the largest nonzero exponent. Therefore, the general form for a cubic (degree 3) polynomial is

$$g(x) = a_0x^3 + a_1x^2 + a_2x + a_3$$

and a specific example of a cubic polynomial is

$$h(x) = x^3 - 2x^2 + 0.5x - 6.5$$

Note that, for each term in the equation, the sum of the coefficient subscript and the variable exponent is equal to the polynomial degree using the notation in Equation (4.1).

POLYNOMIAL ROOTS

The solutions to many engineering problems involve finding the roots of an equation of the form

$$y = f(x)$$

Roots

where the **roots** are the values of x for which y is equal to zero. Examples of applications in which we need to find roots of equations include designing the control system for a robot arm, designing springs and shock absorbers for an automobile, analyzing the response of a motor, and analyzing the stability of a digital filter.

If a function $f(x)$ is a polynomial of degree N, then $f(x)$ has exactly N roots [15]. These N roots may contain real roots or complex roots, as will be shown in the following examples. If we assume that the coefficients $(a_0, a_1, \ldots, a_N)$ of the polynomial are real values, then complex roots will always occur in complex conjugate pairs. (Recall that a complex number can be expressed as $\alpha + i\beta$, where $i = \sqrt{-1}$. The complex conjugate of $\alpha + i\beta$ is $\alpha - i\beta$.)

If a polynomial is factored into linear terms, it is easy to identify the roots of the polynomial by setting each term to zero. For example, consider the following equation:

$$f(x) = x^2 + x - 6$$
$$= (x - 2)(x + 3)$$

Then, if $f(x)$ is equal to zero, we have the following:

$$(x - 2)(x + 3) = 0$$

The roots of the equation, or the values of x for which $f(x)$ is equal to zero, are then $x = 2$ and $x = -3$. These roots also correspond to the values of x where the polynomial crosses the x axis, as shown in Figure 4.5.

If a quadratic equation (polynomial of degree 2) cannot easily be factored, we can use the quadratic formula to determine the two roots of the equation. Recall that for a general quadratic equation

$$y = ax^2 + bx + c$$

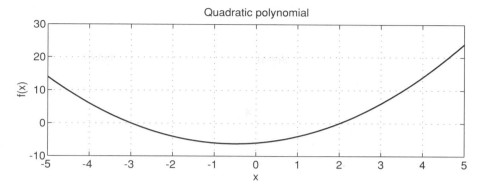

Figure 4.5 *Polynomial with two real roots.*

the roots can be computed as:

$$x_1 = \frac{-b + \sqrt{b^2 - 4ac}}{2a}$$

$$x_2 = \frac{-b - \sqrt{b^2 - 4ac}}{2a}$$

Thus, for this quadratic equation

$$f(x) = x^2 + 3x + 3$$

the roots are

$$x_1 = \frac{-3 + \sqrt{-3}}{2} = -1.5 + 0.87\sqrt{-1}$$

$$x_2 = \frac{-3 - \sqrt{-3}}{2} = -1.5 - 0.87\sqrt{-1}$$

Because a cubic polynomial has degree 3, it has exactly three roots. If we assume that the coefficients are real, then there are only these four possibilities:

  3 real roots at different values (distinct roots)
  3 real roots at the same value (multiple roots)
  1 distinct real root and 2 multiple real roots
  1 real root and a complex conjugate pair of roots

Examples of functions that illustrate each of these cases are as follows:

$$f_1(x) = (x - 3)(x + 1)(x - 1)$$

$$= x^3 - 3x^2 - x + 3$$

$$f_2(x) = (x - 2)^3$$

$$= x^3 - 6x^2 + 12x - 8$$

$$f_3(x) = (x + 4)(x - 2)^2$$
$$= x^3 - 12x + 16$$
$$f_4(x) = (x + 2)[x - (2 + i)][x - (2 - i)]$$
$$= x^3 - 2x^2 - 3x + 10$$

Figure 4.6 contains plots of these functions. Note again that the real roots correspond to the points where the function crosses the x axis.

It is relatively easy to determine the roots of polynomials of degree 1 or 2, but it can be difficult to determine the roots of polynomials of degree 3 and higher. A number of numerical techniques exist [9] for determining the roots of polynomials. Techniques such as the incremental search, the bisection method, and the false-position technique identify the real roots by searching for intervals in which the function changes sign because this indicates that the function has crossed the x axis. Additional techniques, such as the Newton–Raphson method, can be used to find complex roots.

INCREMENTAL-SEARCH TECHNIQUE

Incremental-search

The **incremental-search** technique is often used to determine the real roots of a function in an interval $[a, b]$. This technique searches for a subinterval $[a_k, b_k]$ such

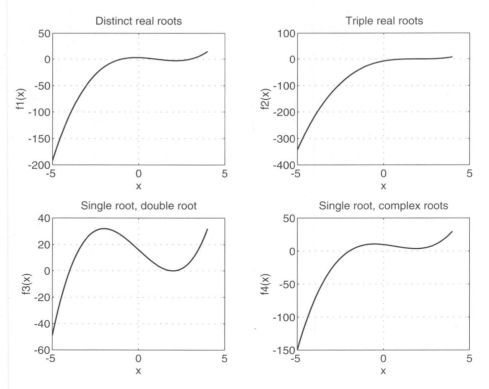

Figure 4.6 *Cubic polynomials.*

that the function value is negative on one end and positive on the other. We are then assured that there is at least one root in this subinterval.

There are many variations of the incremental-search technique. The one that we discuss begins with the selection of a step size that is used to subdivide the original interval into a group of smaller subintervals, as shown in Figure 4.7. For

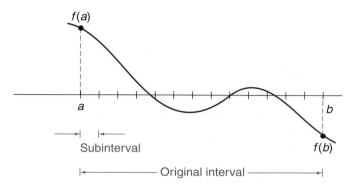

Figure 4.7 *Incremental search.*

each subinterval, we evaluate the function at both endpoints. If the product of the function values is negative, then there is a root in this subinterval. (A negative product implies that one function value is positive, whereas the other function value is negative; hence, the function must cross the x axis in the interval.) At this point, we can estimate the root to be the midpoint of this small segment, as shown in Figure 4.8 (a). It is also possible that one of the subinterval endpoints might be a root, or be very close to a root, as shown in Figure 4.8 (b). Remember that it is not likely that a floating-point value will be exactly equal to zero, so the test to determine if an endpoint is a root should compare the function value to a very small number, but not to zero.

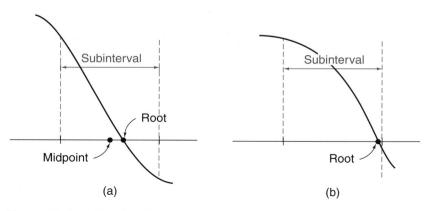

Figure 4.8 *Subinterval analysis.*

It is also important to recognize that there are cases in which this incremental-search technique fails. For example, suppose that there are two roots in one of the subintervals. In this case, because the function values at the endpoints will have the same sign, their product will be positive, and the algorithm will skip to the next subinterval. As another example, consider the case with three roots in one of the subintervals. In this case, because the function values at the endpoints have different signs, the estimate of the root is the midpoint of the subinterval. We then continue with the next subinterval, and thus miss the other two roots in the previous subinterval. These examples are used to illustrate the fact that the incremental-search technique has some flaws, although in general, it works reasonably well. If a technique is needed that has better performance characteristics, other root-finding methods [16] should be investigated.

4.6   Problem Solving Applied: System Stability*

System

The term **system** is often used to represent instrumentation or equipment for which specified inputs generate specified outputs or actions. Examples of systems include the cooling equipment connected to the supports of a pipeline, a robot arm used in a manufacturing facility, and a fast "bullet" train. A simple de-

Stable system

finition of a **stable system** is the following: A system is stable if a reasonable input causes a reasonable output. For example, consider the control system of a robot arm. A reasonable input to the system would specify that the arm should move in a direction that is valid for the robot arm. If a reasonable input causes the arm to become erratic or to attempt to move in invalid directions, then the system is not stable. The analysis of the stability of the design of a system involves determining dynamic properties of the system. A discussion of the types of analyses involved, or of the functions involved, is beyond the scope of this text, but one component of the analysis requires the determination of the roots of polynomials. Usually, both the real and complex roots are needed, but the techniques for finding complex roots involve using the derivative of the polynomial, and thus become more involved mathematically. Therefore, we reduce the scope of this problem to finding only the real roots of a polynomial given a specified interval in which to search. We also assume that the polynomial is a cubic polynomial, but the solution developed can easily be extended to handle higher-degree polynomials.

Develop a program to determine the real roots of a cubic polynomial. Allow the user to enter the coefficients of the polynomial, the interval to be searched, and the step size of the subintervals used in the search.

1.   **PROBLEM STATEMENT**

Determine the real roots of a cubic polynomial.

*Optional section.

2.   INPUT/OUTPUT DESCRIPTION

The I/O diagram shows that the input values are the polynomial coefficients, the interval endpoints, and the step size of the subintervals. The output values are the roots identified in the specified interval.

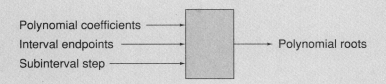

3.   HAND EXAMPLE

For the hand example, we use the equation

$$y = 2x - 4$$

This function can be described as a cubic polynomial with $a_0 = 0$, $a_1 = 0$, $a_2 = 2$, and $a_3 = -4$. If we set the polynomial to zero, we easily observe that the root is equal to 2. To examine the incremental-search technique, we first use a step size such that the root falls on one of the endpoints of a subinterval, and then we use a step size such that the root does not fall on one of the endpoints of a subinterval. If the root falls on an endpoint, we can easily identify it because the polynomial value will be very close to zero. If the root falls within a subinterval, the product of the function values at the endpoints will be negative, and we then estimate the root to be the midpoint of the interval.

First, consider the interval [1, 3] with a step size of 0.5. The subintervals and the corresponding information derived from them are as follows:

Subinterval 1:	[1.0, 1.5]
	$f(1.0) \cdot f(1.5) = (-2) \cdot (-1) = 2$
	No root in this interval.
Subinterval 2:	[1.5, 2.0]
	When we evaluate the endpoints, we detect the root at x = 2.0.
Subinterval 3:	[2.0, 2.5]
	When we evaluate the endpoints, we again detect the root at x = 2.0. Note that we will need to be careful that we do not identify this root twice in the program.
Subinterval 4:	[2.5, 3.0]
	$f(2.5) \cdot f(3.0) = (1) \cdot (2) = 2$
	No root in this interval.

We now consider the interval [1,3] with a step size of 0.3. The subintervals and the corresponding information derived from them are as follows:

Subinterval 1:   [1.0, 1.3]
$f(1.0) \cdot f(1.3) = (-2) \cdot (-1.4) = 2.8$
No root in this interval.

Subinterval 2:   [1.3, 1.6]
$f(1.3) \cdot f(1.6) = (-1.4) \cdot (-0.8) = 1.12$
No root in this interval.

Subinterval 3:   [1.6, 1.9]
$f(1.6) \cdot f(1.9) = (-0.8) \cdot (-0.2) = 1.6$
No root in this interval.

Subinterval 4:   [1.9, 2.2]
$f(1.9) \cdot f(2.2) = (-0.2) \cdot (0.4) = -0.08$
The root in this interval is estimated to occur at the midpoint:

$$x = \frac{1.9 + 2.2}{2} = 2.05$$

Subinterval 5:   [2.2, 2.5]
$f(2.2) \cdot f(2.5) = (0.4) \cdot (1.0) = 0.4$
No root in this interval.

Subinterval 6:   [2.5, 2.8]
$f(2.5) \cdot f(2.8) = (1.0) \cdot (1.6) = 1.6$
No root in this interval.

Subinterval 7:   [2.8, 3.1]
Note that the right endpoint exceeds the overall endpoint. In the program, we will modify such an interval so that it ends on the original right endpoint.
$f(2.8) \cdot f(3.0) = (1.6) \cdot (2.0) = 3.2$
No root in this interval.

4.   ALGORITHM DEVELOPMENT

We first develop the decomposition outline because it breaks the solution into a series of sequential steps.

Decomposition Outline
1. *Read polynomial coefficients, interval of interest, and step size.*
2. *Locate roots using subintervals.*

Step 1 involves prompting the user to enter the necessary information and then reading it. Step 2 requires a loop to compute the subinterval endpoints, and then to determine if a root occurs on an endpoint or in the subinterval. When a root is located, a corresponding message is printed. There are a number of operations involved in step 2, so we should consider using functions to keep the **main** function from getting long. Because we need to evaluate the cubic polynomial several places in the program, it is a good candidate for a function. Within each subinterval, we need to search for a root; this search is also a good candidate for a function. The structure chart for this solution was shown in Figure 4.1 on page 152. The refinement in pseudocode is the following:

Refinement in Pseudocode

main: read coefficients, interval endpoints a and b,
         and step size
    compute the number of subintervals, n
    set k to 0
    while k<= n −1
        compute left subinterval endpoint
        compute right subinterval endpoint
        check_roots (left, right, coefficients)
        increment k by 1
    check_roots (b,b,coefficients)

check_roots (left, right, coefficients):
    set f_left to poly(left,coefficients)
    set f_right to poly(right,coefficients)
    if f_left is near zero
        print root at left endpoint
    else
        if f_left · f_right <0
            print root at midpoint of subinterval
    return

poly(x,a₀,a₁,a₂,a₃):
    return $a_0x^3 + a_1x^2 + a_2x + a_3$

Note in the pseudocode for the **check_root** function that we check to see if the left subinterval endpoint is a root, but we do not check the right subinterval endpoint. This is necessary to avoid identifying the same root twice—when it is a right endpoint for one interval, and also when it is a left endpoint for the next subinterval. Because we only check the left endpoints, we need to check the final point in the interval because it never becomes a left endpoint.

The steps in the pseudocode are detailed enough to convert to C.

ch4_6.c

```c
/*----------------------------------------------------------*/
/*  Program chapter4_6                                      */
/*                                                          */
/*  This program estimates the real roots of a             */
/*  polynomial function using incremental search.          */

#include <stdio.h>
#include <stdlib.h>
#include <math.h>

main()
{
    /*  Declare variables and function prototypes.  */
    int n, k;
    double a0, a1, a2, a3, a, b, step, left, right;
    void check_roots(double left, double right, double a0,
                     double a1, double a2, double a3);

    /*  Get user input. */
    printf("Enter coefficients a0, a1, a2, a3: \n");
    scanf("%lf %lf %lf %lf",&a0,&a1,&a2,&a3);
    printf("Enter interval limits a, b (a<b): \n");
    scanf("%lf %lf",&a,&b);
    printf("Enter step size: \n");
    scanf("%lf",&step);

    /*  Check subintervals for roots.  */
    n = ceil((b - a)/step);
    for (k=0; k<=n-1; k++)
    {
        left = a + k*step;
        if (k == n-1)
            right = b;
        else
            right = left + step;
        check_roots(left,right,a0,a1,a2,a3);
    }
    check_roots(b,b,a0,a1,a2,a3);

    /*  Exit program.  */
    return EXIT_SUCCESS;
}
/*----------------------------------------------------------*/
/*  This function checks a subinterval for a root.     */

void check_roots(double left, double right, double a0,
                 double a1, double a2, double a3)
{
    /*  Declare variables and function prototypes.  */
    double f_left, f_right;
    double poly(double x, double a0, double a1,
                double a2, double a3);
```

```
    /*  Evaluate subinterval endpoints and  */
    /*  test for roots.                      */
    f_left = poly(left,a0,a1,a2,a3);
    f_right = poly(right,a0,a1,a2,a3);
    if (fabs(f_left) < 0.1e-04)
       printf("Root detected at %.3f \n",left);
    else
       if (fabs(f_right) < 0.1e-04)
          ;
       else
          if (f_left*f_right < 0)
             printf("Root detected at %.3f \n",(left+right)/2);


    /* Exit function.  */
    return;
}
/*------------------------------------------------------*/
/*  This function evaluates a cubic polynomial.         */

double poly(double x, double a0, double a1, double a2,
            double a3)
{
    return a0*x*x*x + a1*x*x + a2*x + a3;
}
/*------------------------------------------------------*/
```

5.   **TESTING**

If we use the data from the hand example, we have the following interaction with the program. The roots match the ones that we computed by hand:

```
Enter coefficients a0, a1, a2, a3:
0 0 2 -4
Enter interval limits a, b (a<b):
1 3
Enter step size:
0.5
Root detected at 2.000

Enter coefficients a0, a1, a2, a3:
0 0 2 -4
Enter interval limits a, b (a<b):
1 3
Enter step size:
0.3
Root detected at 2.050
```

Use the polynomials given on pages 179–180 to test this program. Use intervals and step sizes so that the roots do not always fall on subinterval endpoints.

Modify!

ch4_6.c

1. The size of the interval affects the estimate of the root if the root is not on an endpoint of a subinterval. Using the polynomial from the hand example, experiment with several step sizes including 1.1, 0.75, 0.5, 0.3, and 0.14, for the interval [0.5, 3].

2. Using the first cubic polynomial given on page 179, test the program using intervals in which the roots fall on the endpoints of the interval [a, b] entered as input.

3. Using the first cubic polynomial given on page 179, find a step size that cause the program to miss some of the roots for an initial interval of [−10, 10]. Explain why the roots were missed by the program. Is this an error in the program?

4. Modify the program so that it checks to see if the right endpoint of a subinterval is a root, instead of checking the left endpoint of a subinterval. Be sure to include a check for the first point of the interval [a, b].

5. Modify the program so that it can accept and locate the real roots of a fourth-degree polynomial.

6. Use this program to help answer problem 4 of the previous Modify! problems on page 177.

4.7   Macros*

Before compilation of a program, the preprocessor performs any actions specified by preprocessing directives, such as the inclusion of header files or the symbolic definition of constants. A simple operation can also be specified by a preprocessing directive called a **macro**, which has the following general form:

Macro

> #define macro_name(parameters) macro_text

The macro_text replaces references to the macro_name in the program. If the macro does not have parameters, then it is essentially a symbolic constant. If a macro has parameters, then it can represent a simple function. If the description of the macro takes more than one line, a backslash (\) must be used at the end of each line but the last to indicate that the line is continued on the next line.

An advantage of using a macro instead of a function is that the macro does not need to be defined in a separate module; thus, the compilation and

*Optional section.

linking/loading process is simplified, and the execution time is reduced. During preprocessing, each reference to the macro is replaced with the macro text.

To illustrate, consider the following simple program that converts degrees Fahrenheit to degrees Centigrade:

ch4_7.c

```
/*------------------------------------------------------*/
/*   Program chapter4_7                                 */
/*                                                      */
/*   This program converts a temperature in            */
/*   Fahrenheit to Centigrade.                          */

#include <stdio.h>
#include <stdlib.h>
#define degrees_C(x)  (((x) - 32)*(5.0/9.0))

main()
{
   /*  Declare variables.  */
   double temp;

   /*  Get temperature in Fahrenheit.  */
   printf("Enter temperature in degrees Fahrenheit: \n");
   scanf("%lf",&temp);

   /*  Convert and print temperature in Centigrade.  */
   printf("%f degrees Centigrade \n",degrees_C(temp));

   /*  Exit program.  */
   return EXIT_SUCCESS;
}
/*------------------------------------------------------*/
```

When the **printf** statement from the program is compiled, the macro text replaces the macro reference, giving the following:

```
printf("%f degrees Centigrade \n",(((temp) - 32)*(5.0/9.0)));
```

When this statement is executed, the value in **temp** is correctly converted from degrees Fahrenheit to degrees Centigrade before it is printed.

It is important to include parentheses around each individual argument and around the complete macro_text in the macro definition so that the macro will work properly when it is referenced with an expression as an actual parameter. To illustrate, consider these macros that convert temperatures in degrees Centigrade to degrees Fahrenheit:

```
#define degrees1_F(x)  ((x)*(9.0/5.0) + 32)
#define degrees2_F(x)  x*(9.0/5.0) + 32
```

When these macros are used with a variable as an actual parameter, they both work properly. For example, these statements

```
max_temp1 = degrees1_F(temp);
max_temp2 = degrees2_F(temp);
```

are correctly compiled as the following equivalent computations:

```
max_temp1 = ((temp)*(9.0/5.0) + 32);
max_temp2 = temp*(9.0/5.0) + 32;
```

However, these statements

```
max_temp1 = degrees1_F(temp+10);
max_temp2 = degrees2_F(temp+10);
```

are compiled as the following statements, which do not yield the same values:

```
max_temp1 = ((temp+10)*(9.0/5.0) + 32);
max_temp2 = temp+10*(9.0/5.0) + 32;
```

Therefore, the parentheses around the macro arguments and around the macro_text are necessary to ensure correct calculations.

The following macro computes the area of a triangle with a specified base and height as shown in Figure 4.9:

```
#define area_tri(base,height) (0.5*(base)*(height))
```

Note that parentheses are included around each argument and around the complete macro_text in the macro definition.

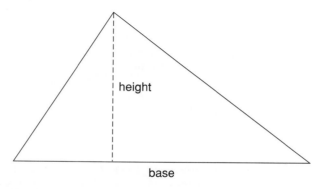

height

base

Figure 4.9 *Triangle.*

Practice!

Give macros to compute these following values. Along with each macro, give an example of a statement that references it.

1. Area of a square:

    $A = \text{side}^2$

2. Area of a rectangle:

    $A = \text{side}_1 \cdot \text{side}_2$

3. Area of a parallelogram:

    $A = \text{base} \cdot \text{height}$

4. Area of trapezoid:

    $A = \frac{1}{2} \cdot base \cdot (height_1 + height_2)$

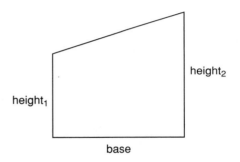

5. Volume of a sphere:

    $V = \frac{4}{3} \cdot \pi \cdot \text{radius}^3$

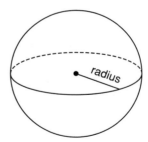

6. Volume of a pyramid:

    $V = \frac{1}{3} \cdot \text{area of the base} \cdot \text{height}$

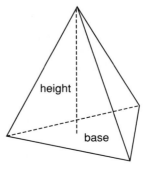

7. Volume of a right circular cone:

$V = \frac{1}{3} \cdot \pi \cdot \text{radius}^3 \cdot \text{height}$

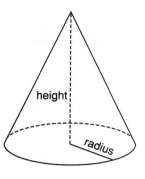

8. Volume of a cube:

$V = \text{side}^3$

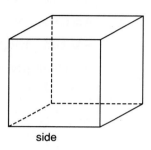

9. Volume of a rectangular parallelepiped:

$V = \text{length} \cdot \text{width} \cdot \text{height}$

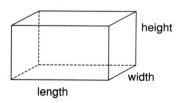

4.8   Recursion*

Recursive function

A function that invokes itself (or calls itself) is a **recursive function**. Recursion can be a powerful tool for solving certain classes of problems in which the solution can be defined in terms of a similar but smaller problem, and then the smaller problem can be defined in terms of a similar but still smaller problem. This redefinition of the problem into smaller problems continues until the smaller problem has a unique solution that is then used to determine the overall solution. There are system-dependent limitations to the number of times that a recursive function can call itself as it is continually redefining a problem into smaller and smaller problems, but these limitations do not usually cause difficulties.

*Optional section.

In the following two examples, we illustrate problems that can be solved with a recursive algorithm. In the examples, note the two parts to a recursive solution: first, the solution has to be redefined in terms of a similar but smaller problem, and, second, the smaller problems must reach a point at which there is a unique solution.

FACTORIAL COMPUTATION

Factorial

A simple example of recursion can be shown using the **factorial** computation. Recall that $k!$ (read as k factorial) is defined in the following way:

$$k! = (k)(k-1)(k-2)\ldots(3)(2)(1)$$

where k is a nonnegative integer, and where $0! = 1$. Thus,

$$5! = 5 \cdot 4 \cdot 3 \cdot 2 \cdot 1 = 120$$

We could also compute 5! using the following steps:

$$5! = 5 \cdot 4!$$
$$4! = 4 \cdot 3!$$
$$3! = 3 \cdot 2!$$
$$2! = 2 \cdot 1!$$
$$1! = 1 \cdot 0!$$
$$0! = 1$$

Thus, we have defined a factorial in terms of a product that involves smaller factorials. The smaller factorial is continually redefined until we reach 0!. We substitute the value of 0! in the last equation, and then begin going back up the list of equations, substituting values for the factorials:

$$1! = 1 \cdot 1$$
$$2! = 2 \cdot 1! = 2$$
$$3! = 3 \cdot 2! = 6$$
$$4! = 4 \cdot 3! = 24$$
$$5! = 5 \cdot 4! = 120$$

We have now developed a recursive algorithm for computing a factorial.

We present a program with two functions to compute a factorial: The first function is a nonrecursive (iterative) function, and the second is a recursive function. A factorial value becomes large quickly, so we use long integers for the factorial value. Note that both functions are referenced similarly in the `main` function.

ch4_8.c

```
/*-------------------------------------------------------*/
/*  Program chapter4_8                                   */
/*                                                       */
/*  This program compares a recursive function and       */
/*  a nonrecursive function for computing factorials.   */

#include <stdio.h>
#include <stdlib.h>

main()
{
   /*  Declare variables and function prototypes.  */
   int n;
   long factorial(int k);
   long factorial_r(int k);

   /*  Get user input.  */
   printf("Enter positive integer: \n");
   scanf("%i",&n);

   /*  Compute and print factorials.  */
   printf("Nonrecursive: %i! = %li \n",n,factorial(n));
   printf("Recursive: %i! = %li \n",n,factorial_r(n));

   /*  Exit program.  */
   return EXIT_SUCCESS;
}
/*-------------------------------------------------------*/
/*  This function computes a factorial with a loop.   */

long factorial(int k)
{
   /*  Declare variables.  */
   int j;
   long term;

   /*  Compute factorial with multiplications.  */
   term = 1;
   for (j=2; j<=k; j++)
   {
      term *= j;
   }

   /*  Return factorial value.  */
   return term;
}
/*-------------------------------------------------------*/
/*  This function computes a factorial recursively.   */

long factorial_r(int k)
{
   /*  Recursive reference until k is equal to 0.  */
```

```
      if (k == 0)
         return 1;
      else
         return k*factorial_r(k - 1);
   }
   /*-------------------------------------------------------*/
```

The condition **k == 0** keeps the recursive routine from becoming an infinite loop; this routine calls itself recursively with an argument that is continually being decremented by 1, until the argument reaches zero.

For large values of *k*, the value of *k*! can exceed even long integers. In these cases, the computations should be done using **double** or **long double** values. An interesting approximation to *k*! is also discussed in the end-of-chapter problems.

FIBONACCI SEQUENCE

Fibonacci
sequence

A **Fibonacci sequence** is a sequence of numbers $\{f_0, f_1, f_2, f_3, \ldots\}$ in which the first two values (f_0 and f_1) are equal to 1, and each succeeding number is the sum of the previous two numbers. Thus, the first few values of the Fibonacci sequence are

$$1 \quad 1 \quad 2 \quad 3 \quad 5 \quad 8 \quad 13 \quad 21 \quad 34 \quad \ldots$$

This sequence was first described in the year 1202 [17], and it has applications that range from biology to electrical engineering. For example, Fibonacci sequences are often used in studies of rabbit population growth.

A function to compute the *k*th value in the Fibonacci sequence is a good candidate for a recursive function because each new value in the sequence is computed from the two previous values. The following functions implement both nonrecursive and recursive algorithms for computing a Fibonacci number.

fib.c

```
   /*-------------------------------------------------------*/
   /*  This function computes the kth Fibonacci             */
   /*  number using a nonrecursive algorithm.               */

   int fibonacci(int k)
   {
      /*  Declare variables.  */
      int term, prev1, prev2, n;

      /*  Compute kth Fibonacci number with a loop.  */
      term = 1;
      if (k > 1)
      {
         prev1 = prev2 = 1;
         for (n=2; n<=k; n++)
         {
            term = prev1 + prev2;
            prev2 = prev1;
            prev1 = term;
         }
      }
```

```
                    /*  Return kth Fibonacci number.  */
                    return term;
                }
                /*-----------------------------------------------------*/
                /*                                                     */
                /*  This function computes the kth Fibonacci           */
                /*  number using a recursive algorithm.                */

                int fibonacci_r(int k)
                {
                    /*  Declare variables.  */
                    int term;

                    /*  Compute kth Fibonacci number recursively  */
                    /*  until k is equal to 1.                    */
                    term = 1;
                    if (k > 1)
                        term = fibonacci_r(k-1) + fibonacci_r(k-2);

                    /* Return kth Fibonacci number.  */
                    return term;
                }
                /*-----------------------------------------------------*/
```

In the recursive function, the condition `k > 1` keeps the function from getting into an infinite loop.

Modify!

ch4_8.c

1. Use program **chapter4_8** to compute values of 1!, 2!, and so on, until you reach the limits for long integers. What kind of error message occurred when the value of *k*! exceeded the limits on your system?

2. Modify **chapter4_8** so that it uses **double** values instead of integers to compute factorials. Explain why the number of digits of precision determines the maximum value of *k*! that can be correctly computed using **double** values. What is the maximum value of *k*! that can be computed using **double** values on your system?

3. Write a **main** function to test the Fibonacci functions. What is the maximum Fibonacci value that can be correctly computed with integers on your system?

SUMMARY

Most programs in C benefit from using both library and programmer-defined functions. Functions allow us to reuse software and to employ abstraction in our solution, and, hence, reduce development time and increase the quality of the software. Numerous examples were developed to illustrate using programmer-defined functions to solve problems, including examples of macros and recursive functions. Specific applications were presented to illustrate generating random numbers (integers or floating-point values) and to implement the incremental search technique for identifying real roots of polynomials.

KEY TERMS

abstraction	macro
actual parameter	modularity
automatic class	module
call by reference	module chart
call by value	programmer-defined function
coercion of arguments	random number
computer simulation	random number seed
external class	recursion
factorial	register class
Fibonacci sequence	reliability
formal parameter	reusability
function	root
function prototype	scope
global variable	stable system
incremental search	static class
invoke	storage class
library function	structure chart
local variable	system

C STATEMENT SUMMARY

Function definition:

```
return_type function_name (parameter types)
{
    declarations;
    statements;
}
```

Return statement:

```
return;
return (a + b)/2;
```

Function prototype:

```
double sinc(double x);
double sinc(double);
void check_roots(double left, double right, double a0,
                 double a1, double a2, double a3)
```

Macro:

```
#define degrees_C(x) (((x) - 32)*(5.0/9.0))
```

Style NOTES

1. A program with several modules is easier to read and understand than one long **main** function.
2. Select the name of the function to indicate the purpose of the function.
3. Use a special line, such as a line of dashes, to separate programmer-defined functions from the **main** function and other programmer-defined functions.
4. Use a consistent order for functions, such as the **main** function first, followed by additional functions in the order in which they are referenced.
5. Use parameter identifiers in prototype statements to help document the order and definition of the parameters.
6. List the function prototypes on separate lines so that they are easy to identify.
7. Use the parameter list instead of external variables to transmit information to a function.

DEBUGGING NOTES

1. If you are having difficulty understanding the error messages from a compiler, try running the program on another compiler to obtain different error messages.
2. When debugging a long program, add comment indicators (/* and */) around some sections of the code so that you can focus on other parts of the program.
3. Test a complicated function by itself using a driver program.
4. Make sure that the value returned from a function matches the function return type. If necessary, use the cast operator to convert a value to the proper type.
5. Functions can be defined before or after the **main** function, but not within it.
6. Always use function prototype statements to avoid errors in parameter passing.

7. Use `printf` statements to generate memory snapshots of the actual arguments before a function is referenced, and of the formal arguments at the beginning of the function.

8. Carefully match the type, order, and number of actual parameters with the formal parameters of a function.

9. In a macro definition, each argument and the entire body should be enclosed in its own set of parentheses.

10. System-dependent limitations can occasionally cause problems with recursive solutions to a problem.

PROBLEMS

rand_rtn.c

Simple Simulations. In the following problems develop simple simulations using the functions `rand_int` and `rand_float` developed in this chapter.

1. Write a program to simulate tossing a "fair" coin. Allow the user to enter the number of tosses. Print the number of tosses that yielded heads, and the number of tosses that yielded tails. What should be the percentage distribution of heads and tails?

2. Write a program to simulate tossing a coin that has been weighted such that it lands with heads up 60% of the time. Allow the user to enter the number of tosses. Print the number of tosses that yielded heads, and the number of tosses that yielded tails.

3. Write a program to simulate rolling a six-sided "fair" die with one dot on one side, two dots on another side, three dots on another side, and so on. Allow the user to enter the number of rolls. Print the number of rolls that gave one dot, the number of rolls that gave two dots, and so on. What should be the percentage distribution of the number of dots from the rolls?

4. Write a program to simulate an experiment rolling two six-sided "fair" dice. Allow the user to enter the number of rolls of the dice to simulate. What percentage of the time does the sum of the dots on the dice equal 8 in the simulation?

5. Write a program to simulate a lottery drawing that uses balls numbered from 1 to 10. Assume that three balls are drawn at random. Allow the user to enter the number of lottery drawings to simulate. What percentage of the time does the result contain three even numbers in the simulation? What percentage of the time does the number 7 occur in the three numbers in the simulation? What percentage of the time do the numbers 1–2–3 occur in the simulation?

rand_rtn.c

Component Reliability. The following problems specify computer simulations to evaluate the reliability of several component configurations. Use the function `rand_float` developed in this chapter.

6. Write a program that simulates the design shown in Figure 4.10 using a component reliability of 0.8 for component 1, 0.85 for component 2, and 0.95 for component 3. Print the estimate of the reliability using 5000 simulations. (The analytical reliability of this system is 0.794.)

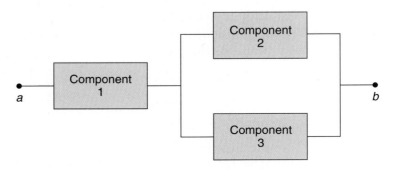

Figure 4.10 *Configuration 1.*

7. Write a program that simulates the design shown in Figure 4.11 using a component reliability of 0.8 for components 1 and 2, and 0.95 for components 3 and 4. Print the estimate of the reliability using 5,000 simulations. (The analytical reliability of this system is 0.9649.)

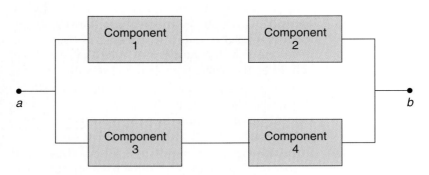

Figure 4.11 *Configuration 2.*

8. Write a program that simulates the design shown in Figure 4.12 using a component reliability of 0.95 for all components. Print the estimate of the reliability using 5000 simulations. (The analytical reliability of this system is 0.99976.)

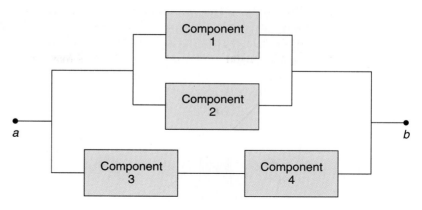

Figure 4.12 *Configuration 3.*

Flight Simulator Wind Speed. This set of problems relates to a computer simulation of wind speed for a flight simulator. Assume that the wind speed for a particular region can be modeled using an average value and a range of gust values that is added to the average. For example, the wind speed might be 10 miles an hour, with added noise (that represents gusts) that range from −2 miles per hour to 2 miles per hour, as shown in Figure 4.13. Use the function **rand_float** developed in this chapter.

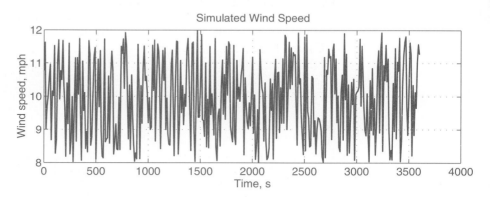

Figure 4.13 *Simulated wind speed.*

9. Write a program to generate a data file named **wind.dat** that contains 1 hour of simulated wind speeds. Each line of the data file should contain the time in seconds and the corresponding wind speed. The time should start with 0 seconds. The increment in time should be 10 seconds and the final line of the data file should correspond to 3600 seconds. The user should be prompted to enter the average wind speed and the range of values of the gusts.

rand_rtn.c

10. In problem 9, assume that we want the flight simulator wind data to include a 0.5% possibility of encountering a small storm at each time step. Therefore, modify the solution to problem 9 so that the average wind speed is increased by 10 mph for a period of 5 minutes when a storm is encountered. A plot of an example data file with three storms is shown in Figure 4.14.

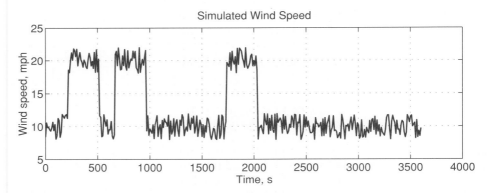

Figure 4.14 *Simulated wind speeds with three storms.*

11. In problem 10, assume that there is a 1% possibility of encountering a microburst at each time step in a small storm. Therefore, modify the solution to problem 10 so that the wind speed is increased by 50 mph over the storm values for a period of 1 minute if a microburst is encountered. A plot of an example data file with a microburst within a storm is shown in Figure 4.15.

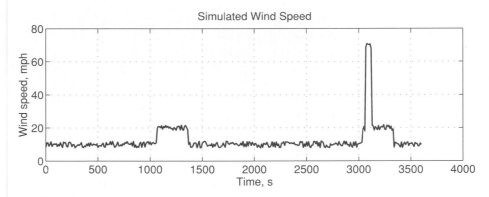

Figure 4.15 *Simulated wind speeds with a microburst.*

12. Modify the program in problem 10 so that the user enters the possibility of encountering a storm.

13. Modify the program in problem 10 so that the user enters the length in minutes for the duration of a storm.

14. Modify the program in problem 10 so that the length of a storm is a random number that varies between 3 and 5 minutes.

Roots of Functions. The following problems relate to finding real roots for functions.

ch4_6.c

15. Write a program to determine the real roots of a quadratic equation, assuming that the user enters the coefficients of the quadratic equation. If the roots are complex, print an appropriate message.

16. Modify problem 15 so that the program also computes the real and imaginary parts of the roots if they are complex.

17. Write a C function to evaluate this mathematical function:

$$f(x) = 0.1x^2 - x \ln x$$

Assume that the corresponding function prototype is

```
double f(double x);
```

Then modify the program developed in Section 4.6 so that it searches for roots of this new function instead of searching for roots of polynomials. Test the program by searching for a root in [1, 2] for this new function.

18. Modify the program developed in Section 4.6 to find the roots of this function in a user-specified interval:

$$f(x) = \text{sinc}(x)$$

Use the **sinc** function developed in this chapter.

19. In the program developed in Section 4.6, we searched for subintervals for which the function values at the endpoints had different signs; we then estimated the root location to be the midpoint of the subinterval. A more accurate estimate of the root location is usually the intersection of a straight line through the function values with the x axis, as shown in Figure 4.16. Using similar triangles, it can be shown that the intersection point c can be computed using this equation:

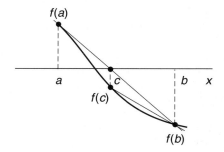

Figure 4.16 *Straight line intersection in (a,b).*

$$c = \frac{a \cdot f(b) - b \cdot f(a)}{f(b) - f(a)}$$

Modify program **chapter4_6** to estimate the root of a subinterval using this approximation.

ch4_8.c

Factorials.   The following set of problems relates to computing factorials. If you did not cover the section on recursion, read the material on page 193 for the definition of a factorial and then review the nonrecursive function for computing the factorial.

20.   A convenient approximation for computing the factorial $n!$ for large values of n is given by the Stirling formula [18]:

$$n! \approx \sqrt{2\pi n}\left(\frac{n}{e}\right)^n$$

where e is the base for natural logarithms, or approximately 2.718282. Write an integer function for computing this approximation to a factorial. Assume that the corresponding prototype is

```
int n_fact(int n);
```

21.   Suppose that we have n distinct objects. There are many different orders that we can select to line up the objects in a row. In fact, there are $n!$ orderings, or **permutations**, that can be obtained with n objects. If we have n objects, and select k of the objects, then there are $n!/(n - k)!$ possible orderings of k objects. That is, the number of different permutations of n different objects taken k at a time is $n!/(n - k)!$. Write a function named **permute** that receives values for n and k, and then returns the number of permutations of the n objects taken k at a time. (If we consider the set of digits {1, 2, 3}, the different permutations of two digits are {1, 2}, {2, 1}, {1, 3}, {3, 1}, {2, 3}, and {3, 2}.) Assume that the corresponding prototype is:

```
int permute(int n; int k);
```

22.   Whereas permutations (problem 21) are concerned with order, combinations are not. Thus, given n distinct objects, there is only one combination of n objects taken k at a time, but there are $n!$ permutations of n distinct objects taken n at a time. The number of **combinations** of n objects, taken k at a time is equal to $n!/((k!)(n - k)!)$. Write a function named **combine** that receives values for n and k, and then returns the number of combinations of the n objects taken k at a time. (If we consider the set of digits {1, 2, 3}, the different combinations of two digits are {1, 2}, {1, 3}, and {2, 3}.) Assume that the corresponding prototype is

```
int combine(int n, int k);
```

23.   The cosine of an angle can be computed from the following infinite series:

$$\cos x = 1 - \frac{x^2}{2!} + \frac{x^4}{4!} - \frac{x^6}{6!} + \ldots$$

Write a program that reads an angle x (in radians) from the keyboard. Then, in a function, compute the cosine of the angle using the first five terms of this series. Print the value computed along with the value of the cosine computed using the C library function.

24.   Modify the program in problem 23 so that the approximation uses terms from the series as long as the absolute value of a term is greater than 0.0001. Also print the number of terms used in the series approximation.

Courtesy of United Airlines.

GRAND CHALLENGE:
Speech Recognition

The modern jet cockpit has literally hundreds of switches and gauges. Several research programs are investigating the feasibility of using a speech-recognition system in the cockpit to serve as a pilot's assistant. The system would respond to verbal requests from the pilot for information such as fuel status or altitude. The pilot would use words from a small vocabulary that the computer had been trained to understand. In addition to understanding a specific vocabulary, the system would also have to be trained using the speech of the pilot who would be using the system. This training information could be stored on a diskette, and inserted into the onboard computer at the beginning of a flight so that the system could recognize the current pilot. The computer system would also use speech synthesis to respond to the pilot's request for information.

Arrays and Matrices

Objectives

OBJECTIVES

This chapter introduces the array, a data structure used frequently in solving engineering problems. Both one-dimensional and two-dimensional arrays are discussed in detail, with examples that illustrate defining and initializing arrays, that perform computations with arrays, that use arrays in input and output statements,

[*]Optional section.

207

and that use arrays as function arguments. A set of functions for performing statistical measurements on one-dimensional arrays is developed and used to analyze a speech signal. Two-dimensional arrays are used to solve a terrain navigation problem. In addition, matrices and vectors are defined, along with some of the common operations performed with them. Finally, the Gauss elimination technique for solving a system of simultaneous equations is presented, and a program is developed to solve a system of equations using arrays.

5.1   One-Dimensional Arrays

Array
One-dimensional array

When solving engineering problems, it is important to be able to visualize the data related to the problem. Sometimes the data consist of just a single number, such as the radius of a circle. Other times the data may be a coordinate in a plane that can be represented as a pair of numbers, with one number representing the x coordinate and the other number representing the y coordinate. There are also times when we want to work with a set of similar data values, but we do not want to give each value a separate name. For example, suppose that we have a set of 100 temperature measurements that we want to use to perform several computations. Obviously, we do not want to use 100 different names for the temperature measurements, so we need a method for working with a group of values using a single identifier. One solution to this problem uses a data structure called an **array**. A **one-dimensional array** can be visualized as a list of values arranged in either a row or a column, as follows:

5	0	−1	2	15	2
s[0]	s[1]	s[2]	s[3]	s[4]	s[5]

t[0]	0.0
t[1]	0.1
t[2]	0.2
t[3]	0.3

Elements
Subscripts

We assign an identifier to an array, and then distinguish between **elements** or values in the array using **subscripts**. In C, the subscripts always start with 0 and increment by 1. Thus, by using the example arrays, the first value in the **s** array is referenced by **s[0]**, and the third value in the **t** array is referenced by **t[2]**.

Arrays are convenient for storing and handling large amounts of data, so there is a tendency to use them in algorithms when they are not necessary. Arrays are more complicated to use than simple variables, and thus make programs longer and more difficult to debug. Therefore, use arrays only when it is necessary to have the complete set of data available in memory.

DEFINITION AND INITIALIZATION

An array is defined using declaration statements. An integer expression in brackets follows the identifier and specifies the number of elements in the array. Note that all elements in an array must be the same data type. The declaration statements for the two example arrays are as follows:

```
int s[6];
double t[4];
```

An array can be initialized with declaration statements or with program statements. To initialize the array with the declaration statement, the values are specified in a sequence that is separated by commas and enclosed in braces. The following statements define and initialize the example arrays **s** and **t**:

```
int s[6]={5, 0, -1, 2, 15, 2};
double t[4]={0.0, 0.1, 0.2, 0.3};
```

If the initializing sequence is shorter than the array, then the rest of the values are initialized to zero. Hence, the following statement defines an integer array of 100 values; each value is also initialized to zero:

```
int s[100]={0};
```

If an array is specified without a size but with an initialization sequence, the size is defined to be equal to the number of values in the sequence:

```
int s[]={5, 0, -1, 2, 15, 2};
double t[]={0.0, 0.1, 0.2, 0.3};
```

The size of an array must be specified in the declaration statement, using either a constant within brackets or by an initialization sequence within braces.

Arrays can also be initialized with program statements. For example, suppose that we want to fill a **double** array **g** with the values 0.0, 0.5, 1.0, 1.5, . . . , 10.0. Because there are 21 values, listing the values on the declaration statement would be tedious. Thus, we use the following statements to define and initialize this array:

```
/*  Declare variables.  */
int k;
double g[21];
...
/*  Initialize the array g.  */
for (k=0; k<=20; k++)
{
   g[k] = k*0.5;
}
```

It is important to recognize that the condition in this **for** statement must specify a final subscript value of 20, and not 21 (since the array elements are g[0] through g[20]). It is a common mistake to specify a subscript that is one value more than the largest valid subscript, and this error can be very difficult to find because it accesses values outside the array. Because this error is generally not detected during the program execution, it is important to be careful about exceeding the array subscripts. In our programs, we select conditions in **for** loops that specifically use the final value as a reminder to ourselves to carefully write the condition to avoid errors. Thus, in this example, we use the condition **k<=20** instead of **k<21**, although both work properly. *Also, we will generally use* k *as the subscript for a one-dimensional array.*

Style

Arrays are often used to store information that is read from data files. For example, suppose that we have a data file named **sensor3.dat** that contains 10 time and motion measurements collected from a seismometer. To read these values into arrays named **time** and **motion**, we could use these statements:

```
/*  Declare variables.   */
int k;
double time[10], motion[10];
FILE *sensor3;
...
/*  Open file and read data into arrays.   */
sensor3 = fopen("sensor3.dat","r");
for (k=0; k<=9; k++)
{
    fscanf(sensor3,"%lf %lf",&time[k],&motion[k]);
}
```

Practice!

Show the contents of the arrays defined in each of the following sets of statements.

1. `int x[10]={-5,  4,  3};`

2. `doublez[4];`
    `...`
    `z[1] = -5.5;`
    `z[2] = z[3] = fabs(z[1]);`

3. `int k`
    `double time[9];`
    `...`
    `for (k=0; k<=8; k++)`
    `{`
    `    time[k] = (k-4)*0.1;`
    `}`

COMPUTATIONS AND OUTPUT

Computations with array elements are specified just like computations with simple variables, but a subscript must be used to specify an individual array element. To illustrate, the following program reads an array **y** of 100 floating-point values from a data file. The program determines the average value of the array, and stores it in **y_ave**. Then, the number of values in the array **y** that are greater than the average are counted and printed.

ch5_1.c
lab.dat

```
/*----------------------------------------------------------*/
/*   Program chapter5_1                                     */
/*                                                          */
/*   This program reads 100 values from a data file         */
/*   and determines the number of values greater            */
/*   than the average.                                      */

#include <stdio.h>
#include <stdlib.h>
#define N 100
#define FILENAME "lab.dat"

main()
{
   /*  Declare and initialize variables.  */
   int k, count=0;
   double y[N], y_ave, sum=0;
   FILE *lab;

   /*  Open file, read data into an array, */
   /*  and compute a sum of the values.    */
   lab = fopen(FILENAME,"r");
   for (k=0; k<=N-1; k++)
   {
      fscanf(lab,"%lf",&y[k]);
      sum += y[k];
   }

   /*  Compute average and count values that  */
   /*  are greater than the average.          */
   y_ave = sum/N;
   for (k=0; k<=N-1; k++)
   {
      if (y[k] > y_ave)
         count++;
   }

   /*  Print count.  */
   printf("%i values greater than the average \n",count);

   /*  Close file and exit program.  */
   fclose(lab);
   return EXIT_SUCCESS;
}
/*----------------------------------------------------------*/
```

If the purpose of this program had been to determine the average of the values in the data file, an array would not have been necessary. The loop to read values could read each value into the same variable, adding its value to a sum before the next value is read. However, because we needed to compare each value to the average in order to count the number of values greater than the average, an array was needed so that we could access each value again.

Array values are printed using a subscript to specify the individual value desired. For example, the following statement prints the first and last values of the array **y** used in the previous example:

```
printf("first and last array values: \n");
printf("%f %f \n",y[0],y[N-1]);
```

The following loop prints all 100 values of **y**, one per line:

```
printf("y values: \n");
for (k=0; k<=N-1; k++)
{
    printf("%f \n",y[k]);
}
```

When printing a large array, such as this one, we probably would like to print several numbers on the same line. The following statements use the modulus operator to skip to a new line before each group of five values is printed:

```
printf("y values: \n");
for (k=0; k<=N-1; k++)
{
    if (k%5 == 0)
        printf("\n %f ",y[k]);
    else
        printf("%f ",y[k]);
}
printf("\n");
```

Statements similar to the ones illustrated here can also be used to write array values to a data file. For example, the following statement will print the value of **y[k]** on a line in a data file with a file pointer **sensor**:

```
fprintf(sensor,"%f \n",y[k]);
```

Since the new line indicator is included, the next value written to the file will be on a new line.

The number of elements in an array is used in the array declaration and in loops used to access the elements in the array. If the number of elements is changed, then there are several places in the program that need to be modified. *Changing the size of an array is simplified if a symbolic constant is used to specify the size of the array.* Then, to change the size, only the preprocessor directive

Style

needs to be changed. This style suggestion is especially important in programs that contain many modules, or in programming environments in which several programmers are working on the same software project. Many of the following programs illustrate the use of a symbolic constant to define the size of an array.

Table 5.1 gives an updated precedence order that includes subscript brackets. Brackets and parentheses are associated before the other operators. If parentheses and brackets are in the same statement, they are associated from left to right; if they are nested, the innermost set is evaluated first.

Practice!

Assume that the variable **k** and the array **s** have been defined with the following statement:

```
int k, s[]={3, 8, 15, 21, 30, 41};
```

Determine by hand, the output for each of the following sets of statements.

1.
```
for (k=0; k<=5; k+=2)
{
    printf("%i %i \n",s[k], s[k+1]);
}
```

2.
```
for (k=0; k<=5; k++)
{
    if (s[k]%2 == 0)
        printf("%i ",s[k]);
}
printf("\n");
```

TABLE 5.1 Operator Precedence

Precedence	Operation	Associativity
1	( ) [ ]	innermost first
2	++ -- + - ! (type)	right to left (unary)
3	* / %	left to right
4	+ -	left to right
5	< <= > >=	left to right
6	== !=	left to right
7	&&	left to right
8	||	left to right
9	?:	right to left
10	= += -= *= /= %=	right to left
11	,	left to right

FUNCTION ARGUMENTS

When the information in an array is passed to a function, two parameters are usually used; one parameter specifies the specific array and the other parameter specifies the number of elements used in the array. By specifying the number of elements of the array that are to be used, the function becomes more flexible. For example, if the function specifies an integer array, then the function can be used with any integer array; the parameter that specifies the number of elements assures that we use the correct size. Also, the number of elements used in an array may vary from one time to another. For example, the array may use elements read from a data file; the number of elements then depends on the specific data file used when the program is run. In all these examples, though, the array must be declared to be a maximum size, and then the actual number of elements used can be less than or equal to that maximum size.

Consider the following program that reads an array from a data file and then references a function to determine the maximum value in the array. The variable **npts** is used to specify the number of values in the array; the value of **npts** can be less than or equal to the defined size of the array, which is 100. The function has two arguments—the name of the array and the number of points in the array, as indicated in the function prototype statement.

ch5_2.c
lab.dat

```
/*------------------------------------------------------*/
/*  Program chapter5_2                                  */
/*                                                      */
/*  This program reads values from a data file and      */
/*  determines the maximum value with a function.        */

#include <stdio.h>
#include <stdlib.h>
#define N 100
#define FILENAME "lab.dat"

main()
{
    /*  Declare variables and function prototypes.  */
    int k=0, npts;
    double y[N];
    FILE *lab;
    double max(double x[], int n);

    /*  Open file and read data into an array, */
    lab = fopen(FILENAME,"r");
    while ((fscanf(lab,"%lf",&y[k])) == 1)
    {
        k++;
    }
    npts = k;

    /*  Find and print the maximum value.  */
    printf("Maximum value: %f \n",max(y,npts));
```

```
    /*  Close file and exit program.  */
    fclose(lab);
    return EXIT_SUCCESS;
}
/*----------------------------------------------------*/
/*  This function returns the maximum                 */
/*  value in the array x with n elements.             */

double max(double x[], int n)
{
    /*  Declare variables.  */
    int k;
    double max_x;

    /*  Determine maximum value in the array.  */
    max_x = x[0];
    for (k=1; k<=n-1; k++)
    {
        if (x[k] > max_x)
            max_x = x[k];
    }

    /*  Return maximum value.  */
    return max_x;
}
/*----------------------------------------------------*/
```

This program assumes that there will not be more than 100 values in the file; otherwise, this program will not work correctly. Arrays must be specified to be as large as, or larger than, the maximum number of values to be read into them.

The purpose of program **chapter5_2** was to illustrate the use of an array as a function argument. If the purpose of this program was to determine the maximum of the data values in the file, an array would not have been necessary; the maximum could have been determined as the data values were read.

There is a very significant difference in using arrays as parameters, and using simple variables as parameters. When a simple variable is used as a parameter, the value is passed to the formal argument in the function, and thus the value of the original value cannot be changed; this is a call-by-value reference. When an array is used as a parameter, the memory address of the array is passed to the function instead of the entire set of values in the array. Therefore, the function references values in the original array; this is a **call-by-address** reference. Because a function accesses the original array values, we must be very careful that we do not inadvertently change values in an array within a function. Of course, there may be occasions when we wish to change the values in the array, as we will see in examples in this chapter.

Call-by-address

Practice!

Assume that the following variables are defined:

```
int k=6;
double data[]={1.5, 3.2, -6.1, 9.8, 8.7, 5.2};
```

Give the values of the following expressions that reference the **max** function presented in this section.

1.   `max(data,6);`

2.   `max(data,5);`

3.   `max(data,k-3);`

4.   `max(data,k%5);`

5.2   Statistical Measurements

Analyzing data collected from engineering experiments is an important part of evaluating the experiments. This analysis ranges from simple computations on the data, such as calculating the average value, to more complicated analyses. Many of the computations or measurements using data are statistical measurements because they have statistical properties that change from one set of data to another. For example, the sine of 60° is an exact value that is the same value every time we compute it, but the number of miles to the gallon that we get with our car is a statistical measurement because it varies somewhat depending on parameters such as the temperature, the speed that we travel, the type of road, and whether we are in the mountains or the desert.

SIMPLE ANALYSIS

When evaluating a set of experimental data, we often compute the maximum value, minimum value, mean or average value, and the median. In this section, we develop functions that can be used to compute these values using an array as input. These functions (stored in a file **stat_lib.c**) will be useful in many of the programs that we develop later in the text and in solutions to problems at the end of the chapters; however, it is important to note that these functions assume that there is at least one value in the array.

Maximum, Minimum. A function for determining the maximum value in an array was presented in the previous section; a similar function for determining the minimum value is presented here. The functions assume that the array contains **double** values; simple changes could be used to convert these functions to specify integer values.

stat_lib.c

```
/*-----------------------------------------------------------*/
/*   This function returns the minimum              */
/*   value in an array x with n elements.           */

double min(double x[], int n)
{
   /*  Declare variables.  */
   int k;
   double min_x;
```

```
    /*  Determine minimum value in the array.  */
    min_x = x[0];
    for (k=1; k<=n-1; k++)
    {
        if (x[k] < min_x)
            min_x = x[k];
    }

    /*  Return minimum value.  */
    return min_x;
}
/*------------------------------------------------------*/
```

Average. The Greek symbol μ (mu) is used to represent the average or **mean value**, as shown in the following equation which uses summation notation:

Mean value

$$\mu = \frac{\sum_{k=0}^{n-1} x_k}{}$$

where $\sum_{k=0}^{n-1} x_k = x_0 + x_1 + x_2 + \ldots + x_{n-1}$. The average of a set of values is always a floating-point value, even if all the data values are integers. This function computes the mean value of a **double** array of **n** values:

stat_lib.c

```
/*------------------------------------------------------*/
/*  This function returns the average or                */
/*  mean value of an array with n elements.             */

double mean(double x[], int n)
{
    /*  Declare and initialize variables.  */
    int k;
    double sum=0;

    /*  Determine mean value.  */
    for (k=0; k<=n-1; k++)
    {
        sum += x[k];
    }

    /*  Return mean value.  */
    return sum/n;
}
/*------------------------------------------------------*/
```

Note that the variable **sum** was initialized to zero on the declaration statement. It could also have been initialized to zero with an assignment statement. In either case, the value of **sum** is initialized to zero when the function is referenced.

Median

Median. The **median** is the value in the middle of a group of values, assuming that the values are sorted. If there is an odd number of values, the median is the value in the middle; if there is an even number of values, the median is the average of the values in the two middle positions. For example, the median of the values {1, 6, 18, 39, 86} is the middle value, or 18; the median of the values {1, 6, 18, 39, 86, 91} is the average of the two middle values, or (18 + 39)/2, or 28.5. Assume that a group of sorted values are stored in an array, and that **n** contains the number of values in the array. If **n** is odd, then the subscript of the middle value can be represented by **floor(n/2)**, as in **floor(5/2)**, which is 2. If **n** is even, then the subscripts of the two middle values can be represented by **floor(n/2)-1** and **floor(n/2)**, as in **floor(6/2)-1** and **floor(6/2)**, which are 2 and 3. The following function determines the median of a set of values stored in an array. We assume that the values are sorted (into either ascending or descending order). If the array is not sorted, a function developed later in this chapter can be referenced from the **median** function to sort the values.

stat_lib.c

```
/*-----------------------------------------------------------*/
/*   This function returns the median              */
/*   value in an array x with n elements           */

double median(double x[], int n)
{
   /*  Declare variables.  */
   int k;
   double median_x;

   /*  Determine median value. */
   k = floor(n/2);
   if (n%2 != 0)
      median_x = x[k];
   else
      median_x = (x[k-1] + x[k])/2;

   /*  Return median value.  */
   return median_x;
}
/*-----------------------------------------------------------*/
```

Go through this function by hand using the two sets of data values given in this discussion.

VARIANCE AND STANDARD DEVIATION

One of the most important statistical measurements for a set of data is the variance. Before we give the mathematical definition for variance, it is useful to develop an intuitive understanding. Consider the values of arrays **data1** and **data2** that are plotted in Figure 5.1. If we attempted to draw a horizontal line through the middle of the values in each plot, this line would be at approximately 3.0. Thus, both arrays have approximately the same average or mean value of 3.0. However, the data in the two arrays clearly have some distinguishing characteristics. The values in **data2** vary more from the mean, or deviate more from the mean value. The **variance** of a set of values is defined to be the average squared deviation from the mean; the **standard deviation** is defined to be the square root of the variance. Thus, the variance and the standard deviation of the values in **data2** are greater than the variance and standard deviation for the values in

Variance
Standard
deviation

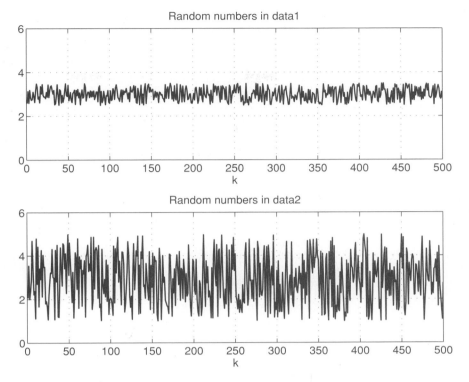

Figure 5.1 *Random sequences.*

data1. Intuitively, the larger the variance (or the standard deviation), the further the values fluctuate around the mean value.

Mathematically, the variance is represented by σ^2, where σ is the Greek symbol sigma. The variance for a set of data values (which we assume are stored in an array **x**) can be computed using the following equation:

$$\sigma^2 = \frac{\displaystyle\sum_{k=0}^{n-1}(x_k - \mu)^2}{n-1} \tag{5.2}$$

This equation is a bit intimidating at first, but if you look at it closely, it becomes much simpler. The term $x_k - \mu$ is the difference between x_k and the mean, or the deviation of x_k from the mean. This value is squared so that we always have a positive value. We then add the squared deviations for all data points. This sum is then divided by $n-1$, which approximates an average. The definition of variance has two forms: The denominator of a sample variance is $n-1$, and the denominator of a population variance is n [14]. Most engineering applications use the sample variance, as shown in Equation (5.2.) Thus, Equation (5.2) computes the average squared deviation of the data from the mean. The standard deviation is defined to be the square root of the variance:

$$\sigma = \sqrt{\sigma^2} \tag{5.3}$$

Both the variance and the standard deviation are commonly used in analyzing engineering data, so we give functions for computing both values. Note that the function for computing the standard deviation references the **variance** function, and that the **variance** function references the **mean** function; thus, these functions must include the proper function prototype statements. Also, note that there must be at least two values in the array, or the **variance** function will attempt to perform a division by zero.

stat_lib.c

```
/*----------------------------------------------------*/
/*  This function returns the variance                */
/*  of an array with n elements.                      */

double variance(double x[], int n)
{
   /*  Declare variables and function prototypes.  */
   int k;
   double sum=0, mu;
   double mean(double x[], int n);

   /*  Determine variance.  */
   mu = mean(x,n);
   for (k=0; k<=n-1; k++)
   {
      sum += (x[k] - mu)*(x[k] - mu);
   }

   /*  Return variance.  */
   return sum/(n-1);
}
/*----------------------------------------------------*/
/*  This function returns the standard deviation      */
/*  of an array with n elements.                      */

double std_dev(double x[], int n)
{
   /*  Declare function prototypes.  */
   double variance(double x[], int n);

   /*  Return standard deviation.  */
   return sqrt(variance(x,n));
}
/*----------------------------------------------------*/
```

CUSTOM HEADER FILE

The functions developed in this section are frequently used in solving engineering problems. To facilitate their use, we generate a custom header file that contains the prototype statements for these functions. Then, instead of including all the prototype statements in a **main** function, a preprocessor directive can be used that includes the custom header file.

The custom header file named **stat_lib.h** contains the following function prototype statements:

stat_lib.h

```
double max(double x[], int n);
double min(double x[], int n);
double mean(double x[], int n);
double median(double x[], int n);
double variance(double x[], int n);
double std_dev(double x[], int n);
```

The statement that includes these in a `main` function is:

```
#include "stat_lib.h"
```

The use of this custom header is illustrated in the program in the next section.

In addition to accessing the custom header file with the **include** statement, a program must also have access to the file **stat_lib.c** containing the statistical functions. The specific details of providing this access are system-dependent, and may involve adding a file name to the operating system command that performs the compilation and linking/loading operations.

Practice!

Assume that the array **x** is defined and initialized with the following statement:

```
double x[]={2.5, 5.5, 6.0, 6.25, 9.0};
```

Compute by hand the values returned by the following function references.

1. `max(x,5)`   2. `median(x,5)`
3. `variance(x,5)`   4. `std_dev(x,5)`
5. `min(x,4)`   6. `median(x,4)`

5.3   Problem Solving Applied: Speech Signal Analysis

A speech signal is an acoustical signal that can be converted into an electrical signal with a microphone. The electrical signal can then be converted into a series of numbers that represents the amplitudes of the electrical signal values. These numbers can be stored in data files so that the speech signal can be analyzed using computer programs. Suppose that we are interested in analyzing speech signals for the words "zero," "one," "two," . . . , "nine." The goal of this analysis would be to develop ways of identifying the correct digit from a data file containing the **utterance** of an unknown digit.

Utterance

Figure 5.2 contains a plot of an utterance of the digit "zero." The analysis of a complicated signal like this one often starts with computing some of the statistical measurements discussed in the last section. Other measurements used with

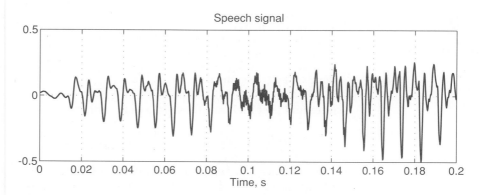

Figure 5.2 *Utterance of the word "zero."*

Magnitude

speech signals include the average **magnitude**, or average absolute value, which is computed as shown, where n is the number of data values:

$$\text{Average magnitude} = \frac{\sum_{k=0}^{n-1} |x_k|}{n} \tag{5.4}$$

Power

Another metric used in speech analysis is the average **power** of the signal, which is the average squared value:

$$\text{Average power} = \frac{\sum_{k=0}^{n-1} x_k^2}{n} \tag{5.5}$$

Zero crossings

The number of **zero crossings** in a speech signal is also a useful statistical measurement. This value is the number of times that the speech signal transitions from a negative to a positive value or from a positive value to a negative value; transition from a nonzero value to a zero value is not a zero crossing.

Write a program to read a speech signal from a data file named **zero.dat**. This file contains values that represent an utterance of the word "zero." Each line of the file contains a single value representing a measurement from the microphone taken in time increments of 0.0002 second, so 5000 measurements represent 1 second of data. The data file contains only valid data, with no header or trailer line; a maximum of 2500 values is contained in the file. Compute and print the following statistical measurements from the file: mean, standard deviation, variance, average power, average magnitude, and number of zero crossings.

1. PROBLEM DESCRIPTION

Compute the following statistical measurements for a speech utterance: mean, standard deviation, variance, average power, average magnitude, and number of zero crossings.

2. **INPUT/OUTPUT DESCRIPTION**

The I/O diagram shows the data file as the input and the statistical measurements as output.

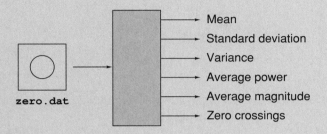

zero.dat

- Mean
- Standard deviation
- Variance
- Average power
- Average magnitude
- Zero crossings

3. **HAND EXAMPLE**

For a hand example, assume that the file contains the following values:

    2.5 8.2 -1.1 -0.2 1.5

Using a calculator, we can compute the following values:

$$\text{Mean} = \mu = \frac{(2.5 + 8.2 - 1.1 - 0.2 + 1.5)}{5}$$

$$= 2.18$$

$$\text{Variance} = [(2.5 - \mu)^2 + (8.2 - \mu)^2 + (-1.1 - \mu)^2$$

$$+ (-0.2 - \mu)^2 + (1.5 - \mu)^2]/4$$

$$= 13.307$$

$$\text{Standard deviation} = \sqrt{13.307}$$

$$= 3.648$$

$$\text{Average power} = \frac{[(2.5)^2 + (8.2)^2 + (-1.1)^2 + (-0.2)^2 + 1.5^2)]}{5}$$

$$= 15.398$$

$$\text{Average magnitude} = \frac{(|2.5| + |8.2| + |-1.1| + |-0.2| + |1.5|)}{5}$$

$$= 2.7$$

Number of zero crossings $= 2$

4.   **ALGORITHM DEVELOPMENT**

We first develop the decomposition outline because it divides the solution into a series of sequential steps.

Decomposition Outline

1. *Read the speech signal into an array.*
2. *Compute and print statistical measurements.*

Step 1 involves reading the data file and determining the number of data points. Step 2 involves computing and printing the statistical measurements, using the functions already developed when possible. The refinement in pseudocode for the **main** function and for the additional statistical functions needed is shown next; the structure chart was shown in Figure 4.1 on page 152 to illustrate an example of a **main** function that references several programmer-defined functions.

Refinement in Pseudocode

main: read speech signal from data file and
                        determine the number of points, n
               compute and print mean
               compute and print standard deviation
               compute and print variance
               compute and print average power
               compute and print average magnitude
               compute and print zero crossings

Additional Functions

ave_power(x, n):
               set sum to zero
               set k to zero
               while $k \leq n - 1$
                        add $(x[k])^2$ to sum
                        increment k by 1
               return sum/n

ave_magn(x, n):
               set sum to zero
               set k to zero
               while $k \leq n - 1$
                        add $|x[k]|$ to sum
                        increment k by 1
               return sum/n

crossings(x, n):

        set count to zero

        set k to zero

        while k ≤ n − 2

            if x[k] · x[k + 1] < 0

                increment count by 1

            increment k by 1

        return count

Note that the number of potential zero crossings for a set of **n** data points is **n-1** crossings because each crossing is determined by a pair of values. Thus, the last pair of values tested will be at subscripts **n-2** and **n-1**.

ch5_3.c
stat_lib.c
stat_lib.h
zero.dat

```
/*-------------------------------------------------------*/
/*  Program chapter5_3                                   */
/*                                                       */
/*  This program computes a set of statistical           */
/*  measurements from a speech signal.                   */

#include <stdio.h>
#include <stdlib.h>
#include <math.h>
#include "stat_lib.h"
#define MAXIMUM 2500
#define FILENAME "zero.dat"

main()
{
    /*  Declare variables and function prototypes.  */
    int k=0, npts;
    double speech[MAXIMUM];
    FILE *file_1;
    double ave_power(double x[], int n);
    double ave_magn(double x[], int n);
    int crossings(double x[], int n);

    /*  Read information from a data file.  */
    file_1 = fopen(FILENAME,"r");
    while ((fscanf(file_1,"%lf",&speech[k])) == 1)
    {
        k++;
    }
    npts = k;

    /*  Compute and print statistics.  */
    printf("Digit Statistics \n");
    printf("     mean: %f \n",mean(speech,npts));
    printf("     standard deviation: %f \n",
          std_dev(speech,npts));
    printf("     variance: %f \n",variance(speech,npts));
```

```
        printf("      average power: %f \n",
               ave_power(speech,npts));
        printf("      average magnitude: %f \n",
               ave_magn(speech,npts));
        printf("      zero crossings: %i \n",
               crossings(speech,npts));

        /*  Close file and exit program.  */
        fclose(file_1);
        return EXIT_SUCCESS;
}
/*-------------------------------------------------------*/
/*  This function returns the average power              */
/*  of an array x with n elements.                       */

double ave_power(double x[], int n)
{
        /*  Declare and initialize variables.  */
        int k;
        double sum=0;

        /*  Determine average power.  */
        for (k=0; k<=n-1; k++)
        {
           sum += x[k]*x[k];
        }

        /*  Return average power.  */
        return sum/n;
}
/*-------------------------------------------------------*/
/*  This function returns the average magnitude          */
/*  of an array x with n values.                         */

double ave_magn(double x[], int n)
{
        /*  Declare and initialize variables.  */
        int k;
        double sum=0;

        /*  Determine average magnitude.  */
        for (k=0; k<=n-1; k++)
        {
           sum += fabs(x[k]);
        }

        /*  Return average magnitude.  */
        return sum/n;
}
/*-------------------------------------------------------*/
```

```
/*  This function returns a count of the number    */
/*  of zero crossings in an array x with n values.  */

int crossings(double x[], int n)
{
   /*  Declare and initialize variables.  */
   int count=0, k;

   /*  Determine number of zero crossings.  */
   for (k=0; k<=n-2; k++)
   {
      if (x[k]*x[k+1] < 0)
         count++;
   }

   /*  Return number of zero crossings.  */
   return count;
}
/*-------------------------------------------------------*/
```

5.   TESTING

This program requires access to the **stat_lib.h** header file and to the **stat_lib.c** file developed in the previous section. The following values were computed for the utterance "zero" using the file **zero.dat**.

```
Digit Statistics
     mean:   0.002931
     standard deviation:   0.121763
     variance:   0.014826
     average power:   0.014820
     average magnitude:   0.089753
     zero crossings:   106
```

Modify!

ch5_3.c
stat_lib.c
stat_lib.h
two_a.dat
two_b.dat
two_c.dat

1.   Run this program using the files from the text diskette named **two_a.dat**, **two_b.dat**, and **two_c.dat**. These utterances are all of the word "two", but they are spoken by different people.

2.   Compare the program output from Problem 1 for the three files. The output illustrates some of the difficulty in designing speech-recognition systems that are speaker-independent.

5.4   Sorting Algorithms

Sorting

Sorting a group of data values is another operation that is routinely used when analyzing data. Entire texts are available that present many different sorting algorithms. One of the reasons that there are so many sorting algorithms is that there is not one "best" sorting algorithm. Some algorithms are faster if the data are already close to the correct order, but these algorithms may be very inefficient if the order is random, or is close to the opposite order. Therefore, in order to choose the best sorting algorithm for a particular application, you usually need to know something about the order of the original data. Rather than try to present a complete discussion of sorting algorithms, we present two algorithms in this text, and then refer you to reference [19] for more information. In this section, we present a selection sort that is simple to understand and simple to code in a function. In Chapter 6, we present a quicksort function that uses a recursive algorithm to sort a set of values; this algorithm is presented in Chapter 6 because it requires material presented in that chapter.

Selection sort

The **selection sort** algorithm begins by finding the minimum value and exchanging the minimum with the value in the first position in the array. Then, the algorithm finds the minimum value beginning with the second element, and exchanges this minimum with the second element. This process continues until reaching the next-to-last element, which is compared to the last element; the values are exchanged if they are out of order. At this point, the entire array of values is now in ascending order. This process is illustrated in the following sequences that reorder an array:

Original order:

5	3	12	8	1	9

Exchange the minimum with the value in the first position:

1	3	12	8	5	9

Exchange the next minimum with the value in the second position:

1	3	12	8	5	9

Exchange the next minimum with the value in the third position:

1	3	5	8	12	9

Exchange the next minimum with the value in the fourth position:

1	3	5	8	12	9

Exchange the next minimum with the value in the fifth position:

1	3	5	8	9	12

Array values are now in ascending order:

1	3	5	8	9	12

The steps in the following function are short, but it is still a good idea to go through this function using the data in this example. Follow the changes in the subscripts k, m, and j within the loops. Also, note that it takes three steps (not two) to exchange values in two variables. Because the function does not return a value, its return type is void.

sorts.c

```
/*-------------------------------------------------*/
/*  This function sorts an array with n elements    */
/*  into ascending order.                           */

void sort(double x[], int n)
{
   /*  Declare variables.  */
   int k, j, m;
   double hold;

   /*  Implement selection sort algorithm.  */
   for (k=0; k<=n-2; k++)
   {
      /*  Exchange minimum with next array value.  */
      m = k;
      for (j=k+1; j<=n-1; j++)
      {
         if (x[j] < x[m])
            m = j;
      }
      hold = x[m];
      x[m] = x[k];
      x[k] = hold;
   }

   /*  Void return.  */
   return;
}
/*-------------------------------------------------*/
```

To change this function into one that sorts an array in descending values, the inner loop should search for a maximum instead of a minimum.

The function prototype statement that should be used to refer to this sort function is

```
void sort(double x[], int n);
```

It is also important to note that this function modifies the original array. To keep the original order, an array should be copied into another array before this function is executed; then, the data are available in the original order and in the sorted order.

Modify!

sorts.c

1. Write a **main** function that initializes an array, then references this **sort** function, and then prints the array values in the new order.
2. Modify the **sort** function so that it sorts values in descending order instead of ascending order. Test the function with the program written in problem 1.

5.5 Two-Dimensional Arrays

A set of data values that is visualized as a row or column is easily represented by a one-dimensional array. However, there are many examples in which the best way to visualize a set of data is with a grid or a table of data, which has both rows and columns, as shown in this array, which has four rows and three columns:

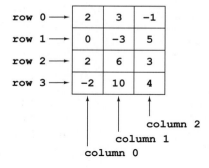

Two-dimensional array

In C, a grid or table of data is represented with a **two-dimensional array**. Each element in a two-dimensional array is referenced using an identifier followed by two subscripts—a row subscript and a column subscript. The subscript values for both rows and columns begin with 0, and each subscript has its own set of brackets. Thus, assuming that the previous array has an identifier **x**, then the value in position **x[2][1]** is 6. Common errors in array references include using parentheses instead of brackets, as in **x(2)(3)**, or using only one set of brackets or parentheses, as in **x[2,3]** or **x(2,3)**.

We can also visualize this grid or table of data as a one-dimensional array, each of whose elements is also an array. Thus, the array in the previous diagram can be interpreted as a one-dimensional array with four elements, each of which is a one-dimensional array with three elements:

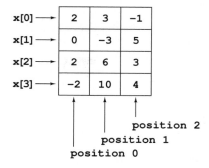

By using this representation, the notation `x[2][1]` can be interpreted as referring to position `[1]` within the one-dimensional array represented by `x[2]`; thus, the value of `x[2][1]` is 6. *In general, we prefer to discuss two-dimensional arrays in terms of a grid with rows and columns, as opposed to an array of arrays.*

Style

All values in an array must have the same type. An array cannot have a column of integers followed by a column of floating-point numbers, and so on.

DEFINITION AND INITIALIZATION

To define a two-dimensional array, we specify the number of rows and the number of columns in the declaration statement, with the row number first. Both the row number and the column number are in brackets, as shown in this statement:

```
int x[4][3];
```

A two-dimensional array can be initialized with a declaration statement. The values are specified in a sequence separated by commas, and each row is contained in braces. An additional set of braces is included around the complete set of values, as shown here:

```
int x[4][3] = {{2,3,-1},{0,-3,5},{2,6,3},{-2,10,4}};
```

If the initializing sequence is shorter than the array, then the rest of the values are initialized to zero. If the array is specified with the first subscript empty, but with an initialization sequence, the size is determined by the sequence. Thus the following statement also defines the array **x**:

```
int x[][3] = {{2,3,-1},{0,-3,5},{2,6,3},{-2,10,4}};
```

Style

Arrays can also be initialized with program statements. *For two-dimensional arrays, two nested `for` loops are usually required to initialize an array; i and j are commonly used as subscripts.* The following statements define and initialize an array such that each row contains the row number:

```
/*  Declare variables.  */
int i,j, t[5][4];
...
/*  Initialize array.  */
for (i=0; i<=4; i++)
}
   for (j=0; j<=3; j++)
   {
      t[i][j] = i;
   }
}
```

The values in the array **t** after these statements are executed follow:

0	0	0	0
1	1	1	1
2	2	2	2
3	3	3	3
4	4	4	4

Style

Two-dimensional arrays can also be initialized with values read from a data file. In this set of statements, we assume that a data file contains 50 temperature values that we read and store in the array. Symbolic constants **NROWS** and **NCOLS** are used to represent the number of rows and columns. *Changing the size of an array is easier to do when the numbers of rows and columns are specified as symbolic constants; otherwise, the change requires modifications to several statements.*

```
#define NROWS 10
#define NCOLS 5
#define FILENAME "engine.dat"
...
/*  Declare variables.  */
int i, j;
double temps[NROWS][NCOLS];
FILE *data_1;
...
/*  Open file and read data into array.  */
data_1 = fopen(FILENAME,"r");
for (i=0; i<=NROWS-1; i++)
{
   for (j=0; j<=NCOLS-1; j++)
   {
      fscanf(data_1,"%lf",&temps[i][j]);
   }
}
fclose(FILENAME);
```

Practice!

Show the contents of the arrays defined in each of the following sets of statements. Use a question mark to indicate an element that has not been initialized.

1.
```
int d[3][1]={{1},{4},{6}};
```

2.
```
int g[6][2]={{5,2},{-2,3}};
```

3.
```
float h[4][4]={{0,0}};
```

4.
```
int k, p[3][3]={{0,0,0});
...
for (k=0; k<=2; k++)
{
    p[k][k] = 1;
}
```

5.
```
int i, j, g[5][5];
...
for (i=0; i<=4; i++)
{
    for (j=0; j<=4; j++)
    {
        g[i][j] = i + j;
    }
}
```

6.
```
int i, j, g[5][5];
...
for (i=0; i<=4; i++)
{
    for (j=0; j<=4; j++)
    {
        g[i][j] = pow(-1,j);
    }
}
```

COMPUTATIONS AND OUTPUT

Computations and output with two-dimensional arrays must always specify two subscripts when referencing an array element. To illustrate, consider the following program that reads a data file containing power output for an electrical plant for a 10-week period. Each line of the data file contains seven values representing the daily power output for a week. The data are stored in a two-dimensional array, and then a report is printed giving the average power for the first day of the week during the period, the average power for the second day of the week during the period, and so on.

ch5_4.c
power1.dat

```
/*-----------------------------------------------------------*/
/*   Program chapter5_4                                      */
/*                                                           */
/*   This program computes power averages                    */
/*   over a 10-week period.                                  */

#include <stdio.h>
#include <stdlib.h>
#define NROWS 10
#define NCOLS 7
#define FILENAME "power1.dat"

main()
{
    /*  Declare variables.  */
    int i, j;
    double power[NROWS][NCOLS], col_sum;
    FILE *data1;

    /*  Open file and read data into array.  */
    data1 = fopen(FILENAME,"r");
    for (i=0; i<=NROWS-1; i++)
    {
        for (j=0; j<=NCOLS-1; j++)
        {
            fscanf(data1,"%lf",&power[i][j]);
        }
    }

    /*  Compute and print daily averages.  */
    for (j=0; j<=NCOLS-1; j++)
    {
        col_sum = 0;
        for (i=0; i<=NROWS-1; i++)
        {
            col_sum += power[i][j];
        }
        printf("Day %i: Average = %.2f \n",j+1,col_sum/NROWS);
    }

    /*  Close file and exit program.  */
    fclose(data1);
    return EXIT_SUCCESS;
}
/*-----------------------------------------------------------*/
```

Note that the daily averages are computed by adding each column, and then dividing the column sum by the number of rows (which is also the number of weeks). The column number is then used to compute the day number. A sample output from this program is as follows:

```
Day 1: Average = 238.4
Day 2: Average = 199.5
Day 3: Average = 274.8
Day 4: Average = 239.1
Day 5: Average = 277.0
Day 6: Average = 305.8
Day 7: Average = 276.1
```

Writing information from a two-dimensional array to a data file is similar to writing the information from a one-dimensional array. In both cases, a new line indicator must be used to specify when the values are to begin a new line. The following statements will write a set of distance measurements to a data file named **dist.dat**, with five values per line:

```c
/*  Declare variables.  */
int i, j;
double dist[20][5];
FILE *data_1;
...
/*  Write information from the array to a file.  */
data_1 = fopen("dist.dat","w");
for (i=0; i<=19; i++)
{
    for (j=0, j<=4; j++)
    {
        fprintf(data_1,"%f ",dist[i][j]);
    }
    fprintf(data_1,"\n");
}
```

The space after the conversion specifier in the **fprintf** statement is necessary in order that the values be separated by a space.

Practice!

Assume the following declaration for the array **g**:

```c
int i, j, g[3][3]={{0,0,0},{1,1,1},{2,2,2}};
```

Give the value of **sum** after each of the following sets of statements are executed.

1.
```c
sum = 0;
for (i=0; i<=2; i++)
{
    for (j=0; j<=2; j++)
    {
        sum += g[i][j];
    }
}
```

2.
```
sum = 1;
for (i=1; i<=2; i++)
{
    for (j=0; j<=1; j++)
    {
        sum *= g[i][j];
    }
}
```

3.
```
sum = 0;
for (j=0; j<=2; j++)
{
        sum -= g[2][j];
}
```

4.
```
sum = 0;
for (i=0; i<=2; i++)
{
        sum += g[i][1];
}
```

FUNCTION ARGUMENTS

When arrays are used as function parameters, the references are call-by-address instead of call-by-value. As discussed in Section 5.1 on one-dimensional arrays, this means that array references in a function refer to the original array and not to a copy of the array. Thus, we must be careful that we do not change values in the original array when we do not intend to make changes. Of course, an advantage of a call-by-address reference is that we can make changes in the array values, in addition to returning a value from the function call.

When using a one-dimensional array as a function argument, the function needs only the address of the array, which is specified by the array name; when using a two-dimensional array as a function argument, the function also needs information about the size of the array. In general, the function declaration and prototype statement should give complete information about the size of a two-dimensional array. To illustrate, suppose that we need to write a program that computes the sum of the elements in an array containing four rows and four columns. Computing this sum requires two nested loops, so the program will be more readable if we put the steps to compute the sum in a function. The program can then reference the function with a single statement, as in the following:

```
/*  Declare variables and function prototypes.  */
int a[4][4];
int sum(int x[4][4]);
...
/*  Use function to compute array sum.  */
printf("Array sum = %i \n",sum(a));
```

If we need to recompute the array sum in several places in the program, the function becomes even more effective. And, of course, if there are several different arrays of the same size, we can use the same function to compute their sums, as in the following:

```
/*  Declare variables and function prototypes.  */
int a[4][4], b[4][4];
int sum(int x[4][4]);
...
/*  Use function to compute array sums.  */
printf("Sum of a = %i \n",sum(a));
printf("Sum of b = %i \n",sum(b));
```

We now present the function referenced in these statements:

```
/*-------------------------------------------------------*/
/*  This function returns the sum of the values in      */
/*  an array with four rows and four columns.           */

int sum(int x[4][4])
{
   /*  Declare and initialize variables.  */
   int i, j, total=0;

   /*  Compute a sum of the array values.  */
   for (i=0; i<=3; i++)
   {
      for (j=0; j<=3; j++)
      {
         total += x[i][j];
      }
   }

   /*  Return sum of array values.  */
   return total;
}
/*-------------------------------------------------------*/
```

In this example, we included the numbers of rows and columns in the function definition and prototype. C allows us to omit the first subscript size, and thus the function definition and prototype could also have been the following statements:

```
/*  Declare variables and function prototypes.  */
int sum(int x[][4]);
```

Style

In general, we prefer listing both the row size and the column size of arrays in the formal argument list and in the function prototype for documentation purposes.

In a final example, we develop a function that computes a partial sum of the elements in an array. The elements to be summed are assumed to be in a subarray in the upper-left corner of the array. The arguments of the function include the original array, and the numbers of rows and columns in the subarray. The function prototype is

```
/*  function prototype  */
int partial_sum(int x[4][4], int m, int n);
```

Thus, if we want to sum the elements shown in the shaded area in the array **a** below, we would use the reference `partial_sum(a,2,3)`:

2	3	−1	9
0	−3	5	7
2	6	3	2
−2	10	4	6

This reference should then compute the sum of the elements in the subarray beginning in the upper-left corner, and consisting of two rows and three columns; the function should return a value of 6. This function follows:

```
/*-----------------------------------------------------------*/
/*  This function returns the sum of the values              */
/*  in a subarray of an array with four rows                 */
/*  and four columns.                                        */

int partial_sum(int x[4][4],int m, int n)
{
    /*  Declare and initialize variables.  */
    int i, j, total=0;

    /*  Compute a sum of subarray values.  */
    for (i=0; i<=m-1; i++)
    {
        for (j=0; j<=n-1; j++)
        {
            total += x[i][j];
        }
    }

    /*  Return sum of subarray values.  */
    return total;
}
/*-----------------------------------------------------------*/
```

When working with one-dimensional arrays, we did not have to specify the size of the array in the function; instead, we included an argument in the function definition that gave the number of values in the array. Thus the function could be used with arrays of different sizes. For example, in Section 4.2, Chapter 4, we developed a function to compute the average of a one-dimensional array.

To use the function to compute the mean (or average) of an array **a** with 10 elements, the reference would be **mean(a,10)**. If we want to compute the mean value of an array **y** with 50 elements, we use the reference **mean(y,50)**. To write a function that can be used with two-dimensional arrays of various sizes, it is necessary to use pointers as function arguments; this technique is discussed in Chapter 6.

Practice!

Assume that the following statement is from a **main** function:

```
int a[4][4] = {{2, 3, -1, 9}, {0, -3, 5, 7},
               {2, 6, 3, 2}, {-2, 10, 4, 6}};
```

Determine by hand the values of the following references to the **partial_sum** function developed in this section.

1.   **partial_sum(a,1,4);**
2.   **partial_sum(a,1,1);**
3.   **partial_sum(a,4,2);**
4.   **partial_sum(a,2,4);**

The next four sections contain examples that use two-dimensional arrays. Section 5.6 contains an application related to terrain navigation; Section 5.7 uses two-dimensional arrays to represent matrices; and Sections 5.8 and 5.9 discuss and develop a solution to a system of simultaneous equations using a two-dimensional array to store the equation coefficients.

5.6   Problem Solving Applied: Terrain Navigation

Terrain navigation is a key component in the design of remotely piloted vehicles (RPVs); these vehicles can travel on land, such as a robot or a car, or they can fly above the land, as in a drone or a plane. An RPV system contains an onboard computer that has stored the terrain information for the area in which it is to be operated. By knowing at any time where it is (perhaps with the aid of a global positioning system [GPS] receiver), the vehicle can then select the best path to get to a designated spot. If the destination changes, the vehicle can refer to its internal maps to recompute the new path.

The computer software that guides these vehicles must be tested over a variety of land formations and topologies. Elevation information for large grids of land is available in computer databases. One way of measuring the "difficulty" of a land grid with respect to terrain navigation is to determine the number of peaks in the grid, where a peak is a point that has lower elevations all around it. For this problem we will assume that the values in the four positions shown below are the ones adjacent to grid position [m] [n] for puposes of determining if the value in grid position [m] [n] is a peak:

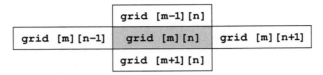

Write a program that reads elevation data from a data file named **grid1.dat**, and then prints the number of peaks and their locations. Assume that the first line of the data file contains the number of rows and the number of columns for the grid of information. These values are then followed by the elevation values, in row order. The maximum size grid is 25 rows by 25 columns.

1.   **PROBLEM STATEMENT**

Determine and print the number of peaks and their locations in an elevation grid.

2.   **INPUT/OUTPUT DESCRIPTION**

The I/O diagram shows that the input is a file containing the elevation data, and that the output is a listing of the locations of the peaks.

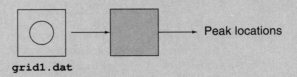

3.   **HAND EXAMPLE**

Assume that the following data represent elevation for a grid that has six points along the side and seven points along the top. The peaks have been underlined in the data.

5039	5127	5238	5259	5248	5310	5299
5150	5392	5410	5401	5320	5820	5321
5290	_5560_	5490	5421	5530	_5831_	5210
5110	5429	5430	5411	5459	5630	5319
4920	5129	4921	_5821_	4722	4921	5129
5023	5129	4822	4872	4794	4862	4245

To specify the location of the peaks, we need to assign an addressing scheme to the data. Because we are going to be implementing this solution in C, we choose its two-dimensional array subscripting notation. Thus, we assume that the top left corner is position [0][0], and that the row numbers increase by 1 as we move down the page, and that the column numbers increase by 1 as we move to the right. These peaks then occur at positions [2][1], [2][5], and [4][3].

To determine the peaks, we compare a potential peak with its four neighboring points. If all four neighboring points are less that the potential peak, then the potential peak is a real peak. Note that the points on the edges of the array or grid cannot be potential peaks because we do not have elevation information on all four sides of the points.

4.   ALGORITHM DEVELOPMENT

We first develop the decomposition outline because it divides the solution into a series of sequential steps.

Decomposition Outline
1. *Read the terrain data into an array.*
2. *Determine and print the location of the peaks.*

Step 1 involves reading the data file and storing the information in a two-dimensional array. Step 2 is a loop that evaluates all potential peaks, and prints their locations if they are determined to be real peaks. There are not obvious candidates for additional functions, so we develop the refinement in pseudcode using only a `main` function:

Refinement in Pseudocode

```
main:    read nrows and ncols from the data file
         read the terrain data into an array
         set i to 1
         while i <= nrows − 2
             set j to 1
             while j <= ncols − 2
                 if grid[i][j] < its four neighbors
                     print peak location
                 increment j by 1
             increment i by 1
```

The steps in the pseudocode are now detailed enough to convert to C.

ch5_5.c
grid1.dat

```
/*-----------------------------------------------------*/
/*   Program chapter5_5                                 */
/*                                                      */
/*   This program determines the locations of           */
/*   peaks in an elevation grid of data.                */

#include <stdio.h>
#include <stdlib.h>
#define N 25
#define FILENAME "grid1.dat"

main()
{
   /*  Declare variables.  */
   int nrows, ncols, i, j;
   double elevation[N][N];
   FILE *file1;

   /*  Read information from data file into array.  */
   file1 = fopen(FILENAME,"r");
   fscanf(file1,"%i %i",&nrows,&ncols);
   for (i=0; i<=nrows-1; i++)
   {
      for (j=0; j<=ncols-1; j++)
      {
         fscanf(file1,"%lf",&elevation[i][j]);
      }
   }

   /*  Determine and print peak locations. */
   printf("Top left point defined as row 0, column 0 \n");
   for (i=1; i<=nrows-2; i++)
   {
      for (j=1; j<=ncols-2; j++)
      {
         if ((elevation[i-1][j]<elevation[i][j]) &&
             (elevation[i+1][j]<elevation[i][j]) &&
             (elevation[i][j-1]<elevation[i][j]) &&
             (elevation[i][j+1]<elevation[i][j]))
                printf("Peak at row: %i column: %i \n",i,j);
      }
   }

   /* Exit program.  */
   return EXIT_SUCCESS;
}
/*-----------------------------------------------------*/
```

5.   TESTING

The following output was printed using a data file that corresponds to the hand example. Recall that this file must contain a special first line that specifies the number of rows and columns in the elevation data.

```
Top Left point defined as row 0, column 0
Peak at row: 2 column: 1
Peak at row: 2 column: 5
Peak at row: 4 column: 3
```

Modify!

ch5_5.c
grid1.dat

Modify the peak-finding program to determine the following information for a grid of elevation data.

1. Print a count of the number of peaks in the grid.
2. Print the location of valleys instead of peaks. Assume that a valley is a point with an elevation lower than the four surrounding elevations.
3. Find and print the location and elevation of the highest point and the lowest point in the elevation data.
4. Assuming that the distance between points in a vertical and horizontal direction is 100 feet, give the location of the peaks in feet from the lower left corner of the grid.
5. Use all eight neighboring points in determining a peak instead of only four neighboring points.

5.7   Matrices and Vectors*

Matrix

A **matrix** is a set of numbers arranged in a rectangular grid with rows and columns, as shown in the following matrix with four rows and three columns; the size of this matrix is also specified as 4 × 3:

$$\mathbf{A} = \begin{bmatrix} -1 & 0 & 0 \\ 1 & 1 & 0 \\ 1 & -2 & 3 \\ 0 & 2 & 1 \end{bmatrix}$$

Note that the values within a matrix are written within large brackets. A matrix with one row is called a **row vector**, and a matrix with one column is called a **column vector.** The term **vector** by itself does not distinguish between a row vector and a column vector.

Vector

In mathematical notation, matrices are usually given names with uppercase boldface letters. To refer to individual elements in the matrix, the row and column number are used, with both the row and column numbers starting with the value 1. In formal mathematical notation, the uppercase name refers to the entire matrix, and the lowercase name with subscripts refer to a specific element. Thus,

*Optional section.

Square matrix

by using the matrix **A**, the value of $a_{3,2}$ is -2. If a matrix has the same number of rows and columns, it is a **square matrix**.

A two-dimensional array can be used to store a matrix, but we must be careful translating equations in matrix notation into C statements because of the difference in subscripting. Matrix notation assumes that the row and column numbers begin with the value 1, whereas C statements assume that the row and column numbers of a two-dimensional array begin with the value 0. Although a vector could be stored as a two-dimensional array with either one row or one column, vectors are more commonly stored as one-dimensional arrays and thus do not usually keep the distinction of a row vector or a column vector.

Matrix operations are frequently used in engineering problem solutions, so we now present common operations with matrices and vectors. C statements for performing some of the operations are included; the problems at the end of the chapter relate to developing C statements for the remaining operations.

DOT PRODUCT

Dot product

The **dot product** is a number computed from two vectors of the same size. This value is the sum of the products of the values in corresponding positions in the vectors, as shown in this summation equation, which assumes that there are n elements in the vectors **A** and **B**:

$$\text{Dot product} = \mathbf{A} \cdot \mathbf{B} = \sum_{k=1}^{n} a_k b_k$$

To illustrate, assume that **A** and **B** are the following vectors:

$$\mathbf{A} = [4 \quad -1 \quad 3] \qquad \mathbf{B} = [-2 \quad 5 \quad 2]$$

The dot product is then

$$\mathbf{A} \cdot \mathbf{B} = 4 \cdot (-2) + (-1) \cdot 5 + 3 \cdot 2$$
$$= (-8) + (-5) + 6$$
$$= -7$$

Inner product

The dot product is also called an **inner product**.

In C, we can compute the dot product of two one-dimensional vectors with a function:

matrix.c

```
/*------------------------------------------------------*/
/*   This function returns the dot product              */
/*   of two vectors.                                    */

double dot_product(double a[], double b[], int n)
{
    /*  Declare and initialize variables.  */
    int k;
    double sum=0;
```

```
/*   Compute dot product.   */
for (k=0; k<=n-1; k++)
{
    sum += a[k]*b[k];
}

/*   Return dot product.   */
return sum;
}
/*-------------------------------------------------------*/
```

Note that the equation subscripts of 1 to n were changed to 0 to $n - 1$ for the C program.

DETERMINANT

Determinant

The **determinant** of a matrix is a value computed from the entries in the matrix. Determinants have various applications in engineering, including computing inverses and solving systems of simultaneous equations. For a 2×2 matrix $\mathbf{A}$, the determinant is defined to be the following:

$$\text{Determinant of } \mathbf{A} = |\mathbf{A}| = a_{1,1}a_{2,2} - a_{2,1}a_{1,2}$$

Therefore, the determinant of $\mathbf{A}$ is equal to 8 for the following matrix:

$$\mathbf{A} = \begin{bmatrix} 1 & 3 \\ -1 & 5 \end{bmatrix}$$

For a 3×3 matrix $\mathbf{A}$, the determinant is defined to be the following:

$$|\mathbf{A}| = a_{1,1}a_{2,2}a_{3,3} + a_{1,2}a_{2,3}a_{3,1} + a_{1,3}a_{2,1}a_{3,2} - a_{3,1}a_{2,2}a_{1,3}$$

$$- a_{3,2}a_{2,3}a_{1,1} - a_{3,3}a_{2,1}a_{1,2}$$

If $\mathbf{A}$ is the following matrix:

$$\mathbf{A} = \begin{bmatrix} 1 & 3 & 0 \\ -1 & 5 & 2 \\ 1 & 2 & 1 \end{bmatrix}$$

then $|\mathbf{A}|$ is equal to $5 + 6 + 0 - 0 - 4 - (-3)$, or 10.

A more involved process is necessary for computing determinants of matrices with more than three rows and columns. This process is discussed in the problems at the end of this chapter.

TRANSPOSE

Transpose

The **transpose** of a matrix is a new matrix in which the rows of the original matrix are the columns of the new matrix. We use a superscript T after a matrix name to refer to the transpose. For example, consider the following matrix and its transpose:

$$\mathbf{B} = \begin{bmatrix} 2 & 5 & 1 \\ 7 & 3 & 8 \\ 4 & 5 & 21 \\ 16 & 13 & 0 \end{bmatrix} \qquad \mathbf{B}^T = \begin{bmatrix} 2 & 7 & 4 & 16 \\ 5 & 3 & 5 & 13 \\ 1 & 8 & 21 & 0 \end{bmatrix}$$

If we consider a couple of the elements, we see that the value in position (3, 1), has now moved to position (1, 3), and the value in position (4, 2) has now moved to position (2, 4). In fact, we have interchanged the row and column subscript so that we are moving the value in position (i, j) to position (j, i). Also, note that the size of the transpose is different than the size of the original matrix unless the original is a square matrix.

We now develop a function that generates the transpose of a matrix. The formal arguments of the function must include two-dimensional arrays that represent the original matrix and the matrix that is to contain the transpose of the original matrix. To allow some flexibility with this function, we assume that symbolic constants have been defined that specify the number of rows and the number of columns in the original matrix; these symbolic constants are **NROWS** and **NCOLS**. Because using a symbolic constant is equivalent to using the value it has been given, we can then use **NROWS** and **NCOLS** in the array definition and in the prototype statement. Note that the function does not return a value; hence, the return type is **void**. Also note that the symbolic constants **NROWS** and **NCOLS** must be defined in a program that uses this function:

matrix.c

```
/*-------------------------------------------------*/
/*   This function generates a matrix transpose.   */
/*   NROWS and NCOLS are symbolic constants        */
/*   that must be defined in the calling program.  */

void transpose(int b[NROWS][NCOLS], int bt[NCOLS][NROWS])
{
    /*  Declare variables.  */
    int i, j;

    /*  Transfer values to the transpose matrix.  */
    for (i=0; i<=NROWS-1; i++)
    {
        for (j=0; j<=NCOLS-1; j++)
        {
            bt[j][i] = b[i][j];
        }
    }

    /*  Void return.  */
    return;
}
/*-------------------------------------------------*/
```

MATRIX ADDITION AND SUBTRACTION

The addition (or subtraction) of two matrices is performed by adding (or subtracting) the elements in corresponding positions in the matrices. Therefore, matrices that are added (or subtracted) must be the same size; the result of the operation is another matrix of the same size. Consider the following matrices:

$$\mathbf{A} = \begin{bmatrix} 2 & 5 & 1 \\ 0 & 3 & -1 \end{bmatrix} \qquad \mathbf{B} = \begin{bmatrix} 1 & 0 & 2 \\ -1 & 4 & -2 \end{bmatrix}$$

Several matrix sums and differences follow:

$$\mathbf{A} + \mathbf{B} = \begin{bmatrix} 3 & 5 & 3 \\ -1 & 7 & -3 \end{bmatrix} \quad \mathbf{A} - \mathbf{B} = \begin{bmatrix} 1 & 5 & -1 \\ 1 & -1 & 1 \end{bmatrix} \quad \mathbf{B} - \mathbf{A} = \begin{bmatrix} -1 & -5 & 1 \\ -1 & 1 & -1 \end{bmatrix}$$

MATRIX MULTIPLICATION

Matrix multiplication

Matrix multiplication is not computed by multiplying corresponding elements of the two matrices. The value in position $c_{i,j}$ of the product $\mathbf{C}$ of two matrices $\mathbf{A}$ and $\mathbf{B}$ is the dot product of row i of the first matrix and column j of the second matrix, as shown in this summation equation:

$$c_{i,j} = \sum_{k=1}^{N} a_{ik} b_{kj}$$

Since the dot product requires that the vectors have the same number of elements, then the first matrix ($\mathbf{A}$) must have the same number of elements in each row as there are in the columns of the second matrix ($\mathbf{B}$). Thus, if $\mathbf{A}$ and $\mathbf{B}$ both have five rows and five columns, their product has five rows and five columns. Furthermore, for these matrices, we can compute both $\mathbf{AB}$ and $\mathbf{BA}$, but, in general, they will not be equal.

If $\mathbf{A}$ has two rows and three columns, and $\mathbf{B}$ has three rows and three columns, the product $\mathbf{AB}$ will have two rows and three columns. To illustrate, consider the following matrices:

$$\mathbf{A} = \begin{bmatrix} 2 & 5 & 1 \\ 0 & 3 & -1 \end{bmatrix} \qquad \mathbf{B} = \begin{bmatrix} 1 & 0 & 2 \\ -1 & 4 & -2 \\ 5 & 2 & 1 \end{bmatrix}$$

The first element in the product $\mathbf{C} = \mathbf{AB}$ is

$$\begin{aligned} c_{1,1} &= \sum_{k=1}^{3} a_{1k} b_{k1} \\ &= a_{1,1} b_{1,1} + a_{1,2} b_{2,1} + a_{1,3} b_{3,1} \\ &= 2 \cdot 1 + 5 \cdot (-1) + 1 \cdot 5 \\ &= 2 \end{aligned}$$

Similarly, we can compute the rest of the elements in the product of **A** and **B**:

$$\mathbf{AB} = \mathbf{C} = \begin{bmatrix} 2 & 22 & -5 \\ -8 & 10 & -7 \end{bmatrix}$$

In this example, we cannot compute **BA**, because **B** does not have the same number of elements in each row as **A** has in each column.

An easy way to decide if a matrix product exists is to write the sizes of the two matrices side by side. If the two inside numbers are the same, the product exists; the size of the product is determined by the two outside numbers. To illustrate, in the previous example, the size of **A** is 2×3 and the size of **B** is 3×3. Therefore, if we want to compute **AB**, we write the sizes side by side:

$$2 \times 3 \qquad 3 \times 3$$

The two inner numbers are both the value 3, so **AB** exists, and its size is determined by the two outer numbers, 2×3. If we want to compute **BA** we again write the sizes side by side:

$$3 \times 3 \qquad 2 \times 3$$

The two inner numbers are not the same, so **BA** does not exist.

We now present a function to compute the product $\mathbf{C} = \mathbf{AB}$. In this function, the arrays are each of size $\mathbf{N} \times \mathbf{N}$, where $\mathbf{N}$ is a symbolic constant:

matrix.c

```
/*-----------------------------------------------------------*/
/*  This function performs a matrix multiplication     */
/*  of two NxN matrices using sums of products.        */
/*  N is a symbolic constant that must be defined      */
/*  in the calling program.                            */

void matrix_mult(int a[N][N], int b[N][N], int c[N][N])
{
   /*  Declare variables.  */
   int i, j, k;

   /*  Compute sums of products.  */
   for (i=0; i<=N-1; i++)
   {
      for (j=0; j<=N-1; j++)
      {
         c[i][j] = 0;
         for (k=0; k<=N-1; k++)
         {
            c[i][j] += a[i][k]*b[k][j];
         }
      }
   }
   /*  Void return.  */
   return;
}
/*-----------------------------------------------------------*/
```

Practice!

Use the following matrices and vectors to evaluate by hand the expressions in these problems. Then write programs to test your answers using the functions developed in this section. Assume that the functions are contained in a file `matrix.c`.

$$A = \begin{bmatrix} 2 & 1 \\ 0 & -1 \\ 3 & 0 \end{bmatrix} \qquad B = \begin{bmatrix} -2 & 2 \\ -1 & 5 \end{bmatrix}$$

$$C = \begin{bmatrix} 3 & 2 \\ -1 & -2 \\ 0 & 2 \end{bmatrix} \qquad D = [1 \quad 2]$$

1. $D \cdot D$
2. $|B|$
3. $C^T + A^T$
4. DB
5. $B(C^T)$
6. $(CB)D^T$

The problems at the end of the chapter use the matrix operations discussed in this section, and also define additional matrix operations.

5.8 Numerical Technique: Solution to Simultaneous Equations*

The need to solve a system of simultaneous equations occurs frequently in engineering problems. A number of methods exist for solving a system of equations, and each method has its advantages and disadvantages. In this section, we present the Gauss elimination method of solving a set of **simultaneous linear equations**; the equations are called linear equations because the equations contain only linear (degree 1) terms such as x, y, and z. However, before we present the details of this technique, we first present a graphical interpretation of the solution to a set of equations.

Simultaneous linear equations

GRAPHICAL INTERPRETATION

A linear equation with two variables, such as $2x - y = 3$, defines a straight line, and is often written in the form $y = mx + b$, where m represents the slope of the line, and b represents the y intercept. Thus, $2x - y = 3$ can also be written as $y = 2x - 3$. If we have two linear equations, they can represent two different lines that intersect in a single point, they can represent two parallel lines that never in-

*Optional section.

tersect, or they can represent the same line; these possibilities are shown in Figure 5.3. Equations that represent two intersecting lines can be easily identified because they will have different slopes, as in $y = 2x - 3$ and $y = -x + 3$. Equations that represent two parallel lines will have the same slope but different y intercepts, as in $y = 2x - 3$ and $y = 2x + 1$. Equations that represent the same line have the same slope and y intercept, as in $y = 2x - 3$ and $3y = 6x - 9$.

If a linear equation contains three variables, x, y, and z, then it represents a plane in three-dimensional space. If we have two equations with three variables, they can represent two planes that intersect in a straight line, they can represent

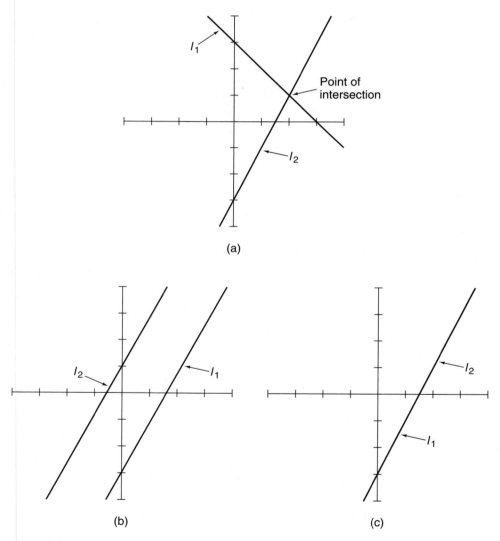

Figure 5.3 *Two lines.*

two parallel planes, or they can represent the same plane; these possibilities are shown in Figure 5.4. If we have three equations with three variables, the three planes can intersect in a single point, they can intersect in a plane, they can have no common intersection point, or they can represent the same plane. Examples of the possibilities that exist if the three equations define three different planes are shown in Figure 5.5.

    These ideas can be extended to more than three variables, although it is harder to visualize the corresponding situations. We call the set of points defined by an equation with more than three variables a **hyperplane**. In general, we consider a set of m linear equations that contain n unknowns, where each equation defines a hyperplane that is not identical to another hyperplane in the set of equations. If $m < n$, then the system is underspecified, and a unique solution does not exist. If $m = n$, then a unique solution will exist if none of the equations represents parallel hyperplanes. If $m > n$, then the system is overspecified and a unique solution does not exist. A set of equations is also called a **system of equations**. A system with a unique solution is called a **nonsingular** system of equations, and a system with no unique solution is called a singular set of equations.

Hyperplane

System of equations
Nonsingular

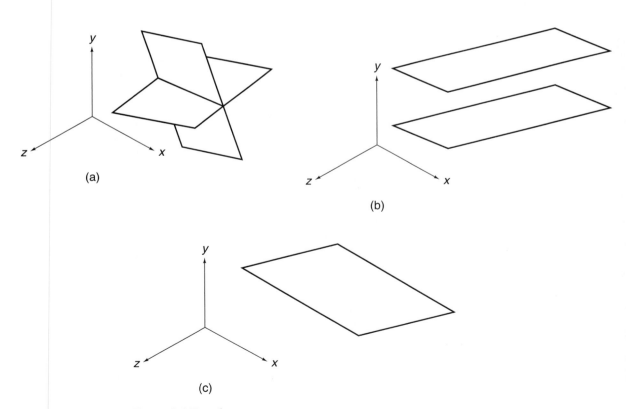

(a)

(b)

(c)

Figure 5.4 *Two planes.*

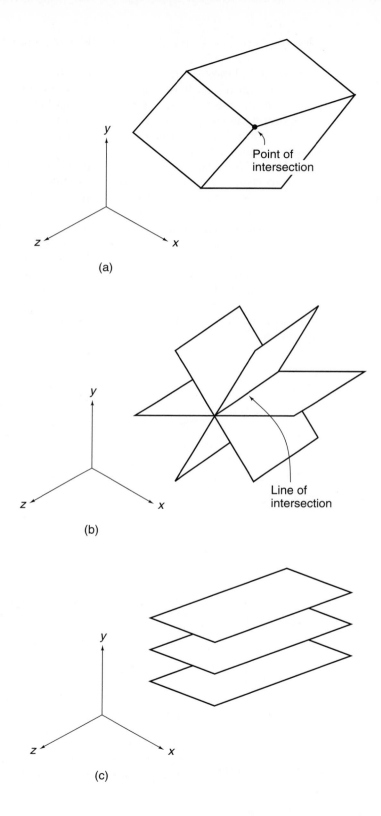

(a)

(b)

(c)

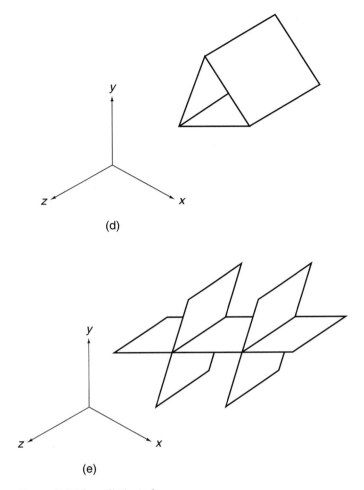

(d)

(e)

Figure 5.5 *Three distinct planes.*

As a specific example, consider this system of equations:

$$3x + 2y - z = 10$$
$$-x + 3y + 2z = 5$$
$$x - y - z = -1$$

The solution to this set of equations is the point $(-2, 5, -6)$. Substitute these values in each of the questions to confirm that this point is a solution to the set of equations.

The material in the previous section on matrices is not required for the development of the solution presented in this section. However, if you did cover that material, it is interesting to observe that a system of linear equations can be expressed in terms of a matrix multiplication. To illustrate, let the information in the previous equations be expressed using the following matrices:

$$\mathbf{A} = \begin{bmatrix} 3 & 2 & -1 \\ -1 & 3 & 2 \\ 1 & -1 & -1 \end{bmatrix} \qquad \mathbf{X} = \begin{bmatrix} x \\ y \\ z \end{bmatrix} \qquad \mathbf{B} = \begin{bmatrix} 10 \\ 5 \\ -1 \end{bmatrix}$$

Then, using matrix multiplication, the system of equations can be written in this form:

$$\mathbf{AX} = \mathbf{B}$$

Go through the multiplication to convince yourself that this matrix equation yields the original set of equations.

In many engineering problems, we are interested in determining if a common solution exists to a system of equations. If the common solution exists, then we want to determine it. In the next part of this section, we present the Gauss elimination technique for solving a set of simultaneous linear equations.

GAUSS ELIMINATION

Before presenting a general description of the Gauss elimination technique, we illustrate the technique with a specific example, using the set of equations presented earlier:

$$3x + 2y - z = 10 \qquad \text{(first equation)}$$

$$-x + 3y + 2z = 5 \qquad \text{(second equation)}$$

$$x - y - z = -1 \qquad \text{(third equation)}$$

The first step is an **elimination** step in which the first variable is eliminated from each equation that follows the first equation. This elimination is achieved by adding a scaled form of the first equation to each of the other equations. The term involving the first variable, x, in the second equation is $-x$. Therefore, if we multiply the first equation by 1/3, and add it to equation 2, we obtain a new equation in which the x variable has been eliminated:

$$-x + 3y + 2z = 5 \qquad \text{(second equation)}$$

$$\underline{x + \tfrac{2}{3}y - \tfrac{1}{3}z = \tfrac{10}{3} \qquad \text{(first equation times } \tfrac{1}{3})}$$

$$0x + \tfrac{11}{3}y + \tfrac{5}{3}z = \tfrac{25}{3} \qquad \text{(sum)}$$

The modified set of equations is then:

$$3x + 2y - z = 10$$

$$0x + \tfrac{11}{3}y + \tfrac{5}{3}z = \tfrac{25}{3}$$

$$x - y - z = -1$$

We now eliminate the first variable from the third equation, using a similar process:

$$x - \ y - \ z = -1 \qquad \text{(third equation)}$$

$$-x - \tfrac{2}{3}y + \tfrac{1}{3}z = -\tfrac{10}{3} \qquad \text{(first equation times } -\tfrac{1}{3})$$

$$0x - \tfrac{5}{3}y - \tfrac{2}{3}z = -\tfrac{13}{3} \qquad \text{(sum)}$$

The modified set of equations is then:

$$3x + \ 2y - \ z = 10$$

$$0x + \tfrac{11}{3}y + \tfrac{5}{3}z = \tfrac{25}{3}$$

$$0x - \tfrac{5}{3}y - \tfrac{2}{3}z = -\tfrac{13}{3}$$

We have now eliminated the first variable in all equations except for the first equation.

The next step is to eliminate the second variable in all equations except for the first and second equations, by adding the equations to a scaled form of the second equation:

$$0x - \tfrac{5}{3}y - \tfrac{2}{3}z = -\tfrac{13}{3} \qquad \text{(third equation)}$$

$$0x + \tfrac{5}{3}y + \tfrac{25}{33}z = \tfrac{125}{33} \qquad \text{(second equation times } \tfrac{5}{11})$$

$$0x + 0y + \tfrac{3}{33}z = -\tfrac{18}{33} \qquad \text{(sum)}$$

The modified set of equations is then

$$3x + \ 2y - \ z = 10$$

$$0x + \tfrac{11}{3}y + \ \tfrac{5}{3}z = \tfrac{25}{3}$$

$$0x + \ 0y + \tfrac{3}{33}z = -\tfrac{18}{33}$$

Because there are no equations following the third equation, this part of the algorithm is completed.

We now perform a **back substitution** to determine the solution to the equations. The last equation has only one variable, so we can multiply the equation by a scale factor chosen to make the variable's coefficient equal to 1. Thus, we multiply the last equation by $\tfrac{33}{3}$, or 11, giving

$$0x + 0y + z = -6$$

This value of z is substituted in the next-to-last equation, giving

$$0x + \tfrac{11}{3}y + \tfrac{5}{3}(-6) = \tfrac{25}{3}$$

Reducing the equation so that all constant terms are on the right side, we have

$$0x + \tfrac{11}{3}y = \tfrac{55}{3}$$

This equation has only one variable, so we now multiply it by a scale factor chosen to make the new coefficient equal to 1:

$$0x + y = 5$$

We back up to the next equation, which is the last equation in this example:

$$3x + 2y - z = 10$$

Substituting the values already determined, we have

$$3x + 2(5) - (-6) = 10$$

or

$$3x = -6$$

Thus, the value of x is -2.

The Gauss elimination technique thus has two parts—elimination and back substitution. First, the equations are modified such that the kth variable is eliminated in all equations following the kth equation. Then, starting with the last equation, we compute the value of the last variable. Then, using this value and the next-to-last equation, we compute the value of the next-to-last variable. This back substitution continues until we have determined the values of all the variables. The system is **ill-conditioned** or does not have a unique solution if all the coefficients for a variable are zero or are very close to zero.

Ill-conditioned

A process called **pivoting** can be applied to improve the accuracy of Gauss elimination. Row pivoting involves reordering the rows before performing Gauss elimination, and column pivoting involves reordering the columns before performing the process. Complete pivoting involves reordering both rows and columns. These processes are discussed in the problems at the end of the chapter.

Practice!

Use the Gauss elimination numerical technique to find the solution to the following sets of simultaneous linear equations.

1. $\begin{aligned} -2x + y &= -3 \\ x + y &= 3 \end{aligned}$

2. $\begin{aligned} 3x + 5y + 2z &= 8 \\ 2x + 3y - z &= 1 \\ x - 2y - 3z &= -1 \end{aligned}$

5.9   Problem Solving Applied: Electrical Circuit Analysis*

The analysis of an electrical circuit frequently involves finding the solution to a set of simultaneous equations. These equations are often derived using either current equations that describe the currents entering and leaving a node or using voltage equations that describe the voltages around mesh loops in the circuit. For example, consider the circuit shown in Figure 5.6. The three equations that describe the voltages around the three loops are the following:

$$
\begin{array}{ccccc}
-V_1 & + & R_1 i_1 & + & R_2(i_1 - i_2) & = 0 \\
R_2(i_2 - i_1) & + & R_3 i_2 & + & R_4(i_2 - i_3) & = 0 \\
R_4(i_3 - i_2) & + & R_5 i_3 & + & V_2 & = 0
\end{array}
$$

If we assume that the values of the resistors (R_1, R_2, R_3, R_4, and R_5) and the voltage sources (V_1 and V_2) are known, then the unknowns in the system of equations are the mesh currents (i_1, i_2, and i_3). We can then rearrange the system of equations to the following form:

$$
\begin{array}{ccccc}
(R_1 + R_2)i_1 & - & R_2 i_2 & + & 0i_3 & = V_1 \\
-R_2 i_1 & + & (R_2 + R_3 + R_4)i_2 & - & R_4 i_3 & = 0 \\
0i_1 & - & R_4 i_2 & + & (R_4 + R_5)i_3 & = -V_2
\end{array}
$$

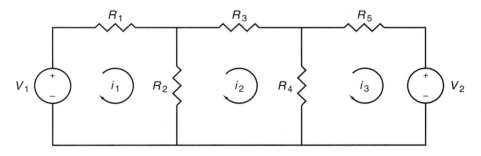

Figure 5.6 *Circuit with two voltage sources.*

Write a program that allows the user to enter the values of the five resistors and the values of the two voltage sources. The program should then compute the three mesh currents.

1.   PROBLEM DESCRIPTION

Compute the three mesh currents in the circuit shown in Figure 5.6.

2.   INPUT/OUTPUT DESCRIPTION

The I/O diagram shows that the resistor values and the voltage values are the input values. The three mesh currents are the output values.

*Optional section.

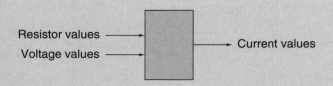

3.   HAND EXAMPLE

By using the resistor values and the voltage values, a system of three equations can be defined using this rearranged set of equations from the problem definition:

$$
\begin{aligned}
(R_1 + R_2)i_1 &- R_2 i_2 &+ 0 i_3 &= V_1 \\
-R_2 i_1 &+ (R_2 + R_3 + R_4)i_2 &- R_4 i_3 &= 0 \\
0 i_1 &- R_4 i_2 &+ (R_4 + R_5)i_3 &= -V_2
\end{aligned}
$$

For example, suppose that each of the resistor values is 1 ohm, and that both of the voltage sources are 5 volts. Then, the corresponding set of equations is the following:

$$
\begin{aligned}
2i_1 &- i_2 &+ 0 i_3 &= 5 \\
-i_1 &+ 3 i_2 &- i_3 &= 0 \\
0 i_1 &- i_2 &+ 2 i_3 &= -5
\end{aligned}
$$

Once the system of equations is determined, the solution follows the steps illustrated in the hand example in the previous section. For this set of equations, the solution is $i_1 = 2.5$, $i_2 = 0$, and $i_3 = -2.5$.

4.   ALGORITHM DEVELOPMENT

We first develop the decomposition outline because it breaks the solution into a series of sequential steps.

Decomposition Outline

1. *Read the resistor values and the voltage values.*
2. *Specify the coefficients for the system of equations.*
3. *Perform Gauss elimination to determine currents.*
4. *Print currents*

In step 1, we read the information necessary to specify the circuit values, and in step 2, we use this information to specify the coefficients for the system of equations. Then, for step 3, we develop the details of the elimination and back substitution steps. To keep the **main** function short and readable, functions are used for both the elimination and back substitution. The structure chart for this solution was used in Figure 4.1 on page 152.

The coefficients of the simultaneous equations are stored in a two-dimensional array; the solution is stored in a one-dimensional array. The variable **index** indicates which variable is being eliminated in the **elimination** function; this variable ranges from 0 to $n - 1$ to match the subscripting in C.

The algorithm for Gauss elimination is a difficult algorithm to describe in pseudocode because of the detailed subscripting that must be specified. Go through this pseudocode with the hand example to be sure that you are comfortable with the subscript handling.

Refinement in Pseudocode

main: *read resistor values and voltage values*
              specify array coefficients, a[i][j]
              set index to zero
              while index$<= n - 2$
                      eliminate(a,n,index)
                      increment index by 1
              back_substitute(a,n,soln)
              print current values

eliminate(a,n,index):
              set row to index $+ 1$
              while row $< = n - 1$

                      set scale_factor to $\dfrac{-a[row][index]}{a[index][index]}$
                      set a[row][index] to zero
                      set col to index $+ 1$
                      while col $< = n$
                              add a[index][col] $\cdot$ scale_factor
                                      to a[row][col]
                              increment col by 1
                      increment row by 1

back_substitute(a,n,soln):

              set soln[n $- 1$] to $\dfrac{a[n - 1][n]}{a[n - 1][n - 1]}$

              set row to n $- 2$
              while row $> = 0$
                      set col to n $- 1$
                      while col $> = row + 1$
                              subtract soln[col] $\cdot$ a[row][col]
                                      from a[row][n]
                              subtract 1 from col
                      set soln[row] to $\dfrac{a[row][n]}{a[row][row]}$
                      subtract 1 from row

Once we are comfortable with the pseudocode, it is relatively straightforward to convert it to C.

ch5_6.c

```c
/*------------------------------------------------------*/
/*   Program chapter5_6                                 */
/*                                                      */
/*   This program uses Gauss elimination to             */
/*   determine the mesh currents for a circuit.         */

#include <stdio.h>
#include <stdlib.h>
#define N 3      /* number of unknowns */

main()
{
   /*  Declare variables and function prototypes.  */
   int i, j, index;
   double r1, r2, r3, r4, r5, v1, v2,
          a[N][N+1], soln[N];
   void eliminate(double a[N][N+1], int n, int index);
   void back_substitute(double a[N][N+1],
                         int n, double soln[N]);

   /*  Get user input.  */
   printf("Enter resistor values in ohms: \n");
   printf("(R1, R2, R3, R4, R5) \n");
   scanf("%lf %lf %lf %lf %lf",&r1,&r2,&r3,&r4,&r5);
   printf("Enter voltage values in volts: \n");
   printf("(V1, V2) \n");
   scanf("%lf %lf",&v1,&v2);

   /*  Specify equation coefficients.  */
   a[0][0] = r1 + r2;
   a[0][1] = a[1][0] = -r2;
   a[0][2] = a[2][0] = a[1][3] = 0;
   a[1][1] = r2 + r3 + r4;
   a[1][2] = a[2][1] = -r4;
   a[2][2] = r4 + r5;
   a[0][3] = v1;
   a[2][3] = -v2;

   /*  Perform elimination step.  */
   for (index=0; index<=N-2; index++)
   {
      eliminate(a,N,index);
   }

   /*  Perform back substitution step.  */
   back_substitute(a,N,soln);

   /*  Print solution.  */
   printf("\nSolution: \n");
   for (i=0; i<=N-1; i++)
   {
      printf("Mesh Current %i: %f \n",i+1,soln[i]);
   }
```

```
    /*  Exit program.  */
    return EXIT_SUCCESS;
}
/*------------------------------------------------*/
/*  This function performs the elimination step.  */

void eliminate(double a[N][N+1], int n, int index)
{
    /*  Declare variables.  */
    int row, col;
    double scale_factor;

    /*  Eliminate variable from equations.  */
    for (row=index+1; row<=n-1; row++)
    {
        scale_factor = -a[row][index]/a[index][index];
        a[row][index] = 0;
        for (col=index+1; col<=n; col++)
        {
            a[row][col] += a[index][col]*scale_factor;
        }
    }

    /*  Void return.  */
    return;
}
/*------------------------------------------------*/
/*  This function performs the back substitution.  */

void back_substitution(double a[N][N+1], int n,
                       double soln[])
{
    /*  Declare variables.  */
    int row, col;

    /*  Perform back substitution in each equation. */
    soln[n-1] = a[n-1][n]/a[n-1][n-1];
    for (row=n-2; row>=0; row--)
    {
        for (col=n-1; col>=row+1; col--)
        {
            a[row][n] -= soln[col]*a[row][col];
        }
        soln[row] = a[row][n]/a[row][row];
    }

    /*  Void return.  */
    return;
}
/*------------------------------------------------*/
```

To handle larger systems of equations, the symbolic constant N must be changed; the steps in the Gauss elimination do not need any modifications.

5.   TESTING

The program interaction using the data from the hand example follows:

```
Enter resistor values in ohms:
(R1, R2, R3, R4, R5)
1 1 1 1 1
Enter voltage values in volts:
(V1, V2)
5 5

Solution:
Mesh Current 1: 2.500000
Mesh Current 2: 0.000000
Mesh Current 3: -2.500000
```

The program assumes that the system of equations has a solution, which means that none of the equations represents the same equation or parallel equations. Modifications to the program to check for these conditions could be added with additional statements or functions.

Modify!

ch5_6.c

Use the program developed in this section to answer the following questions.

1.   Determine the mesh currents if all five resistors are 5 ohms and both voltage sources are 10 volts.

2.   Verify your answer in problem 1 by using matrix multiplication as discussed in this section. (This problem assumes that you covered the previous section on matrices and vectors.)

3.   Determine the mesh currents if the resistors have the values of 2, 8, 6, 6, and 4 ohms, and the voltage sources have the values of 40 and 20 volts.

4.   Verify your answer in problem 3 by substituting back in the original set of three equations.

5.10   Higher-Dimensional Arrays*

C allows arrays to be defined with more than two subscripts. For example, this statement defines a **three-dimensional array**:

```
int b[3][4][2];
```

*Optional section.

The three subscripts, which are necessary to specify a specific element, correspond to the *x, y,* and *z* coordinates if you position the array at the origin of a three-dimensional space, as shown in Figure 5.7. Thus, the position that is shaded corresponds to `b[2][0][1]`.

Most engineering problems that need arrays can be solved using one-dimensional or two-dimensional arrays. However, there are occasionally problems that are good candidates for using higher-dimensional arrays. These problems typically involve data that are specified by several parameters; in addition, the parameters either are integers that are sequential or parameters that can easily be converted into sequential parameters. For example, suppose that a set of data representing temperature measurements is taken from the floor of a large chemical reaction chamber. Furthermore, this set of temperatures is taken at specified intervals of time during a chemical reaction. In this case, we might choose to use a three-dimensional array, using the first subscript to indicate a specific time, and the other two subscripts to indicate the location within the floor. The subscripts would need to begin with zero to match the requirements of C subscripts. The subscripts `[3][2][5]` would then specify the value taken at the fourth time value, and at position `[2][5]` in the grid of temperatures.

Arrays with over three subscripts are seldom used because it is difficult to visualize them. However, a simple way to visualize arrays with over three subscripts can be developed. First, consider a three-dimensional array to be a building. The building has floors, and a rectangular grid of rooms on each floor. Assume each room can contain a single value. The three-dimensional array representing the building uses three subscripts to specify a room; the first subscript is the floor number and the other two subscripts specify the row and column number of the room on the specified floor.

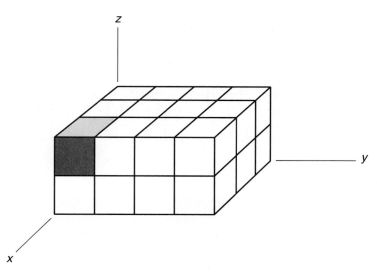

Figure 5.7 *Three-dimensional array.*

A **four-dimensional array** is a row of buildings, as shown in Figure 5.8. The first subscript specifies the building, and the remaining three subscripts specify the room in the building.

A **five-dimensional array** is a block of buildings, as shown in Figure 5.9. The first two subscripts specify the building in the block, and the remaining three subscripts specify the room in the building.

This analogy could continue with a row of blocks, then a city of blocks, then a group of cities, a state of cities, and so on. Although we have shown you how to visualize higher-dimensional arrays, we also want to caution you about using higher-order arrays. Higher-order arrays have a lot of overhead related to the subscripting; not only are there extra subscripts required, but extra loops are necessary each time you want to work with groups of values in the array. In general, higher-order arrays also complicate the debugging and maintenance of the program. Therefore, higher-order arrays should only be used when they simplify the overall visualization of the problem and the steps to solve it.

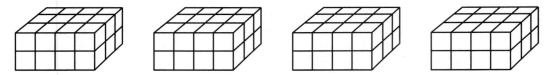

Figure 5.8 *Four-dimensional array.*

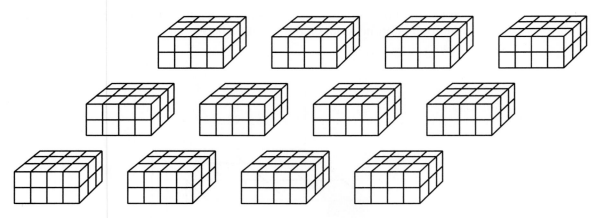

Figure 5.9 *Five-dimensional array.*

SUMMARY

An array is a data structure often used to store engineering data that are analyzed in a program. If the data are best represented by a list of information, a one-dimensional array is used; if the data are best represented by a table or grid of information, a two-dimensional array is used. Many examples were developed in this chapter to illustrate array definitions, array initializations, computations with arrays, input and output with arrays, and arrays as function parameters. A set of statistical functions was developed for computing statistical information for analyzing or sorting one-dimensional arrays. The Gauss elimination technique for solving a system of simultaneous linear equations was also presented, and a C program developed to implement this technique.

KEY TERMS

array	one-dimensional array
call-by-address	power
determinant	selection sort algorithm
dot product	simultaneous linear equations
element	sorting
Gauss elimination	standard deviation
hyperplane	square matrix
ill-conditioned	subscripts
inner product	system of equations
magnitude	transpose
matrix	two-dimensional array
matrix multiplication	utterance
mean	variance
median	vector
nonsingular	zero crossing

C STATEMENT SUMMARY

Array declaration:

```
int a[5], b[]={2, 3, -1};
double x[10][5];
```

Style NOTES

1. The variable **k** is commonly used as a subscript for a one-dimensional array.
2. Use symbolic constants to declare the size of an array so that it is easy to modify.
3. In documentation, describe a two-dimensional array as a grid with rows and columns.

4. The variables i and j are commonly used as subscripts for a two-dimensional array.

5. List both the row size and the column size of arrays in the formal argument list and in the function prototype statement.

DEBUGGING NOTES

1. Only use arrays when it is necessary to keep all the data available in memory.

2. Be careful not to exceed the maximum subscript value when referencing an element in an array.

3. Select conditions in **for** loops to specifically use an equality with the maximum subscript value; this helps avoid errors with subscript ranges.

4. An array must be declared to be as large as, or larger than, the maximum number of values to be stored in it.

5. Because an array reference in a function is a call-by-address reference, be careful that you do not inadvertently change values in an array in the function.

6. Be sure to enclose each subscript in its own set of brackets when referencing elements of a multidimensional array.

7. When translating matrix notation to C, remember that the first row and column in a matrix is referenced with a subscript 1, not zero.

8. Multidimensional matrices complicate the logic of a program, and should be used only when they are necessary.

PROBLEMS

tunnel.dat

Linear Interpolation. The following problems refer to the wind-tunnel test data stored in the file **tunnel.dat**. The file contains the set of data discussed in Chapter 2 on page 66, which consists of a flight-path angle (in degrees) and its corresponding coefficient of lift on each line in the file. The flight-path angles will be in ascending order.

1. Write a program that reads the wind-tunnel test data, and then allows the user to enter a flight-path angle. If the angle is within the bounds of the data set, the program should then use linear interpolation to compute the corresponding coefficient of lift. (You may need to refer to the section on linear interpolation in Section 2.5.)

2. Modify the program in problem 1 so that it prints a message to the user giving the range of angles that are covered in the data file after reading the values.

3. Write a function that could be used to verify that the flight-path angles are in ascending order. The function should return a zero if the angles are not in

order, and a 1 if they are in order. Assume that the corresponding function prototype is

```
int ordered(double x[], int num_pts);
```

4. Write a function that receives two one-dimensional arrays that correspond to the flight-path angles and the corresponding coefficients of lift. The function should sort the flight-path angles into ascending order while maintaining the correspondence between the flight-path angles and the corresponding coefficients of lift. Assume that the corresponding function prototype is

```
void reorder(double x[], double y[], int num_pts);
```

5. Modify the program developed in problem 2 such that it uses the function developed in problem 3 to determine whether or not the data are in the desired order. If they are not in the desired order, use the function developed in problem 4 to reorder them.

rand_rtn.c

Noise Signals. In engineering simulations, we often want to generate a floating-point sequence of values with a specified mean and variance. The function developed in this chapter allows us to generate numbers between limits a and b, but it does not allow us to specify the mean and variance. By using results from probability, the following relationships can be derived between the limits of a uniform random sequence and its theoretical mean μ and variance σ^2:

$$\sigma^2 = \frac{(b-a)^2}{12} \qquad \mu = \frac{a+b}{2}$$

6. Write a program that uses the **rand_float** function developed in Chapter 4 to generate sequences of random floating-point values between 4 and 10. Then compare the computed mean and variance to the theoretical values computed. As you use more and more random numbers, the computed values and the theoretical values should become closer.

7. Write a program that uses the **rand_float** function developed in Chapter 4 to generate two sequences of 500 points. Each sequence should have a theoretical mean of 4, but one sequence should have a variance of 0.5 and the other should have a variance of 2. Check the computed means and compare to the theoretical means. (*Hint*: Use the two previous equations to write two equations with two unknowns. Then solve for the unknowns by hand.)

8. Write a program that uses the **rand_float** function developed in Chapter 4 to generate two sequences of 500 points. Each sequence should have the same variance of 3.0, but one sequence should have a mean of 0.0 and the other should have a mean of −4.0. Compare the theoretical and computed values for mean and variance. (*Hint*: Use the two previous equations to write two equations with two unknowns. Then solve for the unknowns by hand.)

9. Write a function named **rand_mv** that generates a random floating-point value with a specified mean and variance that are input parameters to the function. Assume that the corresponding function prototype is

```
double rand_mv(double mean, double var);
```

Use the **rand_float** function developed in Chapter 4.

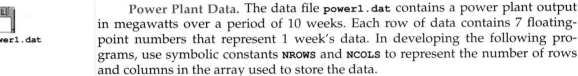

power1.dat

Power Plant Data. The data file **power1.dat** contains a power plant output in megawatts over a period of 10 weeks. Each row of data contains 7 floating-point numbers that represent 1 week's data. In developing the following programs, use symbolic constants **NROWS** and **NCOLS** to represent the number of rows and columns in the array used to store the data.

10. Write a program to compute and print the average power output over this period of time. Also print the number of days with greater-than-average power output.

11. Write a program to print the day of the week and the number of the week on which the minimum power output occurred. If there are several days with the minimum power output, print the information for each day.

12. Write a function to compute the average of a specified column of a two dimensional array that has **NROWS** rows and **NCOLS** columns. The parameters should be the floating-point array and the desired column. Assume that the corresponding function prototype is

```
double col_ave(double x[NROWS,NCOLS],int col);
```

13. Write a program that uses the function written in problem 12 to print a report that lists the average power output for the first day of the week, then for the second day of the week, and so on. Print the information in this format:

```
Day x: Average Power Output in Megawatts:   xxxx.xx
```

14. Write a function to compute the average of a specified row of a two-dimensional array that has **NROWS** rows and **NCOLS** columns. The parameters should be the floating-point array and the desired row. Assume that the corresponding function prototype is

```
double row_ave(double x[NROWS,NCOLS],int row);
```

15. Write a program that uses the function written in problem 14 to print a report that lists the average power output for the first week, then for the second week, and so on. Print the information in this format:

```
Week x: Average Power Output in Megawatts:   xxxx.xx
```

16. Write a program to compute and print the mean and variance of the power plant output data.

Temperature Distribution. The temperature distribution in a thin metal plate with constant (or isothermal) temperatures on each side can be modeled using a two-dimensional grid, as shown in Figure 5.10. Typically, the number of points in the grid are specified, as are the constant temperatures on the four sides. The temperatures of the interior points are usually initialized to zero, but they change according to the temperatures around them. Assume that the temperature of an interior point can be computed as the average of the four adjacent temperatures; the points shaded in Figure 5.10 represent the adjacent temperatures for the point labeled x in the grid. Each time that the temperature of an interior point changes, the temperatures of the points adjacent to it change. These changes continue until a thermal equilibrium is achieved, and all temperatures become constant.

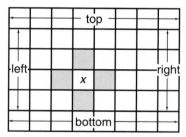

Figure 5.10 *Temperature grid in a metal plate.*

17. Write a program to model this temperature distribution for a grid with six rows and eight columns. Allow the user to enter the temperatures for the four sides. Use one array to store the temperatures. Thus, when a point is updated, its new value is used to update the next point. Continue updating the points, moving across the rows until the temperature differences for all updates are less than a user-entered tolerance value.

18. Modify the program generated in problem 17 so that the updates are performed down the columns. Compare the equilibrium values for the two programs using different tolerance values. The equilibrium values should be very close for small tolerance values.

19. Modify the program in problem 17 so that two arrays are used and so that the program can perform the updates as if they all happen at the same time. Thus, all temperatures are updated using one set of array values. The two arrays are needed so that all the old temperatures are available to compute each new temperature.

Gauss Elimination. The accuracy of the Gauss elimination technique can be improved using a process called pivoting. To perform row pivoting, we first reorder the equations so that the equation with the largest absolute value for the first coefficient is the first equation. We then eliminate the first variable from the

ch5_6.c

equations that follow the first equation. Then, starting with the second equation, we reorder the equations such that the second equation has the largest coefficient (in absolute value) for the second variable. We then eliminate the second variable from all equations after the second equation. The process continues similarly for the rest of the variables. Assume that a symbolic constant N contains the number of equations.

20. Use the program developed in Section 5.8 as a guide to develop a function that receives a **double** array **a** of size **N** by **N+1**. A second parameter is a **double** array **soln** of size **N+1**. The function should solve the system of equations represented by array **a**, and return the solution in array **soln**. Assume that the corresponding function prototype is

```
void gauss(double a[N][N+1], double soln[N+1]);
```

21. Write a function that receives a two-dimensional array and a pivot value that specifies the coefficient of interest, j. The function should then reorder all equations starting with the jth equation such that the jth equation will have the largest coefficient (in absolute value) in the jth position. Assume that the function can reference the size of the array as **N** by **N+1**, and that the corresponding function prototype is

```
void pivot_r(double a[N][N+1], int j);
```

22. Modify the function developed for problem 20 so that the row pivoting is performed before each variable is eliminated. Use the function developed in problem 21.

23. Column pivoting is performed in a similar fashion to row pivoting by exchanging columns such that the largest coefficient (in absolute value) will be in the position of interest. When columns are exchanged, it is important to keep track of the changes in the order of the variables. Write a function to perform column pivoting. Include parameters to specify changes in the order of the variables. Assume that the corresponding function prototype is

```
void pivot_c(double a[N][N+1], int j, int reorder k[N]);
```

24. Modify the function developed for problem 20 so that column pivoting is performed before each variable is eliminated. Use the function developed in problem 23.

25. Modify the function developed for problem 20 so that both row pivoting and column pivoting are performed before each variable is eliminated. Use the functions developed in problems 21 and 23.

Determinants. The following problems define cofactors and minors of a square matrix and then use them to evaluate a determinant.

26. The minor of an element $a_{i,j}$ of a matrix **A** is the determinant of the matrix obtained by removing the row and column to which the given element $a_{i,j}$ belongs. Thus, if the original matrix has four rows and columns, the minor is the determinant of a matrix with three rows and columns. Write a function to compute the minor of a square matrix with four rows and four columns. The input arguments should be the matrix **A** and the values of i and j. Assume that the corresponding function prototype is:

```
double minor(double a[4][4], int i, int j);
```

27. A cofactor $A_{i,j}$ of a matrix **A** is the product of the minor of $a_{i,j}$ and the factor $(-1)^{i+j}$. Write a function to compute a cofactor of a square matrix with four rows and four columns. The arguments should be the matrix **A** and the values of i and j. You may want to reference the function in problem 26. Assume that the corresponding function prototype is:

```
double cofactor(double a[4][4], int i, int j);
```

28. The determinant of a square matrix **A** can be computed in the following way:

(a) Select any column.

(b) Multiply each element in the column by its cofactor.

(c) Add the products obtained in step (b).

Write a function **det_c** to compute the determinant of a square matrix with four rows and four columns using this technique. You may want to reference the function developed in problem 27. Assume that the corresponding function prototype is:

```
double det_c(double a[4][4]);
```

29. The determinant of a square matrix **A** can be computed in the following way:

(a) Select any row.

(b) Multiply each element in the row by its cofactor.

(c) Add the products obtained in step (b).

Write a function **det_r** to compute the determinant of a square matrix with four rows and four columns using this technique. You may want to reference the function developed in problem 27. Assume that the corresponding function prototype is:

```
double det_r(double a[4][4]);
```

stat_lib.c
stat_lib.h
zone1.dat

Correlation Coefficient. In Section 3.7, page 131, we presented a technique to compute a linear model for a set of data points. However, a linear model is not always a good model for a set of data points. Therefore, before computing a linear model, it is a good idea to first determine if a linear model is a reasonable model. The correlation coefficient [14] is a value that is computed from the data that is a measure of the linearity of the data. If this correlation coefficient is exactly 1 or −1, then the data are exactly linear. If the correlation is 0, then there is no linear relationship. For values between 0 and 1, or between 0 and −1, the closer the value is to 1 or −1, the better the linear relationship. By using a set of data points (x_1, y_1), (x_2, y_2), . . . , (x_n, y_n), and the notation from Section 3.7, the correlation coefficient is computed using the following equation:

$$\text{Correlation coefficient} = \frac{\sum_{k=1}^{n} x_k y_k - \mu_x \cdot \mu_y}{}$$

where μ_x and μ_y are the mean values of the x data and the y data, respectively, and σ_x and σ_y are the standard deviations of the x data and the y data, respectively.

30. Write a function that has two one-dimensional arrays x and y as input arguments. Compute and return the value of the correlation coefficient for the data. Assume that the corresponding function prototype is:

```
double corr_coef(double x[], double y[], int num_pts);
```

Use the statistical functions developed in Chapter 3 in your function.

31. Write a program that determines and prints the correlation coefficient for the altitude and ozone mixing ratio values in the data file **zone1.dat**. Use the function developed in problem 30. What does this value indicate about the linear relationship of this data?

Normalization Technique. There are a number of ways to normalize, or scale, a set of values. One common normalization technique scales the values such that the minimum value goes to 0, the maximum value goes to 1, and other values are scaled accordingly. For example, using this normalization, the values in the following array are normalized:

Array values:

−2	−1	2	0

Normalized array values:

0.0	0.25	1.0	0.5

The equation that computes the normalized value from a value x_k in the array is the following:

$$\text{Normalized } x_k = \frac{x_k - \min_x}{\max_x - \min_x}$$

where $\min_x$ and $\max_x$ represent the minimum and maximum values in the array x, respectively. If you substitute the minimum value for x_k in this equation, the numerator is zero, and thus the normalized value for the minimum is zero. If you substitute the maximum value for x_k in this equation, the numerator and denominator are the same value, and hence the normalized value for the maximum is 1.0.

32. Write a function that has a one-dimensional **double** array and the number of values in the array as its arguments. Normalize the values in the array using the technique presented. Assume that the corresponding function prototype is:

    ```
    void norm_1D(double x[], int num_pts);
    ```

33. Write a function that has a two-dimensional **double** array as an argument. Normalize the values in the array using the technique presented. Assume that symbolic contants **NROWS** and **NCOLS** specify the size of the array, and that these are available to the function. Assume that the corresponding function prototype is

    ```
    void norm_2D(double x[NROWS][NCOLS]);
    ```

6

Courtesy of Rainbow.

GRAND CHALLENGE:
Oil and Gas Exploration

The identification of underground oil and gas reserves can be performed using a group of sensors that measure earth motion. These sensors, also called seismometers, are arranged in a predetermined pattern, and are collectively called a sensor array. A ground-shock signal can be generated near the sensor array using an explosive charge in a hole that has been drilled near the array. Ground-shock signals can also be generated by an explosive charge on the surface, or by a special truck that uses a hydraulic hammer to pound the earth several times per second. The ground-shock signals that are transferred into the earth are reflected by the different geologic layer boundaries, and are collected by the sensors on the surface. By using sophisticated signal processing, the boundary layers can be mapped and predictions of the materials (such as sandstone, shale, water, and oil) can be made for the various layers.

An Introduction to Pointers

OBJECTIVES

The relationships between the value stored in a variable, the identifier assigned to a variable, and the address of the memory location used to store the value of a variable are examined. A new pointer data type is defined that can be used to store the address of a value associated with a variable. Examples are presented to demonstrate the use of pointers to reference array elements. Examples of pointers as function arguments illustrate techniques for modifying program variables from

[*]Optional section.

statements within a function. The use of pointers as function arguments is then demonstrated in an example that detects possible earthquakes in a seismic signal. The process of dynamic memory allocation is defined, along with several new functions that are required to implement it. Finally, a quicksort algorithm is presented; this algorithm is implemented in a recursive solution that uses pointers as function arguments.

6.1   Addresses and Pointers

Address

When a C program is executed, memory locations are assigned to the variables used in the program. Each of these memory locations has a positive integer **address** that uniquely defines the location. When a variable is assigned a value, this value is stored in the corresponding memory location. The value of a variable can be used by statements in the program, and it can be changed by statements in the program. The specific addresses used for the variables are determined each time that the program is executed, and may vary from one execution to another.

It is sometimes helpful to compare memory allocation to the allocation of a group of post office boxes. If the post office has 100 boxes numbered from 1 to 100, then the box number corresponds to the memory address. Each box is assigned to an individual, using the individual's name; this name corresponds to the identifier assigned to a memory location. The contents of the box corresponds to the value in the memory location; this value can be examined and it can be changed.

post office box number	individual name	contents
78	John Ruiz	catalog

memory address	identifier	contents
66572	x	105

This analogy is not completely valid because two individuals might have the same name, but two identifiers cannot be exactly the same. Also, a mail box might be empty or it might contain a number of items, whereas a memory location always contains a single value.

ADDRESS OPERATOR

Address operator

In C, the address of a variable can be referenced using the **address operator &**. This operator was introduced in Chapter 2 in conjunction with the `scanf` statement. For example, recall that a statement to read a floating-point value from the keyboard and to store it in the variable **x** is the following:

```
scanf("%f",&x);
```

This statement specifies that the value read from the keyboard is to be stored at the address specified by **&x**, the address of **x**.

To illustrate the use of the address operator to obtain the memory address of a variable, consider the following program:

ch6_1.c

```
/*-------------------------------------------------------*/
/*  Program chapter6_1                                 */
/*                                                     */
/*  This program demonstrates the relationship         */
/*  between variables and addresses.                   */

#include <stdio.h>
#include <stdlib.h>

main()
{
   /*  Declare and initialize variables.  */
   int a=1, b=2;

   /*  Print the contents and addresses of a and b.  */
   printf("a = %i; address of a = %u \n",a,&a);
   printf("b = %i; address of b = %u \n",b,&b);

   /*  Exit program.  */
   return EXIT_SUCCESS;
}
/*-------------------------------------------------------*/
```

Note that the address is printed with a u specification that is used for printing unsigned integers. A sample output from this program is the following:

```
a = 1; address of a = 65524
b = 2; address of b = 65522
```

The following memory snapshot shows the values in the two memory locations at the time that the printf statements are executed:

a | 1 | b | 2 |

We do not usually indicate the memory addresses in these diagrams because the addresses used are system-dependent.

There are no initial values given to variables a and b in this modification to the previous program;

ch6_2.c

```
/*-------------------------------------------------------*/
/*  Program chapter6_2                                 */
/*                                                     */
/*  This program demonstrates the relationship         */
/*  between variables and addresses.                   */

#include <stdio.h>
#include <stdlib.h>
```

```
main()
{
    /*  Declare variables.  */
    int a, b;

    /*  Print the contents and addresses of a and b.  */
    printf("a = %i; address of a = %u \n",a,&a);
    printf("b = %i; address of b = %u \n",b,&b);

    /*  Exit program.  */
    return EXIT_SUCCESS;
}
/*-------------------------------------------------------*/
```

A memory snapshot at the time that the **printf** statements are executed should show a question mark in the variable contents because the values are undefined:

a ☐?☐   b ☐?☐

A sample output from this program is the following:

```
a = 0; address of a = 65524
b = 250; address of b = 65522
```

While we see that there are values in the variables, even though we have not assigned any in the program, we should not assume anything about these values. This example illustrates the importance of being sure that a program initializes a variable before using its value in other statements in a program.

Modify!

ch6_2.c

1. Run program **chapter6_1** two times on the computer that you are using for class assignments. Did your computer use the same addresses or different addresses? Compare the results with your classmates.

2. Run program **chapter6_2** presented in this section. What values were in the locations assigned to **a** and **b**? If these values are zero, your compiler may automatically assign the value of zero to undefined variables. This is not an ANSI standard, and you should not assume that undefined variables will have a value of zero. Do the values change from one execution of the program to another?

POINTER ASSIGNMENT

Pointer

The C language allows us to store the address of a memory location in a special type of variable called a **pointer**. When a pointer is defined, the type of variable to which it will point must also be defined. Thus, a pointer defined to point to an integer variable cannot also be used to point to a floating-point variable. The following statement defines two integer variables and a pointer to an integer value. Note that an asterisk is used to indicate that the variable is a pointer; this asterisk is also called a **dereferencing** or **indirection** operator:

Dereferencing
Indirection

```
int a, b, *ptr;
```

This statement specifies that memory addresses should be assigned to three variables—two integer variables and a pointer to an integer variable. The statement does not specify the initial values for **a** and **b**, and it also does not specify an address to be stored in ptr. Thus, the memory snapshot after this declaration indicates that the initial contents of all variables are not specified; the diagram uses an arrow to indicate that **ptr** is a pointer variable.

a [?]   b [?]   ptr [?] ⟶

To specify that **ptr** should point to the variable **a**, we could use an assignment statement that stores the address of **a** in **ptr**:

```
int a, b, *ptr;
ptr = &a;
```

This assignment could also have been made on the declaration statement:

```
int a, b, *ptr=&a;
```

In either case, the memory snapshot after the declaration is the following:

ptr
  ↘
a [?]   b [?]

Note that it is not necessary to show the contents of **ptr** as long as the variable to which it points is specified.

Consider this set of statements:

```
/*  Declare and initialize variables.  */
int a=5, b=9, *ptr=&a;
. . .
/*  Assign the value pointed to by ptr to b.  */
b = *ptr;
```

This last statement is read as "**b** is assigned the value at the address contained in **ptr**" or "**b** is assigned the value pointed to by **ptr**." The memory snapshot before the declaration statement is executed is the following:

ptr
  ↘
a [5]   b [9]

The memory snapshot after the assignment statement is executed is the following:

Thus, **b** is assigned the value pointed to by **ptr**.

Now consider this set of statements:

```
/*  Declare and initialize variables.  */
int a=5, b=9, *ptr=&a;
. . .
/*  Assign the value of b to the variable  */
/*  to which ptr points.                   */
*ptr = b;
```

The memory snapshot before the assignment statement is executed is the following:

The memory snapshot after the assignment statement is executed is the following:

Thus, the value pointed to by **ptr** is assigned the value in **b**.

We now extend program **chapter6_1** to demonstrate the relationship between variables, addresses, and pointers. Consider the following program:

ch6_3.c

```
/*------------------------------------------------------*/
/*  Program chapter6_3                                  */
/*                                                      */
/*  This program demonstrates the relationship          */
/*  between variables, addresses, and pointers.         */

#include <stdio.h>
#include <stdlib.h>

main()
{
   /*  Declare and initialize variables.  */
   int a=1, b=2, *ptr=&a;

   /*  Print the variable and pointer contents.  */
   printf("a = %i; address of a = %u \n",a,&a);
   printf("b = %i; address of b = %u \n",b,&b);
   printf("ptr = %u; address of ptr = %u \n",ptr,&ptr);
   printf("ptr points to the value %i \n",*ptr);
```

```
        /*  Exit program.  */
        return EXIT_SUCCESS;
}
/*------------------------------------------------------*/
```

A sample output from this program is the following:

```
a = 1; address of a = 65524
b = 2; address of b = 65522
ptr = 65524; address of ptr = 65520
ptr points to the value 1
```

Note that the values of the pointer to **a** and the address of **a** are the same.

Practice!

Give memory snapshots after each of these sets of statements are executed.

1.  ```
    int a=1, b=2, *ptr;
    . . .
    ptr = &b;
    ```

2.  ```
    int a=1, b=2, *ptr=&b;
    . . .
    a = *ptr;
    ```

3.  ```
    int a=1, b=2, c=5, *ptr=&c;
    . . .
    b = *ptr;
    *ptr = a;
    ```

4.  ```
    int a=1, b=2, c=5, *ptr;
    . . .
    ptr = &c;
    c = b;
    a = *ptr;
    ```

Pointers were used in Chapter 3 to access data files. Recall that a pointer to a file (called a file descriptor) was defined using a **FILE** declaration, as in

```
FILE *sensor1;
```

where the **FILE** data type is defined in **<stdio.h>**. The pointer was associated with a specific file using the **fopen** statement, as shown in the following statement:

```
sensor1 = fopen("sensor1.dat","r");
```

This statement also indicates that `sensor1.dat` is an input file because we will be reading information from it, as specified by the parameter `"r."` The pointer is used again with the `fscanf` statement to point to the file from which we want to read data:

```
fscanf(sensor1,"%f %f",&t,&motion);
```

The file pointer is necessary in the `fscanf` function because we may be reading information from several files in the same program. A pointer variable is used in a similar manner with an output file and the `fprintf` function.

ADDRESS ARITHMETIC

The operations that can be performed with pointers (or addresses) are limited to the following: A pointer can be assigned to another pointer of the same type; an integer value can be added to or subtracted from a pointer; and a pointer can be assigned or compared to the integer zero, or, equivalently, to the symbolic constant **NULL**, which is defined in `<stdio.h>`. In addition, pointers to elements of the same array can be subtracted or compared.

NULL

A pointer can point to only one location, but several pointers can point to the same location, as illustrated in this next example. Both `ptr_1` and `ptr_2` point to the same variable after the following statements are executed:

```
/*  Declare and initialize variables.  */
int x=-5, y = 8, *ptr_1, *ptr_2;
...
/*  Assign both pointers to x.  */
ptr_1 = &x;
ptr_2 = ptr_1;
```

The memory snapshot after these statements are executed is

We now present several invalid statements using these variables to illustrate some common errors that can be made when working with pointers:

```
&y = ptr_1;        /*  invalid  statement - attempts  */
                   /*  to change the address of y     */

ptr_1 = y;         /*  invalid statement - attempts   */
                   /*  to change ptr_1 to a           */
                   /*  nonaddress value               */

*ptr_1 = ptr_2;    /*  invalid statement - attempts   */
                   /*  to move an address to an       */
                   /*  integer variable               */
```

```
ptr_1 = *ptr_2;   /*   invalid statement - attempts   */
                  /*   to change ptr_1 to a           */
                  /*   nonaddress value               */
```

It is instructive to attempt to draw memory snapshots of these invalid statements; in each statement we are attempting to store a variable value in a pointer, or we are attempting to store a pointer in a variable. *To help avoid these errors, use identifier names for pointers that clearly indicate that the identifiers are associated with pointers.*

Style

When simple variables are defined, we should not make any assumptions about the relationships of the memory locations assigned to the variables. For example, if a declaration statement defines two integers, **a** and **b**, we should not assume that the values are adjacent in memory; we also should not make assumptions about which value occurs first in memory. The memory assignments of simple variables are system-dependent. However, the memory assignment for an array is guaranteed to be a sequential group of memory locations. Thus, if array **x** contains five integers, then the memory location for **x[1]** will immediately follow the memory location for **x[0]**, and the memory location for **x[2]** will follow the memory location for **x[1]**, and so on. Therefore, if **ptr_x** is a pointer to an integer, we can initialize it to point to the integer **x[0]** with this statement:

```
ptr_x = &x[0];
```

To move the pointer to **x[1]**, we can increment **ptr_x** by 1, which causes it to point to the value that follows **x[0]**, or we can assign **ptr_x** the address of **x[1]**. Thus, any of the following statements would cause **ptr_x**, which currently points to **x[0]**, to be changed to point to **x[1]**:

```
++ptr_x;   /*   increment ptr_x to point to the   */
           /*   next value in memory              */

ptr_x++;   /*   increment ptr_x to point to the   */
           /*   next value in memory              */

ptr_x += 1;   /*   increment ptr_x to point to    */
              /*   the next value in memory       */

ptr_x = &x[1];   /*   ptr_x is assigned the       */
                 /*   address of x[1]             */
```

Similarly, the statement

```
ptr_x += k;
```

refers to the address of the value that is **k** values past the one to which **ptr_x** pointed before this statement was executed. These are all examples of adding integers to pointers. Similarly, integers can also be subtracted from pointers. Section 6.2 expands this discussion for one-dimensional arrays and for multidimensional arrays.

When an integer value is added to or subtracted from a pointer, it is assumed that the integer refers to the number of values from the one referenced by the pointer before the addition or subtraction is performed. For example, the statement

```
ptr++;
```

indicates that **ptr** should be modified such that it points to the next value in memory, which is the value that follows the one referenced by **ptr** before it is incremented. Because different types of values require different amounts of memory, the actual value added to **ptr** depends on the variable type. A floating-point value requires more memory than a short integer, and thus the address increment for a floating-point value will be more than an address increment for a short integer. For example, the memory addresses for consecutive short integers might be 45530 and 45532, and memory addresses for consecutive floating-point values might be 50200 and 50204. Fortunately, the compiler will determine the correct memory address for us when we add an integer to a pointer or when we subtract an integer from a pointer.

A pointer operation can be included in a statement with other operations, so it is important to be sure that the precedence of the operations is specified correctly. An address operator is a unary operation, and thus it is performed before binary operations; unary operations are also performed from right to left if there are more than one in a statement. These precedence rules are summarized in Table 6.1. Remember that parentheses can always be used to change the precedence of operations.

Errors with pointers can cause problems that are difficult to debug. Even worse, pointer errors can often cause a program to give incorrect results while appearing to work properly. Many pointer errors are caused by pointers that were not initialized before being used. Therefore, it is a good habit to initialize all pointers at the beginning of the program. *If a pointer is not initially assigned to a memory location, give it a* NULL *value to indicate that the pointer has not been as-*

Style

TABLE 6.1 Operator Precedence		
Precedence	Operation	Associativity
1	() []	innermost first
2	++ -- + - ! (type) & *	right to left (unary)
3	* / %	left to right
4	+ -	left to right
5	< <= > >=	left to right
6	== !=	left to right
7	&&	left to right
8	||	left to right
9	?:	right to left
10	= += -= *= /= %=	right to left
11	,	left to right

signed to a memory location. You can determine if the pointer named `ptr_1` has been assigned to a memory location at some point in the program in an `if` statement that contains a condition such as `(ptr_1 == NULL)`.

Practice!

For each of the following problems, give a memory snapshot that includes both variables and pointer references after the problem statements are executed. Include as much information as possible. Use question marks to indicate memory locations that have not been initialized.

1.  ```
    double x=15.6, y=10.2, *ptr_1=&y, *ptr_2=&x;
    . . .
    *ptr_1 = *ptr_2 + x;
    ```
2.  ```
    int w=10, x=2, *ptr_2=&x;
    . . .
    *ptr_2 -= w;
    ```
3.  ```
    int x[5]={2,4,6,8,3};
    int *ptr_1=NULL, *ptr_2=NULL, *ptr_3=NULL;
    . . .
    ptr_3 = &x[0];
    ptr_1 = ptr_2 = ptr_3 + 2;
    ```
4.  ```
    int w[4], *first_ptr=NULL, *last_ptr=NULL;
    . . .
    first_ptr = &w[0];
    last_ptr = first_ptr + 3;
    ```

6.2   Pointers to Array Elements

Arrays and array handling were covered in detail in Chapter 5 using subscripts to specify individual array elements. Pointers can also be used to specify individual array elements. Array references using pointers and addresses are almost always faster than references using subscripts; thus, pointer references for arrays are generally preferred if speed is a concern. As discussed in Section 6.1, pointer references to array values are based on the knowledge that memory assignment of array values is always sequential.

ONE-DIMENSIONAL ARRAYS

Consider the following declaration that defines and initializes a one-dimensional array with floating-point values:

```
double x[6]={1.5, 2.2, 4.3, 7.5, 9.1, 10.5};
```

The memory snapshot after this statement is executed is the following:

x[0]	1.5
x[1]	2.2
x[2]	4.3
x[3]	7.5
x[4]	9.1
x[5]	10.5

Reference **x[0]** refers to the first element in the array, reference **x[1]** refers to the second element in the array, and reference **x[k]** refers to the $(k+1)$th element in the array. Similar references can be generated with pointers. Assume that a pointer **ptr** has been defined to reference **double** values, and is then initialized with this statement:

```
ptr = &x[0];
```

The address of the first element in the array is then stored in the pointer. Thus, reference ***ptr** refers to **x[0]**, reference ***(ptr+1)** refers to **x[1]**, and reference ***(ptr+k)** refers to **x[k]**. The value of k in reference ***(ptr+k)** is often referred to **Offset** as an **offset** from the beginning element in the array. The following diagram shows the memory allocation for the array used in this example with the offsets added:

		offset
x[0]	1.5	0
x[1]	2.2	1
x[2]	4.3	2
x[3]	7.5	3
x[4]	9.1	4
x[5]	10.5	5

The following statements compute the sum of the values in the array **x** using subscripts and a **for** loop:

```
/*  Declare and initialize variables.  */
int k;
double x[6], sum=0;
...
/*  Sum the values in the array x.  */
for (k=0; k<=5; k++)
{
    sum += x[k];
}
```

An equivalent set of statements that uses pointers instead of subscripts is the following:

```
/*  Declare and initialize variables.  */
int k;
double x[6], sum=0, *ptr=&x[0];
...
/*  Sum the values in the array x.  */
for (k=0; k<=5; k++)
{
    sum += *(ptr+k);
}
```

Note that reference *(ptr+k) requires parentheses in order to perform the operations in the correct order; k is added to the address in ptr, and then the indirection operator is used to refer to the value pointed to by ptr+k. Reference *ptr+k would not work correctly because it would be computed as if it were (*ptr)+k because a unary operator has precedence over a binary operator.

In the discussion on arrays in Chapter 5, we saw that using an array name as a function parameter passed the address of the first element of the array. An array name can also be used to represent the address of the first element of the array in other statements. For example, the following two statements are equivalent:

```
ptr = &x[0];
ptr = x;
```

Similarly, reference *(ptr+k) is also equivalent to *(x+k). Thus, the statements to sum array x can be simplified to these:

```
/*  Declare and initialize variables.  */
int k;
double x[6], sum=0;
...
/*  Sum the values in the array x.  */
for (k=0; k<=5; k++)
{
    sum += *(x+k);
}
```

This example illustrates the use of an array name as an address. The array name can be used in most statements in place of a pointer, but it cannot be used on the left side of an assignment statement because its value cannot be changed.

Practice!

Assume that an array g is defined with the following statement:

```
int g[] = {2, 4, 5, 8, 10, 32, 78};
int *ptr1=&g[0], *ptr2=&g[3];
```

Give a diagram of the memory allocation, including the array values. Also indicate the offset values from the initial value in the array. Using this information, give the value of the following references.

1. `*g`
2. `*(g+1)`
3. `*g+1`
4. `*(g+5)`
5. `*ptr1`
6. `*ptr2`
7. `*(ptr1 + 1)`
8. `*(ptr2 + 2)`

TWO-DIMENSIONAL ARRAYS

A two-dimensional array is stored in sequential memory locations, in row order, as shown by the following array definition, array diagram, and corresponding memory allocation map. Note that the memory allocation map also shows the offset from the initial value in the array:

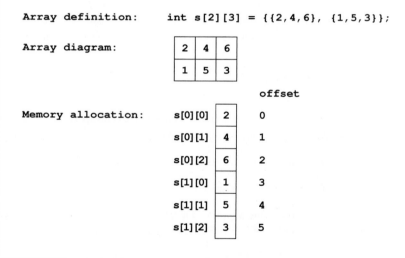

Array definition: `int s[2][3] = {{2,4,6}, {1,5,3}};`

Array diagram:

2	4	6
1	5	3

Memory allocation:

		offset
s[0][0]	2	0
s[0][1]	4	1
s[0][2]	6	2
s[1][0]	1	3
s[1][1]	5	4
s[1][2]	3	5

Practice!

Draw the memory allocation for each of the following arrays, and indicate the values stored in the locations. Use a question mark to indicate positions that are not initially assigned a value. Also indicate the offset from the initial array value for each of the array elements.

1.   `int d[4][2]={{1,6}};`
2.   `int g[3][4]={{5,2,-2,3}, {1,2,3,4}};`
3.   `float h[3][3]={{0}};`

A pointer can be used to reference an element in a two-dimensional array using the offset from the initial element in the array. If pointer `ptr` has been initialized to point to `s[0][0]`, then reference `*(ptr+k)` accesses the array element with the offset of `k`. To illustrate, suppose that we want to compute the sum of the elements in an array `s` with two rows and three columns. The following statements compare a solution using subscripts and a solution using indirection references with pointers.

Solution 1

```
/*   Declare and initialize variables.   */
int s[2][3], srows=2, scols=3, i, j, sum=0;
...
/*   Sum the values in the array s.   */
for (i=0; i<=srows-1; i++)
{
    for (j=0; j<=scols-1; j++)
    {
        sum += s[i][j];
    }
 }
```

Solution 2

```
/*   Declare and initialize variables. */
int s[2][3], s_count=6, k, sum=0, *ptr=&s[0][0];
...
/*   Sum the values in the array s.   */
for (k=0; k<=s_count-1; k++)
{
        sum += *(ptr+k);
}
```

Both solutions correctly compute the sum of the array elements. Note that the first solution required nested loops because both a row subscript and a column subscript were needed, whereas the second solution required only a single loop to specify the offset from the initial array value. It is also interesting to observe that both solutions add the elements in an order that moves across the rows. Solution 1 could be modified to add the elements in an order that moves down the columns by interchanging the two `for` loops.

Practice!

Assume that the following statements define an integer array `x`. Draw a memory allocation diagram, and give the value indicated by each of the following references.

```
int x[2][4]={{1,8,7,6}, {2,4,-1,0}}, *xptr=&x[0][0];
```

1. `*xptr`   2. `*(xptr+2)`

3. `*xptr + 2`   4. `*(xptr+1) + *(xptr+3)`

To convert reference `s[i][j]` to an offset from pointer `sptr` that has been initialized to `&s[0][0]`, the number of columns in the array must be known. If we assume that `scols` contains the number of columns used in the memory allocation for `s`, then the offset for the value in row `i` and column `j` is equal to `i*scols + j`. To demonstrate the validity of this offset formula, consider the memory allocation for array `s` with the offset included:

			offset
Memory allocation:	s[0][0]	2	0
	s[0][1]	4	1
	s[0][2]	6	2
	s[1][0]	1	3
	s[1][1]	5	4
	s[1][2]	3	5

Suppose that we wish to convert reference `s[0][1]` to an offset from the initial value in the array. According to the formula, the offset should be `0*scols + 1`, or 1; a corresponding reference is `*(sptr+1)`. Similarly, because this array has three columns, a reference `s[1][2]` has an offset of `1*scols + 2`, or 5; a corresponding reference is `*(sptr+5)`. Similar formulas can be developed to convert higher-dimensional array references to an offset from the first array value.

In C, a two-dimensional array can also be considered to be a one-dimensional array with each element being another one-dimensional array. For example, array `s` with two rows and three columns can be considered to be a one-dimensional array (with two elements), with each element being another one-dimensional array (with three elements). Thus, reference `s[1][0]` is equivalent to `*s[1]` because `s[1]` represents the address of the first element in row 1. Similarly `*(s[0]+4)` references the value in position `s[1][1]`. For readability, we usually use pointers with an offset instead of a one-dimensional reference with an offset when we want to use an indirect reference to a two-dimensional array.

Practice!

Assume that array `a` has been defined to contain four rows and six columns. Also assume that values have been read into the array from a data file. Use pointers with an offset to perform the following operations:

1. Find the sum of the second row of values.
2. Find the sum of the third column of values.

3.   Find the maximum in the first three rows of values.

4.   Find the minimum in the last four columns of values.

6.3   Pointers in Function References

In C, function references are call-by-value references. Thus, the values of the actual parameters are copied to the formal parameters. All computations in the
function use the formal parameters, and thus an actual parameter cannot be
changed in a function. One exception to this rule was presented in Chapter 4;
when an array name is used as an argument in a function reference, the address
of the array is transferred to the function, and all references to array values use
the actual array locations. Thus, values in an array can be modified by statements
within a function. Other exceptions can be implemented using pointers as function parameters.

To illustrate the use of pointers as function parameters, we develop a function that exchanges the contents of two memory locations. Recall that it takes
three statements to switch the values in two locations, as shown by the following
statements and corresponding memory snapshots.

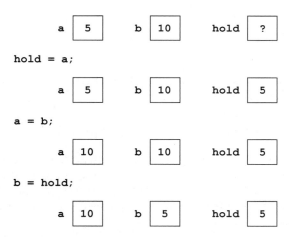

In problem solutions that switch several values, it would be convenient to be able
to access a function to perform the switch. Consider the following function,
which attempts to perform the switch using simple variable parameters (call-by-
value):

```
/*--------------------------------------------------------*/
/*   Incorrect function to switch two values.          */

void switch1(int a, int b)
{
   /* Declare variables.   */
   int hold;
```

```
        /*   Switch values in a and b.   */
        hold = a;
        a = b;
        b = hold;

        /*   Void return.   */
        return;
   }
   /*-----------------------------------------------------------*/
```

Assume that the following statement references this function:

```
    switch1(x, y);
```

If **x** and **y** contain the values 5 and −2, then the transfer of the values from the actual parameters to the formal parameters at the beginning of the function execution is the following:

actual parameters   **formal parameters**

x | 5 | $\longrightarrow$ a | 5 |

y | -2 | $\longrightarrow$ b | -2 |

After the function is executed, the values of the actual parameters and formal parameters are as follows:

actual parameters   **formal parameters**

x | 5 | $\longrightarrow$ a | -2 |

y | -2 | $\longrightarrow$ b | 5 |

Thus, the values have been switched in the formal parameters, but these values are not transferred back to the actual parameters.

After considering this incorrect solution, we are now ready to develop a function that switches the contents of two simple variables using pointers. The function has two parameters that are pointers to the two variables that we want to switch. A prototype statement for this function is the following:

```
    void switch2 (int *a, int *b);
```

Thus, the function does not return a value, and its two parameters are pointers to integers. The function itself now follows:

sorts.c

```
/*----------------------------------------------------------*/
/*  Correct function to switch values in two variables.  */

void switch2(int *a, int *b)
{
    /*  Declare variables.  */
    int hold;

    /*  Switch values pointed to by a and b.  */
    hold = *a;
    *a = *b;
    *b = hold;

    /*  Void return.  */
    return;
}
/*----------------------------------------------------------*/
```

If **x** and **y** are simple variables, then a valid call to this function is

```
switch2(&x,&y);
```

If **ptr_1** points to variable **x**, and **ptr_2** points to the variable **y**, then the values in **x** and **y** can be switched with this reference:

```
switch2(ptr_1,ptr_2);
```

Elements **x[i]** and **x[j]** could also be switched with these statements:

```
switch2(&x[i],&x[j]);
switch2(x+i,x+j);
```

but not with the statement

```
switch2(x[i],x[j]);  /*  invalid statement  */
```

The actual parameter that corresponds to a pointer argument must be an address or pointer.

Practice!

Consider each of the following references to the **switch2** function. For invalid references, explain why the reference is invalid. For valid references, give a memory snapshot before and after the reference.

1.
```
float x=1.5, y=3.0, *ptr_x=&x, *ptr_y=&y;
...
switch2(ptr_x,ptr_y);
```

2.  ```
    int f=2, g=7, *ptr_f=&f, *ptr_g=&g;
    ...
    switch2(ptr_f,ptr_g);
    ```
3.  ```
    int f=2, g=7, *ptr_f=&f, *ptr_g=&g;
    ...
    switch2(*ptr_f,*ptr_g);
    ```
4.  ```
    int f=2, g=7, *ptr_f=&f, *ptr_g=&g;
    ...
    switch2(&ptr_f,&ptr_g);
    ```
5.  ```
    int f=2, g=7, *ptr_f=&f, *ptr_g=&g;
    ...
    switch2(&f,&g);
    ```
6.  ```
    int f=2, g=7, *ptr_f=&f, *ptr_g=&g;
    ...
    switch2(f,g);
    ```

6.4   Problem Solving Applied: Seismic Event Detection

Special sensors called **seismometers** are used to collect earth motion information. These seismometers can be used in a passive environment, in which they record the earth's motion, which includes earthquakes and tidal motion. By analyzing ground motion from an earthquake using data from several seismometers, it is possible to determine the epicenter of the earthquake and the intensity of the earthquake. The earthquake intensity is usually measured using the **Richter scale**, which is a scale from 1 to 10 named after U.S. seismologist C. F. Richter.

Write a program that reads a set of seismometer data from a data file named **seismic.dat**. The first line of the file contains two values—the number of seismometer data readings that follow in the file and the time interval in seconds that occurred between consecutive measurements. This time interval is a floating-point value, and we assume that all the measurements were taken with the same time interval between them. After reading and storing the data measurements, the program should then identify possible earthquakes, which are also called **seismic events**, using a power ratio. At a specific point in time, this ratio is the quotient of a **short-time power** measurement divided by a **long-time power** measurement. If the ratio is greater than a given **threshold**, an event may have occurred at that point in time. Given a specific point in the data measurements, the short-time power is the average power, or average squared value, of the measurements using the specified point plus a small number of points that occurred just previous to the specified point. The long-time power is the average power of the measurements using the specified point plus a larger number of points that occurred just previous to the specified point. (The set of points used in a calculation is sometimes referred to as a **data window**.) The threshold is generally greater than 1 to avoid detecting events in constant data because the short-time power is equal to the long-time power if the data values are all the same value. Assume that the numbers of measurements for the short-time power and for the long-time power are read from the keyboard. Set the threshold value to 1.5.
    ```

1.   PROBLEM STATEMENT

Determine the locations of possible seismic events using a set of seismometer measurements from a data file.

2.   INPUT/OUTPUT DESCRIPTION

The inputs to this program are a data file named **seismic.dat** and the number of measurements to use for short-time power and long-time power. The output is a report giving the times of potential seismic events.

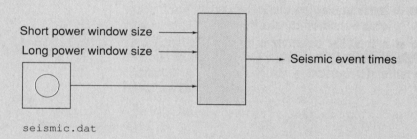

seismic.dat

3.   HAND EXAMPLE

Suppose that a data file contains the following data, which includes number of points to follow (11) and time interval between points (0.01), followed by the eleven values that correspond to a sequence of values $x_0, x_1, \ldots x_{10}$:

seismic.dat

```
11 0.01
 1   2   1   1   1   5   4   2   1   1   1
```

If the short-time power measurement is made using two samples, and the long-time power measurement is made using five measurements, then we can compute power ratios, beginning with the rightmost-point in a window:

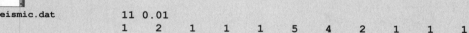

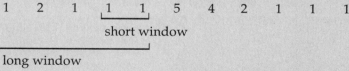

Point x_4:   Short-time power = $(1 + 1)/2 = 1$
Long-time power = $(1 + 1 + 1 + 4 + 1)/5 = 1.6$
Ratio = $1/1.6 = 0.63$

1   2   1   1   1   5   4   2   1   1   1

short window

long window

Point x_5:   Short-time power = $(25 + 1)/2 = 13$
Long-time power = $(25 + 1 + 1 + 1 + 4)/5 = 6.4$
Ratio = $13/6.4 = 2.03$

1   2   1   1   1   5   4   2   1   1   1

short window

long window

Point x_6:   Short-time power = $(16 + 25)/2 = 20.5$
Long-time power = $(16 + 25 + 1 + 1 + 1)/5 = 8.8$
Ratio = $20.5/8.8 = 2.33$

1   2   1   1   1   5   4   2   1   1   1

short window

long window

Point x_7:   Short-time power = $(4 + 16)/2 = 10$
Long-time power = $(4 + 16 + 25 + 1 + 1)/5 = 9.4$
Ratio = $10/9.4 = 1.06$

1   2   1   1   1   5   4   2   1   1   1

short window

long window

Point x_8:   Short-time power = $(1 + 4)/2 = 2.5$
Long-time power = $(1 + 4 + 16 + 25 + 1)/5 = 9.4$
Ratio = $2.5/9.4 = 0.27$

1   2   1   1   1   5   4   2   1   1   1

short window

long window

Point x_9:   Short-time power = $(1 + 1)/2 = 1$
Long-time power = $(1 + 1 + 4 + 16 + 25)/5 = 9.4$
Ratio = $1/9.4 = 0.11$

| 1 | 2 | 1 | 1 | 1 | 5 | 4 | 2 | 1 | 1 | 1 |

short window

long window

Point x_{10}:   Short-time power $= (1 + 1)/2 = 1$
Long-time power $= (1 + 1 + 1 + 4 + 16)/5 = 4.6$
Ratio $= 1/4.6 = 0.22$

By using the previous ratios computed, possible seismic events occurred at points x_5 and x_6. Because the time interval between points is 0.01 second, then the times that correspond to the seismic events are 0.05 and 0.06 second. (We assume that the first point in the file occurred at 0.0 second.)

4.   ALGORITHM DEVELOPMENT

We first develop the decomposition outline because it divides the solution into a series of sequential steps.

Decomposition Outline

1. *Read seismic data from the data file and read numbers of measurement for power from the keyboard.*
2. *Compute power ratios and print possible seismic event times.*

Step 1 involves reading the data file and storing the information in an array. Because we do not know the exact size of the array, we will need to specify a maximum size in the array definition. We will read the numbers of measurements for the power computations from the keyboard. Step 2 involves computing power ratios and comparing them to the threshold to determine if a possible event occurred. Because we need to compute two power measurements for each possible event location, we implement the power measurement as a function. The refinement in pseudocode for the **main** function and the **power** function can now be developed:

Refinement in Pseudocode

```
main:      set threshold to 1.5
           read npts and time-interval
           read the values into sensor array
           read short-window, long-window from keyboard
           set k to long-window - 1
           while k ≤ npts-1
                 set short-power to power(sensor,short-window,k)
                 set long-power to power(sensor,long-window,k)
                 set ratio to short-power/long-power
                 if ratio > threshold
                       print k*time-interval
                 increment k by 1
```

power(x,length,n):
      set xsquare to zero
      set k to n
      while k>n-length+1
         add x[k]*x[k] to xsquare
      return xsquare/length

We are now ready to convert the pseudocode to C.

ch6_4.c
seismic.dat

```
/*-----------------------------------------------------*/
/*  Program chapter6_4                                 */
/*                                                     */
/*  This program reads a seismic data file and then    */
/*  determines the times of possible seismic events.   */

#include <stdio.h>
#include <stdlib.h>
#define FILENAME "seismic.dat"
#define MAX_SIZE 1000
#define THRESHOLD 1.5

main()
{
   /*  Declare variables and function prototypes.  */
   int k, npts, short_window, long_window;
   double sensor[MAX_SIZE], time_incr, short_power,
          long_power, ratio;
   FILE *file_ptr;
   double power_w(double *ptr, int n);

   /*  Read data file.  */
   file_ptr = fopen(FILENAME,"r");
   fscanf(file_ptr,"%i %lf",&npts,&time_incr);
   if (npts > MAX_SIZE)
   {
      printf("Data file too large for array. \n");
      return EXIT_FAILURE;
   }
   else
   {
      /*  Read data into an array.  */
      for (k=0; k<=npts-1; k++)
         fscanf(file_ptr,"%lf",&sensor[k]);
   }

   /*  Read window sizes from the keyboard.  */
   printf("Enter number of points for short-window: \n");
   scanf("%i",&short_window);
   printf("Enter number of points for long-window: \n");
   scanf("%i",&long_window);
```

```
       /*  Compute power ratios and search for events  */
       for (k=long_window-1; k<=npts-1; k++)
       {
          short_power = power_w(&sensor[k],short_window);
          long_power = power_w(&sensor[k],long_window);
          ratio = short_power/long_power;
          if (ratio > THRESHOLD)
             printf("Possible event at %f seconds \n",
                    time_incr*k);
       }

       /*  Close file and exit program.  */
       fclose(file_ptr);
       return EXIT_SUCCESS;
}
/*-------------------------------------------------------*/
/*  This function computes the average power in a       */
/*  specified window of a double array.                 */

double power_w(double *ptr, int n)
{
    /*  Declare and initialize variables.  */
    int k;
    double xsquare=0;

    /*  Compute sum of values squared in the array x.  */
    for (k=0; k<=n-1; k++)
    {
       xsquare += (*(ptr-k))*(*(ptr-k));
    }

    /*  Return the average squared value.  */
    return xsquare/n;
}
/*-------------------------------------------------------*/
```

5.   TESTING

The output from the program using the data file from the hand example is as follows:

```
Enter number of points for short-window:
2
Enter number of points for long-window:
5
Possible event at 0.050000 seconds
Possible event at 0.060000 seconds
```

Modify!

`ch6_4.c`
`seismic.dat`

Modify the event-detection program to include the following new capabilities.

1. Allow the user to enter the threshold value. Check the value to be sure that it is a positive value greater than 1.
2. Print the number of events detected by the program. (Assume that events with contiguous times are all part of the same event. Thus, for the hand example, one event was detected.)

6.5   Dynamic Memory Allocation*

Dynamic memory allocation allows us to allocate memory when a program is executed instead of allocating it when the program is compiled. This is especially important when a program uses an array whose size is not determined until the program is executed; without dynamic memory allocation, the program would have to specify the maximum size anticipated for the array. For systems with limited memory, it is possible that there would not be enough memory to run a program if all arrays had to be specified to the maximum size anticipated.

Dynamic memory allocation is specified using either the **malloc** function or the **calloc** function, which perform a "memory allocation" or a "cleared allocation." Both functions reserve a group of contiguous memory locations; in addition, **calloc** initializes the memory locations to a binary zero. The argument of the **malloc** function is the number of bytes of memory required, where a **byte** is a unit of memory that contains 8 bits; the arguments of the **calloc** function are the number of memory locations needed and the number of bytes for each memory location. We now give the prototype statements (which are contained in the header file **<stdlib.h>**) for these functions, and then give further explanation of the parameters and the values returned by these functions:

Byte

```
void *malloc(size_t m);
void *calloc(size_t n, size_t size);
```

Because the number of bytes used for storing a value with a specific data type (such as an **int**) is system-dependent, a special operator called **sizeof** is used to determine the number of bytes needed for a specific data type. The expression **sizeof(int)** represents the number of bytes used to store an integer, and **sizeof(double)** represents the number of bytes used to store a **double** value. The **sizeof** operator computes an unsigned integer that is a **size_t** type value, where the **size_t** type is system dependent, but is usually either an **unsigned int** or an **unsigned long**. Thus, to request memory for 200 integers, we could use either of these sets of statements:

*Optional section.

```
num_pts = 200;
void *malloc(num_pts*sizeof(int));
num_pts = 200;
void *calloc(num_pts, sizeof(int));
```

Both functions return a value to a pointer. If the memory is available, the pointer will contain the address of the memory; if the allocation cannot be made, the pointer will contain a **NULL** value. The pointer returned by these functions is

void pointer

called a **void pointer** because it does not specify the type of variables to be stored in the memory allocation. Therefore, a cast operator should be used with the pointer value returned by the functions in order to coerce it to the proper pointer type.

To illustrate, assume that we want to dynamically allocate memory to store a double array named **x** containing **npts** elements. (In this example, we give a value to **npts**, but it could be computed by other statements or read from the keyboard or a data file.) Either of the following sets of statements specify the desired allocation:

Solution 1
```
/*  Declare variables.  */
int npts = 500;
double *x;
...
/*  Dynamically allocate memory.  */
x = (double *)malloc(npts*sizeof(double));
```

Solution 2
```
/*  Declare variables.  */
int npts = 500;
double *x;
...
/*  Dynamically allocate memory.  */
x = (double *)calloc(npts,sizeof(double));
```

If the **calloc** function is used, then the memory values will also be initialized to zero. With either of these solutions, we should compare the value of **x** to the constant **NULL** to be sure that the memory was allocated, as shown in this statement:

```
if (x == NULL)
{
   printf("Memory requested not available. \n");
   return EXIT_FAILURE;
}
```

References to the array **x**, such as **x[k]**, are valid in the program after we have determined that the memory has been allocated.

A program can release memory that has been dynamically allocated using the **free** function, which has the following prototype:

```
void free(void *ptr);
```

Thus, the memory allocated to array **x** is released with this statement:

```
free(x);
```

In general, you should free dynamically allocated memory when it is no longer needed so that it becomes available for possible use with another dynamic allocation.

The **realloc** function can be used to change the size of the memory requested by a **calloc**, **malloc**, or previously executed **realloc** function. Its prototype statement is

```
void *realloc(void *ptr, size_t size);
```

If **ptr** contains the value **NULL**, this function operates like the **malloc** function. If ptr contains a value returned earlier in a program by a **calloc**, **malloc**, or previously executed **realloc** function, then the size of the corresponding memory allocation is changed to the new size requested. If the new size is larger, the values of the newly allocated space are undetermined. If the new size is smaller, the values in the new size are unchanged. If the additional space cannot be allocated, the original space is unchanged and the function returns a value of **NULL**.

With the use of dynamic memory allocations and dynamic memory allocation releases, a program can be designed to operate with a minimal amount of memory reserved at any time during its execution. This can allow a program to execute on a system with a small memory when it otherwise could not be executed if it had to specify the maximum possible memory requirements at the beginning of the program. On systems that run multiple programs at the same time, the use of dynamic memory allocation and dynamic memory release may allow more programs to run simultaneously.

The following program allows you to determine the maximum amount of contiguous memory that can be dynamically allocated during its execution. This maximum amount of memory available is generally a function of the other users on the system and the other software that is stored on the system; thus, you may get different results when you run this program on different systems and at different times.

ch6_5.c

```
/*-------------------------------------------------------*/
/*   Program chapter6_5                                  */
/*                                                       */
/*   This program determines the maximum contiguous      */
/*   memory allocation that can be reserved during a     */
/*   specific program execution.                         */

#include <stdio.h>
#include <stdlib.h>
#define UNIT 1000

main()
{
   /*  Declare and initialize variables.  */
   int k=1, *ptr;
```

```
/*  Find maximum amount of contiguous memory      */
/*  available in units of thousands of integers.  */
ptr = (int *)malloc(UNIT*sizeof(int));
while (ptr != NULL)
{
    free(ptr);
    k++;
    ptr = (int *)malloc(k*UNIT*sizeof(int));
}

/*  Print maximum amount of memory available.  */
printf("maximum contiguous memory available: \n");
printf("%i integers \n",(k-1)*UNIT);

/*  Exit program.  */
return EXIT_SUCCESS;
}
/*-----------------------------------------------------*/
```

A typical output for this program using a personal computer is the following:

```
maximum contiguous memory available:
31000 integers
```

Modify!

ch6_5.c

Modify program **chapter6_5** such that it determines the number of thousands of contiguous values that can be stored for the data types indicated in the following problems.

1. long integers
2. doubles
3. long doubles

In the previous section, we developed a program that read a set of seismic data from a data file and determined possible seismic event locations within the data. The program used a symbolic constant **MAX_SIZE** to allocate an array to store the data. If the number of points in the data file exceed the **MAX_SIZE**, then the program terminated with an error message. In the following modification, a main function is presented that uses dynamic memory allocation so that the maximum array size does not have to be allocated when the program is compiled; instead, the array memory is dynamically allocated based on the size of the seismic data file.

ch6_6.c

```
/*-----------------------------------------------------*/
/*  Program chapter6_6                                 */
/*                                                     */
/*  This program reads a seismic data file and then    */
/*  determines the times of possible seismic events.   */
```

```c
/*  Dynamic memory allocation is used.                    */

#include <stdio.h>
#include <stdlib.h>
#define FILENAME "seismic.dat"
#define THRESHOLD 1.5

main()
{
   /*  Declare variables and function prototypes.  */
   int k, npts, short_window, long_window;
   double time_incr, *sensor, short_power, long_power,
          ratio;
   FILE *file_ptr;
   double power_w(double *ptr, int n);

   /*  Read data header and allocate memory.  */
   file_ptr = fopen(FILENAME,"r");
   fscanf(file_ptr,"%i %lf",&npts,&time_incr);
   sensor = (double *)malloc(npts*sizeof(double));
   if (sensor == NULL)
   {
      printf("Not enough memory available \n");
      return EXIT_FAILURE;
   }
   else
   {
      /*  Read data into an array.  */
      for (k=0; k<=npts-1; k++)
         fscanf(file_ptr,"%lf",&sensor[k]);
   }

   /*  Read window sizes from the keyboard.  */
   printf("Enter number of points for short-window: \n");
   scanf("%i",&short_window);
   printf("Enter number of points for long-window: \n");
   scanf("%i",&long_window);

   /*  Compute power ratios and search for events  */
   for (k=long_window-1; k<=npts-1; k++)
   {
      short_power = power_w(&sensor[k],short_window);
      long_power = power_w(&sensor[k],long_window);
      ratio = short_power/long_power;
      if (ratio > THRESHOLD)
         printf("Possible event at %f seconds \n",
                time_incr*k);
   }

   /*  Free memory, close file, and exit program.  */
   free(sensor);
   fclose(file_ptr);
   return EXIT_SUCCESS;
}
/*------------------------------------------------------*/
```

Only the `main` function is shown here because the `power_w` function is not affected by the use of dynamic memory allocation.

6.6   A Quicksort Algorithm*

In this section a **quicksort** algorithm is implemented with a recursive function (see Section 4.8) that uses pointers as function parameters.

The first step in the quicksort algorithm is to select a value, called a **pivot value**, and then separate the rest of the values into two groups—one group containing values less than the pivot value and one group containing values greater than the pivot value. We select the pivot value to be the first element in the list, but the midpoint of the list is also often used as the pivot value. When this separation is done, the correct position in the list for the pivot value is determined; it goes between the two groups of values. Since the values in the two groups are not necessarily in the correct order, we take the group of smaller values, and select a new pivot value. This group is separated into two new groups of values— ones smaller than the new pivot value and ones larger than the new pivot value. This process continues until we eventually have a group of smaller values that contains no values, one value, or two values. If this group contains two values, their order is switched if necessary, and then the original group of values smaller than the original pivot value are in order. We repeat this process with the original group of values that are larger than the original pivot value. When these are in order, the entire list is in order. This algorithm can be described recursively because each step is defined in terms of a similar process with a smaller group of values, and because it has a stopping point that is encountered when the group of values has two or fewer values. A hand example follows:

Original list:

4	10	3	6	−1	0	2	5

Separate into groups of values smaller and larger than the pivot value:

[3	−1	0	2]	4	[10	6	5]

Separate each remaining group into groups of values smaller and larger than the pivot value of each group:

[−1	0	2]	3	4	[6	5]	10

Separate each remaining group into groups of values smaller and larger than the pivot of each group:

−1	[0	2]	3	4	5	6	10

Separate each remaining group into groups of values smaller and larger than the pivot of each group:

−1	0	2	3	4	5	6	10

*Optional section.

The implementation of the quicksort algorithm that we present references an additional function named **separate**. This function switches values in the array that it receives such that the pivot value is correctly positioned in the position referenced by **break_pt**. All values less than the pivot value are to the left in the array (if we visualize the array as a row) and all values greater than the pivot value are to the right. Then, the **quicksort** function is recursively called using a statement which specifies that a total of **break_pt** values, starting with **x[0]**, should be sorted

```
quicksort(x, break_pt);
```

The **quicksort** function is also recursively called using a statement that specifies that a total of **n-break_pt-1** values, starting with **x[break_pt+1]**, should be sorted

```
quicksort(&x[break_pt+1], n-break_pt-1];
```

Note that the actual argument uses **&x[break_pt+1]**, a reference to the address of **x[break_pt+1]**. This address reference is necessary because using **x[break_pt+1]** generates a call-by-value, not a call-by-reference. The **quicksort** function and the **separate** function use the **switch2** function developed on page 293. Since the quicksort algorithm is a complicated algorithm, a good way to begin is to use the hand example, and work through the statements using that data. (The order of the values in the intermediate groups varies from the order in the hand example.)

sorts.c

```
/*-------------------------------------------------------*/
/*  This function implements a quicksort algorithm.  */

void quicksort(int x[], int n)
{
   /*  Declare variables and function prototypes.  */
   int break_pt;
   int separate(int x[], int n);
   void switch2(int *a, int *b);

   /*  If only two elements, order them correctly.  */
   if (n == 2)
   {
      if (x[0] > x[1])
         switch2(&x[0],&x[1]);
   }
   else
   /*  If more than two elements, separate into those  */
   /*  greater than and those less than a breakpoint.  */
   {
      if (n > 2)
      {
         break_pt = separate(x,n);
         quicksort(x,break_pt);
         quicksort(&x[break_pt+1],n-break_pt-1);
      }
   }
```

```
         /*   Void return.   */
         return;
      }
      /*-------------------------------------------------------*/
      /*  This function reorders the array such that           */
      /*  y[0] is correctly positioned and the values          */
      /*  less than it are to the left and the values          */
      /*  greater than it are to the right.                    */

      int separate(int y[], int m)
      {
         /*  Declare variables and function prototypes.   */
         int k1=1, k2=1, count=0, pivot;
         int switch2(int *a, int *b);

         /*  Separate values into two groups.   */
         pivot = y[0];
         while ((k1<m) && (k2<m))
         {
            while ((k1<m) && (y[k1]>pivot))
               k1++;
            while ((k2<m) && (y[k2]<pivot))
               k2++;
            if ((k1<m) && (k2<m))
            {
               switch2(&y[k1],&y[k2]);
               count++;
            }
         }

         /*  Put pivot value in correct position.   */
         if (count > 0)
            switch2(&y[0],&y[count]);
         else
         {
            k1 = 0;
            while ((k1<m-1) && (y[k1]>y[k1+1]))
            {
               switch2(&y[k1],&y[k1+1]);
               k1++;
            }
            count = k1;
         }

         /*  Return count.   */
         return count;
      }
      /*-------------------------------------------------------*/
```

Modify!

sorts.c

1.   Write a program that reads a set of values from the keyboard, calls the **quicksort** function to sort them, and prints the sorted values.

2.   Modify this program so that the values are sorted into descending order.

SUMMARY

The focus of this chapter was pointers, and the relationship between a pointer and the variable to which it points was analyzed. Examples were presented that demonstrated how to define pointers and how to initialize them. The valid types of operations that can be performed with pointers were listed, and the precedence relationships for operators was updated to include the address operator and the indirection operator. Examples of pointers used as function parameters and in references to arrays were given.

KEY TERMS

address	indirection
address operator	**NULL**
byte	offset
dereference	pointer
dynamic memory allocation	**void** pointer

C STATEMENT SUMMARY

Pointer declaration:

```
int *ptr_1;
double a, *ptr_2=&a;
```

Dynamic memory allocation:

```
x =  (double *)malloc(npts*sizeof(double));
x =  (double *)calloc(npts,sizeof(double));
```

Style NOTES

1. Choose identifers for pointers that clearly indicate that the identifiers are associated with pointer variables.

2. If a pointer is not initially assigned to a memory location, give it a value of **NULL** to indicate that it has not yet been assigned.

DEBUGGING NOTES

1. Be sure that a program initializes a variable before using its value in other statements.

2. Be sure that a pointer variable is initialized before it is used to reference a value.

3. The actual parameter that corresponds to a pointer argument in a function must be an address or a pointer.

PROBLEMS

General Functions. Pointers are often used as function arguments when we want to return more than one value from the function. In each of the following problems, write the indicated function, and then develop a `main` function for testing the function.

1. Write a function that converts radius, diameter, and area measurements for a circle from units of inches and square inches to units of feet and square feet. Assume that the corresponding function prototype statement is the following:

   ```
   void convert_ft(double *r, double *d, double *a);
   ```

   where `r`, `d`, and `a` are pointers to the radius, diameter, and area variables.

2. Write a function that reorders the values in three integer variables such that the values are in ascending order. Assume that the corresponding function prototype statement is the following:

   ```
   void reorder(int *a, int *b, int *c);
   ```

   where `a`, `b`, and `c` are pointers to the three variables.

3. Write a function that determines the maximum and minimum values from a one-dimensional integer array. Assume that the corresponding function prototytpe statement is the following:

   ```
   void ranges(int x[], int npts, int *max_ptr,
               int *min_ptr);
   ```

   where `npts` contains the number of values in array `x` and `max_ptr` and `min_ptr` are pointers to the variables in which to store the maximum and minimum values in the array.

4. Write a function that returns the **double** average value of a one-dimensional integer array, in addition to determining the number of values in the array that are greater than the average. Assume that the corresponding function prototype statement is the following:

```
double average(int x[], int npts, int *gtr);
```

where **npts** contains the number of values in array **x** and **gtr** is a pointer to the variable in which to store the number of values in **x** that are greater than the average.

5. Write a function that returns the number of positive values, zero values, and negative values in an integer array. Assume that the corresponding function prototype statement is the following:

```
void signs(int x[], int npts, int *npos,
           int *nzero, int *nneg);
```

where **npts** contains the number of values in the array **x** and **npos**, **nzero**, and **nneg** are pointers to variables to store the numbers of positive values, zero values, and negative values in the array.

Vector Functions. A vector is a group of numerical values that can be represented by a one-dimensional array. These problems develop functions for manipulating values within a vector. Then, a reference to the function is requested to show how to use the function to manipulate groups of values within the vector, instead of manipulating the complete set of values in the vector. Use pointer references instead of subscripts in the functions. Assume that the first position in an array is the position referenced with a zero subscript.

6. Write a function that fills a vector with zeros. Assume that the function prototype statement is the following:

```
void zeros(int x[], int n);
```

where **x** is a one-dimensional array with **n** elements. Give a reference to the function that fills positions 20–25 of an array **a** with zeros.

7. Write a function that fills a vector with ones. Assume that the function prototype statement is the following:

```
void ones(int x[], int n);
```

where **x** is a one-dimensional array with **n** elements. Give a reference to the function that fills positions 5 to **k** of array **y** with ones.

8. Write a function that computes the sum of a vector. Assume that the function prototype statement is the following:

```
int v_sum(int x[], int n);
```

where **x** is a one-dimensional array with **n** elements. Give a reference to the function that computes the sum of the last 10 values in array **y**, which has **npts** elements.

9. Write a function that reverses the order of the values in a vector. Assume that the function prototype statement is the following:

```
void v_rev(int x[], int n);
```

where **x** is a one-dimensional array with **n** elements. Give a reference to the function that reverses the values in positions 5 through 20 of array **z**.

10. Write a function that replaces values in an array with their absolute values. Assume that the function prototype statement is the following:

```
void v_abs(int x[], int n);
```

where **x** is a one-dimensional array with **n** elements. Give a reference to the function that replaces all the values of array **t** except the first five values with their absolute values, where **t** has **npts** elements.

Table Functions. The following problems develop a set of functions for computing values from a two-dimensional array or a table of data. Use pointer references instead of subscript references in the functions.

11. Write a function that computes the sum of the **i**th row in a table containing 10 rows and 8 columns of values. Assume that the function prototype statement is the following:

```
double row_sum(double table[10][8], int i);
```

12. Write a function that computes the sum of the **j**th column in a table containing 10 rows and 8 columns of values. Assume that the function prototype statement is the following:

```
double col_sum(double table[10][8], int j);
```

7

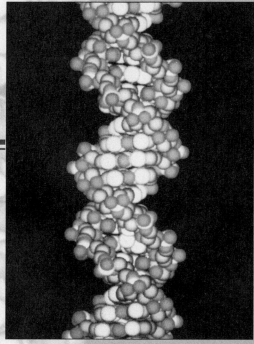

Courtesy of Rainbow.

GRAND CHALLENGE:
Mapping the Human Genome

The deciphering of the human genetic code involves locating, identifying, and determining the function of each of the 50,000 to 100,000 genes that are contained in human DNA. Each gene is a double-helix strand composed of base pairs of adenine bonded with thymine, or cytosine bonded with guanine, that are arranged in a steplike manner with phosphate groups along the side. DNA directs the production of proteins, so the proteins produced by a cell provide a key to the sequence of base pairs in the DNA. Instrumentation developed for genetic engineering is extremely useful in this detective work. A protein sequencer developed in 1969 can identify the sequence of amino acids in a protein molecule. Once the amino acid order is known, biologists can begin to identify the gene that made the protein. A DNA synthesizer, developed in 1982, can build small genes or gene fragments out of DNA. This research and its associated instrumentation are key components in beginning to address the mapping of the human genome.

Characters and Text Processing

Objectives

Summary, Key Terms, C Statement Summary
Style Notes, Debugging Notes, Problems

OBJECTIVES

Character information is an important type of information to represent and to manipulate in engineering problem solutions. Each character is stored using a binary code; the ASCII code is the most commonly-used code, and it is discussed in detail in this chapter. Examples are presented to demonstrate that character information can be processed as character data types or as integers that corresponds to the ASCII code values. The initialization of character variables is discussed, and

*Optional section.

313

new I/O statements are presented for reading and printing characters. A number of functions from the Standard C library that work with characters are presented, and functions are developed that use characters as arguments. An example is then presented that develops a program that reads chemical formulas from the keyboard and then computes and prints the corresponding molecular weight. Finally, character strings are defined, and examples are given in text processing and pattern-detection techniques. A number of library functions that work with character strings is also presented.

7.1   Character Information

Numeric information is represented in a C program as integers or floating-point values. These numeric values can be single, independent values or they can be grouped together in an array. Numeric values are often used in arithmetic computations. In many problem solutions, we also need to store and manipulate nonnumeric information, which may consist of alphabetic characters, digits, and special characters. Even though nonnumeric information can contain digits, these digits are not values generally used in arithmetic computations; instead, they are digits in an address, a phone number, or a social security number.

Character

Binary code
ASCII code
EBCDIC

Recall that all information stored in a computer is represented internally as sequences of binary digits (0 or 1). In general, we do not need to be concerned about this binary representation because the compiler and the computer perform the necessary steps to convert our programs to binary and then to execute them. However, in order to work with **characters**, we need to understand more about their representation in the computer's memory. Each character corresponds to a **binary code** value. The most commonly used binary codes are **ASCII** (American Standard Code for Information Interchange) and **EBCDIC** (Extended Binary Coded Decimal Interchange Code). In the discussions that follow, we assume that ASCII code is used to represent characters. Table 7.1 contains a few characters, their binary form in ASCII, and the integer values that correspond to the binary values. Thus, the character a is represented by the binary value 1100001, which is equivalent to an integer value of 97. A total of 128 characters can be represented in the ASCII code; a complete ASCII code table is given in Appendix B.

TABLE 7.1 Examples of ASCII Codes		
Character	ASCII Code	Integer Equivalent
newline, \n	0001010	10
%	0100101	37
3	0110011	51
A	1000001	65
a	1100001	97
b	1100010	98
c	1100011	99

Once a character is stored in memory as a binary value, the binary value can be interpreted as a character or as an integer, as illustrated in Table 7.1. Thus, when we define variables that are to be used for storing characters, we can define them as either characters or integers. However, it is important to note that the binary representation for a character digit is not equal to the binary representation for an integer digit. From Table 7.1 we see that the binary representation of the digit 3 is equivalent to the binary representation of the integer 51. Thus, performing a computation with the character representation of a digit does not yield the same result as performing the computation with the integer representation of the digit.

Nonnumeric information can be represented by constants or by variables in our programs. A character constant is enclosed in single quotes, as in `'A'`, `'b'`, and `'3'`. A variable that is going to contain a character can be defined as an integer or as a character data type `(char)`. Integer arrays can be used to represent a group of characters. C also allows the definition of a **character string**, which is a sequence of characters stored in an array of characters. A string constant is enclosed in double quotes, as in `"sensor 1"`, `"1536A"`, and `"F18"`. C also contains a large number of library functions for working with character strings that are discussed in Section 7.6.

Character string

Practice!

Give integer values for the following characters using the ASCII code table from Appendix B.

1.   (2.   <
3.   G   4.   g
5.   {   6.   ^

Give the characters (or meaning) that correspond to each of the following binary-code values.

7.   0001111   8.   0100100
9.   0010101   10.   0011110

7.2   Character Initialization and I/O

The binary representation for a character can be interpreted as a character or as an integer. Similarly, the value of a small positive integer can be printed as a character or an integer, and the value of a character variable (defined using the `char` type) can be printed as a character or an integer. To print a value as an integer, the `%i` or `%d` specifier is used; to print a value as a character, the `%c` specifier is used. The following statements illustrate printing the same value as an integer and as a character:

```
/*  Declare and initialize variables.   */
int k=97;
char c='a';
...
/*  Print both values as characters.   */
printf("value of k: %c; value of c: %c \n",k,c);
/*  Print both values as integers.   */
printf("value of k: %i; value of c: %i \n",k,c);
```

The output of these statements is

```
value of k: a; value of c: a
value of k: 97; value of c: 97
```

In many problem solutions, either type of variable can be used to store and manipulate a character. However, there are situations in which a character should be stored in an integer variable, as illustrated in the following discussion on character I/O.

Although the **printf** and **scanf** functions can be used to read characters using the **%c** specifier, C also contains special functions for reading and printing characters. The **getchar** function reads a character from the keyboard and returns the integer value of the character; the **putchar** function prints a character to the computer screen, and then also returns the same character. The prototype statements for these functions are

```
int getchar(void);
int putchar(int);
```

Text stream

EOF

Both functions use a **text stream** that is composed of a sequence of characters. For the **getchar** function, the text stream is the line entered through the keyboard; for the **putchar** function, the text stream is the line printed on the screen. In either case, the text stream can be separated into lines by newline characters. The end of a text stream is indicated with a special value, **EOF**. This special value, **EOF**, is a symbolic constant defined in **stdio.h**.

The execution of the **putchar** function causes the character that corresponds to the integer argument to be written to the computer screen. If several **putchar** function references are made in a row, the characters are printed one after another on the same line, until a newline character is printed. Thus, the following statements cause the characters **ab** to be printed on one line, followed by **c** on the next line:

```
putchar('a');
putchar('b');
putchar('\n');
putchar('c');
```

The same information could be printed using the integer values that correspond to the characters (see Table 7.1):

```
putchar(97);
putchar(98);
putchar(12);
putchar(99);
```

Style

In general, we prefer to use character constants instead of their binary equivalents in order to make the program easier to read.

When a `getchar` function is executed, the next character in the current input text stream is obtained, and returned as the function value. If there is no current text stream, then a line of information is obtained from the keyboard. This line must be ended by pressing the return key, which corresponds to entering a newline character. Thus, when the first `getchar` function is executed in a program, a line of information is read from the keyboard, but only the first character in the line is returned by the function. When the next `getchar` function reference is executed, the second character from the line is returned by the function. Successive references continue to return additional characters, until the character returned is a newline character; this signifies that we have reached the end of the current line. Then, the next reference to the `getchar` function causes a new line of information to be read from the keyboard into the text stream. This processing of the text stream by lines continues until the **EOF** character is entered through the keyboard.

A variable defined with the `char` data type can represent only the 128 ASCII characters, but a variable read by the `getchar` function must be able to represent all 128 ASCII characters and the value representing **EOF**. Because an integer variable can represent more that 128 values, we use an `int` type instead of a `char` type for a variable read by the `getchar` function so that we can also detect the end of the text stream.

The value of the **EOF** character is system-dependent; in the Borland Turbo C++ environment, the **EOF** character is entered by pressing the control (ctrl) key, and then pressing the **z** key while the control key is still pressed. This combination of characters is often written as ^**z**, but this is not the same as pressing the ^ key with the **z** key. In the Borland Turbo C++ environment, this **EOF** character is represented by the integer value −1. (Note that you cannot enter −1 for the **EOF** character because it will be interpreted as a minus sign followed by the digit 1.) To determine the integer value of the **EOF** character on your system, execute the following statement:

```
printf("EOF = %i \n",EOF);
```

The sequence of characters that represents the **EOF** character on many UNIX systems is ^**d**. To determine the sequence of characters that represent the **EOF** character on other systems, consult your instructor or a computing center consultant.

To illustrate the use of the `getchar` and `putchar` functions, consider the following program that reads characters from the keyboard and prints them back to the screen. It also computes and prints a count of the characters read, including spaces and newline characters, but not including the **EOF** character. Note that the user is reminded of the sequence necessary to terminate the text stream.

ch7_1.c

```
/*---------------------------------------------------------*/
/*  Program chapter7_1                                     */
/*                                                         */
/*  This program demonstrates the relationship             */
/*  between a text stream and character I/O by             */
/*  reading characters from the keyboard and then          */
/*  printing them to the screen.                           */

#include <stdio.h>
#include <stdlib.h>

main()
{
   /*  Declare and initialize variables.  */
   int c, count=0;

   /*  Read, print, and count characters.  */
   printf("Enter characters: (^z to quit) \n");
   c = getchar();
   count++;
   while (c != EOF)
   {
      putchar(c);
      c = getchar();
      count++;
   }

   /*  Print the number of characters printed.  */
   printf("%i characters printed. \n",count-1);

   /*  Exit program.  */
   return EXIT_SUCCESS;
}
/*---------------------------------------------------------*/
```

When the first **getchar** function is executed, a line of text is obtained from the keyboard. (Note that this line of text must be ended by pressing the return key, which is equivalent to a newline character.) The **getchar** function returns the value of the first character of the line to the variable **c**, but successive executions of the **getchar** function cause additional characters on the line to be read. Therefore, you may enter as many characters as you want on a line, but processing of the program will not continue until you press the return (or enter) key.

An example of the information displayed on the screen during a sample execution of this program is the following:

```
Enter characters: (^z to quit)
abcd
abcd
z
z
```

```
1w2e3r $
1w2e3r $
^z
16 characters printed.
```

The first line of characters was **abcd** followed by a newline, the second line contained the character **z** followed by a newline, and the third line contained the characters **1w2e3r1 $** followed by a newline. The fourth line contained the **EOF** representation followed by a newline; the **EOF** representation caused the program to be terminated. Thus, a total of $5 + 2 + 9 + 1$, or 17 characters were read, but only 16 were printed.

An interesting variation of program **chapter7_1** is shown in the next program, which prints each character twice, and also counts the number of lines read. Note that each character is read within the evaluation of the condition for the **while** loop:

```
while ((c = getchar()) != EOF)
```

Since the value of the statement

```
c = getchar();
```

is equal to **c**, this is equivalent to referencing the **getchar** function to obtain a value for **c**, and then comparing the value in **c** to **EOF**. The parentheses around the statement **c = getchar()** are necessary since **!=** has a higher priority than **=**.

```
/*------------------------------------------------------*/
/*  Program chapter7_2                                  */
/*                                                      */
/*  This program reads characters from the keyboard     */
/*  and prints them twice on the screen.  It also       */
/*  counts and prints the number of lines read.         */

#include <stdio.h>
#include <stdlib.h>
#define NEWLINE '\n'

main()
{
   /*  Declare and initialize variables.  */
   int c, count=0;

   /*  Read and print characters.  */
   printf("Enter characters: (^z to quit) \n");
   while ((c = getchar()) != EOF)
   {
      putchar(c);
      putchar(c);
      /*  Count the number of lines.  */
      if (c == NEWLINE)
         count++;
   }
```

```
        /*   Print the number of lines read.   */
        printf("%i lines read. \n",count);

        /*   Exit program.   */
        return EXIT_SUCCESS;
    }
    /*-----------------------------------------------------*/
```

Sample output from this program, using the same input as for the previous program, is as follows:

```
Enter characters: (^z to quit)
abcd
aabbccdd

z
zz

1w2e3r $
11ww22ee33rr   $$

^z
3 lines read.
```

Note that the extra line following each line of output is generated by the duplication of the newline character at the end of each input line.

Modify!

ch7_1.c

Modify program **chapter7_1** to perform the following operations.

1. Print each output character on a new line.
2. Insert a space after each output character.
3. Print the bell character after printing the message **Enter characters:
    (^z to quit)**. (The bell character is represented by the integer value 7 or by the escape sequence **\a**.)

Because a character can be stored as an integer, groups of characters can be stored in an integer array. (A group of characters stored in a character array is a string; strings are discussed in Section 7.6.) Characters in an integer array are accessed using subscripts. Integer arrays containing characters can also be used as function arguments. To illustrate, consider the following program that counts the number of words in a data file containing text. We assume that words are not split between lines, and that there is at least one blank between words. We also assume that the maximum number of characters on a line, including the newline character, is 100. Each character is read using the **fgetc** function; this function reads characters from a text stream in a data file. The argument of the **fgetc** function is a file pointer.

ch7_3.c

```
/*------------------------------------------------------*/
/*  Program chapter7_3                                 */
/*                                                     */
/*  This program reads characters from a data file    */
/*  and counts the number of words line by line.       */

#include <stdio.h>
#include <stdlib.h>
#define FILENAME "text1.dat"
#define NEWLINE '\n'

main()
{
   /*  Declare variables and function prototypes.  */
   int line[100], k=0, count=0;
   FILE *text1;
   int word_ct(int x[], int npts);

   /*  Open file.  */
   text1 = fopen(FILENAME,"r");

   /*  Read characters and count words.  */
   while ((line[k]=fgetc(text1)) != EOF)
   {
      if (line[k] == NEWLINE)
      {
         if (k != 0)
            count += word_ct(line,k);
         k = 0;
      }
      else
         k++;
   }
   /*  Count words in last line of data.  */
   if (k != 0)
      count += word_ct(line,k);

   /*  Print number of words read.  */
   printf("%i words read. \n",count);

   /*  Exit program.  */
   return EXIT_SUCCESS;
}
/*------------------------------------------------------*/
/*  This function counts the number of words           */
/*  in an integer array.                               */

int word_ct(int x[], int npts)
{
   /*  Declare and initialize variables.  */
   int count=0, k=0;
```

```
/*  While not at the end of the line,      */
/*  look for the first character of a word. */
while (k <= npts-1)
{
   while (k<=npts-1 && x[k]==' ')
      k++;
   if (k <= npts-1)
      count++;
   while (k<=npts-1 && x[k]!=' ')
      k++;
}

/*  Return word count.  */
return count;
}
/*-----------------------------------------------------*/
```

By using a function to count the number of words in a line, we were able to keep the **main** function short and readable. When the function finds the beginning of a word, it increments the word count. The end of the word is then determined by finding another space or reaching the end of the array. This program was executed with a data file **text2.dat** containing the chapter opening discussion on the human genome; the output gave the correct word count of 170.

Modify!

ch7_3.c
text1.dat
text2.dat

Modify program **chapter7_3** as suggested by the following problems. Use the data files **text1.dat** and **text2.dat** to test the program.

1. Modify program **chapter7_3** so that it assumes that spaces between words can include spaces, vertical tabs, and horizontal tabs. (Refer to Appendix B.)

2. Modify program **chapter7_3** so that it counts hyphenated words as multiple words; thus, state-of-the-art would count as four words, not one.

3. Modify program **chapter7_3** so that it prints the average number of characters per word in the text in the data file. Average word counts are used to determine the reading level of a particular piece of text—the more characters on the average per word, the higher the reading level needed to understand the text.

7.3   Character Comparisons

In programs **chapter7_1** and **chapter7_2**, we compared the contents of the integer variable **c** to the **EOF** character; when the binary representations in **c** and **EOF** were equal, the program was terminated. In this comparison, it was clear that the values must be equal in order for the condition to be true. However, suppose **a** and **b** are integer variables that contain characters, and we evaluate the following condition:

```
a < b
```

At first, it may seem strange to ask if one character is less than another character, but if we consider the comparison in terms of the integer values represented by the characters, then this comparison makes sense. If we want to know if `'?' < 'A'`, we simply need to refer to the ASCII code table in Appendix B. Because the numeric value of `'?'` is 63, and the numeric value of `'A'` is 65, the comparison is true.

Collating
sequence   The ordering of characters in a specific code, from low to high, is a **collating sequence**. If you study the ASCII collating sequence in Appendix B, some interesting characteristics can be observed. The character codes for the digits 0 through 9 are contiguous, the character codes for the uppercase letters A through Z are contiguous, and the character codes for the lowercase letters a through z are contiguous. Also, digits are less than uppercase letters, which are less than lowercase letters. The difference between an uppercase letter and its corresponding lowercase letter is 32. Finally, special characters are not contiguous; some special characters are before digits, others are after digits, and still others are between uppercase and lowercase letters.

Consider the following program that counts the number of digits in an input text stream:

ch7_4.c

```
/*-----------------------------------------------------*/
/*  Program chapter7_4                                 */
/*                                                     */
/*  This program counts and prints the                */
/*  number of digits in an input text stream.         */

#include <stdio.h>
#include <stdlib.h>

main()
{
   /*  Declare and initialize variables.  */
   int c, count=0;

   /*  Read characters and count digits.  */
   printf("Enter characters: (^z to quit) \n");
   while ((c = getchar()) != EOF)
   {
      if ('0'<=c && c<='9')
         ++count;
   }

   /*  Print the number of digits read.  */
   printf("%i digits read. \n",count);

   /*  Exit program.  */
   return EXIT_SUCCESS;
}
/*-----------------------------------------------------*/
```

An example interaction with this program is the following:

```
Enter characters: (^z to quit)
514 East Sixth St.
Hampton, NH 30255-0345
^z
12 digits read.
```

An alternative solution to this program is developed in the next section.

Modify!

ch7_3.c

Modify program **chapter7_3** to compute and print the following information. (You may need to refer to the ASCII code table in Appendix B.)

1.   Print the number of uppercase characters in the input text stream.
2.   Print the number of alphabetic characters in the input text stream.
3.   Print the number of nonalphabetic characters in the input text stream.
4.   Print the number of alphanumeric characters in the input text stream. (An **alphanumeric** character is either a digit or a letter.)

In Section 5.4 (page 228), we developed a function to sort an array with *n* elements into ascending order. Because the collating sequence for ASCII codes is in an increasing order by the integer representation, a sort that reorders a set of integers into ascending order can also be used to sort the corresponding characters into an alphabetical order. In the following program, we read a set of alphabetical characters from the keyboard into an integer array. A function is then called to sort the integers; this sort algorithm is essentially the one from Section 5.4 that has been modified to sort integers instead of **double** values.

ch7_5.c

```
/*----------------------------------------------------*/
/*   Program chapter7_5                                */
/*                                                     */
/*   This program reads characters from the           */
/*   keyboard, sorts them into an alphabetical        */
/*   order, and prints them.                          */

#include <stdio.h>
#include <stdlib.h>

main()
{
   /*  Declare variables and function prototypes.  */
   int letters[20], k=0, count=0;
   void sort(int x[], int n);

   /*  Print message to the user.  */
   printf("Enter a maximum of 20 letters: \n");
   printf("(^z after the last letter) \n");
```

```
    /*  Read characters from the keyboard.  */
    while ((letter[k] = getchar()) != EOF)
    {
        k++;
    }
    count = k;

    /*  Sort and print the characters.  */
    sort(letter,count);
    printf("The alphabetical order is: \n");
    for (k=0; k<=count-1; k++)
    {
        putchar(letter[k]);
    }
    putchar('\n');

    /*  Exit program.  */
    return EXIT_SUCCESS;
}
/*-------------------------------------------------------*/
/*  This function sorts an array with n elements     */
/*  into ascending order.                            */

void sort(int x[], int n)
{
    /*  Declare variables.  */
    int k, j, m, hold;

    /*  Implement selection sort algorithm.  */
    for (k=0; k<=n-2; k++)
    {
        /*  Exchange minimum with next array value.  */
        m = k;
        for (j=k+1; j<=n-1; j++)
        {
            if (x[j] < x[m])
                m = j;
        }
        hold = x[m];
        x[m] = x[k];
        x[k] = hold;
    }

    /*  Void return.  */
    return;
}
/*-------------------------------------------------------*/
```

A sample interaction with this program is the following:

```
Enter a maximum of 20 letters:
(^z after the last letter)
rawybspz^Z
The alphabetical order is:
abprswyz
```

Modify!

ch7_5.c

1. Run program **chapter7_5** using a combination of letters, digits, and special characters. Then use Appendix B to confirm that the output is in alphabetical order.
2. To print the output letters in reverse alphabetical order, we could still sort the values alphabetically, but then print them in reverse order. Modify program **chapter7_5** to implement this technique.
3. To print the output letters in reverse alphabetical order, we could revise the sort so that it reverses the order. Modify program **chapter7_5** to implement this technique.

7.4   Character Functions

The Standard C library contains a set of functions for use with characters. These functions fall into two categories: One set of functions is used to convert characters between uppercase and lowercase, and the other set is used to perform character comparisons. Each function requires an integer argument, and each function returns an integer value; the prototype statements for these functions are included in the header file **ctype.h**. The character comparison functions return a non-zero value if the comparison is true; otherwise, they return a zero.

tolower(c)	If **c** is an uppercase letter, this function returns the corresponding lowercase letter; otherwise, it returns **c**.
toupper(c)	If **c** is a lowercase letter, this function returns the corresponding uppercase letter; otherwise, it returns **c**.
isdigit(c)	This function returns a nonzero value if **c** is a decimal digit; otherwise, it returns a zero.
islower(c)	This function returns a nonzero value if **c** is a lowercase letter; otherwise, it returns a zero.
isupper(c)	This function returns a nonzero value if **c** is an uppercase letter; otherwise, it returns a zero.
isalpha(c)	This functions returns a nonzero value if **c** is an uppercase letter or a lowercase letter; otherwise, it returns a zero.
isalnum(c)	This function returns a nonzero value if **c** is an alphabetic character or a numeric digit; otherwise, it returns a zero.
iscntrl(c)	This function returns a nonzero value if **c** is a control character; otherwise, it returns a zero. (The **control characters** have integer codes of 0 through 21, and 127.)

Control character

isgraph(c)   This function returns a nonzero value if **c** is a character that can be printed, as opposed to a character that cannot be printed, such as a control character or a tab; otherwise, it returns a zero. (The **printing characters** have integer codes from 32 through 126.)

isprint(c)   This function returns a nonzero value if **c** is a printing character (does include a space); otherwise, it returns a zero.

ispunct(c)   This function returns a nonzero value if **c** is a printing character with the exception of a space or a letter or a digit; otherwise, it returns a zero.

isspace(c)   This function returns a nonzero value if **c** is a space, formfeed, newline, carriage return, horizontal tab, or vertical tab (these characters are also referred to as **white space**); otherwise, the function returns a zero.

isxdigit(c)   This function returns a nonzero value if **c** is a hexadecimal digit, which is a decimal digit or an alphabetic character A through F (or *a* through *f*); otherwise, it returns a zero.

White space

Style

These functions perform operations similar to some of the operations that we included in previous programs. *In general, use a library function when possible instead of writing your own statements;* this reduces the length of your programs and also reduces debugging time.

We now rewrite program **chapter7_4** so that it uses a library character function to determine the number of digits in an input text stream. Also, note that an additional **include** statement is needed:

ch7_6.c

```
/*-------------------------------------------------------*/
/*  Program chapter7_6                                   */
/*                                                       */
/*  This program counts and prints the                  */
/*  number of digits in an input text stream.           */

#include <stdio.h>
#include <stdlib.h>
#include <ctype.h>

main()
{
   /*  Declare and initialize variables.  */
   int c, count=0;
```

```
        /*  Read characters and count digits.  */
        printf("Enter characters: (^z to quit) \n");
        while ((c = getchar()) != EOF)
        {
            if (isdigit(c))
                ++count;
        }

        /*  Print the number of digits read.  */
        printf("%i digits read. \n",count);

        /*  Exit program.  */
        return EXIT_SUCCESS;
    }
    /*-------------------------------------------------------*/
```

The sample output with this program is same as with program **chapter7_4**:

```
Enter characters: (^z to quit)
514 East Sixth St.
Hampton, NH 30255-0345
^Z
12 digits read.
```

Modify!

ch7_6.c

Modify program **chapter7_6** to compute and print the following information. Use the character functions as much as possible.

1. Print the percentage of uppercase characters in the input text stream.
2. Print the number of alphabetic characters in the input text stream.
3. Print the number of nonalphabetic characters in the input text stream.
4. Print the percentage of alphanumeric characters in the input text stream.

7.5   Problem Solving Applied: Molecular Weights

Chemical reactions play an important role in many scientific and engineering systems. Understanding and controlling chemical reactions allows petroleum engineers to improve the efficiency of the refineries necessary to process oil and gas resources. Understanding the behavior and reactions of fully ionized gases at very high temperatures under the influence of strong magnetic fields will be an important step in developing controlled nuclear fusion. In genetic engineering, the identification of amino acids in DNA proteins is a key step in developing techniques to synthesize new products.

Computing the molecular weight from a chemical formula is a common task in any application that involves chemical reactions. Write a program that reads a chemical formula from the keyboard and then computes the corresponding molecular weight. We will assume that this program will be used in a genetic engineering laboratory working with the amino acids in proteins. Amino acids contain only atoms of oxygen (O), carbon (C), nitrogen (N), sulfur (S), and hydrogen (H). For example, the chemical formula for alanine is $O_2C_3NH_7$; thus, alanine contains two atoms of oxygen, three atoms of carbon, one atom of nitrogen, and seven atoms of hydrogen. The input to the program is a set of characters that specifies the chemical formula. The valid characters are the abbreviations O, C, N, S, and H, and we will allow these characters to be either uppercase or lowercase. Each element may also be followed by one or two digits that specify the number of atoms of the element. Thus, the input characters for alanine could include O2C3NH7 or o2c3nh7. Errors occur if the element is not one of the five specified elements or if the formula begins with a number. Use the following molecular weights:

oxygen	15.9994	sulfur	32.066
carbon	12.011	hydrogen	1.00794
nitrogen	14.00674		

After computing the molecular weight, the program should then print the value on the terminal screen.

1.   **PROBLEM STATEMENT**

Compute the molecular weight of a chemical formula for an amino acid.

2.   **INPUT/OUTPUT DESCRIPTION**

The input to the program is a chemical formula entered from the keyboard, and the output is the corresponding molecular weight displayed on the computer screen.

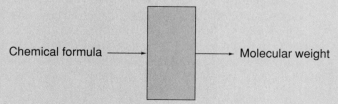

Chemical formula ⟶ ⟶ Molecular weight

3.   **HAND EXAMPLE**

If the input is the chemical formula for alanine, which is O2C3NH7, then the corresponding output should be computed in the following way:

```
Two atoms of oxygen:
     2 x 15.9994 = 31.9988
Three atoms of carbon:
     3 x 12.011 = 36.033
One atom of nitrogen:
     1 x 14.00674 = 14.00674
Seven atoms of hydrogen:
     7 x 1.00794 = 7.05558
The total molecular weight is 89.09412.
```

4.   ALGORITHM DEVELOPMENT

We first develop the decomposition outline because it breaks the solution into a series of sequential steps.

Decomposition Outline
1. *Read the chemical formula.*
2. *Compute the molecular weight.*
3. *Print the molecular weight.*

Parsing

Step 1 involves reading the characters from the keyboard and storing them in an integer array. Step 2 involves examining the characters (also called **parsing**) to first determine each element and then to determine the number of atoms for each element. Because comparing a character to the possible elements and then selecting the corresponding atomic weight will require several steps, we will implement this computation in a function. In the `main` function, we will multiply the individual atomic weights by the appropriate number of atoms and then add the values to a total. Note that we will need to convert the number of atoms from character digits to a numerical value in order to perform the multiplication; because the digits are consecutive in the collating sequence, the numerical equivalent of a digit can be obtained by subtracting the value of '0' from it. Step 3 involves printing the final molecular weight. We will also include in this step the printing of an error message if the input characters could not be analyzed properly. The refinement in pseudocode for the `main` function and the `atomic_wt` function can now be developed:

Refinement in Pseudocode

main: *print message to the user*
            set k to 0
            while more characters
                read formula[k]
                increment k by 1
            set current to 0

while current character is not newline
 if current character is alphabetic
  convert current character to uppercase
 else
  set error to 1.0
 set weight to atomic_wt(current character)
 if weight is equal to 0
  set error to 1.0
 if next character (or characters) are numeric,
  multiple weight by decimal value
  increment current by 1
 add weight to total
 increment current by 1
if no error
 print weight
else
 print error message and formula
atomic_wt(atom):
 if atom is in element list
  return corresponding molecular weight
 else
  return 0.0

ch7_7.c

```
/*-----------------------------------------------------*/
/*  Program chapter7_7                                 */
/*                                                     */
/*  This program computes the molecular weight         */
/*  of an amino acid from its chemical formula.        */

#include <stdio.h>
#include <stdlib.h>
#include <ctype.h>
#define NEWLINE '\n'

main()
{
   /*  Declare variables and function prototypes.  */
   int k=0, formula[20], n, current=0, number;
   double error=0.0, weight, total=0.0;
   double atomic_wt(int atom);

   /*  Read chemical formula from keyboard.  */
   printf("Enter chemical formula for amino acid: \n");
   while ((formula[k] = getchar()) != NEWLINE)
   {
      ++k;
   }
   n = k;
```

```
/*  Identify individual elements and add weights.  */
while (formula[current] != NEWLINE)
{
   /*  Check that formula begins with an element.  */
   if (isalpha(formula[current]))
      formula[current] = toupper(formula[current]);
   else
   {
      /*  Set error code and exit while loop.  */
      error = 1.0;
      break;
   }

   /*  Determine atomic weight of current element.  */
   weight = atomic_wt(formula[current]);
   if (weight == 0.0)
   {
      /*  Set error code and exit while loop.  */
      error = 1.0;
      break;
   }

   /*  Multiply weight by number of atoms  */
   if (isdigit(formula[current+1]) &&
       isdigit(formula[current+2]))
   {
      /*  Number of atoms is between 10 and 99.  */
      number = (formula[current+1]-'0')*10
               + (formula[current+2]-'0');
      weight *= number;
      current += 2;
   }
   else
   {
      /*  Number of atoms is between 1 and 9.  */
      if (isdigit(formula[current+1]))
      {
         weight *= (formula[current+1]-'0');
         ++current;
      }
   }
   /*  Add weight to molecular weight.  */
   total += weight;
   ++current;
}
```

```
      /*  Print molecular weight.  */
      if (error == 0.0)
         printf("Molecular Weight: %f \n",total);
      else
      {
         printf("Error in Formula \n");
         for (k=0; k<=n-1; k++)
            putchar(formula[k]);
      }

      /*  Exit program.  */
      return EXIT_SUCCESS;
}
/*-------------------------------------------------------*/
/*  Function to compute molecular weight                 */
/*  of an element in an amino acid.                      */

double atomic_wt(int atom)
{
   /*  Declare and initialize variables.  */
   int i=0, element[5]={'H','C','N','O','S'};
   double m_wt[5]={1.00794, 12.011, 14.00674, 15.9994, 32.066};

   /*  Search for element.  */
   while ((element[i] != atom) && (i<=4))
      i++;

   /*  Return corresponding atomic weight.  */
   if (element[i] == atom)
      return m_wt[i];
   else
      return 0.0;
}
/*-------------------------------------------------------*/
```

5.   **TESTING**

The output from the program using the data from the hand example follows:

```
Enter chemical formula for amino acid:
O2C3NH7
Molecular Weight:  89.094116
```

Modify!

ch7_7.c

Modify the molecular-weight program to include these capabilities.

1.   Allow the user to compute the molecular weights for several amino acids. The program should terminate when an EOF character is read.

2.   Instead of working with the chemical elements in amino acids, modify the program to work with the combination of elements of Si, Cl, and H. (These elements are used in generating silicon films that are used in the electronics industry.) Because two of the elements have two-letter abbreviations, write the program so that it requires the second letter of a two-letter abbreviation to be lowercase. The additional atomic weights are

> Si   28.0855   Cl   35.4527

Test your program with the following formulas:

> H_2, HCl, $SiCl_4$, $SiCl_2$, $SiHCl_3$, and SiH_2Cl_2

3.   Add a function to program **chapter7_7** that converts several digits in a row to an integer value. Call the function instead of computing the decimal number of atoms in the **main** function. Assume that the corresponding function prototype is

```
int numeric (int formula[20], int start);
```

4.   Modify program **chapter7_7** so that it accepts a prefix to the chemical formula. Thus, 2H2O represents two molecules of water, and the molecular weight is twice the molecular weight of water. (*Hint*: The function developed in Problem 3 might be useful.)

7.6   Character Strings*

A character array is an array in which the individual elements are stored as characters. A **character string** is a character array in which the last array element is a null character, '\0', which has an ASCII integer equivalent of zero. In this section, we focus on character strings.

STRING DEFINITION AND I/O

Character string constants are enclosed in double quotes, as in **"sensor1.dat"**, **"r"**, and **"15762"**. A character string array can be defined using string constants, or using character constants, as shown in the following equivalent statements:

```
char filename[12] = "sensor1.dat";
char filename[] = "sensor1.dat";
char filename[] = {'s','e','n','s','o','r',
                   '1','.','d','a','t','\0'};
```

The following statements read a line from the keyboard, and store it as a character string:

```
/*  Declare variables.  */
int k=0, nchars;
char line[50];
...
/*  Read characters into string.  */
while ((line[k] = getchar()) != '\n')
{
    k++;
}
line[k] = '\0';
nchar = k + 1;
```

A similar set of statements can be used to read a character string from the characters in a line in a data file. To print the values in this character string, we can use statements such as these:

```
for (k=0; k<=nchar-2; k++)
{
    putchar(line[k]);
}
putchar('\n');
```

Note that we did not print the last character, `line[nchar-1]`, since it is a null character; however, we did print a newline character so that the information printed will be on a separate line from any remaining output. We can also print a character string using the `%s` specifier; the null character is not printed by this specifier. Thus, the string `line` could be printed using this statement:

```
printf("String: %s \n",line);
```

If a string printed with an `%s` specifier does not end with a null character, the characters following the string will be printed until a null character is encountered.

STRING FUNCTIONS

We first present programmer-defined functions that use character string arguments, and then we present a group of library functions that use character strings. The following three programmer-defined functions determine the length of a character string argument, where the length of a character string is defined to be the number of characters up to, but not including, the null character. The first function uses subscripting within a `while` loop, the second function uses pointers within a `while` loop, and the third function uses pointers within a `for` loop. All three functions are equivalent, and all have essentially the same function prototype statements:

```
int strg_len_1(char s[]);
int strg_len_2(char *s);
int strg_len_3(char *s);
```

Function 1

```
/*----------------------------------------------------*/
/*  This function determines the length of a string   */
/*  using subscripts within a while loop.             */

int strg_len_1(char s[])
{
   /*  Declare variables.  */
   int k=0;

   /*  Count characters.  */
   while (s[k] != '\0')
   {
     k++;
   }

   /*  Return string length.  */
   return k;
}
/*----------------------------------------------------*/
```

Function 2

```
/*----------------------------------------------------*/
/*  This function determines the length of a string   */
/*  using a pointer within a while loop.              */

int strg_len_2(char *s)
{
   /*  Declare variables.  */
   int count=0;

   /*  Count characters.  */
   while (*s != '\0')
   {
      s++;
      count++;
   }

   /*  Return string length.  */
   return count;
}
/*----------------------------------------------------*/
```

Function 3

```
/*----------------------------------------------------*/
/*  This function determines the length of a string   */
/*  using a pointer within a for loop.                */

int strg_len_3(char *s)
{
   /*  Declare variables.  */
   int count;
```

```
/*  Count characters.  */
for (count=0; *s != '\0'; s++)
{
    count++;
}

/*  Return string length.  */
return count;
}
/*-------------------------------------------------*/
```

These functions demonstrate the variety of techniques that can be used with character strings.

The Standard C library contains a number of functions for working with strings. In the following discussion of these functions and their arguments, assume that **s** and **t** are character strings, and that **ps** and **pt** are pointers to **s** and **t**, respectively. The variable **n** is of type `size_t`, which is an unsigned integer; **c** is an integer that is converted to a character. The prototype statements for these functions are included in the header file `string.h`.

`strlen(ps)`	This function returns the length of the string **s**.
`strcpy(ps,pt)`	This function copies string **t** to string **s**. The function returns a pointer to **s**.
`strncpy(ps,pt,n)`	This function copies at most n characters from string **t** to string **s**. If **t** has fewer characters than **s**, then **s** is padded with null characters. The function returns a pointer to **s**.
`strcat(ps,pt)`	This function **concatenates** string **t** to the end of string **s**. Thus, string **s** will contain the characters of **s** followed by the characters of **t**; the first character of **t** overwrites the null character at the end of **s**. The function returns a pointer to **s**.
`strncat(ps,pt,n)`	This function concatenates at most **n** characters of string **t** to string **s**. If **t** has more than **n** characters, then only the first **n** characters of **t** are concatenated to **s**. The initial character of **t** overwrites the null character at the end of **s**; a null character is added to the new end of **s**. The function returns a pointer to **s**.
`strcmp(ps,pt)`	This function compares string **s** to string **t** in an element-by-element comparison, starting with `s[0]` and `t[0]`. A negative value is returned if s<t, zero is returned if **s** is equal to **t**, and a positive value is returned if s>t.
`strncmp(ps,pt,n)`	This function compares at most **n** characters of string **s** to string **t** in an element-by-element comparison, starting with `s[0]` and `t[0]`. A

	negative value is returned if **s<t**, zero is returned if **s** is equal to **t**, and a positive value is returned if **s>t**.
strchr(ps,c)	This function returns a pointer to the first occurrence of the character **c** in the string **s**. If the character does not occur in **s**, a **NULL** pointer is returned.
strrchr(ps,c)	This function returns a pointer to the last occurrence of the character **c** in the string **s**. If the character does not occur in **s**, a **NULL** pointer is returned.
strstr(ps,pt)	This function returns a pointer to the start of the string **t** within the string **s**. If **t** does not occur in **s**, a **NULL** pointer is returned.
strspn(ps,pt)	This function returns the initial number of characters of string **s** that consists entirely of characters in string **t**.
strcspn(ps,pt)	This function returns the initial number of characters of string **s** that consists entirely of characters not in string **t**.
strpbrk(ps,pt)	This function returns a pointer to the first occurrence in string **s** of any character of string **t**. If none of the characters in **t** occurs in **s**, a **NULL** pointer is returned.

To illustrate the use of these functions, we now present several examples. Consider the following string definitions and operations:

```
/*  Declare and initialize variables.  */
char strg1[]="Engineering Problem Solving: ";
char strg2[]="Fundamental Concepts", strg3[50];
char *ptr1=strg1, *ptr2=strg2, *ptr3=strg3;

/*  Print the length of strings.  */
printf("String lengths: %i %i \n",
       strlen(ptr1),strlen(ptr2));

/*  Combine two strings into one.  */
strcpy(ptr3,ptr1);
strcat(ptr3,ptr2);
printf("strg3: %s \n",strg3);
printf("strg3 length: %i \n",strlen(ptr3));
```

The output from these statements is the following:

```
String lengths: 29 20
strg3: Engineering Problem Solving: Fundamental Concepts
strg3 length: 49
```

Note that the statement that determined and printed the string lengths could also have been replaced with

```
printf("String lengths: %i %i \n",
       strlen(strg1),strlen(strg2));
```

since an array name is also a pointer to the first element in the array.

Assume that we want to count the occurrences of one string in another string using the `strstr` function. For example, suppose that we want to count the number of times that `"bb"` occurs in the string `"abbcfgwdbibbw"`. The `strstr` function will return a pointer to the start of the first occurrence of `"bb"` in `"abbcfgwdbibbw"`, or a `NULL` pointer if `"bb"` is not found. In this example, the `strstr` function will return a pointer to the beginning of the first occurrence of `"bb"`, as follows:

```
"abbcfgwdbibbw"
  ↑
```

In order to find the next occurrence of the string `"bb"`, we need to search the portion of the string that follows the first position of the occurrence of `"bb"` Specifically, we want the next `strstr` reference to search for the string `"bb"` in the string `"bcfgwdbiddw."` The `strstr` function will then return a pointer to the beginning of the first occurrence of `"bb"` in this new portion, as follows:

```
"bcfgwdbibbw"
       ↑
```

We repeat the process, using this portion of the string:

```
"bw"
```

At this point, the `strstr` function will return a `NULL` value. The statements to implement these steps follow:

```
/*  Declare and initialize variables.  */
int count=0;
char strg1[]="abbcfgwdbibbw", strg2[]="bb";
char *ptr1=strg1, *ptr2=strg2;
...
/*  Count the number of occurrences of strg2 in strg1.  */
while ((ptr1=strstr(ptr1,ptr2)) != NULL)
{
    count++;
    ptr1++;
}
printf("Count: %i \n",count);
```

The output from these statements is the following:

```
Count: 2
```

Suppose the previous statements were used with the string **"abbcfgwdbb bibbw."** The **strstr** function would identify the following four occurrences of the string **"bb"**:

"abbcfgwdbbbibbw"
　↑　　　　↑↑　↑

Thus, the substring **"bbb"** contains two occurrences of the string **"bb."** If we did not want to allow overlapping occurrences, then we should increment **ptr1** in the **while** loop by the number of characters in the substring for which we are searching.

Style

Although the string functions presented in this section are very specific, they should be used when possible instead of adding user-defined functions . The use of library functions makes programs both more readable and easier to debug.

Practice!

Give the output of the following statements, assuming the following strings and pointer definitions:

```
char strg1[]="Engineering Problem Solving: ";
char strg2[]="Fundamental Concepts", strg3[50];
char *ptr1=strg1, *ptr2=strg2, *ptr3=strg3;
```

1.  ```
    strncpy(ptr3,ptr1,12);
    strcat(ptr3,ptr2);
    printf("%s \n",*ptr3);
    ```
2.  ```
    if (strcmp(ptr1,ptr2) != 0)
       printf("not equal \n");
    else
       printf("equal \n");
    ```
3.  ```
    printf("%i \n",strspn(ptr1,ptr2));
    ```
4.  ```
    printf("%i \n",strspn(ptr2,ptr1));
    ```
5.  ```
    printf("%i \n",strcspn(ptr1,ptr2));
    ```
6.  ```
    printf("%s \n",*strpbrk(ptr1,ptr2));
    ```

SUMMARY

Using the ASCII binary code to represent characters, we presented techniques for initializing, manipulating, and printing character information. The variables containing the character information were generally defined as integers, and then referenced as either integers or characters, depending on the problem to be solved. A number of examples were presented that used character information as function arguments, including an alphabetical sort function. The molecular weight computation program developed in this chapter combined many of the techniques presented; it read a chemical formula from the keyboard and then used both library character functions and a user-defined function in the determination of the corresponding molecular weight. Finally, character strings and related library functions were presented.

KEY TERMS

alphanumeric character	EBCDIC code
ASCII code	EOF character
binary code	null character
character	parsing
character string	text stream
collating sequence	white space
control character	

C STATEMENT SUMMARY

Include character function header files

```
#include <ctype.h>
#include <string.h>
```

Declare and initialize character variable

```
char c = '*';
```

Read character from the keyboard

```
c = getchar();
```

Print character to the screen

```
putchar(c);
```

Style NOTES

1. Use character constants instead of their binary equivalents in program statements.
2. Use character library functions instead of writing similar ones yourself.

DEBUGGING NOTES

1. Remember that the integer representation for a character digit is not the same as the integer representation for the numerical digit.

2. Store the value read by the `getchar` function in an integer variable so that you can compare it to the `EOF` character.

3. If unexpected characters are printed at the end of a string, the null character may be missing.

4. Use the character library functions instead of writing similar ones yourself to reduce the debugging time of your program.

PROBLEMS

Data Filters. Programs called data filters are often used to read the information in a data file and then analyze the contents. In many cases, this data filter program is designed to remove any data errors that would cause problems with other programs that read the information from the data file. The following set of programs are designed to perform error checking and data analysis on information in a data file. Generate data files to test all features of the programs.

1. Write a program that reads a data file that should contain only integer values, and thus should contain only digits, plus or minus signs, and white space. The program should print any invalid characters located in the file, and at the end, it should print a count of the invalid characters located.

2. Write a program that analyzes a data file that has been determined to contain only integer values and white space. The program should print the number of lines in the file and the number of integer values (not integer digits).

3. Write a program that reads a file that contains only integers, but some of the integers have embedded commas, as in 145,020. The program should copy the information to a new file, removing any commas from the information. Do not change the number of values per line in the file.

4. Write a program that reads a file containing integer and floating-point values separated by commas, which may or may not be followed by additional white space. Generate a new file that contains the integers and floating-point values separated only by spaces; remove all white space characters between the values and insert a single space between the values. Do not change the number of values per line in the file.

5. Write a program that reads a file containing data values computed by an accounting software package. While the file contains only numerical information, the values may contain embedded commas and dollar signs, as in

gram to generate a new file that contains the values with the commas and dollar signs removed, and with a leading minus sign instead of the parentheses. Do not change the number of values per line in the file.

6. A very useful program is one that compares two files, character by character, to determine if they are exactly the same. Write a program to compare two files. The program should print a message indicating that the files are exactly the same, or that there are differences. If the files are different, the program should print the line numbers for lines that are not the same.

Bar Graphs. Characters can be used to print a bar graph that corresponds to a set of numerical values. For example, the following bar graph corresponds to the integers 5,9,2,4,10,7:

```
5    *****
9    *********
2    **
4    ****
10   **********
7    *******
```

7. Write a function that receives an integer array and an integer variable that contains the number of integer values in the array. If all the values are between 0 and 50, print a bar graph similar to one shown above and return a value of 0; otherwise, do not print a bar graph, and return a value of 1. Assume that the corresponding function prototype statement is

```
int bargraph_1(int count, int data[]);
```

8. Modify the function developed in Problem 7 such that it prints two lines of asterisks for each bar. Assume that the corresponding function prototype statement is

```
int bargraph_2(int count, int data[]);
```

9. Modify the function developed in Problem 7 such that it computes the average of the data values. For each bar, print asterisks for any part of the bar up to the average value, and then print plus signs for any part of the bar that is over the average. Thus, if a data value is below the average, its bar is composed entirely of asterisks. If a data value is above the average, its bar is composed of asterisks and plus signs, as in *****++. Assume that the corresponding function prototype statement is

```
int bargraph_3(int count, int data[]);
```

10. Write a function that generates a bar graph that corresponds to scaled integers computed from integers in an array. Thus, instead of requiring the integers in the array to be between 0 and a maximum of 50, scale the values to the range [0,50], and then print a corresponding bargraph. To scale the values, use the following computation that normalizes a value x (that is between the minimum value and the maximum value) so that it is between 0 and 1:

$$\frac{x - \text{minimum}}{\text{maximum} - \text{minimum}}$$

Note that if x is equal to the minimum, this expression is equal to zero, and if x is equal to the maximum, this expression is equal to 1.0. To scale the normalized values between 0 and 50, we simply multiply the normalized values by 50. Since the scaled values are floating-point values, round them to the nearest integer before printing the corresponding bargraph. The bar graph should contain the original values next to the bars, not the scaled values. Also, be sure not to change the original values in the array. Assume that the corresponding function prototype statement is

```
void bar_4(int count, int data[]);
```

11. Modify the function developed in problem 10 such that the maximum number of asterisks in a bar (which was 50 in problem 10) is an input parameter. Assume that the corresponding function prototype statement is

```
void bar_5(int count, int data[], int max_bar);
```

Cryptography. The science of developing secret codes has interested many people for centuries. Some of the simplest codes involve replacing a character, or a group of characters with another character, or group of characters. To easily decode these messages, the decoder needs the "key" that shows the replacement characters. In recent times, computers have been used very successfully to decode many codes that initially were assumed to be unbreakable. The next set of problems considers simple codes and schemes for decoding them. Generate files to test the programs.

12. A simple code can be developed by replacing each character by another character that is a fixed number of positions away in the collating sequence. For example, if each character is replaced by the character that is two characters to the right, then the letter 'a' is replaced by the letter 'c,' the letter 'b' is replaced by the letter 'd,' and so on. Write a program that reads the text in a file, and then generates a new file that contains the coded text using this scheme. Do not change the newline characters or the EOF character.

13. Write a program to decode the scheme presented in Problem 12. Test the program using files generated by Problem 12. Use the program developed in Problem 6 to compare the original file and the decoded files.

14. One step in decoding a simple code such as the one described in Problem 12 without knowing the coding scheme, involves counting the number of occurrences of each character. Then, knowing that the most common letter in English is 'e,' the letter that occurs most commonly in the coded message is replaced by 'e.' Similar replacements are then made based on the number of occurrences of characters in the coded message and the known occurrences of characters in the English language. This decoding often provides enough of the correct replacements that the incorrect replacements can then be determined. For this problem, write a program that reads a data file and determines the number of occurrences of each of the characters in the file. Then, print the characters and the number of times that they occurred. If a character does not occur, do not print it. (HINT: Use an array to store the occurrences of the characters, based on their ASCII codes.)

15. Another simple code encodes a message in text such that the true message is represented by the first letter of each word. There are no spaces between the words, but the decoded string of characters can easily be separated into words by a person. Write a program to read a data file and determine the secret message stored by the sequence of first letters of the words.

16. Assume that the true secret message in Problem 15 is stored in the second letter of each word. Write a program to read a data file and determine the secret message stored in the file.

17. Assume that the true secret message in Problem 15 is represented by the characters that are three characters to the right in the collating sequence from the first letters of the words. Write a program to read a data file and determine the secret message stored in the file using this decoding scheme.

18. Write a program that encodes the text in a data file using an integer array named **key** that contains 26 characters. This key is read from the keyboard; the first letter contains the character that is to replace the letter **a** in the data file, the second letter contains the letter that is to replace the letter **b** in the data file, and so on. Assume that all punctuation is to be replaced by spaces. Check to be sure that the key does not map two different characters to the same one during the encoding.

19. Write a program that decodes the file that is the output of Problem 18. Assume that the same integer **key** is read from the keyboard by this program, and is used in the decoding steps. Note that you will not be able to restore the punctuation characters.

Atomic Elements. Assume that we have three arrays that contain information from the periodic table of the elements. The one-dimensional array **atomic_num** contains atomic numbers, the two-dimensional array **atomic_sym** contains three columns which contain the characters that compose the symbols for the elements that correspond to the elements in the array **atomic_num**, and the one-dimensional array **atomic_wt** contains the atomic weights that correspond to the elements in the array **atomic_num**. The variable **n_elts** contains the number of elements in `atomic_num`. Assume that each of the arrays is defined with 103 rows so that it could conceivably hold all 103 elements from the periodic table. A typical set of values for these arrays is shown below:

```
n_elts     6

atomic_num     atomic_sym     atomic_wt
2              He             4.00260
10             Ne             20.1797
18             Ar             39.948
36             Kr             83.80
54             Xe             131.29
86             Rn             222.0176
```

20. Write a function that prints the information in these arrays in a table with a title and column headings. Assume that the corresponding function prototype statement is

```
void print_elts(int n_elts, int atomic_num[],
                int atomic_sym[103][3], double atomic_wt[]);
```

21. Write a function that checks each atomic symbol to be sure that the first letter is upper-case, and that the remaining letters are lowercase. If a letter is found with the wrong case, the function should replace it with the correct case. Assume that the corresponding function prototype statement is

```
void check_symbol(int n_elts, int atomic_sym[103][3]);
```

22. Write a function that prints the atomic symbol and the atomic weight for each element whose weight is above a specified weight. Assume that the corresponding function prototype statement is

```
int select_wt(int n_elts, int atomic_sym[103][3],
              double atomic_wt[], double limit);
```

The function should return the number of atomic symbols printed.

23. Write a function that prints the atomic symbol and the atomic weight for each element whose weight is between a specified lower weight and an upper weight. Assume that the corresponding function prototype statement is

```
int limit_wt(double lower, double upper, int n_elts,
             int atomic_sym[103][3], double atomic_wt[]);
```

The function should return the number of atomic symbols printed.

24. Write a function that copies the `atomic_sym` array into another array, sorts the new array of symbols, and prints an alphabetical listing of the symbols. Assume that the corresponding function prototype statement is

```
void sort_sym(int n_elts, int atomic_sym[103][3]);
```

25. Write a function that reorders the values in the three arrays such that the symbols are alphabetical, and such that the order of the values in the other two arrays is changed to correspond to the new order of the symbols. Assume that the corresponding function prototype statement is

```
void reorder(int n_elts, int atomic_num[],
             int atomic_sym[103][3], double atomic_wt[]);
```

Conversion Functions. We occasionally need to convert a group of characters to a numerical value, and to convert a numerical value to a character array. The following functions perform these types of functions.

26. Write a function that converts an integer numerical value to an integer array that contains the characters of the original integer. Thus, given the input integer 351, the function should determine array values '3', '5', '1'. Assume that the corresponding function prototype statement is

```
int int_to_char(int x, int ch[], max_ch);
```

where `max_ch` contains the maximum number of characters that can be stored in the integer array `ch`. If the conversion works properly, return the number of characters in the array; if the conversion requires more than `max_ch`, return a value of 0. If the value of `x` is negative, the first character should be a minus sign, but no sign is used if the value is positive.

27. Write a function that converts characters in an integer array to an integer numerical value. Thus, given array values '−', '5', '4', the function should return the value −54. Assume that the corresponding function prototype statement is

```
int char_to_int(int ch[], int max_ch);
```

The variable `max_ch` contains the number of characters to convert. If the characters cannot be converted correctly to an integer, the function should return a value of 0. (Note that if a value of 0 is returned, the program must check array `ch` to determine if an error occurred in the conversion.)

Pattern Recognition. Many areas of engineering use problem solutions in which we search for a specific pattern of information in a signal. In the following problems, use character string functions as much as possible.

28.   Write a function that receives a pointer to a character string and a character. The function should return the number of times that the character occurred in the string. Assume that the function has the following prototype statement:

```
int charcnt(char *ptr, char c);
```

29.   Write a function that receives a pointer to a character string and returns the number of repeated characters that occur in the string. For example, the string "Mississippi" has three repeated characters. Do not count repeated blanks in the string. If a character occurs more than two times, it should still only count as one repeated character; thus, "hisssss" would have only one repeated character. Assume that the function has the following prototype statement:

```
int repeat(char *ptr);
```

30.   Rewrite the function from Problem 29 such that each pair of characters is counted as a repeat. Thus, the string "hisssss" would have four repeated characters. Assume that the function has the following prototype statement:

```
int repeat2(char *ptr);
```

31.   Write a function that receives pointers to two character strings and returns a count of the number of times that the second character string occurs in the first character string. Do not allow overlap of the occurrences. Thus, the string "110101" contains only one occurrence of "101." Assume that the function has the following prototype statement:

```
int pattern(char *ptr1, char *ptr2);
```

32.   Rewrite the function from Problem 31 such that overlap of the occurrences of the second string in the first string is allowed. Thus, the string "110101" contains two occurrences of "101." Assume that the function has the following prototype statement:

```
int overlap(char *ptr1, char *ptr2);
```

Appendix A
ANSI C Standard Library

While entire texts [7] have been written to discuss the ANSI C Standard Library, the intent of this appendix is to present only a short discussion on the information defined in each of the header files in the ANSI C Standard Library. These brief discussions are not intended to provide all the details necessary to use the functions, but to provide enough information so that you can determine if the functions may be of use in a particular application; you can then obtain more details from other references. The following discussions assume that you are familiar with the various data types, including pointers and character strings.

`<assert.h>`

The header file `<assert.h>` provides a definition of the assert function that can be used to provide diagnostic information when testing a program. This system-dependent diagnostic information is stored in the standard error file, which can be accessed after a program is completed.

`<ctype.h>`

The header file `<ctype.h>` defines several functions for testing and converting characters; they are also discussed in Chapter 7. The function prototype statements and corresponding discussions use the following definitions:

digit	one of the characters `0123456789`
hexadecimal digit	a digit or one of the characters `ABCDEFabcdef`
uppercase letter	one of the characters `ABCDEFGHIJKLMNOPQRSTUVWXYZ`
lowercase letter	one of the characters `abcdefghijklmnopqrstuvwxyz`
alphabetic character	an uppercase or a lowercase letter
alphanumeric character	a digit or an alphabetic character
punctuation character	one of the characters `!"#%&'();<=>?[\]*+,-./:^`
graph character	an alphanumeric character or a punctuation character
print character	a graph character or the space character

motion control character   one of the control characters FF (form feed), NL (new line), CR (carriage return), HT (horizontal tab), VT (vertical tab)

white space   the space character or one of the motion control characters

control character   one of the motion control characters or BEL (bell) or BS (backspace)

We now list each function prototype and give a brief definition for the corresponding function:

```
int isalnum(int c);
```
returns a nonzero (true) value if and only if the input character is a digit or an uppercase or lowercase letter

```
int isalpha(int c);
```
returns a nonzero (true) value if and only if the input character is an uppercase or lowercase letter

```
int iscntrl(int c);
```
returns a nonzero (true) value if and only if the input character is one of the control characters

```
int isdigit(int c);
```
returns a nonzero (true) value if and only if the input character is a digit

```
int isgraph(int c);
```
returns a nonzero (true) value if and only if the input character is a graph character

```
int islower(int c);
```
returns a nonzero (true) value if and only if the input character is a lowercase letter

```
int isprint(int c);
```
returns a nonzero (true) value if and only if the input character is a printing character

```
int ispunct(int c);
```
returns a nonzero (true) value if and only if the input character is a punctuation character

```
int isspace(int c);
```
returns a nonzero (true) value if and only if the input character is a white space character

```
int isupper(int c);
```
returns a nonzero (true) value if and only if the input character is an uppercase character

```
int isxdigit(int c);
```
returns a nonzero (true) value if and only if the input character is a hexadecimal character

```
int tolower(int c);
```
converts an uppercase letter to a lowercase letter

```
int toupper(int c);
```
converts a lowercase letter to an uppercase letter

`<errno.h>`

The header file `<errno.h>` provides a definition of macros **EDOM** and **ERANGE** and an external function **errno**. The macros **EDOM** and **ERANGE** are integer constants with nonzero values that are system-dependent. The purpose of the **errno** function is to report error conditions, and its use is system dependent.

`<float.h>`

The header file `<float.h>` provides several macros that give various limits and characteristics for floating-point values, where a normalized floating-point value has been expressed in an exponential notation with a mantissa greater than or equal to 1 and less than 10. These macros and their corresponding definitions are listed below:

```
int FLT_ROUNDS;
```
specifies the rounding mode for floating-point addition
```
int FLT_RADIX;
```
radix of the exponent representation for floating-point values
```
int FLT_MANT_DIG;
int DBL_MANT_DIG;
int LDBL_MANT_DIG;
```
number of radix base digits in the normalized mantissa for a **float**, **double**, or **long double** value
```
int FLT_DIG;
int DBL_DIG;
int LDBL_DIG;
```
number of decimal digits in the normalized mantissa for a **float**, **double**, or **long double** value
```
int FLT_MIN_EXP;
int DBL_MIN_EXP;
int LDBL_MIN_EXP;
```
integer used to determine the minimum radix exponent for a normalized value for a **float**, **double**, or **long double** value
```
int FLT_MIN_10_EXP;
int DBL_MIN_10_EXP;
int LDBL_MIN_10_EXP;
```
integer used to determine the minimum exponent for a base 10 normalized value for a **float**, **double**, or **long double** value
```
int FLT_MAX_EXP;
int DBL_MAX_EXP;
int LDBL_MAX_EXP;
```
integer used to determine the maximum exponent for the radix base for a normalized value for a **float**, **double**, or **long double** value
```
int FLT_MAX_10_EXP;
int DBL_MAX_10_EXP;
int LDBL_MAX_10_EXP;
```
integer used to determine the maximum exponent for a base 10 normalized value for a **float**, **double**, or **long double** value

```
float FLT_MIN;
double DBL_MIN;
long double LDBL_MIN;
```
   minimum representable value for a **float**, **double**, or **long double** value

```
float FLT_MAX;
double DBL_MAX;
long double LDBL_MAX;
```
   maximum representable value for a **float**, **double**, or **long double** value

```
float FLT_EPSILON;
double DBL_EPSILON;
long double LDBL_EPSILON;
```
   difference between 1 and the smallest value greater than one for a **float**, **double**, or **long double** value

<limits.h>

The header file **<limits.h>** provides several macros that give various limits and characteristics for integer values. These macros and their definitions are listed below:

```
int CHAR_BIT;
```
   number of bits for the smallest nonbit value

```
int CHAR_MIN;
int CHAR_MAX;
```
   minimum and maximum values for type **char**

```
int INT_MIN;
int INT_MAX;
```
   minimum and maximum values for type **int**

```
int LONG_MIN;
int LONG_MAX;
```
   minimum and maximum values for type **long int**

```
int MB_LEN_MAX;
```
   maximum number of bytes in a multibyte character

```
int SCHAR_MIN;
int SCHAR_MAX;
```
   minimum and maximum values for type **signed char**

```
int SHRT_MIN;
int SHRT_MAX;
```
   minimum and maximum values for type **short int**

```
int UCHAR_MAX;
```
   maximum values for type **unsigned char**

```
int UINT_MAX;
```
   maximum value for type **unsigned int**

```
int ULONG_MAX;
```
   maximum value for type **unsigned long int**

```
int USHRT_MAX;
```
   maximum value for type **unsigned short int**

`<locale.h>`

The header file `<locale.h>` defines two functions, one type, and several macros relative to the formatting of numeric values. This information allows numeric values to be formatted in ways to address internationalization issues, and includes information relative to monetary formatting and times.

`<math.h>`

The header file `<math.h>` defines functions that are often needed to perform engineering calculations. These functions are also described in detail in Chapter 2.

`double acos(double x);`
> computes the arccosine or inverse cosine of **x**, where **x** must be in the range $[-1,1]$; returns an angle in radians in the range $[0, \pi]$

`double asin(double x);`
> computes the arcsine or inverse sine of **x**, where **x** must be in the range $[-1,1]$; returns an angle in radians in the range $[\frac{-\pi}{2}, \frac{\pi}{2}]$

`double atan(double x);`
> computes the arctangent or inverse tangent of **x**; returns an angle in radians in the range $[\frac{-\pi}{2}, \frac{\pi}{2}]$

`double atan2(double y, double x);`
> computes the arctangent or inverse tangent of the value $\frac{y}{x}$; returns an angle in radians in the range $[-\pi, \pi]$

`int ceil(double x);`
> rounds **x** to the nearest integer towards ∞ (infinity)

`double cos(double x);`
> computes the cosine of **x**, where **x** is in radians

`double cosh(double x);`
> computes the hyperbolic cosine of **x**, which is equal to $\frac{e^x + e^{-x}}{2}$

`double exp(double x);`
> computes the value of e^x, where e is the base for natural logarithms, or approximately 2.718282

`double fabs(double x);`
> computes the absolute value of **x**

`int floor(double x);`
> rounds **x** to the nearest integer towards $-\infty$ (negative infinity)

`double log(double x);`
> computes ln **x**, the natural logarithm of **x** to the base e; errors occur if **x**≤ 0

`double log10(double x);`
> computes $\log_{10}$**x**, the common logarithm of **x** to the base 10; errors occur if **x**≤ 0

```
double pow(double x, double y);
```
computes the value of **x** to the **y** power, or x^y; errors occur if **x** = 0 and **y** ≤ 0, or if **x** < 0 and **y** is not an integer

```
double sin(double x);
```
computes the sine of **x**, where **x** is in radians

```
double sinh(double x);
```
computes the hyperbolic sine of **x**, which is equal to $\dfrac{e^x - e^{-x}}{2}$

```
double sqrt(double x);
```
computes the square root of **x** where **x** ≥ 0

```
double tan(double x);
```
computes the tangent of **x**, where **x** is in radians

```
double tanh(double x);
```
computes the hyperbolic tangent of **x**, which is equal to $\dfrac{\sinh x}{\cosh x}$

`<setjmp.h>`

The header file **`<setjmp.h>`** contains a macro, a function, and a type declaration used to bypass the normal function call and return processes. These operations are not generally recommended, and thus are not discussed here.

`<signal.h>`

The header file **`<signal.h>`** contains a type definition, two functions, and several macros for handling various signals, which are conditions that may be reported during the execution of a program and that are generally considered to be fatal errors. Since signal handling is nonportable, we do not discuss the information in this header file here. In general, the default handling provided by a system is sufficient for handling signals.

`<stdarg.h>`

The header file **`<stdarg.h>`** contains a type definition, and three macros for working with functions that allow a variable number of arguments. While this capability is very powerful, it is not generally commonly used in engineering applications.

`<stddef.h>`

The header file **`<stddef.h>`** contains type definitions and macros that are essentially unrelated. These types and macros are not commonly used in engineering applications and thus are not addressed here.

`<stdio.h>`

The header file **`<stdio.h>`** defines the types, macros, and functions required to perform input and output. Of the new types defined, the type **FILE** is the one most useful in engineering applications because it is used in conjunction with data files. Many of the input/output functions are discussed in Chapters 2 and 3; those functions and several additional functions are now summarized here.

```
void clearerr(FILE *stream);
```
clears the end-of-file and error indicators for the stream pointed to by `stream`

```
int fclose(FILE *stream);
```
closes the file associated with the file pointer

```
int feof(FILE *stream);
```
tests the end-of-file indicator for the stream pointed to by `stream`

```
int ferror(FILE *stream);
```
tests the error indicator for the stream pointed to by `stream`

```
int fflush(FILE *stream);
```
causes unwritten data for the stream to be written to the file

```
int fgetc(FILE *stream);
```
returns the integer equivalent of the next character in the stream

```
int fgetpos(FILE *stream, fpos_t *pos);
```
returns the current value of the file position indicator for the stream pointed to by `stream` in the object pointed to by `pos`

```
char *fgets(char *s, int n, FILE *stream);
```
reads into the array pointed to by `s` at most one less than the number of characters specified by `n` from the stream pointed to by `stream`

```
FILE *fopen(const char *filename, const char *mode);
```
opens the file whose name is a string pointed to by `filename`

```
int fprintf(FILE *stream, const char *format, ...);
```
writes the output to the stream pointed to by `stream` using the format specified and the values that follow the format reference; returns the number of characters printed

```
int fputc(int c, FILE *stream);
```
writes the character specified by `c` to the output stream pointed to by `stream`

```
int fputs(const char *s, FILE *stream);
```
writes the string pointed to by `s` to the stream pointed to by `stream`; does not write the terminating null character

```
size_t fread(void *ptr, size_t size, size_t nmemb, FILE *stream);
```
reads into the array pointed to by `ptr` up to `nmemb` elements whose size is specified by `size` from the stream pointed to by `stream`

```
FILE *freopen(const char *filename, const char *mode, FILE
    *stream);
```
reopens the file whose name is a string pointed to by `filename`

```
int fscanf(FILE *stream, const char *format, ...);
```
reads input from the stream pointed to by `stream` using the format specified and the addresses that follow the format reference; returns the number of input values assigned

```
int fseek(FILE *stream, long int offset, int whence);
```
sets the file position indicator for the stream pointed to by **stream**

```
int fsetpos(FILE *stream, const fpos_t *pos);
```
sets the file position indicator for the stream pointed to by **stream** according to the value of the object pointed to by **pos**

```
long int ftell(FILE *stream);
```
returns the current value of the file position indicator for the stream pointed to by **stream**

```
size_t fwrite(const void *ptr, size_t size, size_t nmemb,
      FILE *stream);
```
writes from the array pointed to by **ptr** up to **nmemb** elements whose size is specified by **size** to the stream pointed to by **stream**

```
int getc(FILE *stream);
```
returns the integer equivalent of the next character in the stream

```
int getchar(void);
```
returns the integer equivalent of the next character from the standard input stream

```
char *gets(char *s);
```
reads characters from the input stream into the array pointed to by **s** until a new-line character or end-of-file is encountered; the new-line character is replaced by a null character in the array

```
void perror(const char *s);
```
maps the error number in the integer expression **errno** to an error message

```
int printf(const char *format, ...);
```
writes the output to the standard output stream using the format specified and the values that follow the format reference; returns the number of characters printed

```
int putc(int c, FILE *stream);
```
writes the character specified by **c** to the output stream pointed to by **stream**

```
int putchar(int c);
```
writes the character specified by **c** to the standard output stream

```
int puts(const char *s);
```
writes the string pointed to by **s** to the standard output stream and adds a new-line character to the output in place of the null character

```
int remove(const char *filename);
```
removes accessibility of the file pointed to by **filename**

```
int rename(const char *old, const char *new);
```
changes the file originally pointed to by **old** to the one pointed to by **new**

```
void rewind(FILE *stream);
```
sets the file position indicator for the stream pointed to by **stream** to the beginning of the file

```
int scanf(const char *format, ...);
```
reads input from the standard input stream using the format specified

and the addresses that follow the format reference; returns the number of input values assigned

```
void setbuf(FILE *stream, char *buf);
```
specifies the type of buffering to be used with the stream pointed to by **stream**

```
int setvbuf(FILE *stream, char *buf, int mode, size_t size);
```
specifies the type of buffering to be used with the stream pointed to by **stream**

```
int sprintf(char *s, const char *format, ...);
```
writes the output to the array pointed to by **s** using the format specified and the values that follow the format reference, and a null character is written at the end of the characters written; returns the number of characters printed, not including the null character

```
int sscanf(const char *s, const char *format, ...);
```
reads input from the string pointed to by **s** using the format specified and the addresses that follow the format reference; returns the number of input values assigned

```
FILE *tmpfile(void);
```
creates a temporary binary file that is automatically removed when it is closed

```
char *tmpnam(char *s);
```
generates a string that is a valid file name and is not the same as an existing file

```
int ungetc(int c, FILE *stream);
```
pushes the character specified by **c** back onto the input stream pointed to by **stream**

```
int vfprintf(FILE *stream, const char *format, va_list arg);
```
writes the output to the stream pointed to by **stream** using the format specified and the values contained in the variable argument list; returns the number of characters printed

```
int vprintf(const char *format, va_list arg);
```
writes the output to the standard output stream using the format specified and the values contained in the variable argument list; returns the number of characters printed

```
int vsprintf(char *s, const char *format, va_list arg);
```
writes the output to the array pointed to by **s** using the format specified and the values contained in the variable argument list, and a null character is written at the end of the characters written; returns the number of characters printed, not including the null character

```
<stdlib.h>
```

The header file **<stdlib.h>** defines types, macros, and functions that did not fit in any of the other header files. The types **div_t** and **ldiv_t** are structures for storing a quotient and a remainder. The macros are the following:

NULL
> an integer value of binary zero

EXIT_FAILURE
EXIT_SUCCESS
> integral expressions used to return unsuccessful or successful termination status, respectively, to the host

RAND_MAX
> an integral expression that is the maximum value returned by the **RAND** function

MB_CUR_MAX
> a positive integer expression whose value is the maximum number of bytes in a multibyte character

The functions that are most likely to be used in engineering application are listed below, with the function prototype statement and a brief description. Many of these functions are discussed in Chapter 3 and in Chapter 7.

```
void a bort(void);
```
> causes an abnormal program termination of the program

```
int abs(int k);
long int labs(long int k);
```
> computes the absolute value of the integer **k**

```
int atexit(void (*func)(void));
```
> registers the function pointed to by **func** to be called without arguments at normal program termination

```
double atof(const char *s);
int atoi(const char *s);
long int atol(const char *s);
double strtod(const char *s, char **endptr);
long int strtol(const char *s, char **endptr, int base);
unsigned long int strtoul(const char *s, char **endptr,
                          int base);
```
> converts the initial portion of the string pointed to by **s** to a numerical representation

```
void *bsearch(const void *key, const void *base, size_t n, size_t
              size, int(*compar)(const void *,const void *));
```
> searches an array of **n** objects searching for the value pointed to by **key**

```
void *calloc(size_t n, size_t size);
```
> allocates space for an array of **n** objects, each of size **size**

```
div_t div(int numer, int denom);
ldiv_t ldiv(long int numer, long int denom);
```
> computes the quotient and remainder of the division of **numer** by **denom**

```
void exit(int status);
```
> causes normal program termination to occur

```
void free(void *ptr);
```
> deallocates the space pointed to by **ptr**

```
void *malloc(size_t size);
```
allocates space for an object of size **size**

```
void qsort(void *base, size_t nmemb, size_t size, int
             (*compar)(const void*, const void *));
```
sorts an object of **n** objects into ascending order

```
int rand(void);
```
returns a pseudo-random integer in the range of 0 to **RAND_MAX**

```
void *realloc(void *ptr, size_t size);
```
changes the size of the object pointed to by **ptr**

```
void srand(unsigned int seed);
```
uses the seed to initialize a new sequence of values from the **RAND** function

<string.h>

The header file **<string.h>** defines the type **size_t**, which is an unsigned integer, and the macro **NULL**, which has the value of binary zero. In addition, the header file defines a number of functions for handling strings; these functions are also discussed in Chapter 7.

```
void *memchr(const void *s, int c, size_t n);
```
returns a pointer to the first occurrence of **c** in the initial **n** characters of the object pointed to by **s**

```
int memcmp(const void *s, const void *t, size_t n);
```
returns an integer greater than, equal to, or less than zero, accordingly, as the string pointed to by **s** is greater than, equal to, or less than the string pointed to by **t**

```
void *memcpy(void *s, const void *t, size_t n);
```
copies n characters from the object pointed to by **t** into the object pointed to by **s**

```
void *memmove(void *s, const void *t, size_t n);
```
copies n characters from the object pointed to by **t** into the object pointed to by **s**, using a temporary area

```
void *memset(void *s, int c, size_t n);
```
copies the value of **c** into the first **n** characters of the object pointed to by **s**

```
char *strcat(char *s, const char *t);
```
concatenates string pointed to by **t** to the end of string pointed to by **s**; returns a pointer to string pointed to by **s**

```
char *strchr(const char *s, int c);
```
returns a pointer to the first occurrence of the character **c** in the string pointed to by **s**

```
int strcmp(const char *s, const char *t);
```
compares string **s** to string **t** in an element-by-element comparison; returns an integer greater than, equal to, or less than zero, accordingly, as the string pointed to by **s** is greater than, equal to, or less than the string pointed to by **t**

```
int strcoll(const char *s, const char *t);
```
   returns an integer greater than, equal to, or less than zero, accordingly, as the string pointed to by **s** is greater than, equal to, or less than the string pointed to by **t**

```
char *strcpy(char *s, const char *t);
```
   copies string pointed to by **t** to string pointed to by **s**; returns a pointer to string pointed to by **s**

```
size_t strcspn(const char *s, const char *t);
```
   returns the initial number of characters of string pointed to by **s** that consists entirely of characters not in string pointed to by **t**

```
size_t strlen(const char *s);
```
   returns the length of the string pointed to by **s**

```
char *strncat(char *s, const char *t, size_t n);
```
   concatenates at most n characters of string **t** to string **s**; returns a pointer to string pointed to by **s**

```
int strncmp(const char *s, const char *t, size_t n);
```
   compares at most n characters of string **s** to string **t** in an element-by-element comparison; returns an integer greater than, equal to, or less than zero, accordingly, as the string pointed to by **s** is greater than, equal to, or less than the string pointed to by **t**

```
char *strncpy(char *s, const char *t, size_t n);
```
   copies at most **n** characters from string pointed to by **t** to string pointed to by **s**; if **t** has fewer characters than **s**, then **s** is padded with null characters; returns a pointer to **s**

```
char *strpbrk(const char *s, const char *t);
```
   returns a pointer to the first occurrence in string pointed to by **s** of any character of string pointed to by **t**

```
char *strrchr(const char *s, int c);
```
   returns a pointer to the last occurrence of the character **c** in the string pointed to by **s**

```
size_t strspn(const char *s, const char *t);
```
   returns the initial number of characters of string pointed to by **s** that consists entirely of characters in string pointed to by **t**

```
char *strstr(const char *s, const char *t);
```
   returns a pointer to the start of the string pointed to by **t** within the string pointed to by **s**

<time.h>

The header file **<time.h>** defines two macros, four types, and several functions for representing and manipulating calendar time and local time. The types **clock_t** and **time_t** are arithmetic types capable of representing times, and the structure **tm** contains a calendar time broken into seconds **(tm_sec)**, minutes **(tm_min)**, hours **(tm_hour)**, day of the month **(tm_mday)**, months since January **(tm_mon)**, years since 1900 **(tm_year)**, days since Sunday **(tm_wday)**, days since

January 1 `(tm_yday)`, and a daylight saving time flag `(tm_isdst)`; the order of the values in the structure is system dependent. The related macros are the following:

CLOCKS_PER_SEC
    number per second of the value returned by the clock function
NULL
    an integer representing binary zero

Function prototypes and brief descriptions of their related computations follow:

```
char *asctime(const struct tm *timeptr);
```
    returns a pointer to the string containing a converted time
```
clock_t clock(void);
```
    returns the current processor time
```
char *ctime(const time_t *timer);
```
    returns a pointer to a string containing a converted time
```
double difftime(time_t time1, time_t time0);
```
    computes the difference between two calendar times
```
struct tm *gmtime(const time_t *timer);
```
    returns a pointer to a time expressed in Coordinated Universal Time
```
struct tm *localtime(const time_t *timer);
```
    returns a pointer to a time converted from calendar time
```
time_t mktime(struct tm *timeptr);
```
    converts the broken-down time to a calendar time value
```
time_t time(time_t *timer)
```
    returns the current calendar time
```
size_t strftime(char *s, size_t maxsize, const char *format,
                const struct tm *timeptr);
```
    converts time into a formatted multibyte character sequence

Appendix B
ASCII Character Codes

The following table contains the 128 ASCII characters and their equivalent integer values and binary values. The characters that correspond to the integers 1 through 31 have special significance to the computer system. For example, the character BEL is represented by the integer 7, and causes the bell to sound on the keyboard.

The order of the characters from low to high is the collating sequence, and has several interesting characteristics. Note that the digits are less than uppercase letters, and uppercase letters are less than lowercase letters. Also, note that special characters are not grouped together—some are before digits, some are after digits, and some are between uppercase and lowercase characters.

Character	Integer Equivalent	Binary Equivalent
NUL (Binary Zero)	0	0000000
SOH (Start of Header)	1	0000001
STX (Start of Text)	2	0000010
ETX (End of Text)	3	0000011
EOT (End of Transmission)	4	0000100
ENQ (Enquiry)	5	0000101
ACK (Acknowledge)	6	0000110
BEL (Bell)	7	0000111
BS (Backspace)	8	0001000
HT (Horizontal Tab)	9	0001001
LF (Line Feed or New Line)	10	0001010
VT (Vertical Tabulation)	11	0001011
FF (Form Feed)	12	0001100
CR (Carriage Return)	13	0001101
SO (Shift Out)	14	0001110
SI (Shift In)	15	0001111
DLE (Data Link Escape)	16	0010000
DC1 (Device Control 1)	17	0010001
DC2 (Device Control 2)	18	0010010
DC3 (Device Control 3)	19	0010011

DC4 (Device Control 4-Stop)	20	0010100
NAK (Negative Acknowledge)	21	0010101
SYN (Synchronization)	22	0010110
ETB (End of Text Block)	23	0010111
CAN (Cancel)	24	0011000
EM (End of Medium)	25	0011001
SUB (Substitute)	26	0011010
ESC (Escape)	27	0011011
FS (File Separator)	28	0011100
GS (Group Separator)	29	0011101
RS (Record Separator)	30	0011110
US (Unit Separator)	31	0011111
SP (Space)	32	0100000
!	33	0100001
"	34	0100010
#	35	0100011
$	36	0100100
%	37	0100101
&	38	0100110
' (Closing Single Quote)	39	0100111
(	40	0101000
)	41	0101001
*	42	0101010
+	43	0101011
, (Comma)	44	0101100
- (Hyphen)	45	0101101
. (Period)	46	0101110
/	47	0101111
0	48	0110000
1	49	0110001
2	50	0110010
3	51	0110011
4	52	0110100
5	53	0110101
6	54	0110110
7	55	0110111
8	56	0111000
9	57	0111001
:	58	0111010
;	59	0111011
<	60	0111100
=	61	0111101
>	62	0111110
?	63	0111111
@	64	1000000
A	65	1000001
B	66	1000010

C		67	1000011
D		68	1000100
E		69	1000101
F		70	1000110
G		71	1000111
H		72	1001000
I		73	1001001
J		74	1001010
K		75	1001011
L		76	1001100
M		77	1001101
N		78	1001110
O		79	1001111
P		80	1010000
Q		81	1010001
R		82	1010010
S		83	1010011
T		84	1010100
U		85	1010101
V		86	1010110
W		87	1010111
X		88	1011000
Y		89	1011001
Z		90	1011010
[		91	1011011
\		92	1011100
]		93	1011101
^	(Circumflex)	94	1011110
_	(Underscore)	95	1011111
'	(Opening Single Quote)	96	1100000
a		97	1100001
b		98	1100010
c		99	1100011
d		100	1100100
e		101	1100101
f		102	1100110
g		103	1100111
h		104	1101000
i		105	1101001
j		106	1101010
k		107	1101011
l		108	1101100
m		109	1101101
n		110	1101110
o		111	1101111
p		112	1110000
q		113	1110001

r	114	1110010
s	115	1110011
t	116	1110100
u	117	1110101
v	118	1110110
w	119	1110111
x	120	1111000
y	121	1111001
z	122	1111010
{	123	1111011
|	124	1111100
}	125	1111101
~	126	1111110
DEL (Delete/Rubout)	127	1111111

Appendix C
Using MATLAB to Plot Data From ASCII Files

To understand engineering problems and engineering solutions to problems, it is important to be able to visualize the numerical information that is involved. Therefore, the ability to easily obtain simple xy plots from data files is an important capability in solving engineering problems.

In this appendix, we present a simple C program that generates a data file, and we then show how to use MATLAB to obtain a plot of the data. We chose MATLAB (MATrix LABoratory) to generate the plots in this appendix and also in the text chapters because it is an extremely powerful software environment for interactive numeric computations, data analysis, and graphics. An extensive discussion on generating different types of plots and on additional options that can be specified within the plots is included in Chapter 7 of *Engineering Problem Solving with MATLAB*, by D. M. Etter, Prentice Hall Publishing, 1993.

In the following example, we use a C program to generate an ASCII (American Standard Code for Information Interchange) data file, and we then plot the information using MATLAB. An ASCII data file can also be generated using a word processor, and then the same steps can be used to plot the information using MATLAB. If the data file is generated with a word processor, it is important to select the options for saving the file such that it is saved as a text file instead of as a word processor file.

The following program generates a data file containing 100 lines of information. Each line contains the corresponding time and function value from the following equation for a damped sine function:

$$f(t) = e^{-t} \sin(2\pi t)$$

where $t = 0.0, 0.1, 0.2, \ldots, 9.9$ seconds. The statements that open the data file, write information to it, and close it are discussed in Chapter 3 of this text.

C Program to Generate a Data File

app_c.c

```
/*-----------------------------------------------------*/
/*   Program app_c                                     */
/*                                                     */
/*   This program generates a data file of values     */
/*   from a damped sine function.                      */

#include <stdio.h>
#include <stdlib.h>
#include <math.h>
#define PI 3.141593

main()
{
   /*  Define variables.  */
   int k;
   double t, f;
   FILE *dsine;

   /*  Generate data file.  */
   dsine = fopen("dsine.dat","w");
   for (k=1; k<=100; k++)
   {
      t = 0.1*(k-1);
      f = exp(-t)*sin(2*PI*t);
      fprintf(dsine,"%f %f \n",t,f);
   }

   /*  Close data file and exit program. */
   fclose(dsine);
   return EXIT_SUCCESS;
}
/*-----------------------------------------------------*/
```

ASCII Data File Generated by the C Program

The data file generated by this program is an ASCII file that contains two numbers per line. The first few lines of information and the last line of information are shown below:

```
0.0   0.000
0.1   0.532
0.2   0.779
...
9.9   0.000
```

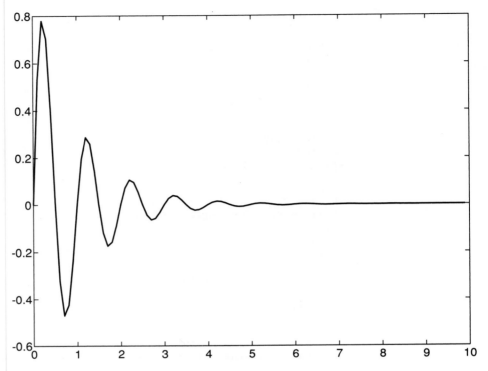

Figure C.1 *Plot of a damped sine function.*

Generating a Plot with MATLAB

To generate a plot of this information with MATLAB, we only need two statements. The first statement loads the file into the MATLAB workarea, and the second statement generates the xy plot:

```
>>load dsine.dat
>>plot(dsine(:,1),dsine(:,2))
```

These steps generate the plot shown in Figure C-1.

Since it is important to label the information in a plot, we could also add the statements to give the plot a title, to label the axes, and to add a background grid:

```
>>load dsine.dat
>>plot(dsine(:,1),dsine(:,2)),
>>title('Damped Sine Function'),
>>xlabel('Time, s'), ylabel('f(t)'), grid
```

The plot with these labels is shown in Figure C-2.

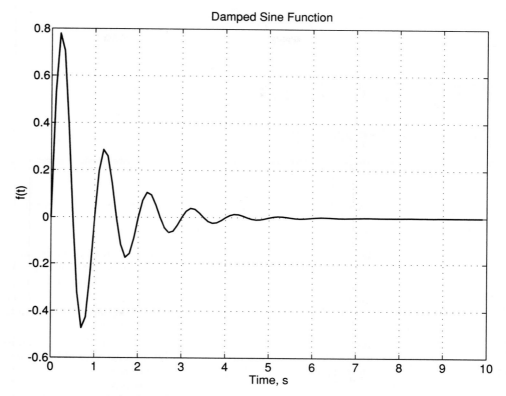

Figure C.2 *Enhanced plot of a damped sine function.*

Appendix D
References

These references were cited at various locations throughout this text.

[1] "10 Outstanding Achievements, 1964–1989." National Academy of Engineering, Washington, DC, 1989.

[2] Etter, D. M. *Structured FORTRAN 77 for Engineers and Scientists*, 4th Ed. Benjamin/Cummings, Redwood City, CA, 1993.

[3] "The Federal High Performance Computing Program." Executive Office of the President, Office of Science and Technology Policy, Washington, DC, September 8, 1989.

[4] Etter, D. M., and J. Bordogna. "Engineering Education for the 21st Century." IEEE International Conference on Acoustics, Speech, and Signal Processing, April 1994.

[5] Fairley, R. *Software Engineering Concepts*. McGraw-Hill, New York, 1985.

[6] Etter, D. M. *Engineering Problem Solving with MATLAB®*. Prentice Hall, Englewood Cliffs, NJ, 1993.

[7] Plauger, P. J. *The Standard C Library*. Prentice Hall, Englewood Cliffs, NJ, 1992.

[8] Jones, E. R., and R. L. Childers. *Contemporary College Physics*. Addison-Wesley, Reading, MA, 1990.

[9] Etter, D. M. *FORTRAN 77 with Numerical Methods for Engineers and Scientists*. Benjamin/Cummings, Redwood City, CA, 1992.

[10] Spanier, Jerome and Keith B. Oldham. *An Atlas of Functions*. Hemisphere Publishing Corporation, 1987.

[11] Edwards, Jr., C. H. and D. E. Penney. *Calculus and Analytic Geometry*. 3rd Ed. Prentice Hall, Englewood Cliffs, NJ, 1990.

[12] Master, G. M. *Introduction to Environmental Engineering and Science*. Prentice Hall, Englewood Cliffs, NJ, 1991.

[13] Gille, J. C., and J. M. Russell, III. "The Limb Infrared Monitor of the Stratosphere: Experiment Description, Performance, and Results," Journal of Geophysical Research, Vol. 89, No. D4, pp. 5125-5140, June 30, 1984.

[14] Roberts, Richard A. *An Introduction to Applied Probability*. Addison-Wesley, Reading, MA, 1992.

[15] Richardson, M. *College Algebra*, 3rd Ed. Prentice Hall, Englewood Cliffs, NJ, 1966.

[16] Kahaner, D., Cleve Moler, and Stephen Nash. *Numerical Methods and Software*. Prentice Hall, Englewood Cliffs, NJ, 1989.

[17] *Encyclopedia of Computer Science*, 3rd Ed. edited by Anthony Ralston and Edwin D. Reilly, Van Nostrand Reinhold Publishing Company, New York, NY, 1993.

[18] Kreyszig, E. *Advanced Engineering Mathematics*. John Wiley & Sons, New York, 1979.

[19] Wirth, Niklaus. *Algorithms + Data Structures = Programs*. Prentice Hall, Englewood Cliffs, NJ, 1976.

Complete Solutions to Practice! Problems

SECTION 2.2, PAGE 41

1. valid
2. valid
3. valid
4. valid
5. valid
6. invalid character (-), replacement `tax_rate`
7. valid
8. invalid character (^), replacement `sec_sqrd`
9. valid
10. invalid, keyword, replacement `break_1`
11. invalid character (#), replacement `num_123`
12. invalid character (&), replacement `x_and_y`
13. valid
14. invalid, keyword, replacement `void_term`
15. invalid characters ((,)), replacement `fx`
16. valid
17. valid
18. invalid character (.), replacement `w1_1`
19. valid
20. valid
21. invalid character (/), replacement `m_per_s`

SECTION 2.2, PAGE 42

1. 3.5004×10^1 4 digits of precision
2. 4.2×10^{-4} 1 digit of precision
3. -5.0×10^4 0 digits of precision
4. 3.15723×10^0 5 digits of precision
5. -9.9×10^{-2} 2 digits of precision
6. $1.00000028 \times 10^{-2}$ 8 digits of precision
7. 0.0000103
8. -105000
9. -3552000
10. 0.000667
11. -0.0902
12. -0.022

SECTION 2.2, PAGE 45

1. `#define light_speed 2.99792e08`
2. `#define charge_e 1.602177e-19`
3. `#define N_A 6.022e23`
4. `#define g_mss 9.8`
5. `#define g_ftss 32`
6. `#define mass 5.98e24`
7. `#define moon_radius 1.74e06`

SECTION 2.3, PAGE 49

1. `6`   2. `4.5`   3. `3.1`   4. `3`

SECTION 2.3, PAGE 51

1. `distance = x0 + v0*t + 0.5*a*t*t;`
2. `tension = (2*m1*m2*g)/(m1 + m2);`
3. `P2 = P1 + rho*v2^2*(A2^2 - A1^2)/(2*A1^2);`
4. centripetal = $\dfrac{4\pi^2}{T^2}$

5. potential energy = $\dfrac{GM_Em}{r}$

6. change = $GM_Em\left(\dfrac{1}{R_E} - \dfrac{1}{R_E + h}\right)$

SECTION 2.3, PAGE 55

1.   x $\boxed{3}$ y $\boxed{4}$ z $\boxed{12}$

2.   x $\boxed{3}$ y $\boxed{4}$ z $\boxed{12}$

3.   x $\boxed{6}$ y $\boxed{3}$

4.   x $\boxed{2}$ y $\boxed{0}$

SECTION 2.4, PAGE 59

1.   `Sum =    150; Average =    12.4`
2.   `Sum =  150`
     `Average =  12.3680`
3.   `Sum and Average`

     `150 12.4`
4.   `12.37 is the average;`
     `    150 is the sum`
5.   `12.37 is the average;    150 is the sum`

SECTION 2.5, PAGE 64

1.   75.92°   89.35°   111.25°   109.92°
2.   0.69   1.6   1.71   1.87
3.   There are 5 times that correspond to 110°, as can be seen from Figure 2.5. These values can be computed to be the following:
     1.71   2.84   3.39   4.42   5.33

SECTION 2.7, PAGE 72

1.   `-3`   2.   `-2`   3.   `0.125`   4.   `3.16`
5.   `25`   6.   `11`   7.   `-1`   8.   `32`

SECTION 2.7, PAGE 73

1.   `velocity = sqrt(v0^2 + 2*a*(x - x0));`
2.   `length = k*sqrt(1 - (v/c)^2);`
3.   `center = 38.1972*(r*r*r - s*s*s)*sin(a)/((r*r - s*s)*a);`

4.   frequency $= \dfrac{1}{\sqrt{\dfrac{2\pi c}{L}}}$

5.   range $= \dfrac{v_0^2}{g} \sin 2\theta$

6. $v = \sqrt{\dfrac{2gh}{1 + \dfrac{I}{mr^2}}}$

SECTION 2.7, PAGE 75

```
1.    cothx = cosh(x)/sinh(x);
2.    secx = 1/cos(x);
3.    cscx = 1/sin(x);
4.    acothx = 0.5*log((x + 1)/(x - 1));
5.    acoshx = log(x + sqrt(x*x - 1));
6.    acscx = asin(1/x);
```

SECTION 3.2, PAGE 98

1.	true	2.	true	3.	true	4.	false
5.	true	6.	true	7.	true	8.	false

SECTION 3.3, PAGE 103

```
1.    if (time > 15)
          time += 1;
2.    if (sqrt(poly) < 0.5)
          printf("poly = %f \n",poly);
3.    if (abs(volt_1-volt_2) > 10)
          printf("volt_1: %f,   volt_2: %f \n",volt_1,volt_2);
4.    if (den < 0.5)
          result = 0;
      else
          result = num/den;
5.    if (log(x) > 3)
      {
          time = 0;
          count--;
      }
6.    if (dist<50.0 && time>10)
          time += 2;
      else
          time += 2.5;
7.    if (dist >= 100)
          time += 2;
      else
          if (50<dist && dist<100)
              time += 1;
      else
          time += 0.5;
```

SECTION 3.3, PAGE 105

```
1.  switch (rank)
    {
       case 1: case 2:
          printf("Lower division \n");
          break;
       case 3: case 4:
          printf("Upper division \n");
          break;
       case 5:
          printf("Graduate student \n");
          break;
       default:
          printf("Invalid rank \n");
          break;
    }
```

SECTION 3.4, PAGE 111

1.	18	2.	18	3.	17
4.	9	5.	infinite loop		

SECTION 4.2, PAGE 162

1.   Actual Parameters   Formal Parameters

   x

   sqrt(x) | 25 | $\longrightarrow$ a | 25 |

   x-30 | 5 | $\longrightarrow$ b | 5 |

2.   2 | -5 | $\longrightarrow$ c | -5 |

SECTION 4.2, PAGE 164

1.   external identifiers: none
2.   local variables and scope:
     main function:
          `seed, n, k, component_reliability, a_series,`
          `a_parallel, series_success, parallel_success,`
          `num1, num2, num3, rand_float`
     rand_float prototype statement:
          `a, b`
     rand_float function:
          `a, b`

3.   external identifiers: none
4.   local variables and scope:
      `main` function:
          `n, k, a0, a1, a2, a3, a, b, step, left, right`
      `check_roots` prototype statement:
          `left, right, a0, a1, a2, a3`
      `check_roots` function:
          `left, right, a0, a1, a2, a3, f_left, f_right`
      `poly` prototype statement:
          `x, a0, a1, a2, a3`
      `poly` function:
          `x, a0, a1, a2, a3`

SECTION 4.7, PAGE 191

1.    ```
      #define area_sq(side) ((side)*(side))
      printf("area: %f \n",area_sq(side1));
      ```
2.    ```
      #define area_rect(side1,side2) ((side1)*(side2))
      sum = area_rect(sidea,sideb) + area_rect(sidec,sided);
      ```
3.    ```
      #define area_par(base,height) ((base)*(height))
      area1 = area_par(b,h1);
      ```
4.    ```
      #define area_trap(base,height1,height2)
              (0.5*(base)((height1)+(height2)))
      area += area_trap(base,left,right);
      ```
5.    ```
      #define vol_sph(radius) (4.0/3.0*3.141593*pow((radius),3))
      printf("volume: %f \n",vol_sph(5.5);
      ```
6.    ```
      #define vol_pyr(area,height) (1.0/3.0*(area)*(height))
      vol1 = vol_pyr(0.5*baseb*baseht,pyrht);
      ```
7.    ```
      #define vol_cone(radius,height)
              (1.0/3.0*3.141593*pow((radius),3)*(height))
      vol2 = vol_cone(diameter/2,ht);
      ```
8.    ```
      #define vol_cube(side) ((side)*(side)*(side))
      vol3 = vol_cube(sqrt(base_area));
      ```
9.    ```
      #define vol_par(length,width,height)
              ((length)*(width)*(height))
      vol4 = vol_par(side1,side1,side1);
      ```

SECTION 5.1, PAGE 210

1.

-5	4	3	0	0	0	0	0	0	0

2.

0	-5.5	5.5	5.5
      ```

3.

–.4	–.3	–.2	–.1	0	.1	.2	.3	.4

SECTION 5.1, PAGE 213

1.
3 8
15 21
30 41

2.
8 30

SECTION 5.1, PAGE 215

1.   9.8   2.   9.8   3.   3.2   4.   1.5

SECTION 5.2, PAGE 221

1.   9   2.   6   3.   21.44   4.   4.63
5.   2.5   6.   5.75

SECTION 5.5, PAGE 233

1.

1
4
6

2.

5	2
–2	3
?	?
?	?
?	?
?	?

3.

0	0	0	0
0	0	0	0
0	0	0	0
0	0	0	0

4.

1	0	0
0	1	0
0	0	1

5.

0	1	2	3	4
1	2	3	4	5
2	3	4	5	6
3	4	5	6	7
4	5	6	7	8

6.

1	-1	1	-1	1
1	-1	1	-1	1
1	-1	1	-1	1
1	-1	1	-1	1
1	-1	1	-1	1

SECTION 5.5, PAGE 235

1. **9**
2. **0**
3. **-6**
4. **3**

SECTION 5.5, PAGE 239

1. **13**
2. **0**
3. **18**
4. **22**

SECTION 5.7, PAGE 249

1. 5
2. −8
3. $\begin{bmatrix} 5 & -2 & 3 \\ 3 & -3 & 2 \end{bmatrix}$
4. $\begin{bmatrix} 2 \\ 9 \end{bmatrix}$
5. $\begin{bmatrix} -2 & -2 & 4 \\ 7 & -9 & 10 \end{bmatrix}$

6. $\begin{bmatrix} 24 \\ -20 \\ 22 \end{bmatrix}$

SECTION 5.8, PAGE 256

1.   x=2, y=1
2.   x=3, y=−1, z=2

SECTION 6.1, PAGE 281

1.

```
                 ptr
                  ↘
   a  1      b  2
```

2.

```
                 ptr
                  ↘
   a  2      b  2
```

3.

```
                          ptr
                           ↘
   a  1      b  5      c  1
```

4.

```
                          ptr
                           ↘
   a  2      b  2      c  2
```

SECTION 6.1, PAGE 285

1.

```
   ptr_2          ptr_1
      ↘              ↘
   x  15.6       y  31.2
```

2.

```
                    ptr_2
                      ↘
   w  10        x  −8
```

3.

```
              ptr_3
              ptr_1
              ptr_2
                ↓
   x  2  4  6  8  3
```

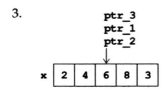

4.   **first_ptr**   **last_ptr**

```
     w | ? | ? | ? | ? |
```

SECTION 6.2, PAGE 287

		offset
g[0]	2	0
g[1]	4	1
g[2]	5	2
g[3]	8	3
g[4]	10	4
g[5]	32	5
g[6]	78	6

1.	2	5.	2
2.	4	6.	8
3.	3	7.	4
4.	32	8.	32

SECTION 6.2, PAGE 288

			offset
1.	d[0][0]	1	0
	d[0][1]	6	1
	d[1][0]	?	2
	d[1][1]	?	3
	d[2][0]	?	4
	d[2][1]	?	5
	d[3][0]	?	6
	d[3][1]	?	7

			offset
2.	g[0][0]	5	0
	g[0][1]	2	1
	g[0][2]	-2	2
	g[0][3]	3	3
	g[1][0]	1	4
	g[1][1]	2	5
	g[1][2]	3	6
	g[1][3]	4	7
	g[2][0]	?	8
	g[2][1]	?	9
	g[2][2]	?	10
	g[2][3]	?	11

			offset
3.	h[0][0]	0	0
	h[0][1]	0	1
	h[0][2]	0	2
	h[1][0]	0	3
	h[1][1]	0	4
	h[1][2]	0	5
	h[2][0]	0	6
	h[2][1]	0	7
	h[2][2]	0	8

SECTION 6.2, PAGE 289

		offset
g[0][0]	1	0
g[0][1]	8	1
g[0][2]	7	2
g[0][3]	6	3
g[1][0]	2	4
g[1][1]	4	5
g[1][2]	-1	6
g[1][3]	0	7

1. 1   3. 3
2. 7   4. 14

SECTION 6.2, PAGE 290

1.
```
int a[4][6], sum=0, *ptr=&a[1][0];
...
for (k=0; k<=5; k++)
    sum += *(ptr+k);
```

2.
```
int a[4][6], sum=0, *ptr=&a[0][2];
...
for (k=0; k<=3; k++)
    sum += *(ptr+k*4);
```

3.
```
int a[4][6], *ptr=&a[0][0];
...
max = a[0][0];
for (k=0; k<=17; k++)
    if (max<*(ptr+k))
        max = *(ptr+k);
```

4.
```
int a[4][6], *ptr=&a[0][0];
...
min = a[0][2];
for (i=0; i<=3; i++)
    for(j=2; j<=5; j++)
        if (min > *(ptr+i*6+j))
            min = *(ptr+i*6+j);
```

SECTION 6.3, PAGE 293

1. invalid, arguments are not pointers to integers

2.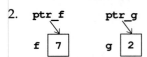

3. invalid, arguments are not pointers

4. invalid, arguments are not pointers to integers

5.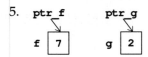

6. invalid, arguments are not pointers to integers

SECTION 7.1, PAGE 315

1. 40
2. 60
3. 71
4. 103
5. 123
6. 94
7. SI (Shift In)
8. $
9. NAK (Negative Acknowledge)
10. RS (Record Separator)

SECTION 7.6, PAGE 340

1. `Engineering Fundamental Concepts`
2. `not equal`
3. `2`
4. `0`
5. `0`
6. `Engineering Problem Solving`

Selected Solutions to Modify! Problems

1.
```
/*-----------------------------------------------------------*/
/*  Program chapter2_mod                                     */
/*                                                           */
/*  This program includes a division by zero                */
/*  to determine the system response.                       */

#include <stdio.h>
#include <stdlib.h>

main()
{
   /*  Declare and initialize variables.  */
   double a=5, b=0, c;

   /*  Execute a division by zero.  */
   c = a/b;

   /*  Print the value of c.  */
   printf("c = %f \n",c);

   /*  Exit program.  */
   return EXIT_SUCCESS;
}
/*-----------------------------------------------------*/
```

4.
```
/*-----------------------------------------------------------*/
/*  Program chapter3_4mod                                    */
/*                                                           */
/*  This program prints a table of height and               */
```

```
/*   velocity values for a weather balloon.          */
/*   A modification is added so that it will print    */
/*   the last time that the maximum height occurred   */
/*   instead of the first time it occurred.          */
```

(No changes in the first part of the program.)

```
   if (height >= max_height)
   {
      max_height = height;
      max_time = time;
   }
```

(No changes in the last part of the program.)

```
/*------------------------------------------------*/
```

SECTION 4.3, PAGE 170

```
/*------------------------------------------------*/
/*   Program chapter4_4mod                         */
/*                                                 */
/*   This program generates and prints ten random  */
/*   floating-point values between user-entered limits. */

#include <stdio.h>
#include <stdlib.h>

main()
{
   /*  Declare variables and function prototypes.  */
   unsigned int seed;
   int k;
   double a, b;
   double rand_float(double a, double b);

   /*  Get seed value and interval limits.  */
   printf("Enter a positive integer seed value: \n");
   scanf("%u",&seed);
   srand(seed);
   printf("Enter limits a and b (a<b): \n");
   scanf("%f %f",&a,&b);

   /*  Generate and print ten random numbers.  */
   printf("Random Numbers: \n");
   for (k=1; k<=10; k++)
   {
      printf("%f ",rand_float(a,b));
   }

   /* Exit program.  */
   return EXIT_SUCCESS;
}
/*------------------------------------------------*/
```
(No changes in the rand_float function from page 170.)
```
/*------------------------------------------------*/
```

SECTION 5.4, PAGE 230

1.
```c
/*------------------------------------------------------*/
/*  Program chapter5_mod                                */
/*                                                      */
/*  This program initializes an array and then uses     */
/*  the selection sort to reorder it.                   */

#include <stdio.h>
#include <stdlib.h>

main()
{
   /*  Declare variables and function prototypes.   */
   int k;
   double x[10]={4,8,-2,16,19,6,-4,0,20,3};
   void sort(double x[], int n);

   /*  Print original order.  */
   printf("Original Order \n");
   for (k=0; k<=9; k++)
      printf("%.1f ",x[k]);
   printf("\n");

   /*  Sort values.  */
   sort(x,10);

   /*  Print new order.  */
   printf("New Order \n");
   for (k=0; k<=9; k++)
      printf("%.1f ",x[k]);
   printf("\n");

   /*  Exit program.  */
   return EXIT_SUCCESS;
}
/*------------------------------------------------------*/
```
            (No changes in the sort function from page 229.)
```c
/*------------------------------------------------------*/
```

SECTION 6.4, PAGE 300

2.
```c
/*------------------------------------------------------*/
/*  Program chapter6_4mod                               */
/*                                                      */
/*  This program reads a seismic data file and then     */
/*  determines the times of possible seismic events.    */
/*  The modification checks to be sure that the         */
/*  short window is shorter than the long window.       */
```
       (No changes in the first part of the program.)

```
    /*  Read window sizes from the keyboard.  */
    short_window = long_window = 0;
    while (short_window >= long_window)
    {
        printf("The short-window must be shorter "
               " than the long-window. \n");
        printf("Enter data points in short-window: \n");
        scanf("%i",&short_window);
        printf("Enter data points in long-window: \n");
        scanf("%i",&long_window);
    }
```

(No changes in the last part of the program.)
```
/*-------------------------------------------------------*/
```

SECTION 7.2, PAGE 320

3.
```
    /*-------------------------------------------------------*/
    /*  Program chapter7_2_mod                              */
    /*                                                      */
    /*  This program reads characters from the keyboard     */
    /*  and prints them twice on the screen.  It also       */
    /*  counts and prints the number of lines read.         */
    /*  The modification causes the bell to sound when      */
    /*  the user is prompted to enter characters.           */
```

(No changes in the first part of the program.)

```
    /*  Read and print characters.  */
    putchar("\a");
    printf("Enter characters: (^z to quit) \n");
```

(No changes in the last part of the program.)
```
/*-------------------------------------------------------*/
```

Selected Solutions to End-of-Chapter Problems

CHAPTER 2

19.

```
/*-------------------------------------------------------*/
/*    Program chapter2_prob19                            */
/*                                                       */
/*    This program computes the molecular weight         */
/*    for an amino acid.                                 */

#include <stdio.h>
#include <stdlib.h>
#define O 15.9994
#define C 12.011
#define N 14.00674
#define S 32.066
#define H 1.00794

main()
{
    /* Declare variables.   */
    int num_o, num_c, num_n, num_s, num_h;
    double weight;

    /* Prompt the user for numbers of atoms.  */
    printf("Enter number of oxygen atoms: \n");
    scanf("%i",&num_o);
    printf("Enter number of carbon atoms: \n");
    scanf("%i",&num_c);
    printf("Enter number of nitrogen atoms: \n");
    scanf("%i",&num_n);
    printf("Enter number of sulfur atoms: \n");
    scanf("%i",&num_s);
    printf("Enter number of hydrogen atoms: \n");
    scanf("%i",&num_h);
```

```
        /*  Compute molecular weight.  */
        weight = O*num_o + C*num_c + N*num_n +
                S*num_s + H*num_h;

        /*  Print the molecular weight.  */
        printf("amino acid molecular weight = %.5f \n",
                weight);

        /* Exit program.  */
        return EXIT_SUCCESS;
    }
    /*-------------------------------------------------------*/
```

CHAPTER 3

20.
```
    /*-------------------------------------------------------*/
    /*  Program chapter3_prob20                              */
    /*                                                       */
    /*  This program prints a table showing the              */
    /*  number of acres of land reforested at the            */
    /*  end of each year, for 20 years.                      */

    #include <stdio.h>
    #include <stdlib.h>
    #define UNCUT 2500
    #define RATE 0.02

    main()
    {
        /* Declare variables.  */
        int year;
        double old_forest=UNCUT, new_forest;

        /* Print report.  */
        printf("Reforestation Summary \n");
        printf("Year    Total Acres Forested \n");
        for (year=1; year<=20; year++)
        {
            new_forest = old_forest*RATE;
            old_forest += new_forest;
            printf("%4i    %10.2f \n",year,old_forest);
        }

        /* Exit program.  */
        return EXIT_SUCCESS;
    }
    /*-------------------------------------------------------*/
```

CHAPTER 4

4.
```
    /*-------------------------------------------------------*/
    /*  Program chapter4_prob4                               */
    /*                                                       */
    /*  This program simulates rolling two six-sided         */
```

```
/*  dice and estimates the percentage of time that     */
/*  the sum of the dots on the dice equals 8.          */

#include <stdio.h>
#include <stdlib.h>

main()
{
   /* Declare variables and function prototypes.  */
   unsigned int seed;
   int rolls, k, die_1, die_2, sum=0;
   int rand_int(int a, int b);

   /*  Get seed value.  */
   printf("Enter a positive integer seed value: \n");
   scanf("%u",&seed);
   srand(seed);

   /*  Prompt user for number of rolls.  */
   printf("Enter number of rolls of dice: \n");
   scanf("%i",&rolls);

   /*  Simulate rolls of the dice.  */
   for (k=1; k<=rolls; k++)
   {
      die_1 = rand_int(1,6);
      die_2 = rand_int(1,6);
      if (die_1+die_2 == 8)
      sum++;
   }

   /*  Compute and print percentage  */
   /*  of rolls with a sum of 8.      */
   printf("Number of rolls: %i \n",rolls);
   printf("Percent with sum of eight: %.2f \n",
           sum*100.0/rolls)

   /*  Exit program.  */
   return EXIT_SUCCESS;
}
/*---------------------------------------------------------*/
        (Include function rand_int from page 168.)
/*---------------------------------------------------------*/
```

CHAPTER 5

```
/*---------------------------------------------------------*/
/*  Program chapter5_prob30                                */
/*                                                         */
/*  This function computes the correlation                 */
/*  coefficient for two one-dimensional arrays.            */

double correlation(double x[], double y[], int npts)
{
    /* Declare variables and function prototypes.  */
```

```
    int k;
    double mean_x, mean_y, sd_x, sd_y, sumxy=0;
    double mean(double x[], int n);
    double std_dev(double x[], int n);

    /* Use statistical functions for calculations.  */
    mean_x = mean(x,npts);
    mean_y = mean(y,npts);
    sd_x = std_dev(x,npts);
    sd_y = std_dev(y,npts);

    /*  Compute sum of products x*y.  */
    for (k=0; k<=npts-1; k++)
    {
        sumxy += x[k]*y[k];
    }

    /*  Compute and return correlation coefficient.  */
    return (sumxy - mean_x*mean_y)/(sd_x*sd_y);
}
/*------------------------------------------------------*/
```

> *(Include function mean from page 217 and*
> *function std_dev from page 220.)*

```
/*------------------------------------------------------*/
```

CHAPTER 6

```
/*------------------------------------------------------*/
/*  Program chapter6_prob5                            */
/*                                                    */
/*  This function determines the number of positive,  */
/*  negative, and zero values in an array.            */

void signs(int x[], int npts, int *npos,
           int *nzero, int *nneg)
{
    /*  Declare variables.  */
    int k;

    /* Set sums to zero.  */
    *npos = *nzero = *nneg = 0;

    /* Update corresponding sums.  */
    for (k=0; k<=npts-1; k++)
    {
        if (x[k] < 0)
            *nneg += 1;
        else
            if (x[k] > 0)
                *npos += 1;
            else
                *nzero += 1;
    }
```

```
      /*  Void return.  */
      return;
   }
   /*------------------------------------------------------*/
```

CHAPTER 7

```
   /*------------------------------------------------------*/
   /*  Program chapter7_prob7                           */
   /*                                                   */
   /*  This function prints a bar graph.                */

   int bargraph_1(int count, int data[])
   {
      /*  Declare and initialize variables.  */
      int k, error = 0, m;

      /*  Check to see if all values between 0 and 50.  */
      for (k=0; k<=count-1; k++)
      {
         if (data[k]<0 || data[k]>50)
            error = 1;
      }

      /* If no data errors, print bar chart.  */
      if (error == 0)
      {
         printf("\n");
         for (k=0; k<=count-1; k++)
         {
            printf("%3i    ",data[k]);
            for (m=1; m<=data[k]; m++)
               printf("*");
         }
         printf("\n");
      }

      /*  Return error code.  */
      return error;
   }
   /*------------------------------------------------------*/
```

Glossary

abbreviated assignment   an assignment statement that uses a shortened format

abstraction   a concept in which a programmer can use modules to accomplish specific tasks without needing to know the details of the steps within the modules

actual parameter   a value that corresponds to a formal parameter when a function is invoked

address   a positive integer that uniquely defines a memory location

address operator   a unary operator that determines the memory address of an identifier

algorithm   a step-by-step outline of a problem solution

alphanumeric character   a character that is either an alphabetic character or a digit

ANSI C   an American National Standards Institute standard that provides a system independent and unambiguous definition of the C language

argument   an input to a function

arithmetic logic unit (ALU)   the part of the computer that performs the arithmetic operations

array   a data structure that allows a group of values to be represented using a common name and distinguished using subscripts

ASCII code   American Standard Code for Information Interchange

assembler   a program that converts an assembly language program to binary

assembly language   a language specific to a particular CPU design that is written in English-like statements

assignment statement   a statement that assigns a value to an identifier

associativity   the order for grouping the operations in an expression

automatic class   a class used to represent local variables

binary   two states, which are usually represented by 0 and 1

binary code   a code composed of 0's and 1's

binary operator   an operator that operates on two values, such as addition

bug   an error in a program

byte   a unit of memory that contains 8 bits or binary digits

call by address   a function reference in which the address of the actual parameter is used as the address of the corresponding formal parameter

call by reference   a function reference in which the address of the actual parameter is used as the address of the corresponding formal parameter

call by value   a function reference in which the value of the actual parameter is passed to the corresponding formal parameter

case label   the expression used to control a case structure

case sensitive   lowercase and uppercase letters are perceived as different characters

case structure   a structure in which groups of statements are performed based on the value of a controlling expression

cast operator   a unary operator that specifies a type change in the value before the next computation

central processing unit (CPU)   the combination of the processor and the ALU

character   a data type that represents information that is not restricted to numeric information

character string   a character array that ends with a null character

coercion of arguments   the process of converting the type of a value to another type before using the value in a computation

collating sequence   an ordering of characters for a specific code, from low to high

comment   a statement in a program that is not an instruction but that is used to document the steps in the program

compile   the process of translating a program from a high-level language to machine language

compiler   a program that translates a program in a high-level language into machine language

compiler error   errors that are identified during the compilation of a program

composition   nesting of functions

compound statement   a set of statements that are enclosed in braces

computer   a machine that is designed to perform operations that are specified with a set of instructions called a program

computer simulation   a computer program that uses random numbers to model an event

condition   an expression that can be evaluated as either true or false

constant   a value such as 3.141593 that does not change during the execution of a program

control character   one of the following characters: FF (form feed), NL (new line), CR (carriage return), HT (horizontal tab), VT (vertical tab), BEL (bell), BS (backspace)

control string   a string in an output statement that specifies the format to use for an output line

controlling expression   the expression used in a `switch` statement

conversion specifier   a specifier that describes the format to be used in printing a value

data file   a file that contains data that can accessed by a program or that can be generated by a program

database management tool   a software tool for manipulating and retrieving information from large amounts of data

debug   the process of identifying and removing bugs or errors from a program

debugger   a program that assists in identifying and removing bugs or errors from a program

declaration   a statement that defines variables to be stored in memory

decomposition outline   an outline of the general steps necessary to solve a problem

default label   a label in a `switch` statement that is used to indicate statements to execute if none of the other statements are executed

dereference   an operation that references the value contained in an address that is stored in a pointer

desktop publishing   a powerful word processor with a high-quality printer to produce professional-looking documents

determinant   a specific value computed from the entries in a matrix

divide and conquer   strategy for solving a large problem by breaking it into smaller problems

dot product   the sum of the products of the values in corresponding positions in two vectors

dynamic memory allocation   a technique that allows a programmer to specify a memory allocation during the execution of the program

EBCDIC code   Extended Binary Coded Decimal Interchange Code

electronic copy   information that is stored in a computer or in a form that the computer can read, such as on a diskette

element   a value in an array

end-of-file character   a special character at the end of a file to indicate that the end of the file has been reached

EOF character   a special character that indicates the end of a text stream

error condition   a condition that should not occur in the desired execution of a program

execution   the process of executing the steps described by a program

exponential notation   notation that uses the letter e to separate the mantissa from the exponent in scientific notation, as in 3.1e02

expression   a group of terms composed of constants, variables, and operators that can be evaluated as a single value

external class   a class used to represent global variables which have the entire program as their scope

factorial   a function of a positive integer that is the product of the integer and all integers between it and 1

Fibonacci sequence   a sequence of values that begins with the values 1,1; each succeeding value is the sum of the two previous values

field width   the value specified that controls the minimum number of positions used to print a value

file open mode   a character that indicates the status of a data file

file pointer   a pointer variable that is associated with a data file

floating-point value   a value that can represent both integer and non-integer values

flowchart   a diagram used to describe the steps in an algorithm

for loop   a loop that is executed a specified number of times

formal parameter   an identifier used in the definition of a function to represent an input value

function   a module that returns at most one value to the invoking statement

function prototype   a statement that identifies the information necessary to properly invoke a function

Gauss elimination   a numerical technique for finding the solution to a set of simultaneous equations

grand challenges   a group of fundamental problems in engineering and science with broad potential impact

graphics tool   a software tool for visually displaying information

hardware   the computer equipment, such as the keyboard, the mouse, and the hard disk

high-level language   a language with English-like commands that is not specific to a particular CPU design

hyperbolic function   a common function that is a function of the natural logarithm function or of the natural exponential function

hyperplane   the space represented by an equation with more than three variables

I/O diagram   a simple block diagram that defines the input and the output information for a program

identifier   name used to reference the value stored in a memory location

ill-conditioned   a term used to describe a system of equations that does not have a unique solution

incremental search   a numerical technique for estimating the roots of a function

indirection   an operation that references the value contained in an address that is stored in a pointer

initial value   the initial value given to a variable; often included in the declaration statement

inner product   a dot product

invoke   call or reference a function (or module)

iteration   one pass through a loop

keyword   words with special meaning to the C compiler

least squares   a technique that minimizes the square of the difference between a model and a given function or a given set of data points

library function   a function that is included in the files that accompany a compiler

linear interpolation   a numerical technique for estimating a function value by assuming that it falls between two points on a straight line

linear modeling   modeling a set of data values with a straight line

linear regression   a numerical technique for determining the equation of a straight line that best fits a set of data values

loader/linker   the software that prepares a machine language program to be executed

local variable   a variable whose scope is the function in which it is defined

logic error   an error in the logic of the steps to solve a problem

logical operator   an operator that is used to compare conditions

loop   a set of statements that are repeated

loop control variable   a variable used to control a `for` loop

low-level language   machine language

machine language   a language in which instructions are written as binary strings

macro   a preprocessing directive that can be used to define a simple function

magnitude   absolute value

mantissa   the value that is multiplied by a power of 10 when a value is expressed in scientific notation

math function   a function that computes the value of a common function, such as the square root of x

mathematical tool   a software tool for performing mathematical computations

matrix   a set of numbers arranged in a rectangular grid with rows and columns

matrix multiplication   an operation between two matrices that determines a new matrix

mean   average value of a list of values

median   the middle value in a group of sorted values if there are an odd number of values; otherwise, the average of the two middle values

memory   the part of a computer that stores information

memory snapshot   a diagram that shows the contents of a memory location at a specified point in the execution of a program

microprocessor   a CPU that is contained in a single integrated circuit chip that is smaller than a postage stamp

modularity   the result of the process of separating a problem solution into a group of modules

module   a set of statements that perform an operation or that compute a value that can be considered to be a unit in terms of functionality

module chart   a diagram that shows the module structure of a program

modulus   an operation that computes the remainder in a division between two integers

multiple assignment   a statement that allows multiple variables to be assigned values

network   an interconnection of computers so that they can share resources and information

nonsingular   a characteristic of a set of equations that have a unique solution

NULL constant   a constant with the value of binary zero

object program   a program in machine language

offset   an integer value that gives a number of positions from the first element in the memory allocation for an array

one-dimensional array   a data structure that can be visualized as a list of values arranged in either a row or a column

operating system   software that provides an interface between the user and the hardware

overflow   an error caused when the result of an arithmetic operation is too large to store in the memory assigned to it

parameter   the input to a function, also called an argument

parsing   examining the individual characters in an array or string of characters

personal computer (PC)   a small inexpensive computer that is designed around a microprocessor chip

pointer   a variable that contains the memory address of another variable

postfix   a position after an identifier

power   average squared value of a set of values

precedence   the order in which operations are evaluated in an expression

precision   the accuracy specified by the mantissa of a value in scientific notation

prefix   a position before an identifier

preprocessor directive   a statement that gives an instruction to the compiler

problem solving process   a methodology for approaching new problems

processor   the part of the computer that controls all the other parts

program   instructions to describe a set of operations to be performed by a computer

program walkthrough   a technique in which an algorithm or a program for a complicated problem is presented in detail to a new group of people to get feedback and suggestions

programmer-defined function   a function that is written by a programmer

prompt   a message printed by a program to indicate that information should be entered

prototype   a system that does not have all the functions of the final system but that has much of the user interface so that it can be evaluated by the user

pseudocode   English-like statements used to describe the steps in an algorithm

random number   a number that is defined by statistical properties rather than an equation

random number seed   a value that is used to initialize a random sequence

range   the number of digits allowed for the exponent in a scientific notation

real-time program   a program usually written in assembly language so that it can execute very fast

recursion   a methodology that implements a problem solution using a process that invokes itself

register class   a class used to represent variables that need to be accessed frequently

relational operator   an operator that is used to compare two expressions

reliability   a measure of the proportion of the time that a component works

repetition   a control structure that contains a set of steps that are repeated as long as a condition is true

reusability   the result of a process in which software is developed in modules that can be used in a variety of problem solutions

root   a value of x for which $f(x)$ is equal to zero

scientific notation   notation that expresses a value as a mantissa times a power of 10, as in 3.1×10^2

scope   the portion of a program in which it is valid to reference a function or a variable

selection   a control structure that contains one set of steps to perform if a condition is true and another set of steps to perform if the condition is false

selection sort algorithm   a sort algorithm that performs several passes through an array, exchanging minimum values with values in specified positions

sequence   a control structure composed of steps performed one after another

sentinel signal   a value included at the end of a data file to indicate that the end of the file has been reached

simultaneous equations   a set of equations with a common solution

software   the programs that describe the steps that we want the computer to perform

software life cycle   the steps or cycles in the development of a large software project

software maintenance   the work necessary to add enhancements to existing software, to fix errors identified in the software, and to adapt the software to work with new hardware and software

software tool   a program written to perform common operations, such as generating a report or a graph

sorting   a technique in which a group of values are ordered in ascending order or in descending order

source program   a program in a high-level language

spreadsheet   a software tool that works with information that can be displayed in a grid of rows and columns

Standard C library   a library of constants and functions that can be accessed from a C program

standard deviation   square root of the variance

square matrix   a matrix with the same number of rows as columns

stable system   a system in which reasonable inputs cause reasonable outputs

statement   a comment or an instruction in a program

static class   a designation that specifies that the memory for a variable should be retained during the entire program execution

stepwise refinement   the process of breaking a problem solution into a sequence of smaller and smaller steps

storage class   a designation that determines the scope of a variable

structure chart   a diagram that shows the module structure of a program

subscripts   integers used to distinguish elements in an array

summation notation   a mathematical notation used to describe the sum of a set of values

supercomputer   the fastest of computers that can process billions of instructions per second

symbolic constant   a constant that is assigned an identifier by a preprocessor directive

syntax   the grammar rules of a language

system   components or a process that defines interactions

system dependent   a capability that may not be available on all computer systems

system of equations   a set of equations with a common solution

test data   data designed to test the correctness of a program

text stream   a sequence of characters

top-down design   a design methodology that starts with a general "big picture" description of a problem solution and then refines the solution

trailer signal   a value included at the end of a data file to indicate that the end of the file has been reached

transpose   a matrix generated from another matrix in which the rows of the original matrix form the columns of the new matrix

trigonometric function   function that computes a value from a trigonometric or inverse trigonometric function

truncate   an operation that drops any fractional portion of a value

two-dimensional array   a data structure that can be visualized as a table or grid of values displayed in rows and columns

type specifier   a term that distinguishes the various types of forms in which C can store numeric values

unary operator   an operator that operates on a single value as in the negative of a value

underflow   an error caused when the result of an arithmetic operation is too small to store in the memory assigned to it

utility   a program for performing common functions such as copying files from a hard disk to a diskette

utterance   a segment of speech

validation and verification   processes to verify that a program is correctly performing its objectives, and that those objectives solve the problem

variable   a memory location that is given a name, and whose contents may or may not change during the execution of a program

variance   average squared deviation of a group of values from their mean

vector   a matrix composed of one row or of one column

void pointer   a pointer returned by a function that does not specify the type of variable to which it is to point

while loop   a loop that is executed as long as a condition is true

white space   the space character or one of the following characters: FF (form feed), NL (new line), CR (carriage return), HT (horizontal tab), VT (vertical tab)

word processor   a software tool for entering and formatting text which may be used in reports or which may be computer programs

workstation   a minicomputer or mainframe computer that is small enough to fit on a desk

zero crossing   a point at which a function crosses the x axis

Index

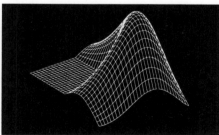

Marketing Manager
Engineering / Computer Science
PRENTICE HALL
Simon & Schuster Education Group
113 Sylvan Avenue, Route 9W
Englewood Cliffs, NJ 07632

BUSINESS REPLY MAIL
FIRST CLASS PERMIT NO. 82 NATICK, MA

POSTAGE WILL BE PAID BY ADDRESSEE

The MathWorks, Inc.
24 Prime Park Way
Natick, MA 01760-9889